Excel

—for Windows® 95—

SIMPLIFIED

VISUAL 3D SERIES

by: maranGraphics' Development Group

Corporate Sales
Contact maranGraphics
Phone: (905) 890-3300, ext.206
(800) 469-6616, ext.206
Fax: (905) 890-9434

Canadian Trade Sales
Contact Prentice Hall Canada
Phone: (416) 293-3621
(800) 567-3800
Fax: (416) 299-2529

Visit our Web site at:
http://www.maran.com

Excel for Windows® 95 Simplified

5755 Coopers Avenue
Mississauga, Ontario, Canada
L4Z 1R9

Screen shots reprinted with permission from Microsoft Corporation.

Canadian Cataloguing in Publication Data

Maran, Ruth, 1970-
Excel for Windows 95 simplified

(Visual 3-D series)
Written by Ruth Maran
Includes index.
ISBN 1-896283-17-9

1. Microsoft Excel for Windows (Computer file).
2. Electronic spreadsheets. 3. Business-
Computer programs. I. maranGraphics'
Development Group. II. Title III. Series.

HF5548.4.M523M3 1996 005.369 C95-933260-X

Trademark Acknowledgments

maranGraphics Inc. has attempted to include trademark information for products, services and companies referred to in this guide. Although maranGraphics Inc. has made reasonable efforts in gathering this information, it cannot guarantee its accuracy.

All other brand names and product names used in this book are trademarks, registered trademarks, or trade names of their respective holders. maranGraphics Inc. is not associated with any product or vendor mentioned in this book.

Printed in the United States of America

10 9 8 7 6 5 4 3 2 1

Excel

—for Windows® 95—

S I M P L I F I E D

maranGraphics™

Every maranGraphics book represents the extraordinary vision and commitment of a unique family: the Maran family of Toronto, Canada.

Back Row (from left to right): *Sherry Maran, Rob Maran, Richard Maran, Maxine Maran, Jill Maran.*
Front Row (from left to right): *Judy Maran, Ruth Maran.*

Richard Maran is the company founder and its inspirational leader. He developed maranGraphics' proprietary communication technology called "visual grammar." This book is built on that technology—empowering readers with the easiest and quickest way to learn about computers.

Ruth Maran is the Author and Architect—a role Richard established that now bears Ruth's distinctive touch. She creates the words and visual structure that are the basis for the books.

Judy Maran is Senior Editor. She works with Ruth, Richard, and the highly talented maranGraphics illustrators, designers, and editors to transform Ruth's material into its final form.

Rob Maran is the Technical and Production Specialist. He makes sure the state-of-the-art technology used to create these books always performs as it should.

Sherry Maran manages the Reception, Order Desk, and any number of areas that require immediate attention and a helping hand.

Jill Maran is a jack-of-all-trades and dynamo who fills in anywhere she's needed anytime she's back from university.

Maxine Maran is the Business Manager and family sage. She maintains order in the business and family—and keeps everything running smoothly.

Oh, and three other family members are seated on the sofa. These graphic disk characters help make it fun and easy to learn about computers. They're part of the extended maranGraphics family.

Credits

Author:
Ruth Maran

Copy Developer:
Kelleigh Wing

Technical Consultant:
Wendi Blouin Ewbank

Editors:
Brad Hilderley
Paul Lofthouse

Proofreaders:
Alison MacAlpine
Lorena Zupancic

Layout Designer:
Tamara Poliquin

Illustrators:
Chris K.C. Leung
Russell Marini
Andrew Trowbridge

Indexer:
Mark Kmetzko

Post Production:
Robert Maran

Acknowledgments

Thanks to the dedicated staff of maranGraphics, including Brad Hilderley, Chris K.C. Leung, Paul Lofthouse, Alison MacAlpine, Jill Maran, Judy Maran, Maxine Maran, Robert Maran, Sherry Maran, Russ Marini, Greg Midensky, Tamara Poliquin, Andrew Trowbridge, Christie Van Duin, Kelleigh Wing, and Lorena Zupancic.

Finally, to Richard Maran who originated the easy-to-use graphic format of this guide. Thank you for your inspiration and guidance.

TABLE OF CONTENTS

CHAPTER 1

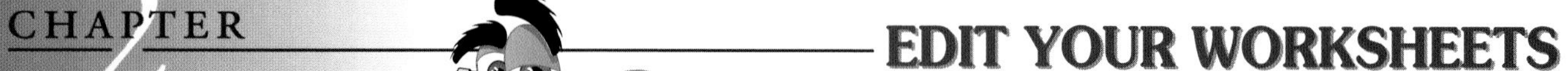

GETTING STARTED

CHAPTER 2

EDIT YOUR WORKSHEETS

CHAPTER 3

SAVE AND OPEN YOUR WORKBOOKS

USING FORMULAS AND FUNCTIONS

WORKING WITH ROWS AND COLUMNS

CHAPTER 6

FORMAT YOUR WORKSHEETS

TABLE OF CONTENTS

CHAPTER 7

PRINT YOUR WORKSHEETS

CHAPTER 8

CHANGE YOUR SCREEN DISPLAY

CHAPTER 9

USING MULTIPLE WORKSHEETS

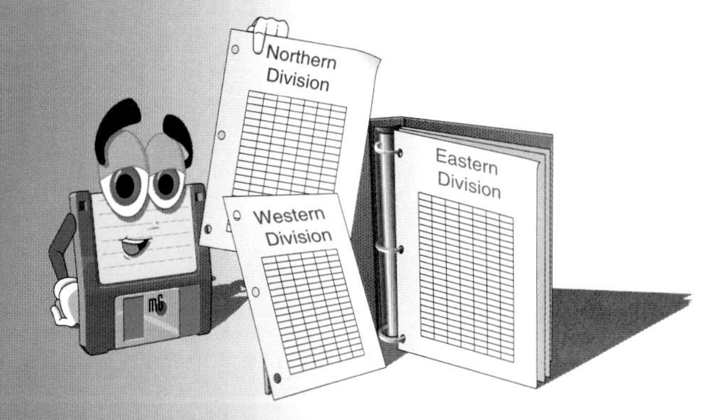

CHAPTER 10

USING MULTIPLE WORKBOOKS

CHAPTER 11

CHARTING DATA

CHAPTER 12

MANAGE DATA IN A LIST

In this chapter you will learn the basic skills needed to use Excel for Windows 95.

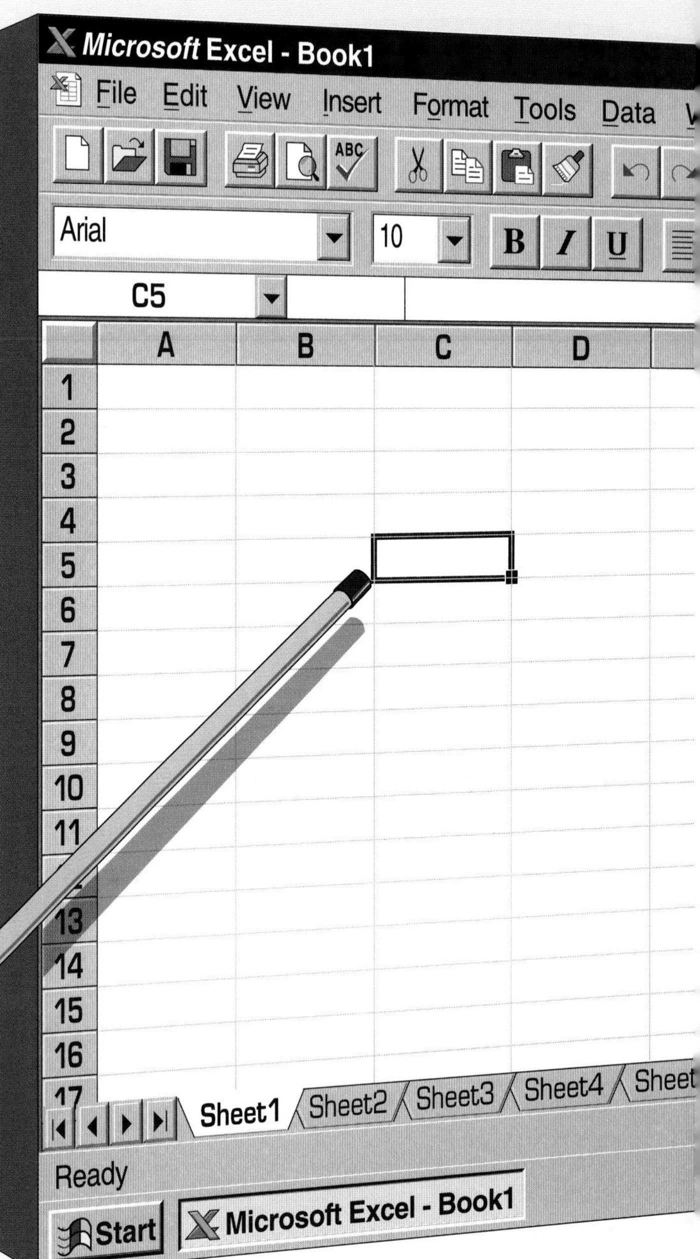

CHAPTER 1

GETTING STARTED

INTRODUCTION

Excel
for Windows® 95
helps you manage, analyze
and attractively present
information.

Typical Business

Excel can help you manage your finances and create professional-looking reports and documents.

EXCEL FEATURES

FORMULAS AND FUNCTIONS

Excel provides powerful tools to calculate and analyze data in your worksheets.

EDITING

Excel lets you efficiently enter and edit data in your worksheets.

MANAGING DATA IN A LIST

Excel provides many tools for organizing, managing, sorting and retrieving data from a large collection of information.

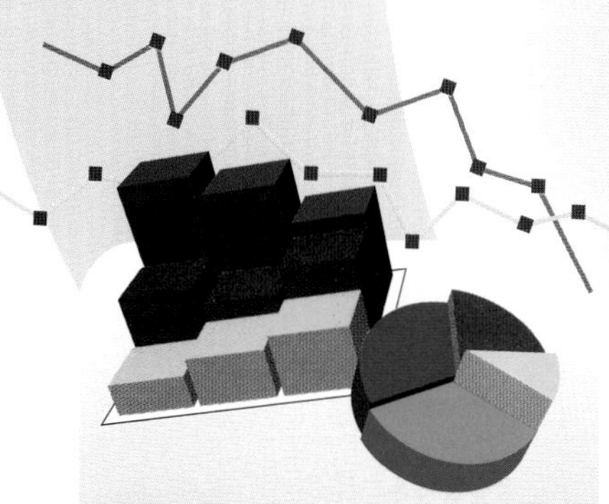

CHARTS

Excel helps you create charts from your worksheet data.

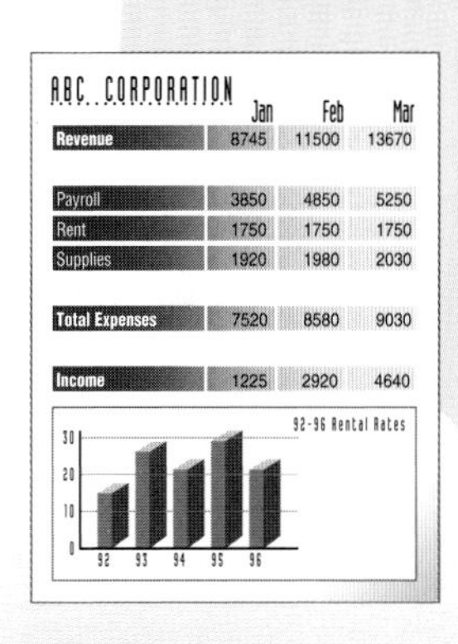

ABC CORPORATION

	Jan	Feb	Mar
Revenue	8745	11500	13670
Payroll	3850	4850	5250
Rent	1750	1750	1750
Supplies	1920	1980	2030
Total Expenses	7520	8580	9030
Income	1225	2920	4640

FORMATTING

Excel offers many features to help you change the appearance of your worksheets.

MOUSE BASICS

The mouse is a hand-held device that lets you select and move items on your screen.

When you move the mouse on your desk, the mouse pointer on your screen moves in the same direction. The mouse pointer assumes different shapes (examples: ,), depending on its location on your screen and the task you are performing.

Hold the mouse as shown in the diagram. Use your thumb and two rightmost fingers to move the mouse while your two remaining fingers press the mouse buttons.

CLICK
Press and release the left mouse button.

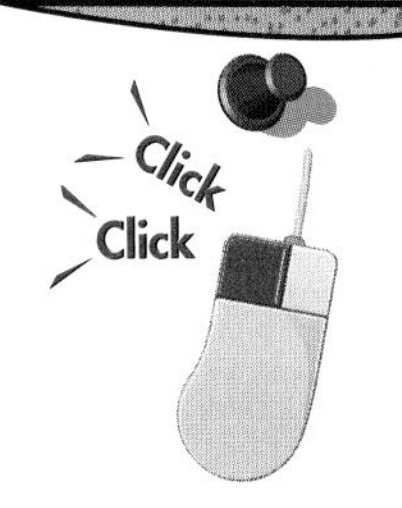

DOUBLE-CLICK
Quickly press and release the left mouse button twice.

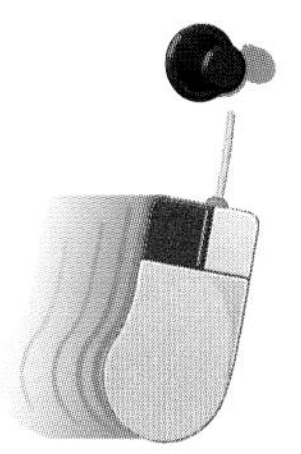

DRAG AND DROP
When the mouse pointer is over an object on your screen, press and hold down the left button. Still holding down the button, move the mouse to where you want to place the object. Then release the button.

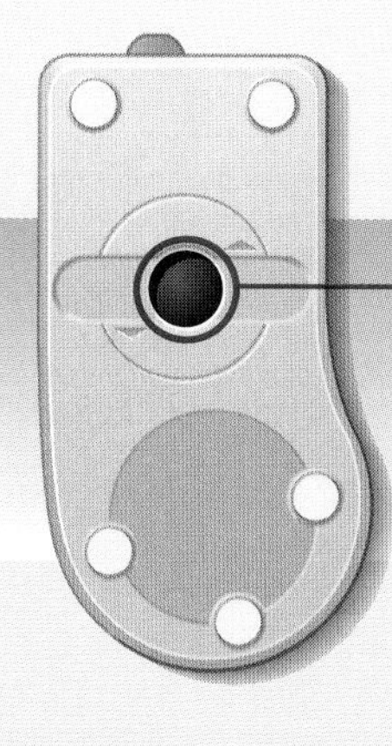

A ball under the mouse senses movement. To ensure smooth motion of the mouse, you should occasionally remove and clean this ball.

START EXCEL

COLUMNS, ROWS AND CELLS

When you start Excel, a blank worksheet appears. You can enter data into this worksheet.

START EXCEL

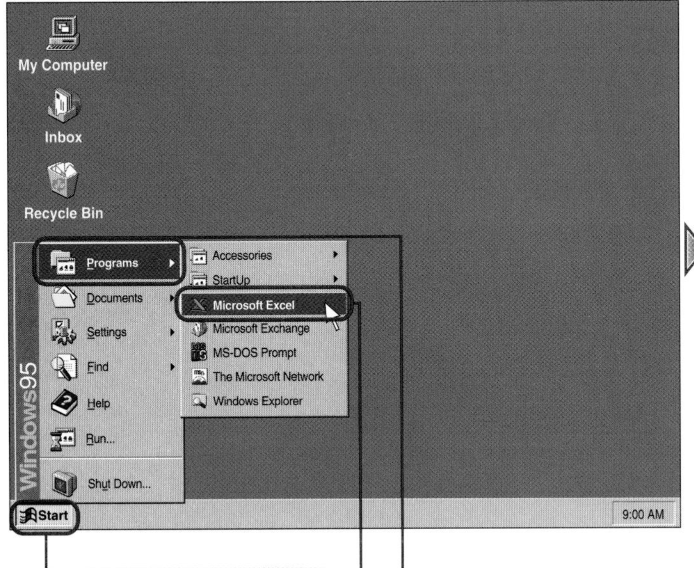

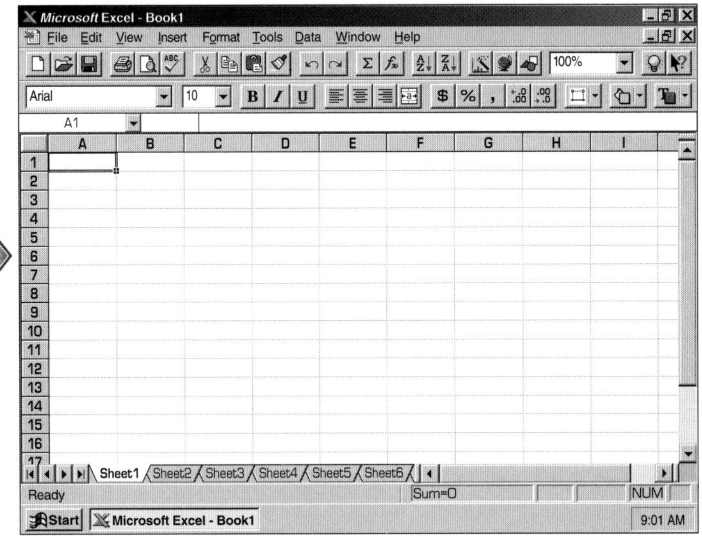

1 Move the mouse over **Start** and then press the left button.

2 Move the mouse over **Programs**.

3 Move the mouse over **Microsoft Excel** and then press the left button.

■ The **Microsoft Excel** window appears, displaying a blank worksheet.

COLUMNS, ROWS AND CELLS

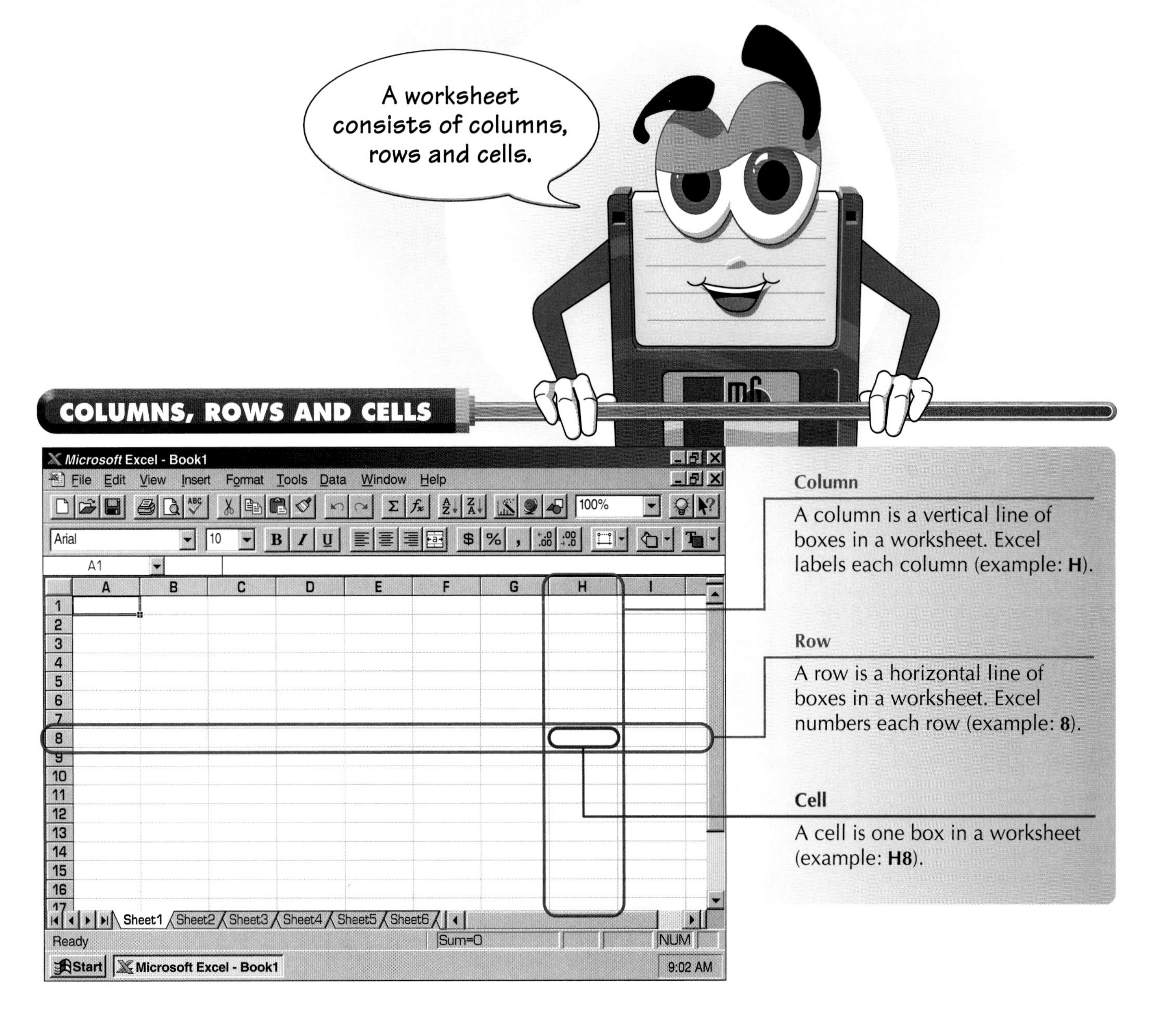

Column

A column is a vertical line of boxes in a worksheet. Excel labels each column (example: **H**).

Row

A row is a horizontal line of boxes in a worksheet. Excel numbers each row (example: **8**).

Cell

A cell is one box in a worksheet (example: **H8**).

THE ACTIVE CELL

The active cell is the cell in your worksheet where you enter data.

CHANGE THE ACTIVE CELL

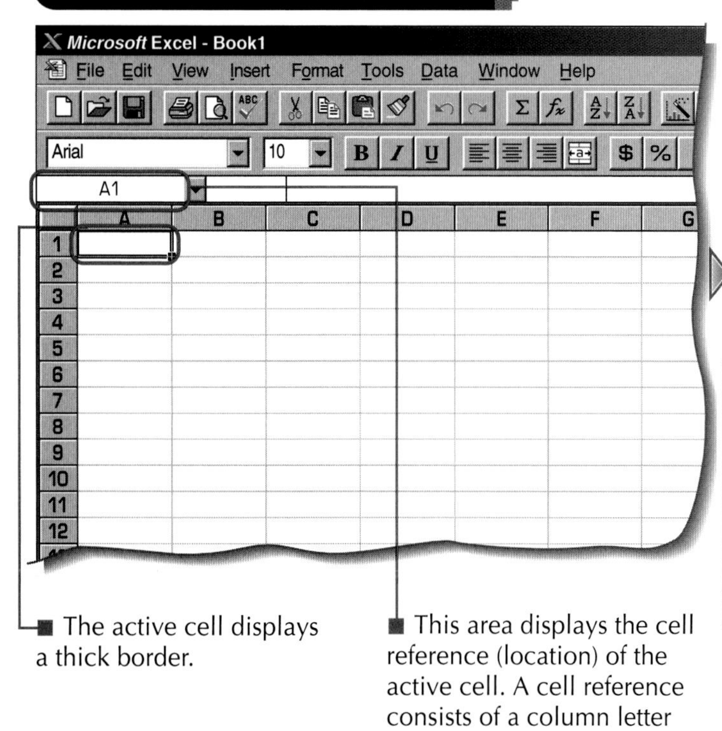

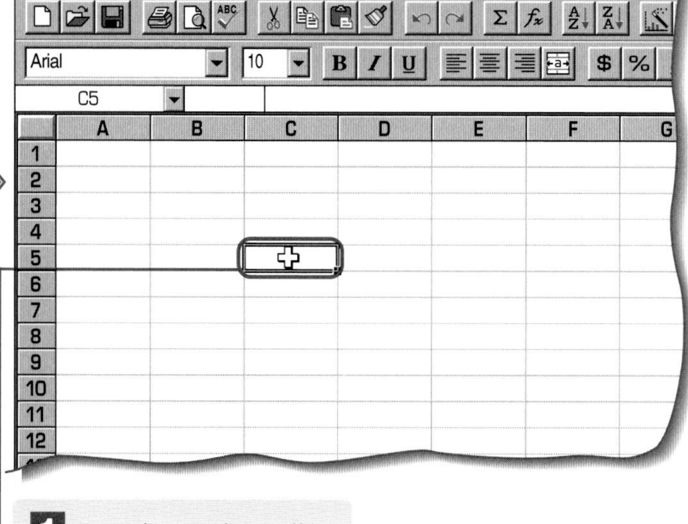

■ The active cell displays a thick border.

■ This area displays the cell reference (location) of the active cell. A cell reference consists of a column letter followed by a row number (example: **A1**).

1 To make another cell active, move the mouse ✜ over the cell and then press the left button.

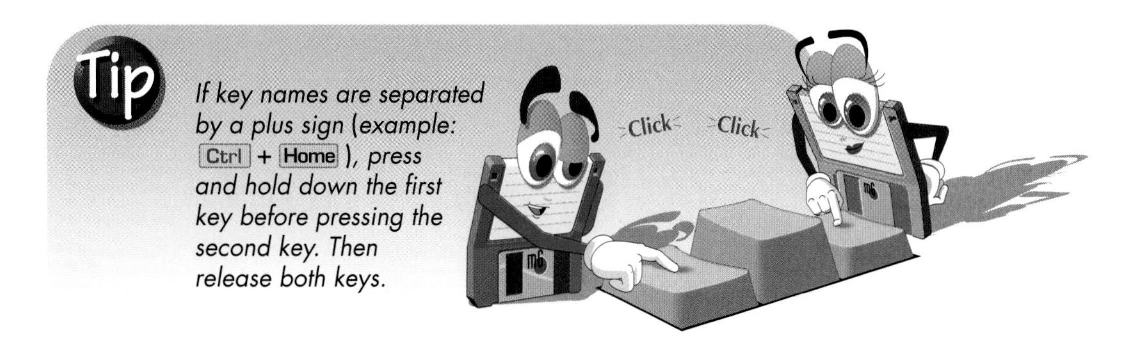

Tip

If key names are separated by a plus sign (example: Ctrl + Home), press and hold down the first key before pressing the second key. Then release both keys.

USING THE KEYBOARD

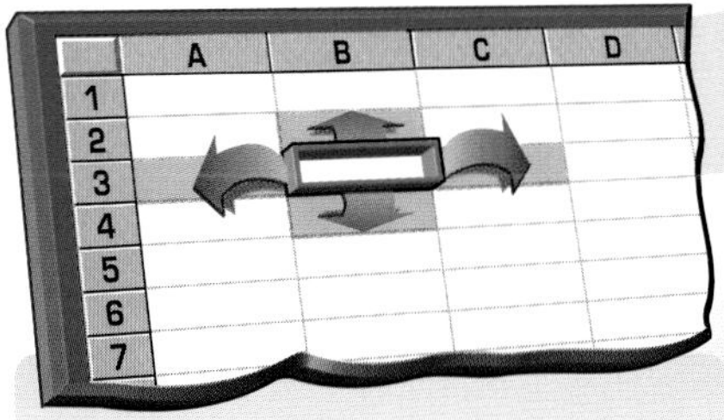

To move one cell in any direction, press ↓, ↑, → or ←.

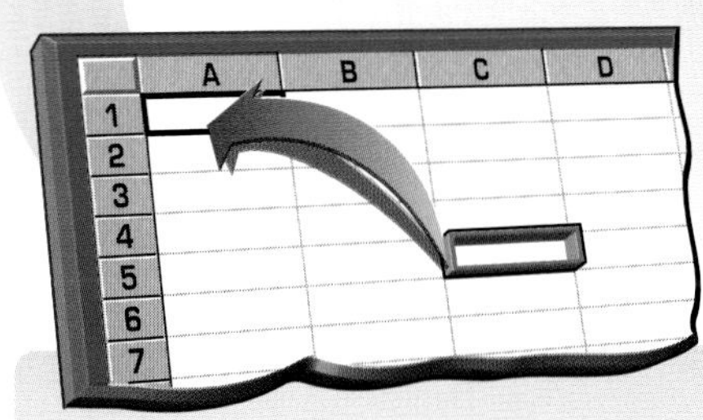

To move to cell A1 from any cell in your worksheet, press Ctrl + Home.

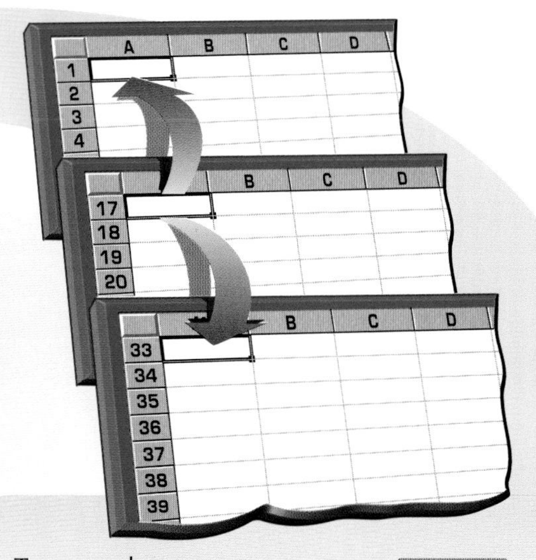

To move down one screen, press PageDown.

To move up one screen, press PageUp.

To move right one screen, press Alt + PageDown.

To move left one screen, press Alt + PageUp.

SELECT CELLS

Before performing many tasks in Excel, you must select the cells you want to work with. Selected cells appear highlighted on your screen.

SELECT ONE CELL

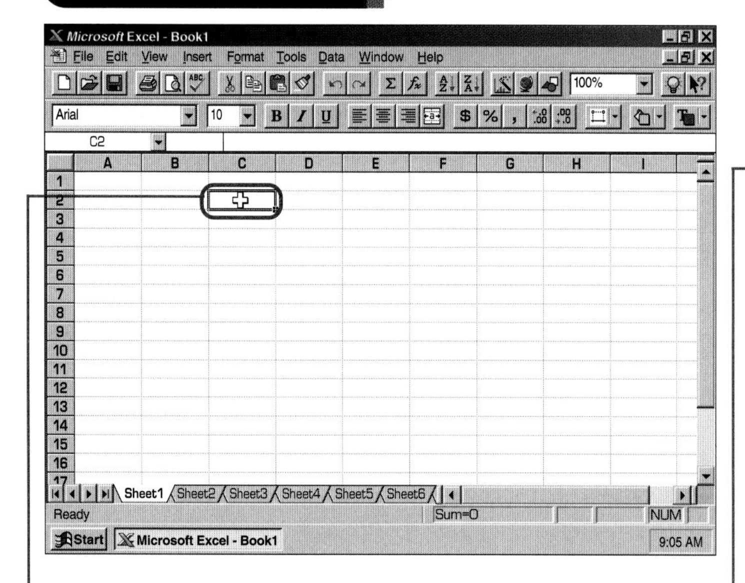

1 Move the mouse over the cell you want to select and then press the left button.

SELECT COLUMNS

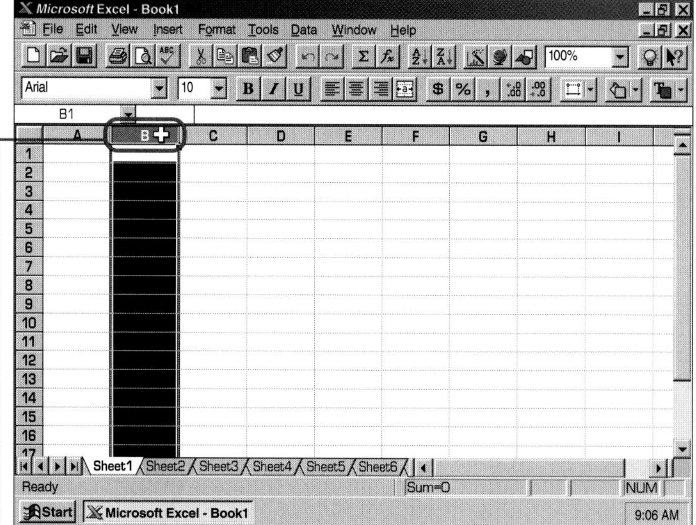

1 Move the mouse over the letter of the column you want to select and then press the left button.

■ To select multiple columns, press and hold down Ctrl on your keyboard as you repeat step **1** for each column.

Note: To deselect columns, move the mouse over any cell and then press the left button.

Tip

You can quickly select your entire worksheet.

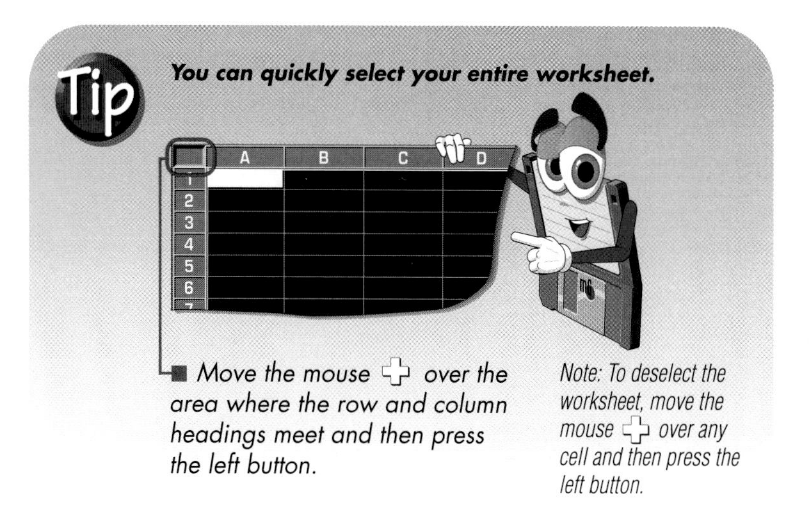

■ *Move the mouse over the area where the row and column headings meet and then press the left button.*

Note: To deselect the worksheet, move the mouse over any cell and then press the left button.

SELECT ROWS

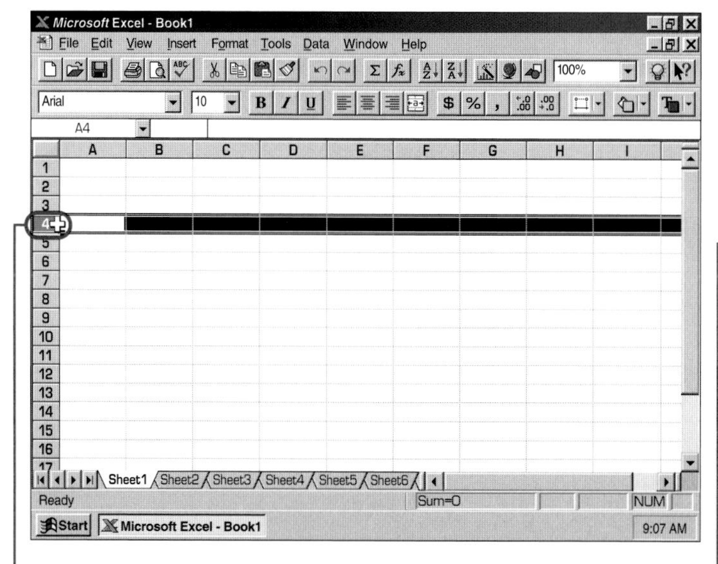

1 Move the mouse over the number of the row you want to select and then press the left button.

■ To select multiple rows, press and hold down Ctrl on your keyboard as you repeat step **1** for each row.

Note: To deselect rows, move the mouse over any cell and then press the left button.

SELECT MULTIPLE CELLS

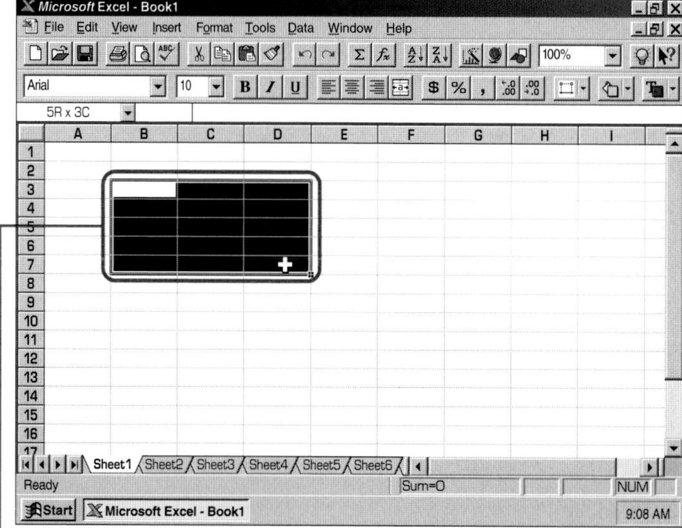

1 Move the mouse over the first cell you want to select.

2 Press and hold down the left button as you move the mouse to highlight all the cells you want to select. Then release the button.

■ To select multiple groups of cells, press and hold down Ctrl on your keyboard as you repeat steps **1** and **2** for each group.

Note: To deselect cells, move the mouse over any cell and then press the left button.

SCROLL THROUGH A WORKSHEET

If your worksheet contains a lot of data, your computer screen cannot display all the data at once. You must scroll through the worksheet to view other areas.

SCROLL UP OR DOWN

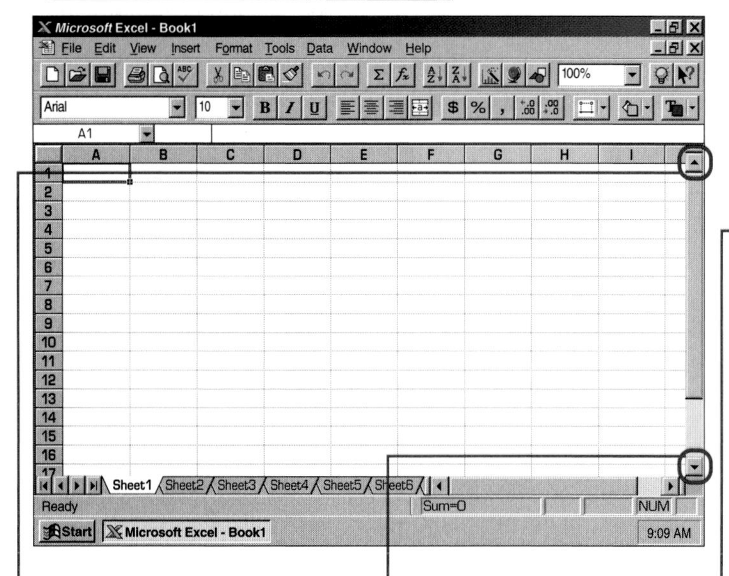

■ To scroll up one row, move the mouse over ▲ and then press the left button.

■ To scroll down one row, move the mouse over ▼ and then press the left button.

SCROLL TO ANY ROW

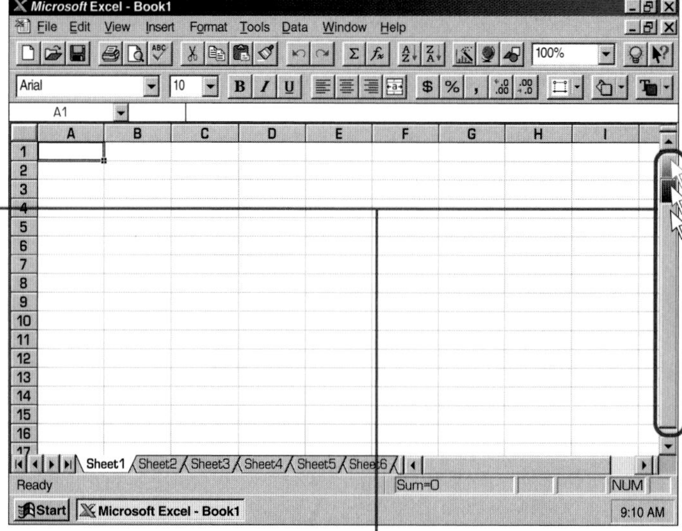

1 To quickly scroll to any row in your worksheet, move the mouse over this box.

2 Press and hold down the left button and then move the mouse up or down the scroll bar. Then release the button.

SCROLL LEFT OR RIGHT

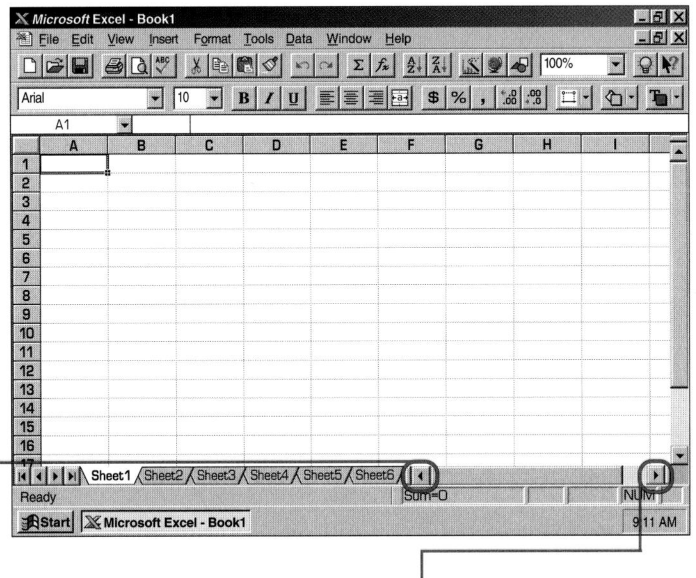

■ To scroll left one column, move the mouse over ◄ and then press the left button.

■ To scroll right one column, move the mouse over ► and then press the left button.

SCROLL TO ANY COLUMN

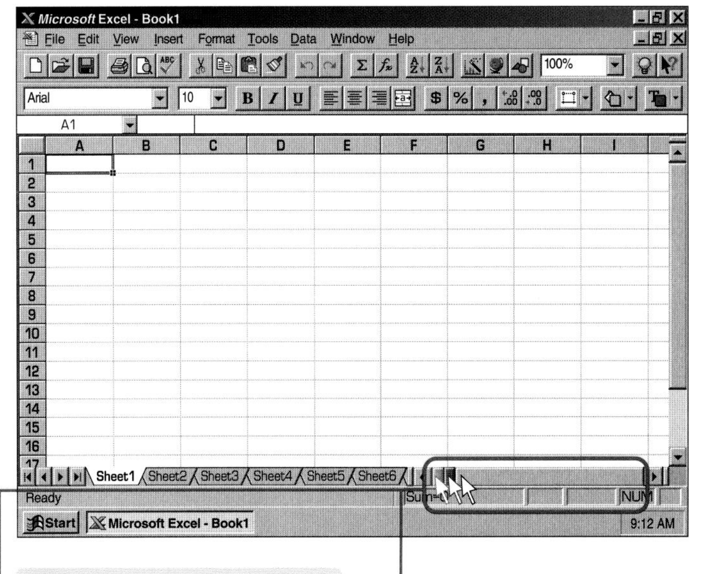

1 To quickly scroll to any column in your worksheet, move the mouse over this box.

2 Press and hold down the left button and then move the mouse across the scroll bar. Then release the button.

GETTING HELP

If you do not know how to perform a task, you can use the Help feature to get information.

GETTING HELP

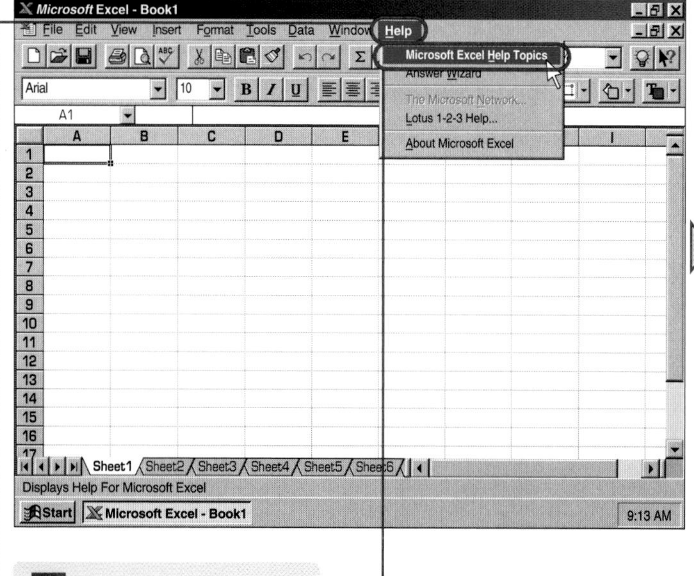

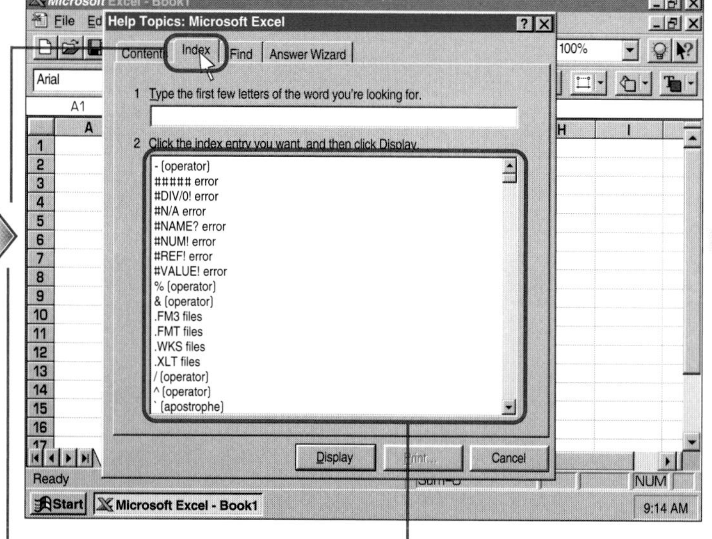

1 Move the mouse over **Help** and then press the left button.

2 Move the mouse over **Microsoft Excel Help Topics** and then press the left button.

■ The **Help Topics** dialog box appears.

3 To display the help index, move the mouse over the **Index** tab and then press the left button.

■ This area displays a list of all the available help topics.

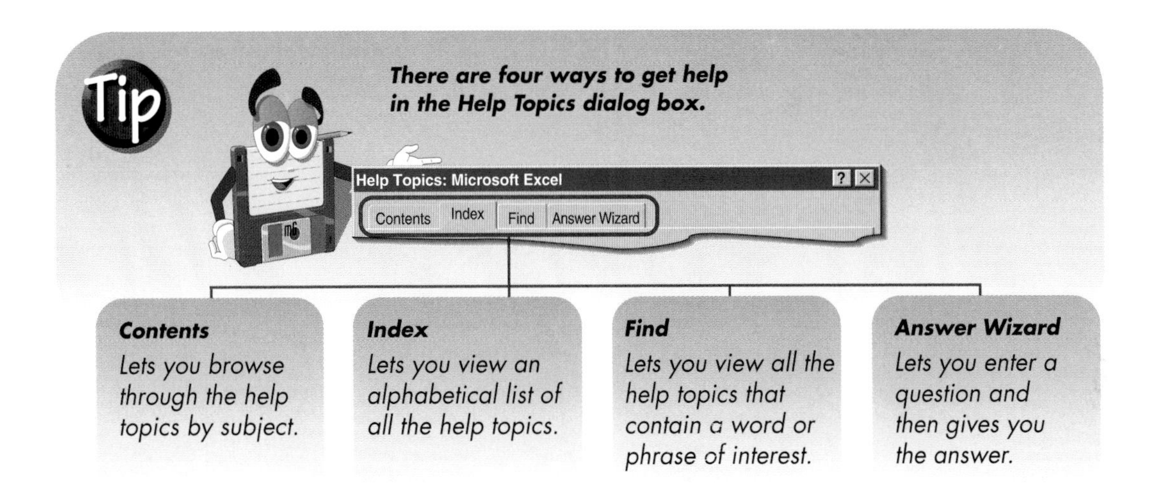

Tip
There are four ways to get help in the Help Topics dialog box.
Help Topics: Microsoft Excel
Contents
Index
Find
Answer Wizard

Contents
Lets you browse through the help topics by subject.

Index
Lets you view an alphabetical list of all the help topics.

Find
Lets you view all the help topics that contain a word or phrase of interest.

Answer Wizard
Lets you enter a question and then gives you the answer.

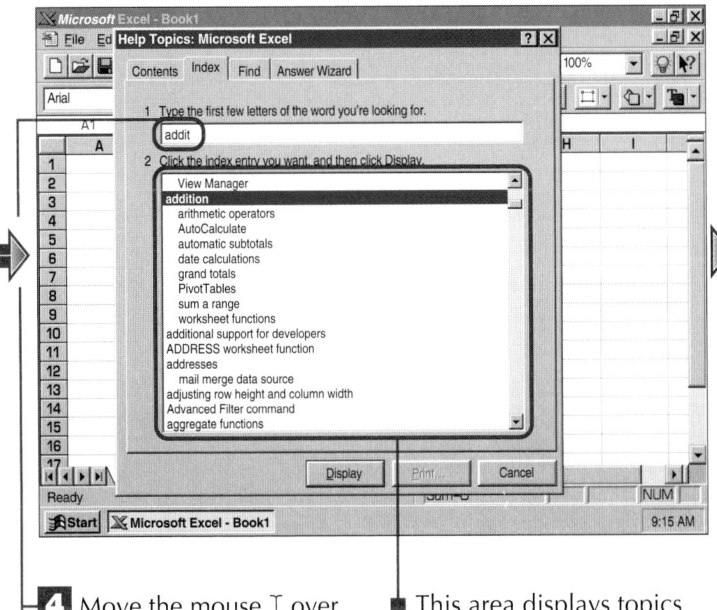

4 Move the mouse I over this area and then press the left button.

5 Type the first few letters of the topic of interest (example: **addit** for **addition**).

■ This area displays topics beginning with the letters you typed.

Note: To browse through the topics, use the scroll bar. For more information, refer to page 14.

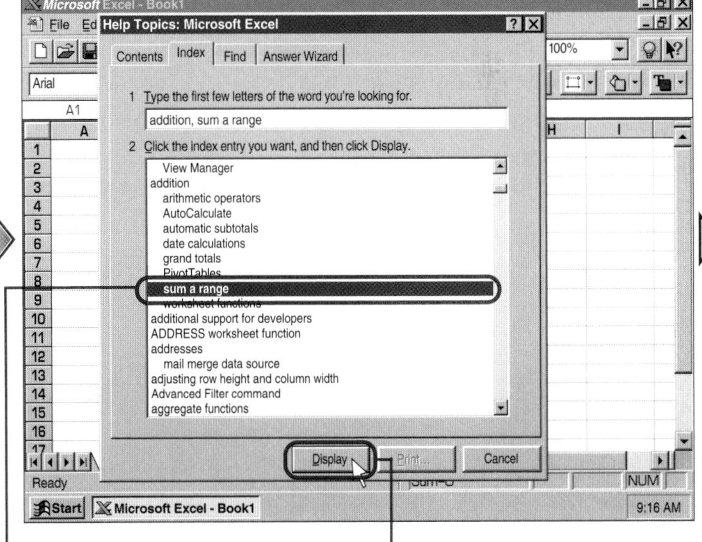

6 Move the mouse over the topic you want information on and then press the left button.

7 Move the mouse over **Display** and then press the left button.

GETTING HELP

GETTING HELP (CONTINUED)

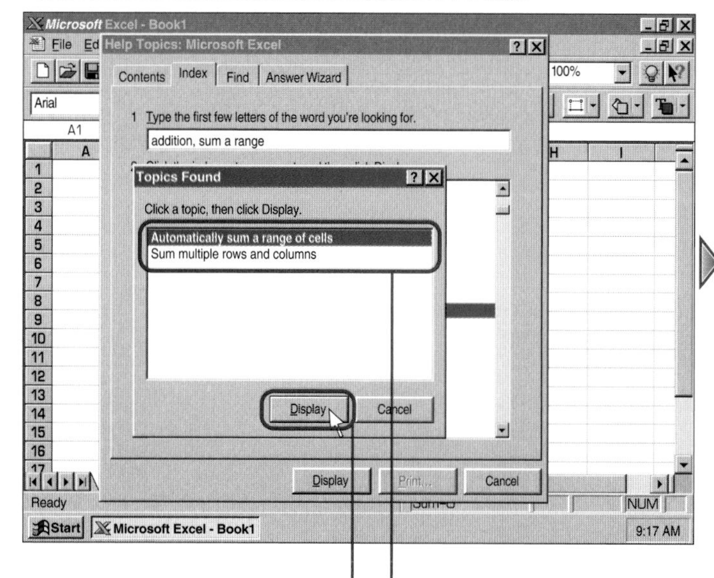

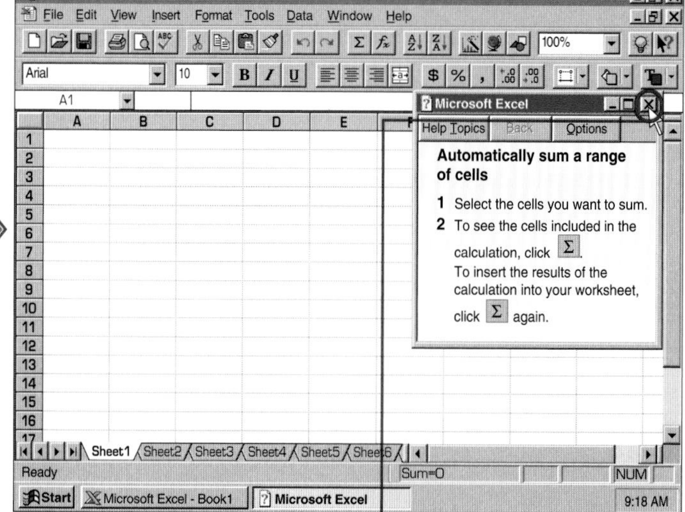

■ A window appears, displaying items related to the topic you selected.

Note: If this window does not appear, skip steps 8 and 9.

8 Move the mouse over the item you want information on and then press the left button.

9 Move the mouse over **Display** and then press the left button.

■ A window appears, displaying information on the item you selected.

10 To close the window, move the mouse over ☒ and then press the left button.

You can display a description of any button on your screen.

GETTING HELP ON A BUTTON

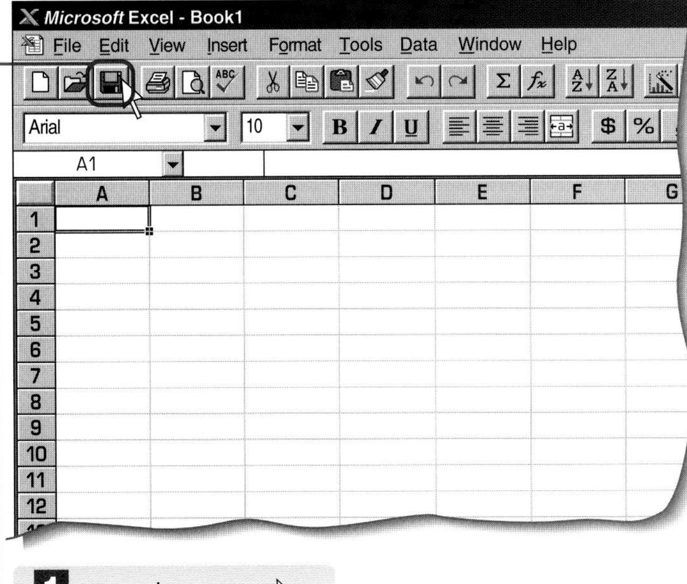

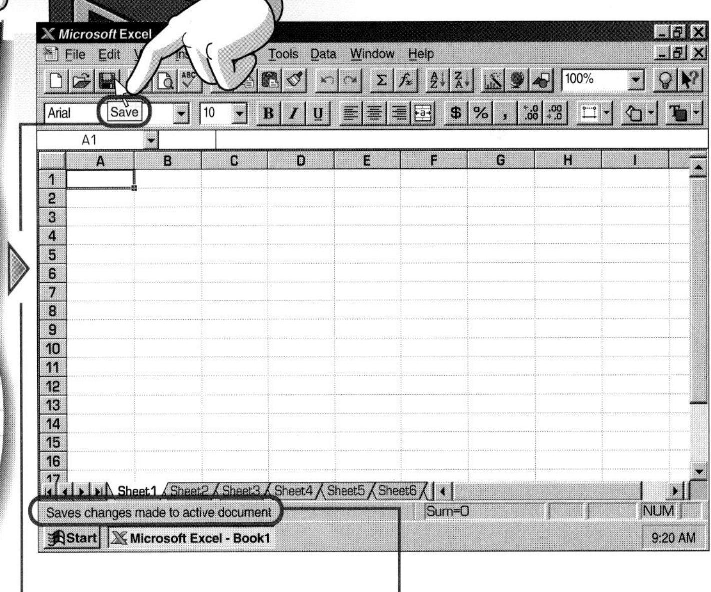

1 Move the mouse over the button of interest.

■ After a few seconds, the name of the button appears.

■ A short description of the button also appears at the bottom of your screen.

In this chapter you will learn how to enter and make changes to data in your worksheets.
INCOME STATEMENT
January
February
REVENUE
8700
11500
Payroll
3850
4850
1750
1920
TOTAL EXPENSES
INCOME

CHAPTER 2

EDIT YOUR WORKSHEETS

Enter Data

Complete a Series

Edit Data

Delete Data

Undo Last Change

Move Data

Copy Data

Check Spelling

ENTER DATA

You can enter data into your worksheet quickly and easily.

ENTER DATA

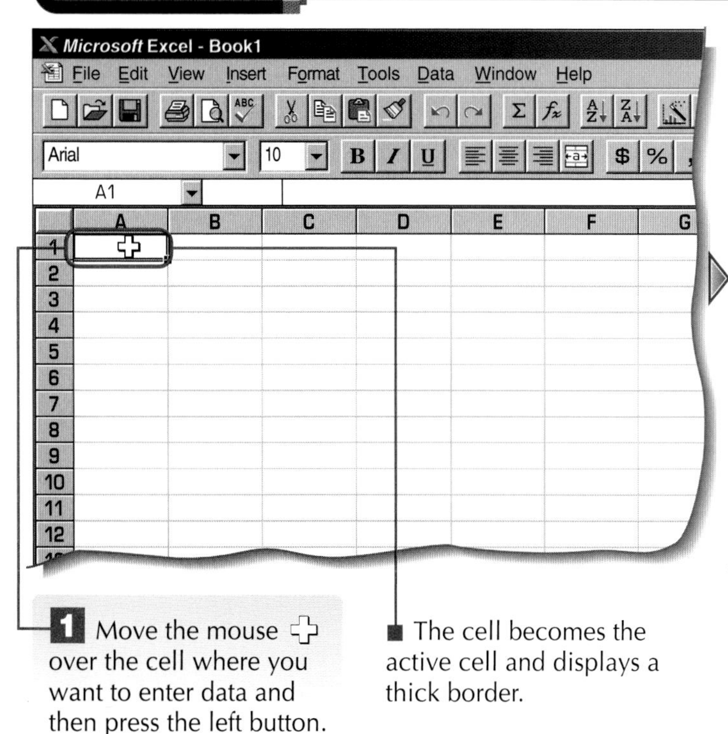

1 Move the mouse ✥ over the cell where you want to enter data and then press the left button.

■ The cell becomes the active cell and displays a thick border.

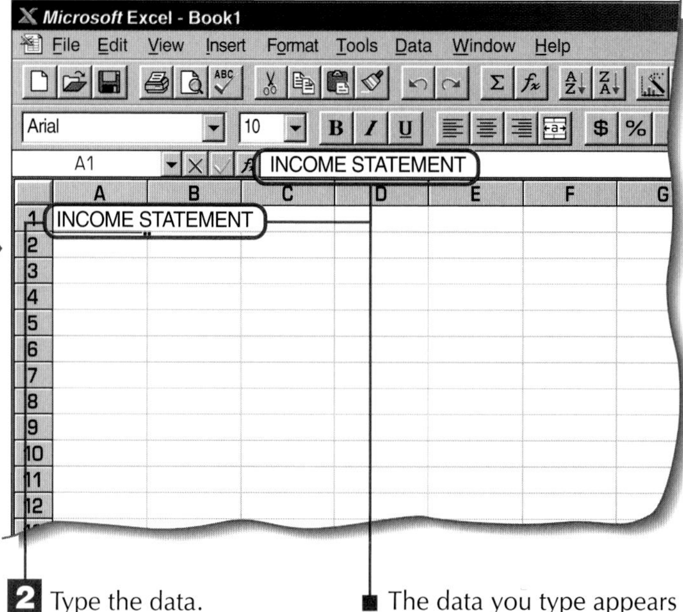

2 Type the data.

■ If you make a typing mistake, press Backspace on your keyboard to remove the incorrect data and then retype.

■ The data you type appears in the active cell and in the formula bar.

- **Enter Data**
- Complete a Series
- Edit Data
- Delete Data
- Undo Last Change
- Move Data
- Copy Data
- Check Spelling

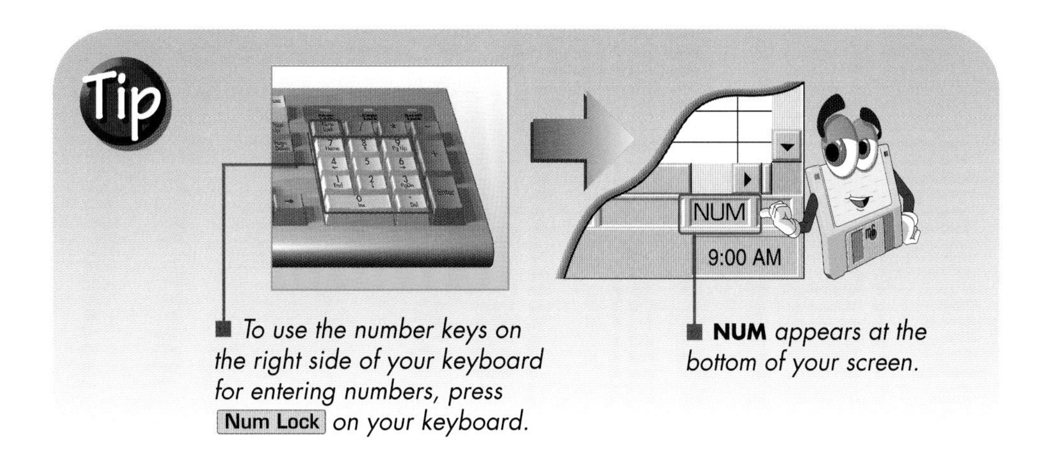

■ *To use the number keys on the right side of your keyboard for entering numbers, press* **Num Lock** *on your keyboard.*

■ ***NUM** appears at the bottom of your screen.*

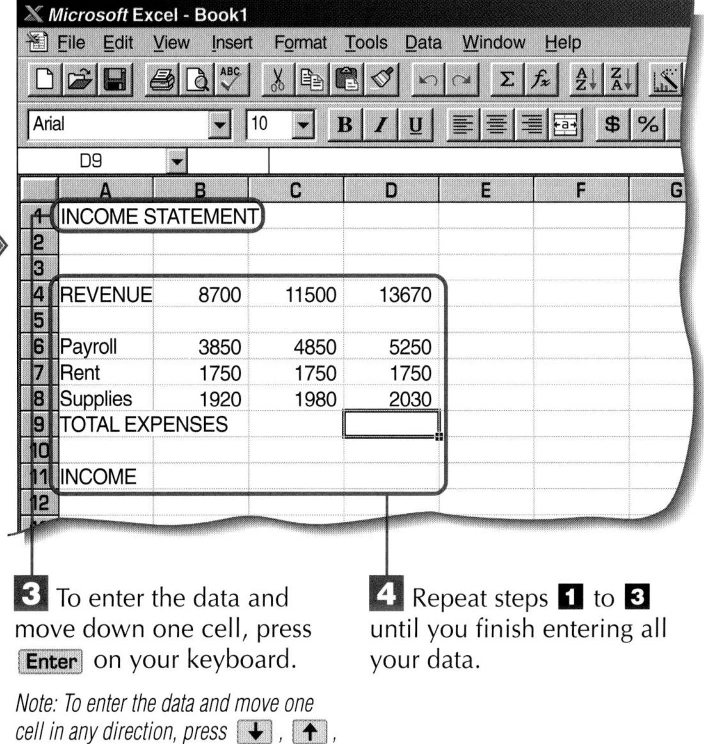

3 To enter the data and move down one cell, press **Enter** on your keyboard.

Note: To enter the data and move one cell in any direction, press ↓, ↑, → or ← on your keyboard.

4 Repeat steps **1** to **3** until you finish entering all your data.

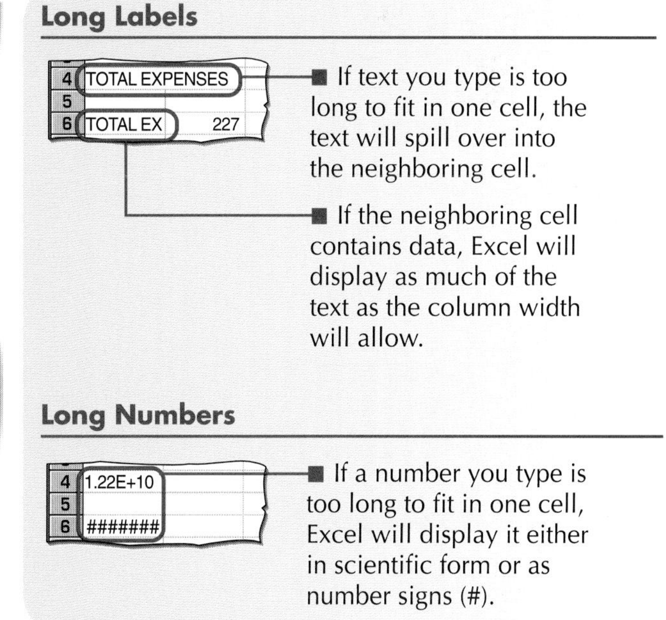

Long Labels

■ If text you type is too long to fit in one cell, the text will spill over into the neighboring cell.

■ If the neighboring cell contains data, Excel will display as much of the text as the column width will allow.

Long Numbers

■ If a number you type is too long to fit in one cell, Excel will display it either in scientific form or as number signs (#).

Note: To display all the text or the entire number in a cell, you must increase the column width. For more information, refer to page 80.

Excel can save you time by completing a series of numbers, text or time periods in your worksheet.

COMPLETE A SERIES

Complete a Series of Labels

Mon	Tue	Wed	Thu
Product 1	Product 2	Product 3	Product 4
1st Quarter	2nd Quarter	3rd Quarter	4th Quarter

■ Excel completes a series of labels based on the label in the first cell.

Complete a Series of Numbers

1995	1996	1997	1998
5	10	15	20
202	204	206	208

■ Excel completes a series of numbers based on the numbers in the first two cells. These numbers tell Excel how much to add to each number to complete the series.

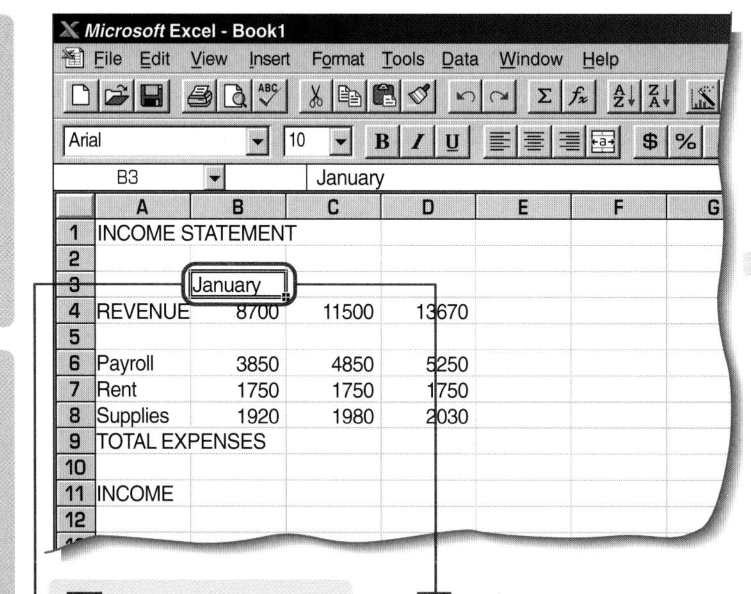

1 Type and enter the first label or the first two numbers in the series.

2 Select the cell(s) containing the label or numbers you entered.

Note: To select cells, refer to page 12.

Tip ***AutoComplete is another feature that can save you time as you enter text.***

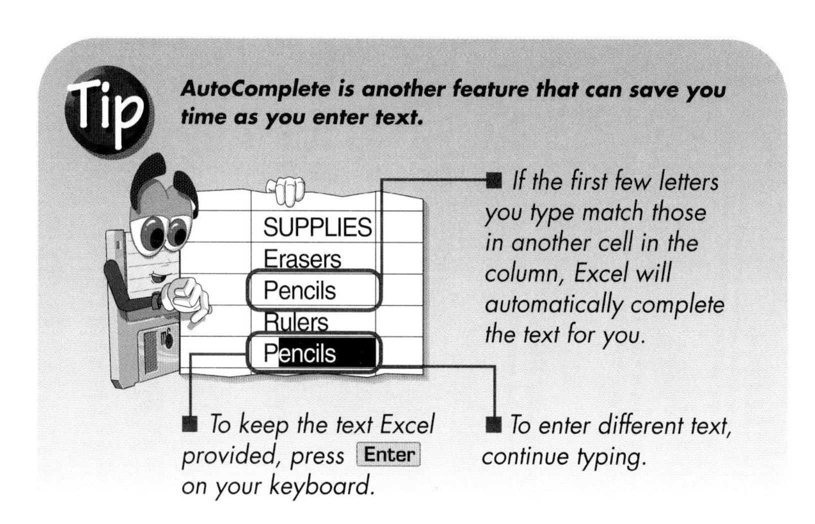

■ *If the first few letters you type match those in another cell in the column, Excel will automatically complete the text for you.*

■ *To keep the text Excel provided, press* Enter *on your keyboard.*

■ *To enter different text, continue typing.*

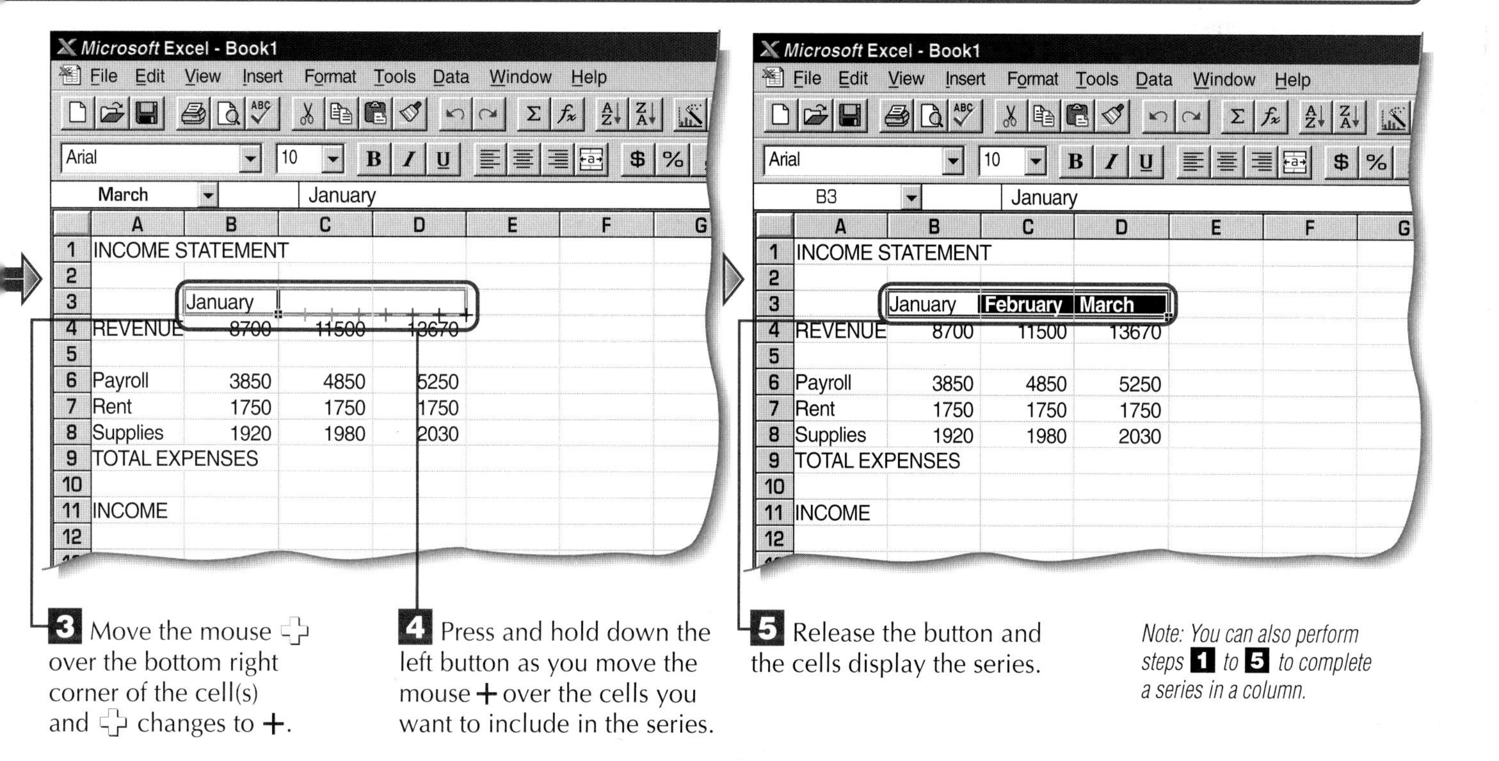

3 Move the mouse ✚ over the bottom right corner of the cell(s) and ✚ changes to +.

4 Press and hold down the left button as you move the mouse + over the cells you want to include in the series.

5 Release the button and the cells display the series.

Note: You can also perform steps **1** *to* **5** *to complete a series in a column.*

EDIT DATA

EDIT DATA IN A CELL

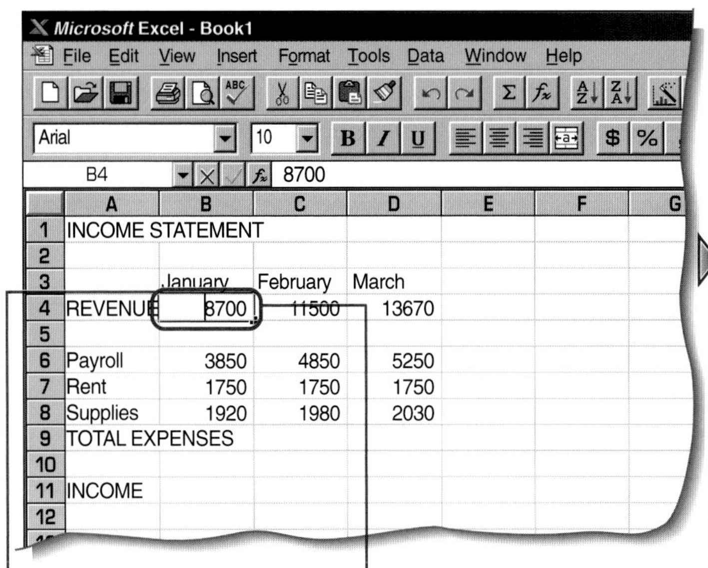

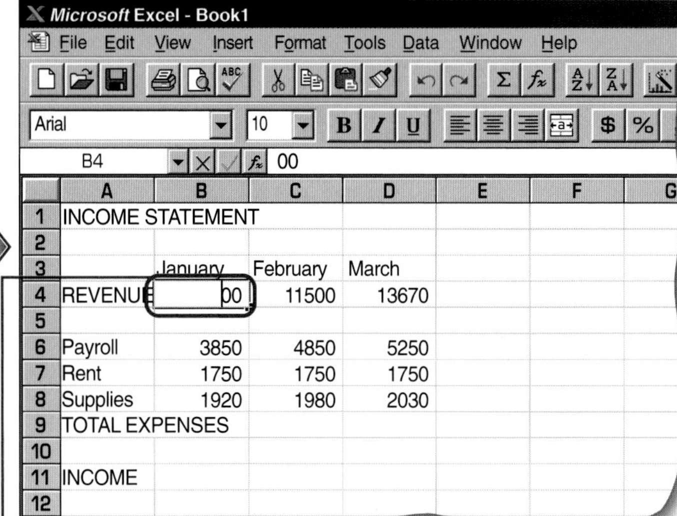

1 Move the mouse over the cell containing the data you want to change and then quickly press the left button twice.

■ A flashing insertion point appears in the cell.

2 Press → or ← on your keyboard to move the insertion point to where you want to add or remove characters.

3 To remove a character, press one of the following keys on your keyboard.

Delete Removes the character to the right of the insertion point.

Backspace Removes the character to the left of the insertion point.

If you make a common typing mistake when entering or editing text, Excel will automatically fix the mistake for you.

Examples

adn	and
comittee	committee
recieve	receive
tuesday	Tuesday
JAnuary	January

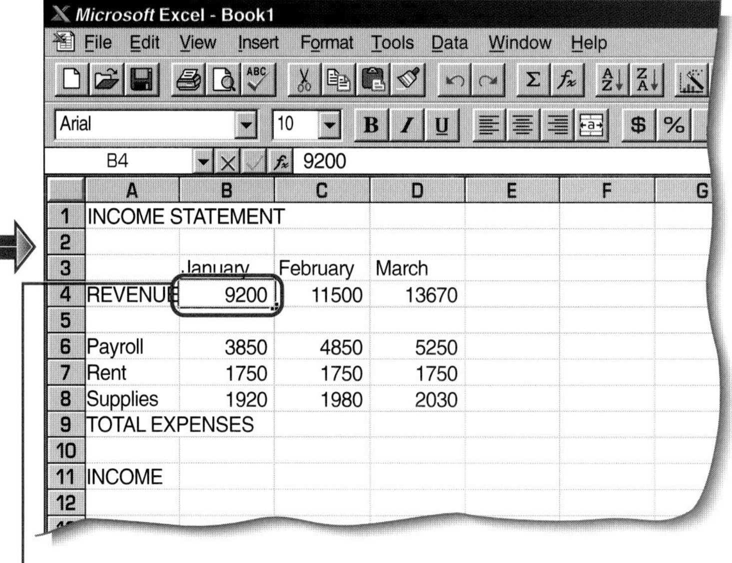

4 To insert data where the insertion point flashes on your screen, type the data.

5 When you finish making changes to the data, press Enter on your keyboard.

REPLACE ALL DATA IN A CELL

Microsoft Excel - Book1

File Edit View Insert Format Tools Data Window Help

B4 8745

	A	B	C	D
1	INCOME STATEMENT			
2				
3		January	February	March
4	REVENUE	8745	11500	13670
5				
6	Payroll	3850	4850	5250
7	Rent	1750	1750	1750
8	Supplies	1920	1980	2030
9	TOTAL EXPENSES			
10				
11	INCOME			
12				

1 Move the mouse over the cell containing the data you want to replace with new data and then press the left button.

2 Type the new data and then press Enter on your keyboard.

DELETE DATA

UNDO LAST CHANGE

You can easily remove data from cells in your worksheet.

DELETE DATA

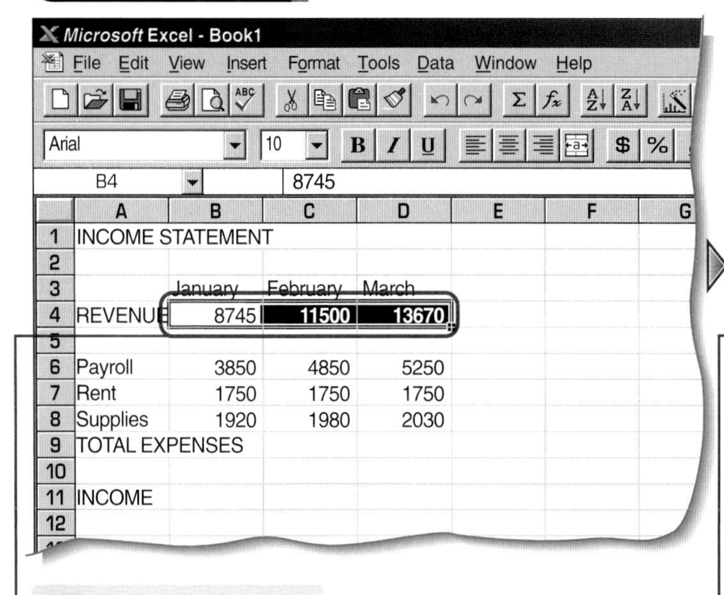

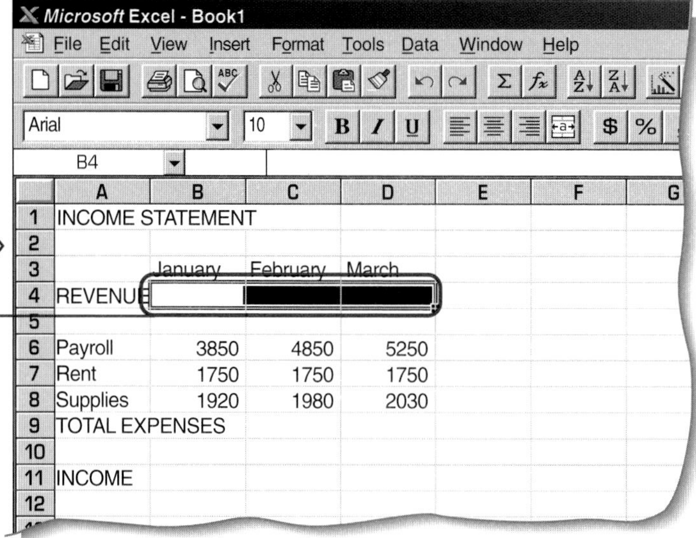

1 Select the cell(s) containing the data you want to remove.

Note: To select cells, refer to page 12.

2 Press Delete on your keyboard and the data in the cell(s) you selected disappears.

- Move Data
- Copy Data
- Check Spelling

Excel remembers the last change you made to your worksheet. If you regret this change, you can cancel it by using the Undo feature.

UNDO LAST CHANGE

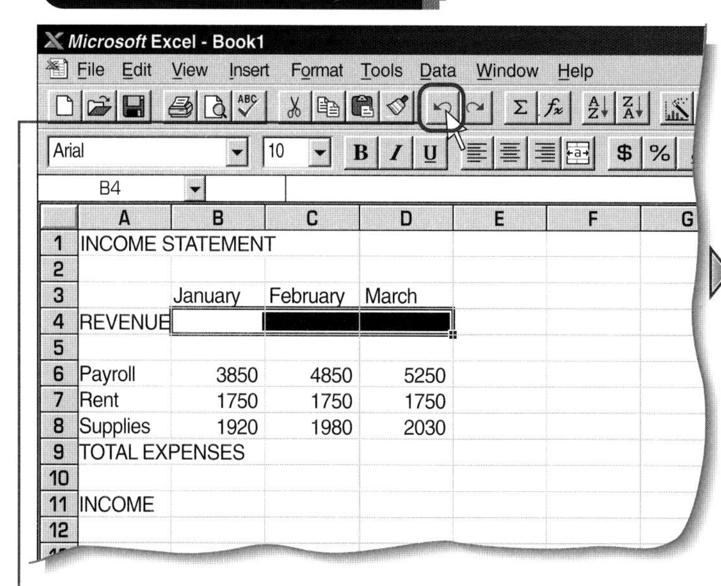

1 Move the mouse over the Undo button and then press the left button.

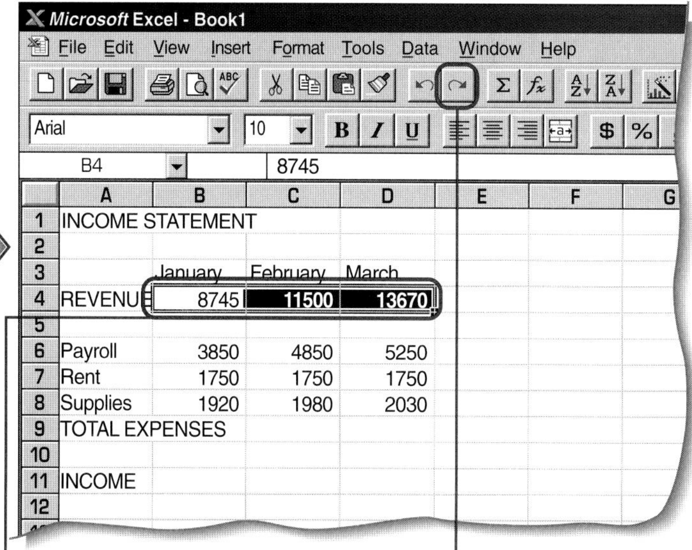

■ Excel cancels the last change you made to your worksheet.

■ To reverse the results of using the Undo feature, move the mouse over the Redo button and then press the left button.

MOVE DATA

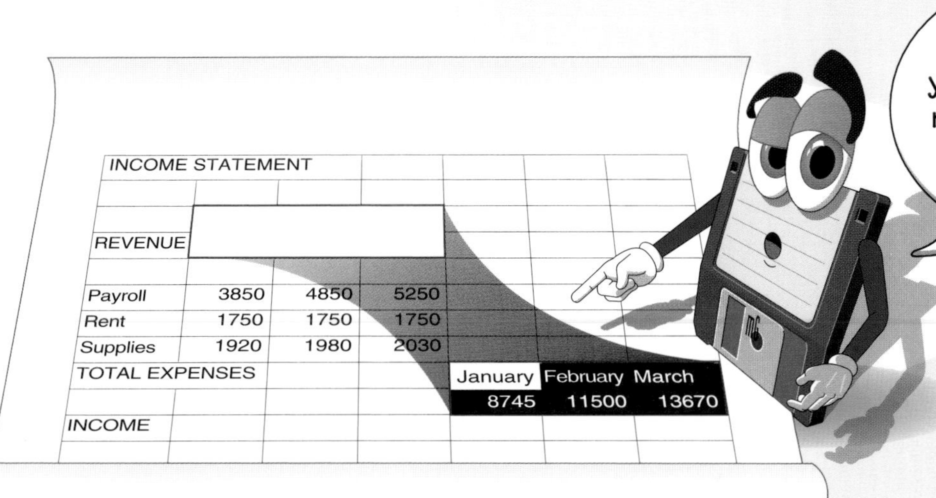

MOVE DATA

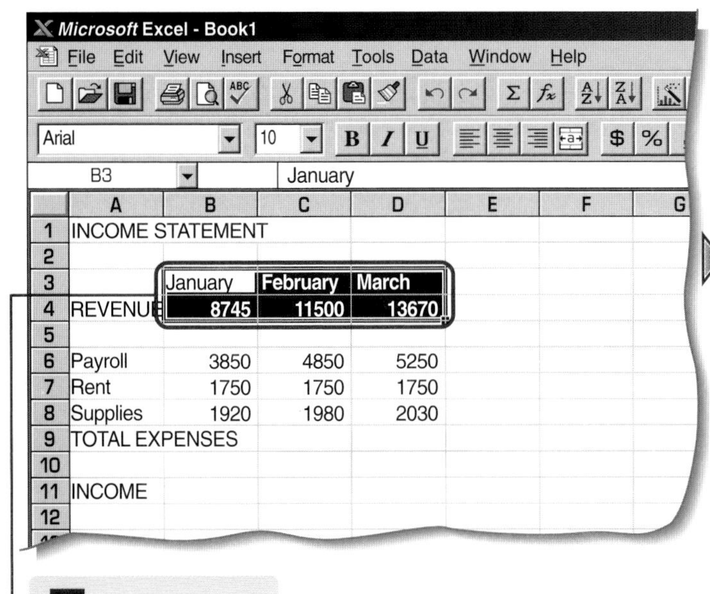

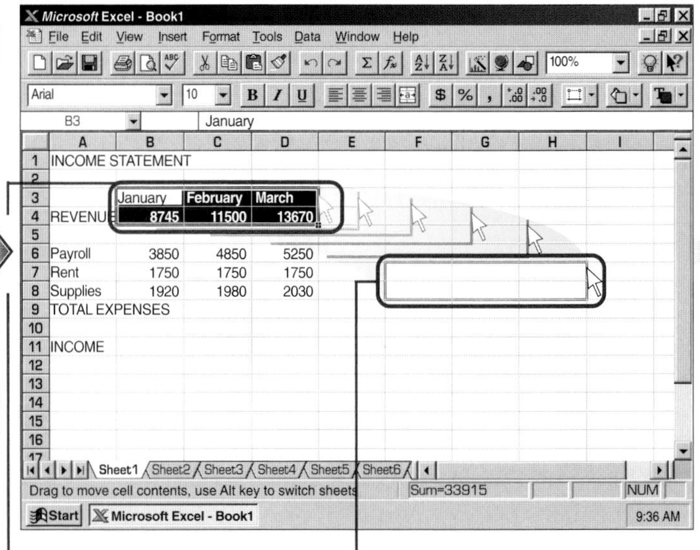

1 Select the cells containing the data you want to move.

Note: To select cells, refer to page 12.

2 Move the mouse ✥ over a border of the selected cells and ✥ changes to ↖.

3 Press and hold down the left button as you move the mouse ↖ to where you want to place the data.

■ A rectangular box shows where the data will appear.

Tip
You can move data from one worksheet to another.
Note: For more information, refer to page 144.
DATA
Worksheet 1
Worksheet 2

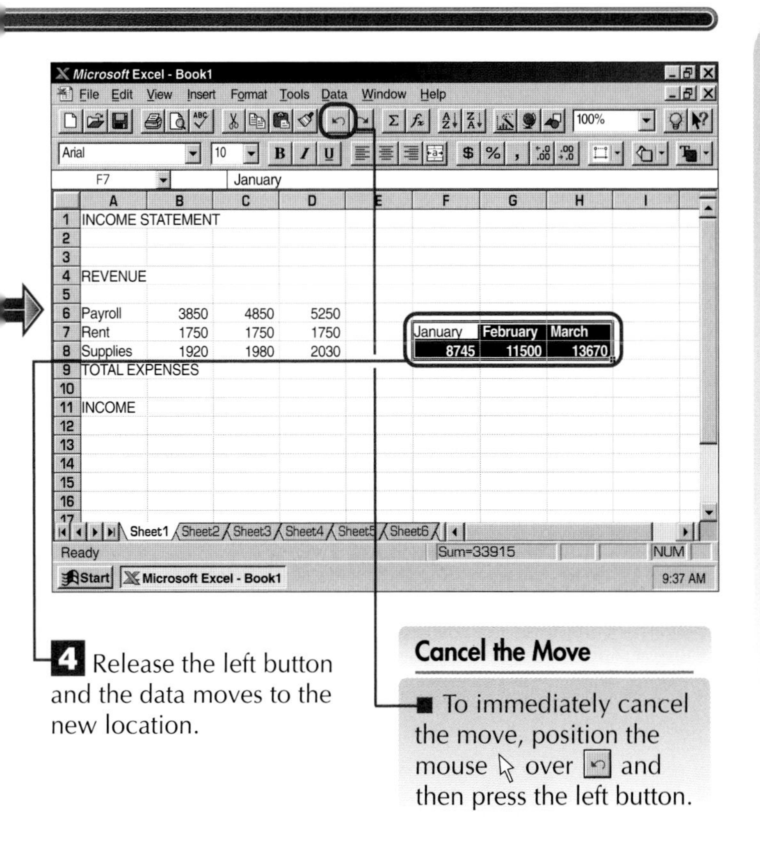

4 Release the left button and the data moves to the new location.

Cancel the Move

■ To immediately cancel the move, position the mouse over and then press the left button.

You can also use the Cut and Paste features to move data.

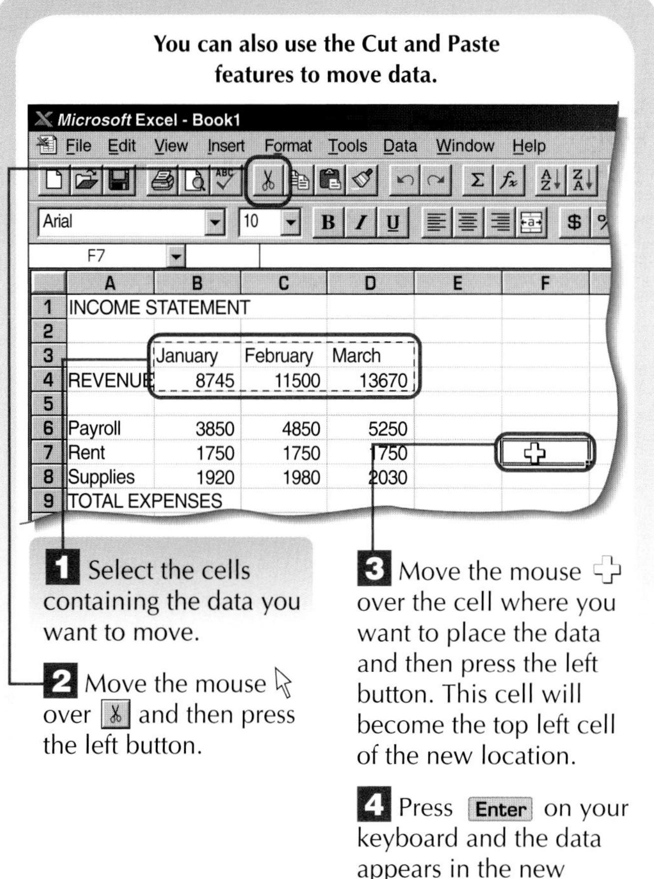

1 Select the cells containing the data you want to move.

2 Move the mouse over and then press the left button.

3 Move the mouse over the cell where you want to place the data and then press the left button. This cell will become the top left cell of the new location.

4 Press **Enter** on your keyboard and the data appears in the new location.

COPY DATA

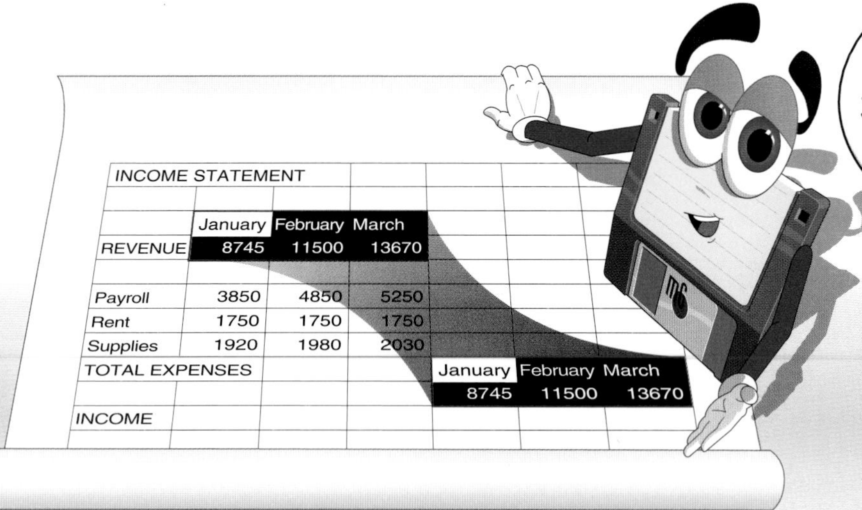

You can place a copy of data in a different location in your worksheet. This will save you time, since you do not have to retype the data.

COPY DATA

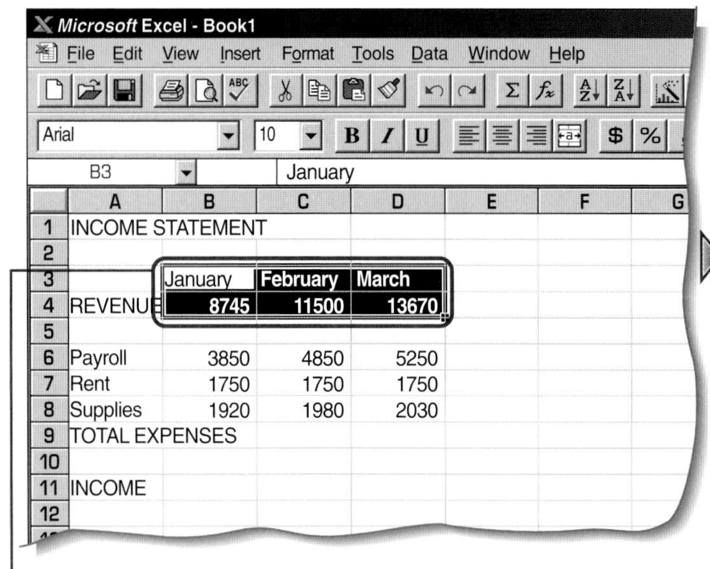

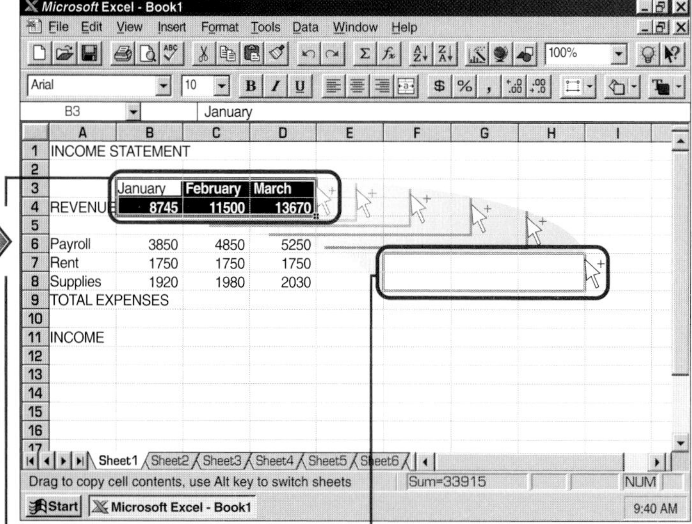

1 Select the cells containing the data you want to copy.

Note: To select cells, refer to page 12.

2 Move the mouse ✥ over a border of the selected cells and ✥ changes to ↖.

3 Press and hold down **Ctrl** on your keyboard and ↖ changes to ↖+.

4 Still holding down **Ctrl**, press and hold down the left button as you move the mouse ↖+ to where you want to place the copy.

■ A rectangular box shows where the data will appear.

Tip
You can copy data from one worksheet to another.
Note: For more information, refer to page 144.
DATA
DATA
Worksheet 1
Worksheet 2

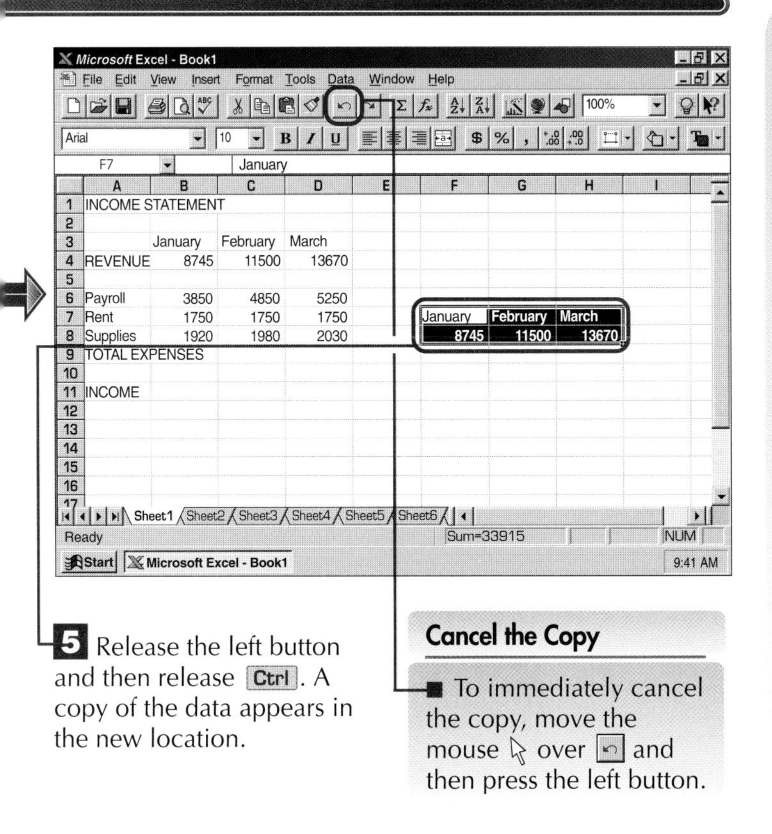

5 Release the left button and then release Ctrl. A copy of the data appears in the new location.

Cancel the Copy

■ To immediately cancel the copy, move the mouse over ↶ and then press the left button.

You can also use the Copy and Paste features to copy data.

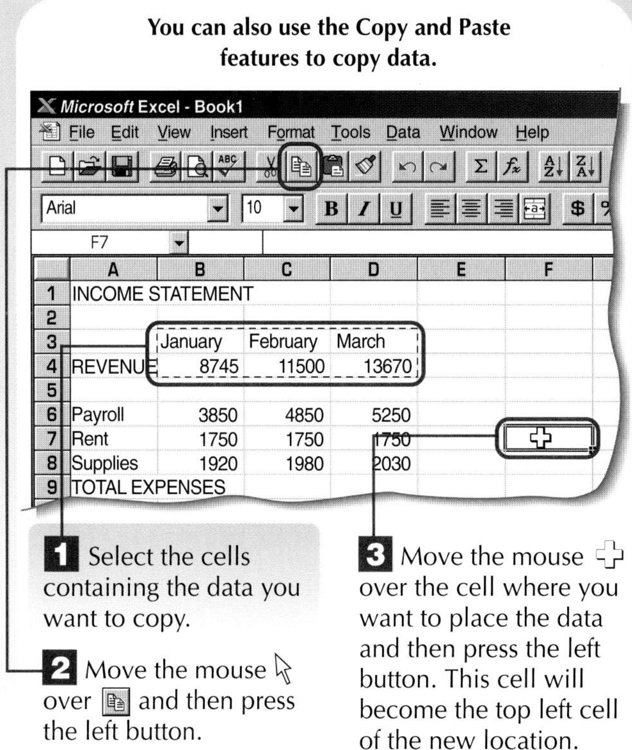

1 Select the cells containing the data you want to copy.

2 Move the mouse over 📋 and then press the left button.

3 Move the mouse ✚ over the cell where you want to place the data and then press the left button. This cell will become the top left cell of the new location.

4 Press Enter on your keyboard and a copy of the data appears in the new location.

CHECK SPELLING

CHECK SPELLING

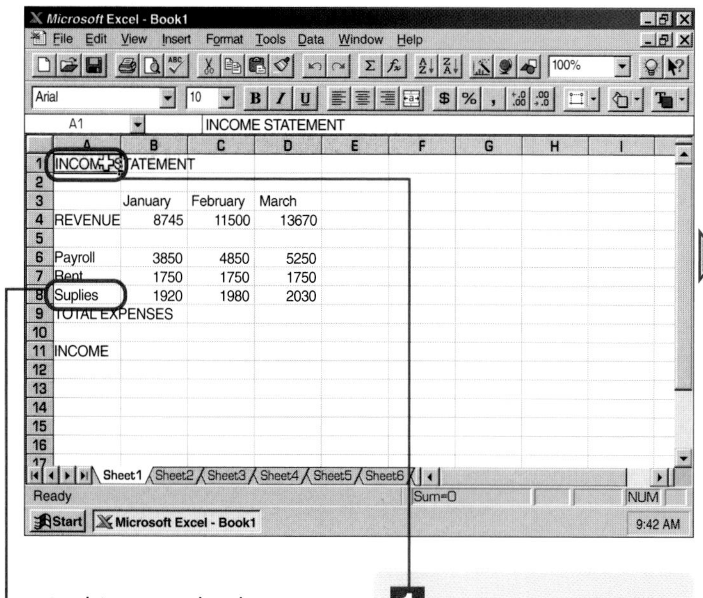

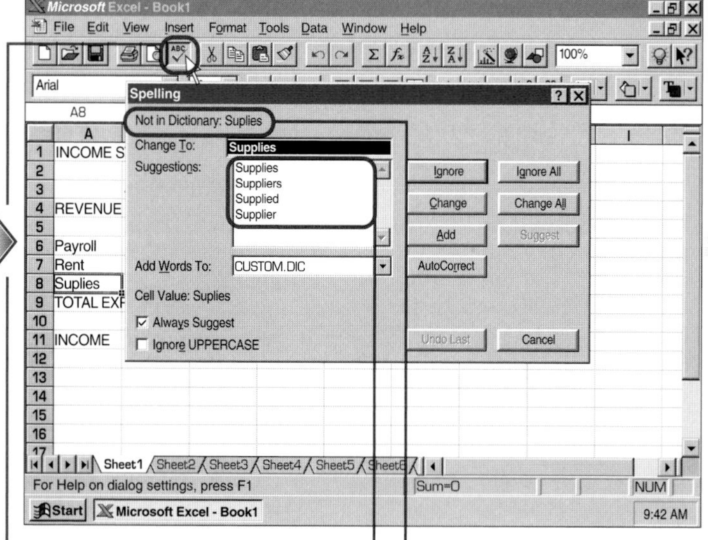

■ In this example, the spelling of **Supplies** was changed to **Suplies**.

1 To start the spell check at the beginning of your worksheet, move the mouse over cell **A1** and then press the left button.

Note: To spell check a section of your worksheet, select the cells you want to check. To select cells, refer to page 12.

2 To start the spell check, move the mouse over and then press the left button.

■ The **Spelling** dialog box appears if Excel finds a misspelled word.

■ This area displays the first word that Excel considers misspelled.

■ This area displays suggestions to correct the word.

Tip

Excel compares every word in your worksheet to words in its dictionary. If a word does not exist in the dictionary, Excel considers it misspelled.

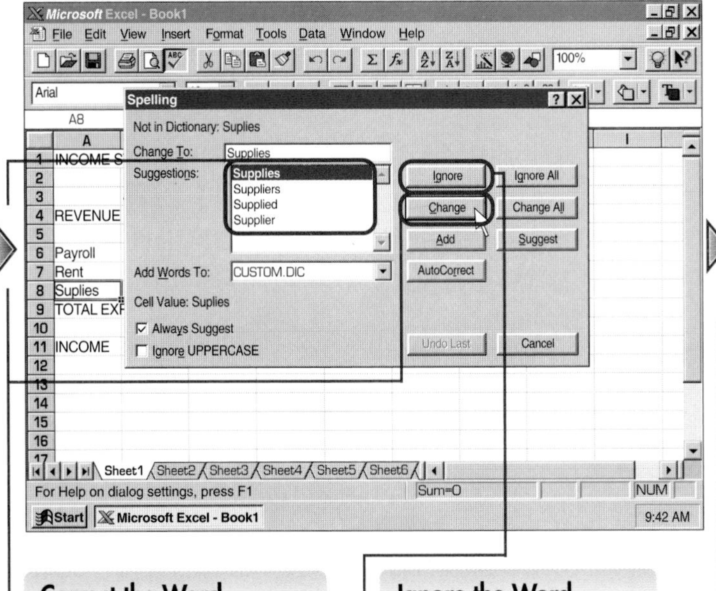

Correct the Word

3 To correct the word, move the mouse over the correct spelling and then press the left button.

4 Move the mouse over **Change** and then press the left button.

Ignore the Word

5 To ignore the word and continue checking your worksheet, move the mouse over **Ignore** and then press the left button.

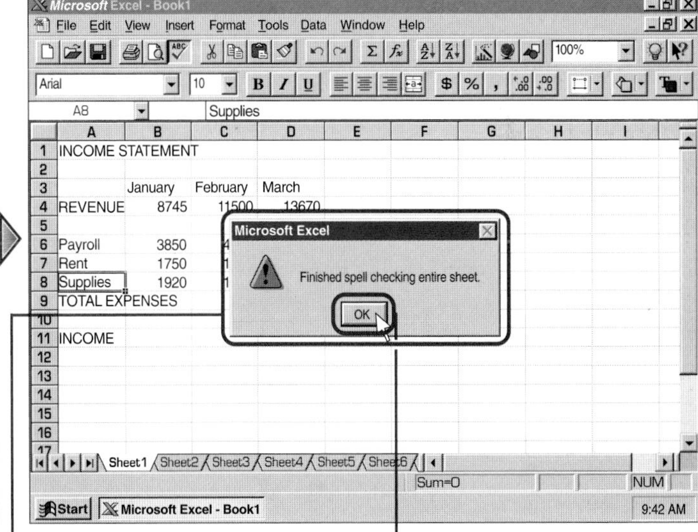

■ Excel corrects or ignores the word in your worksheet and continues checking for misspelled words.

6 Correct or ignore misspelled words until this dialog box appears, telling you the spell check is complete.

7 To close the dialog box, move the mouse over **OK** and then press the left button.

In this chapter you will learn how to save your work and exit Excel. You will also learn how to find and open your workbooks.
Joe's Budget

CHAPTER 3

SAVE AND OPEN YOUR WORKBOOKS

HARD DRIVE (C:)

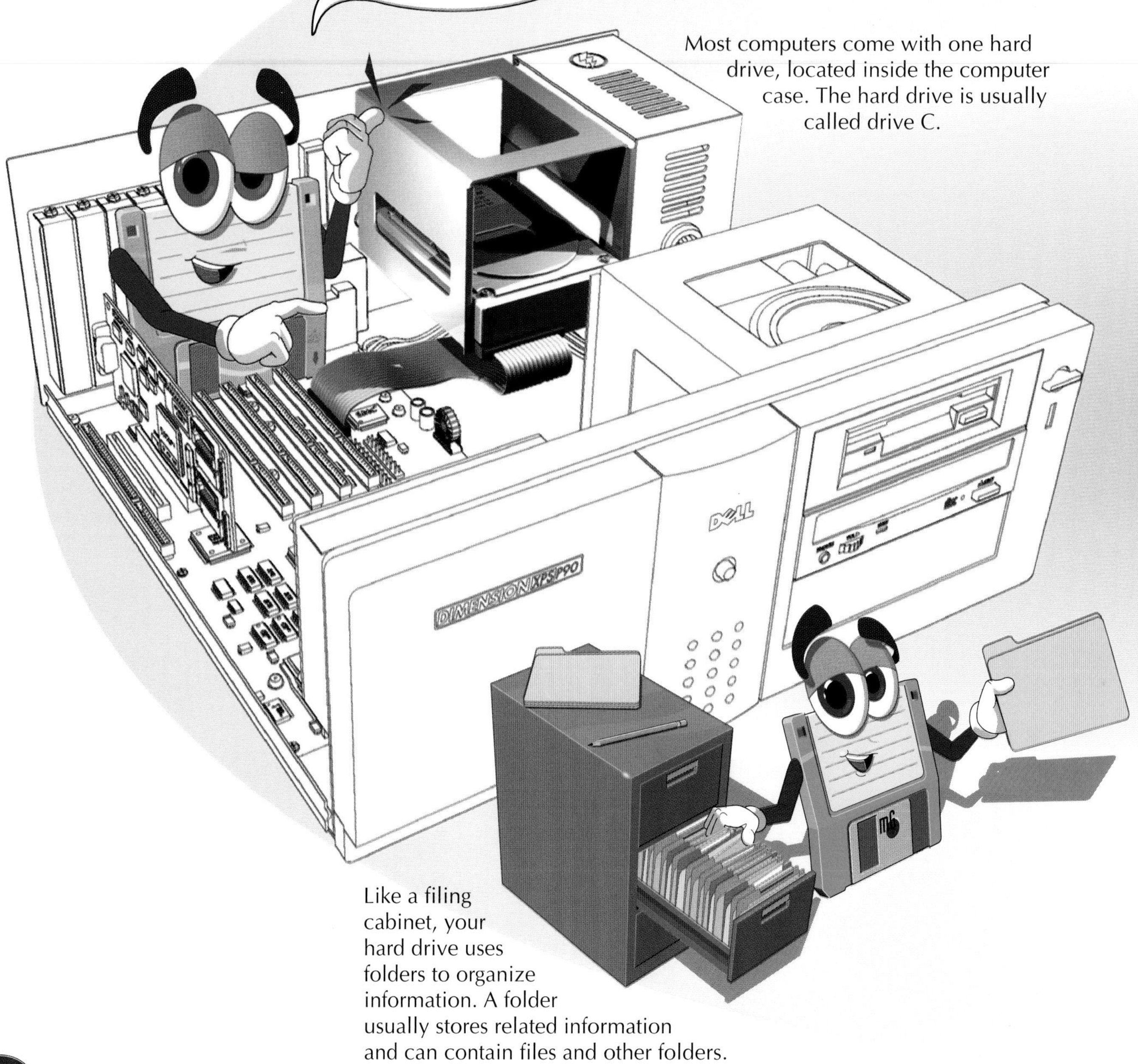
The hard drive is the primary device your computer uses to store information.
DIMENSION XPS P90
DELL

Most computers come with one hard drive, located inside the computer case. The hard drive is usually called drive C.

Like a filing cabinet, your hard drive uses folders to organize information. A folder usually stores related information and can contain files and other folders.

FLOPPY DRIVE (A:)

A floppy drive stores and retrieves information on floppy disks (diskettes). If your computer has only one floppy drive, the drive is called drive A. If your computer has two floppy drives, the second drive is called drive B.

CD-ROM DRIVE (D:)

A CD-ROM drive is a device that reads information stored on compact discs. You cannot change information stored on a compact disc.

Note: Your computer may not have a CD-ROM drive.

SAVE A WORKBOOK

You should save your workbook to store it for future use. This lets you later review and make changes to the data.

SAVE A WORKBOOK

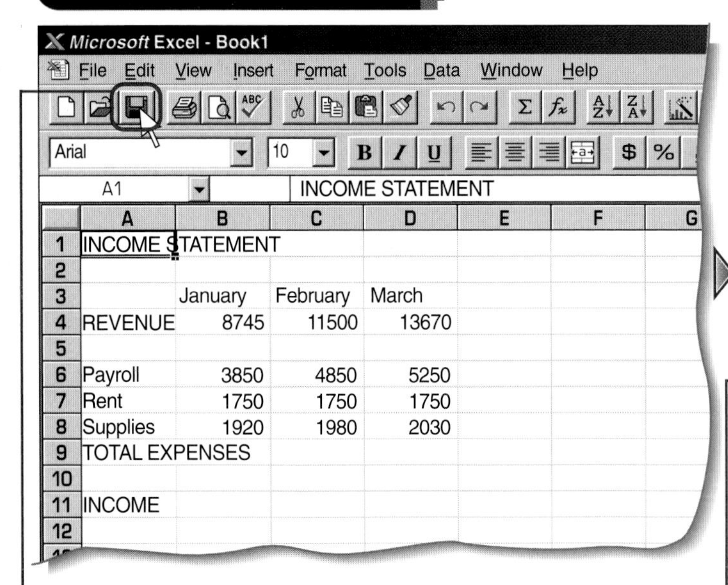

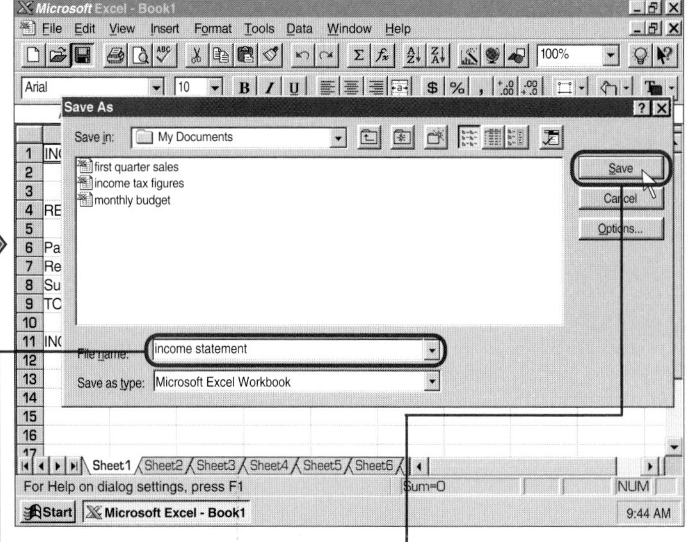

1 Move the mouse over 💾 and then press the left button.

■ The **Save As** dialog box appears.

*Note: If you previously saved your workbook, the **Save As** dialog box will not appear, since you have already named the workbook.*

2 Type a name for your workbook.

*Note: You can use up to 218 characters, including spaces, to name a workbook. The name cannot contain the characters / \ < > * " ? ; : or |.*

3 Move the mouse over **Save** and then press the left button.

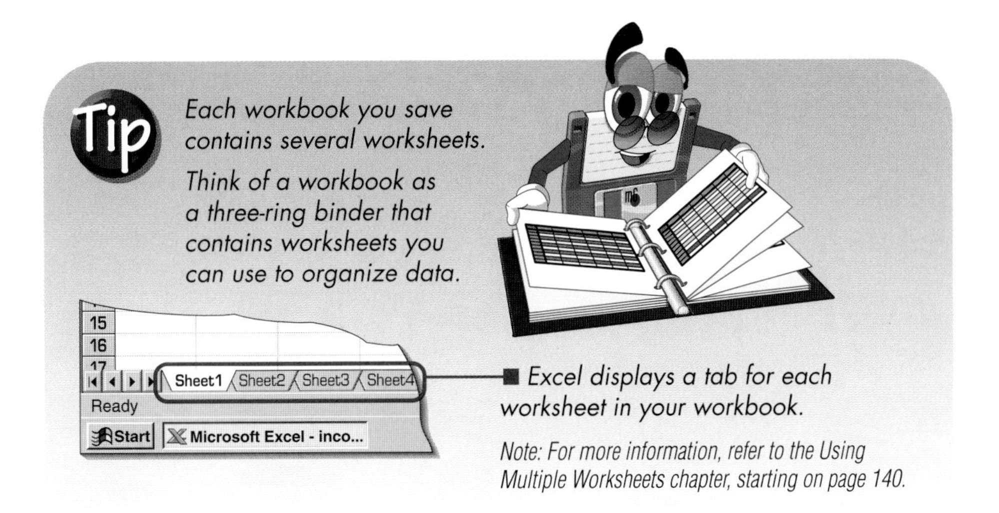

Each workbook you save contains several worksheets.

Think of a workbook as a three-ring binder that contains worksheets you can use to organize data.

■ *Excel displays a tab for each worksheet in your workbook.*

Note: For more information, refer to the Using Multiple Worksheets chapter, starting on page 140.

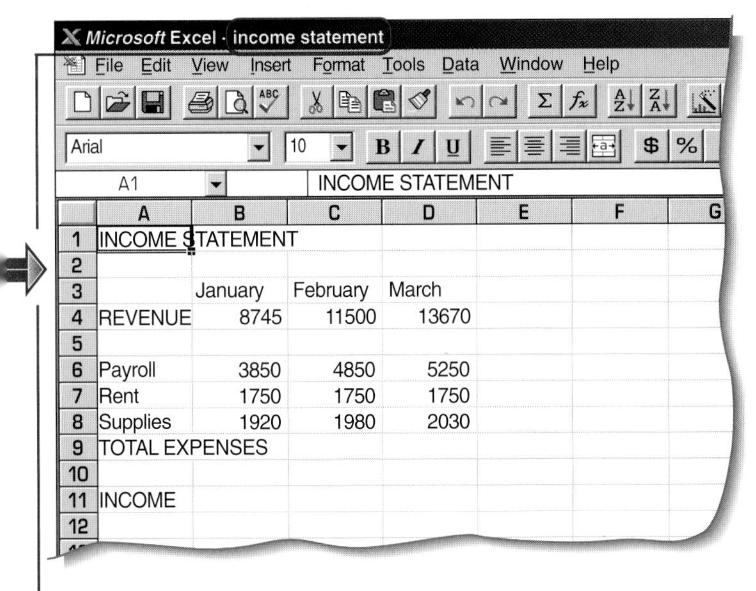

■ Excel saves your workbook and displays the name at the top of your screen.

SAVE YOUR CHANGES

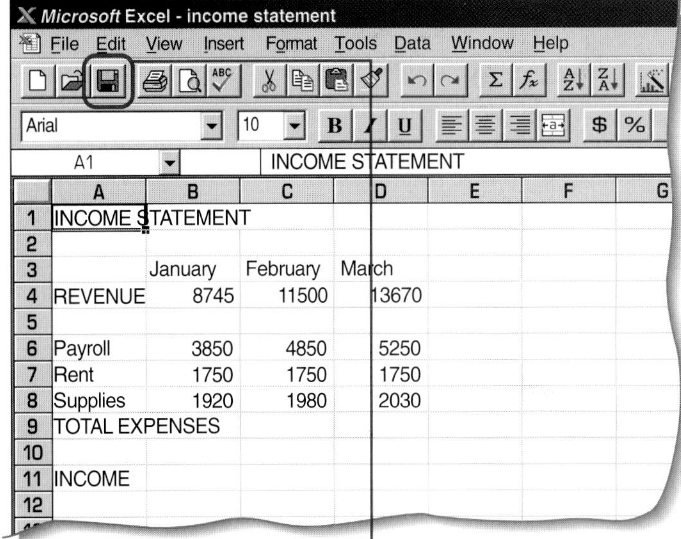

You should save your workbook approximately every ten minutes to avoid losing changes you have made.

■ To save your changes, move the mouse over and then press the left button.

SAVE A WORKBOOK TO A FLOPPY DISK

You can save your workbook to a floppy disk. This is useful if you want to give a copy of the workbook to a colleague.
Bill's disk
MicroFLOPPY
Double Sided
1.44 MB

SAVE A WORKBOOK TO A FLOPPY DISK

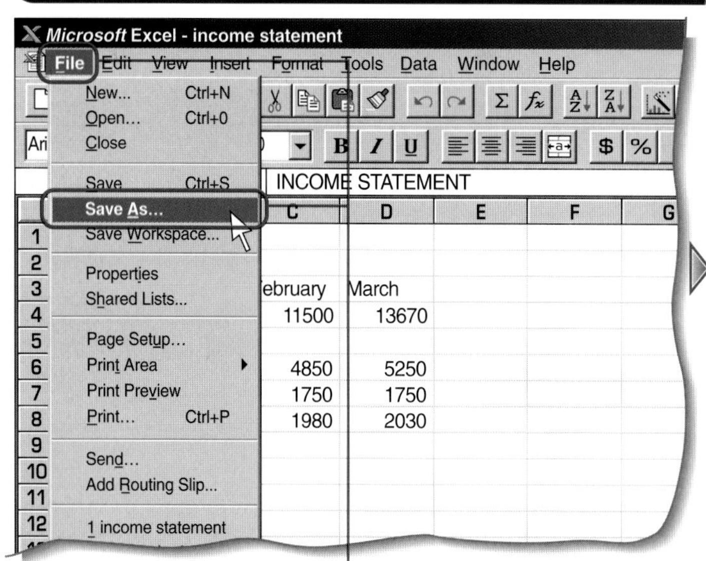

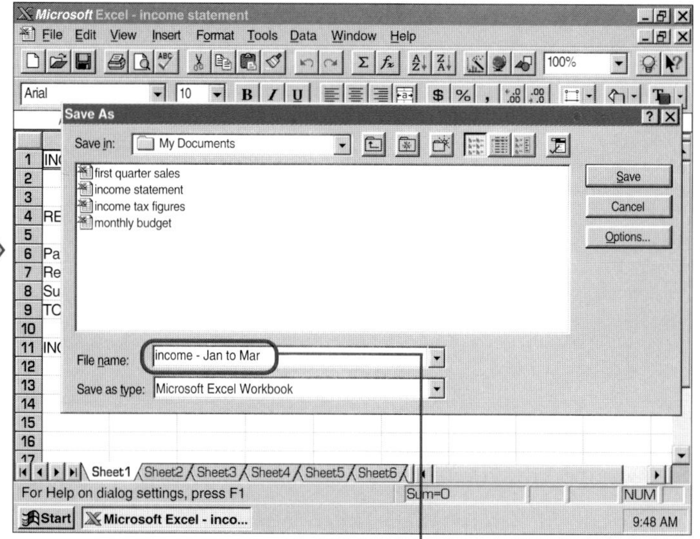

1 Insert a floppy disk into a drive.

2 Move the mouse over **File** and then press the left button.

3 Move the mouse over **Save As** and then press the left button.

■ The **Save As** dialog box appears.

4 This area displays the name of the workbook. To save the workbook with a different name, type a new name.

If you plan to make major changes to your workbook, you may want to save the workbook with a different name before you begin. This gives you two copies of the workbook—the original workbook and a workbook with all the changes.

■ *Perform steps 2 to 4 on page 42. Then perform step 7 below.*

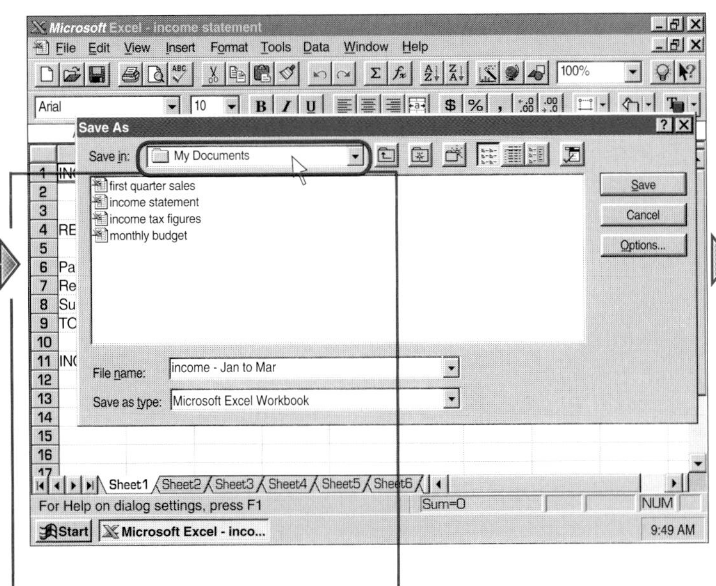

■ This area displays the location where the workbook will be saved.

5 To change the location, move the mouse over this area and then press the left button.

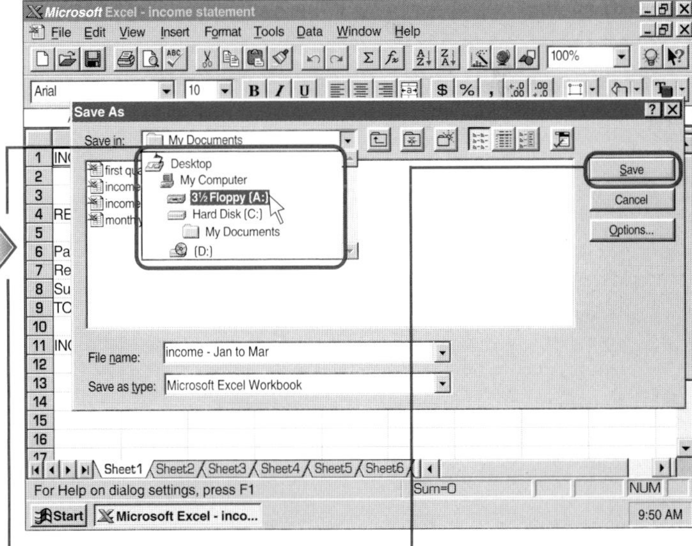

■ A list of the available locations appears.

6 Move the mouse over the location where you want to save the workbook and then press the left button.

7 To save the workbook, move the mouse over **Save** and then press the left button.

EXIT EXCEL

OPEN A WORKBOOK

When you finish using Excel, you can exit the program.
EXIT

EXIT EXCEL

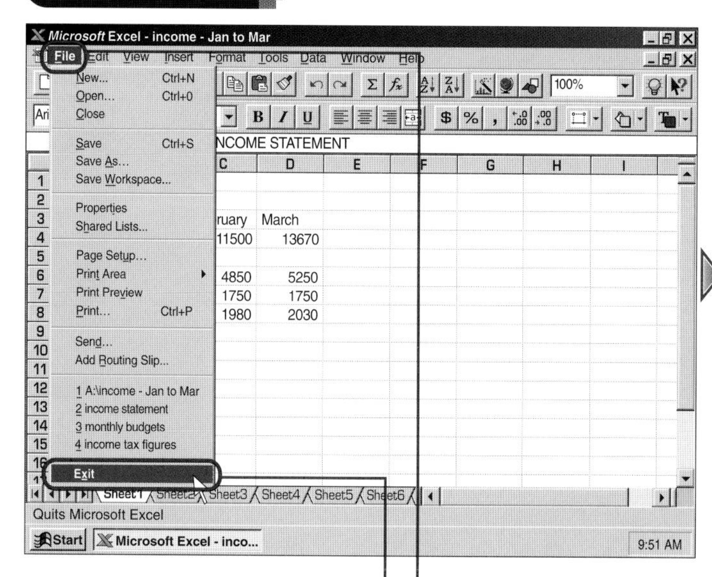

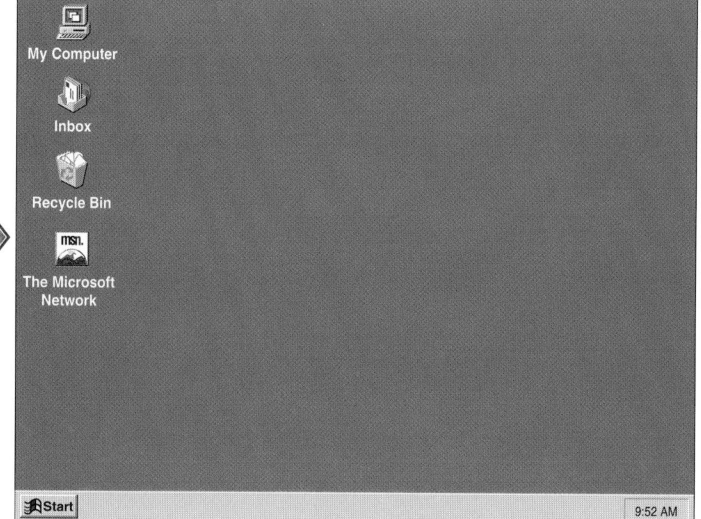

1 Save your workbook before exiting.

Note: For information on saving, refer to page 40.

2 Move the mouse over **File** and then press the left button.

3 Move the mouse over **Exit** and then press the left button.

■ The Excel window disappears from your screen.

Note: To restart Excel, refer to page 8.

■ To avoid damaging your information, always exit Excel and Windows before turning off your computer.

Excel remembers the names of the last four workbooks you opened. You can quickly display any of these workbooks on your screen.

QUICKLY OPEN A WORKBOOK

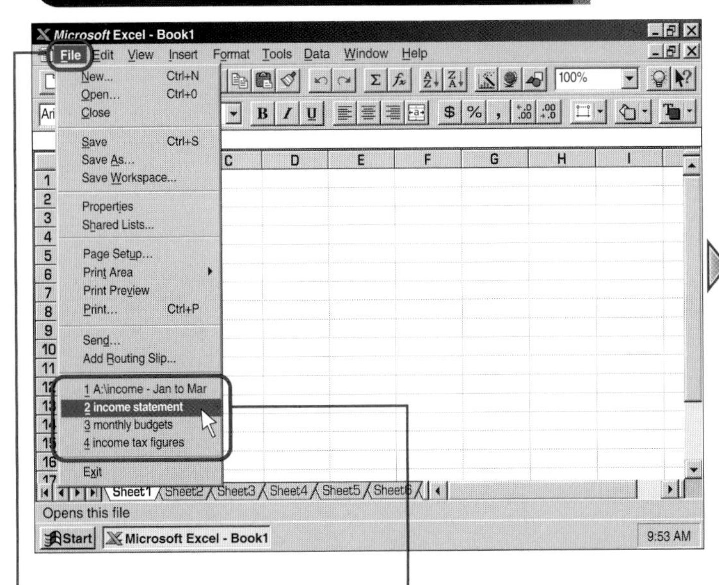

Microsoft Excel - income statement

	A	B	C	D
1	INCOME STATEMENT			
2				
3		January	February	March
4	REVENUE	8745	11500	13670
5				
6	Payroll	3850	4850	5250
7	Rent	1750	1750	1750
8	Supplies	1920	1980	2030
9	TOTAL EXPENSES			
10				
11	INCOME			

1 Move the mouse over **File** and then press the left button.

2 Move the mouse over the name of the workbook you want to open and then press the left button.

Note: If the name of the workbook is not displayed, refer to page 46 to view a list of all your saved workbooks.

■ Excel opens the workbook and displays it on your screen. You can now review and make changes to the workbook.

■ The name of the workbook appears at the top of your screen.

OPEN A WORKBOOK

You can open a saved workbook and display it on your screen. This lets you review and make changes to the workbook.

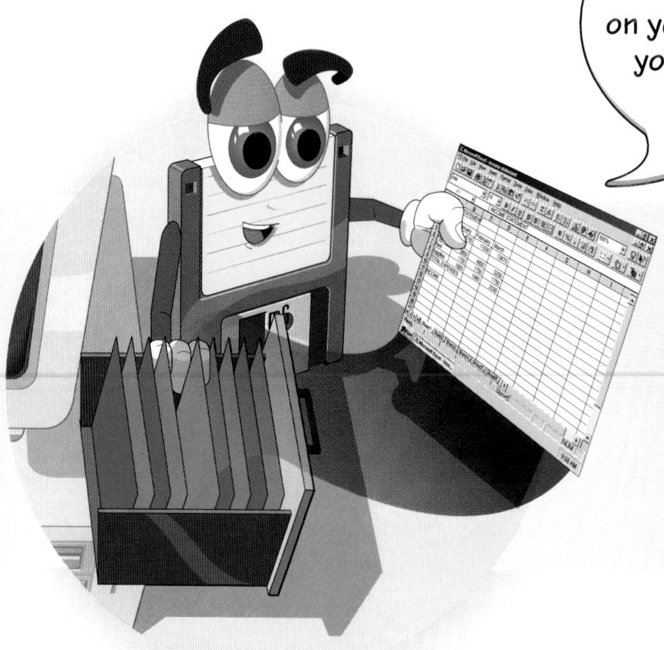

OPEN A WORKBOOK

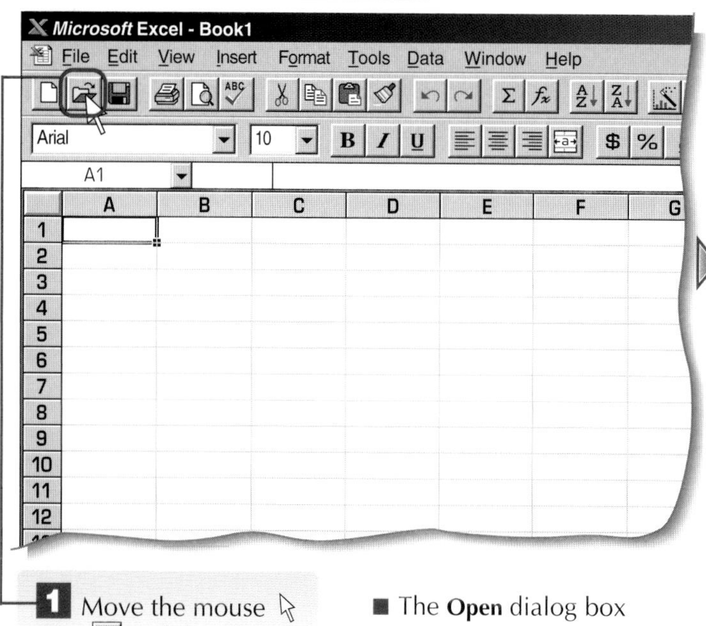

1 Move the mouse over and then press the left button.

■ The **Open** dialog box appears.

2 Move the mouse over the name of the workbook you want to open and then press the left button.

Note: If the name of the workbook you want to open is not displayed, refer to page 48 to find the workbook.

You can easily open a brand new workbook at any time.

Note: For more information, refer to page 154.

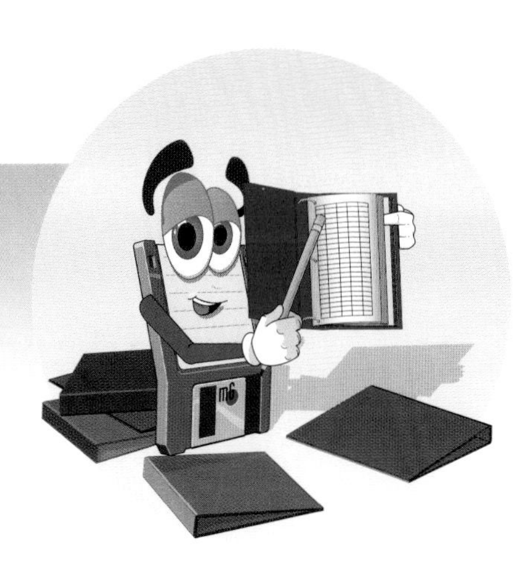

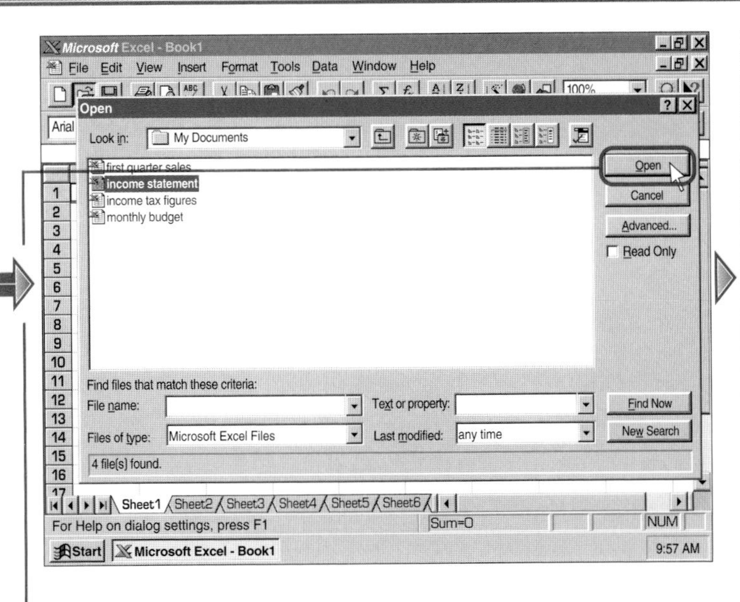

3 To open the workbook, move the mouse over **Open** and then press the left button.

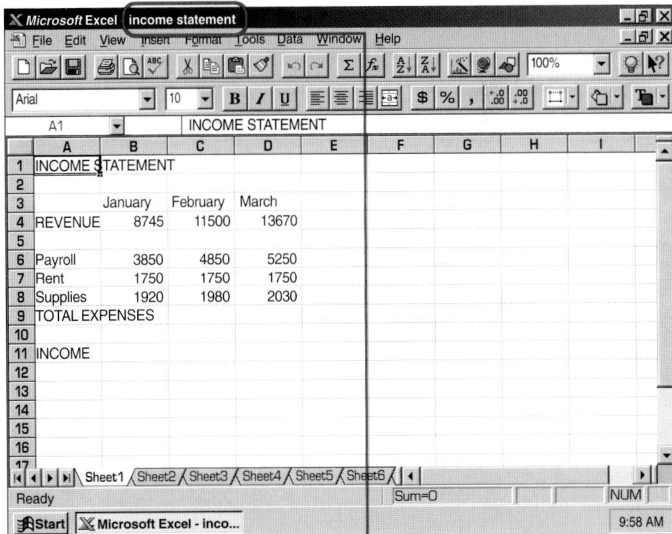

■ Excel opens the workbook and displays it on your screen. You can now review and make changes to the workbook.

■ The name of the workbook appears at the top of your screen.

FIND A WORKBOOK

If you cannot remember the name or location of a workbook you want to open, you can have Excel search for the workbook.
Monthly Statement
Financial Statement 1995
Joe's Budget

FIND A WORKBOOK

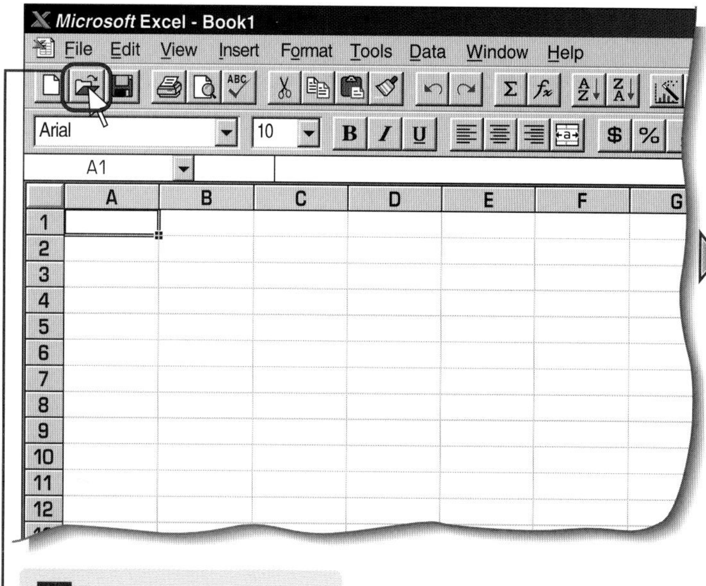

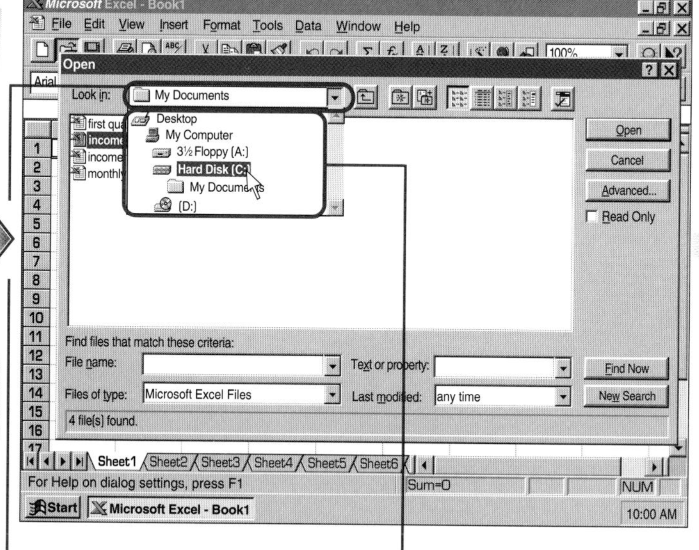

1 Move the mouse over the Open button and then press the left button.

■ The **Open** dialog box appears.

2 To specify where you want Excel to search for the workbook, move the mouse over this area and then press the left button.

3 Move the mouse over the location you want to search and then press the left button.

Tip
If you search for a workbook with a particular name, Excel will find all the workbooks whose names contain the text you specified.
Find:
income
income
tax
Mike's
income
1995
income
income
statement

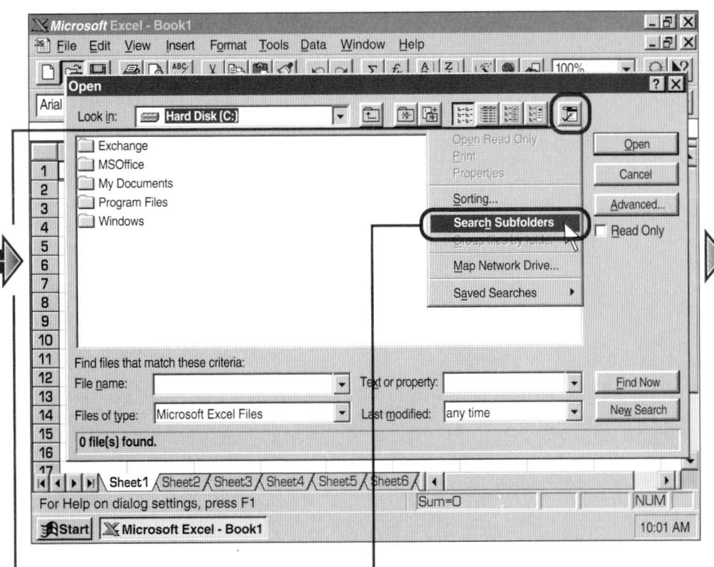

4 To search the contents of all the folders in the location you selected, move the mouse over and then press the left button.

5 Move the mouse over **Search Subfolders** and then press the left button.

*Note: If a check mark (✔) is displayed beside **Search Subfolders**, the feature is already on. To leave the feature on, press Alt on your keyboard.*

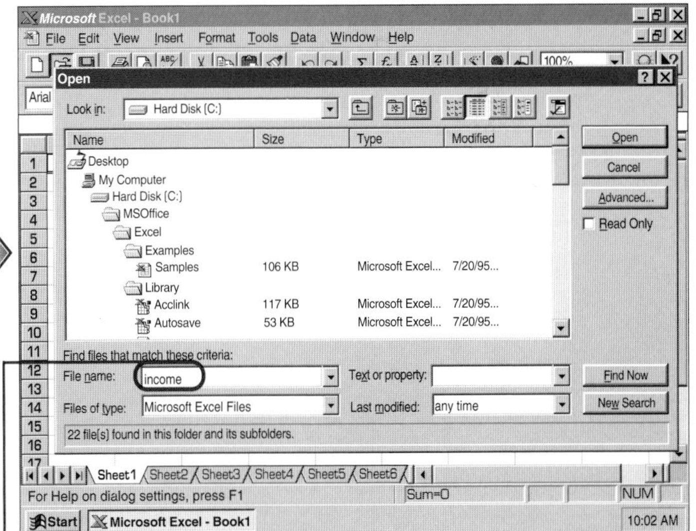

6 If you know all or part of the name of the workbook you want to find, move the mouse over this area and then press the left button. Then type the name.

FIND A WORKBOOK

When the search is complete, Excel displays the names of the workbooks it found.

FIND A WORKBOOK (CONTINUED)

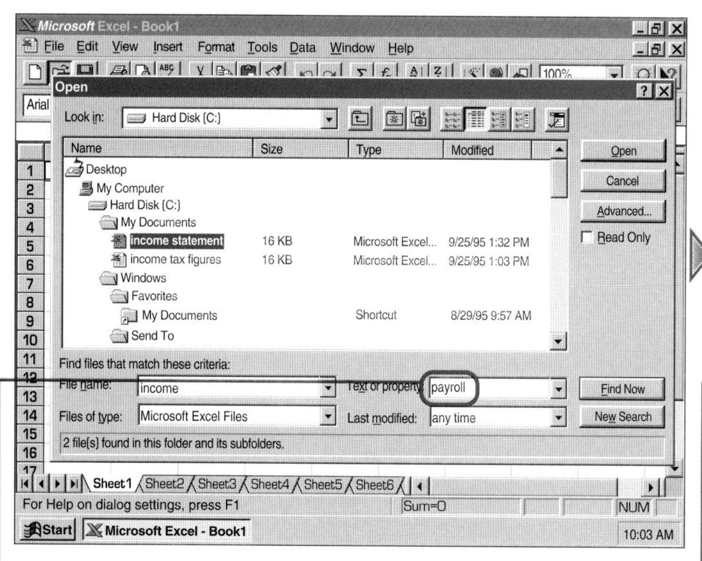

7 If you know a word or phrase in the workbook you want to find, move the mouse over this area and then press the left button. Then type the word or phrase.

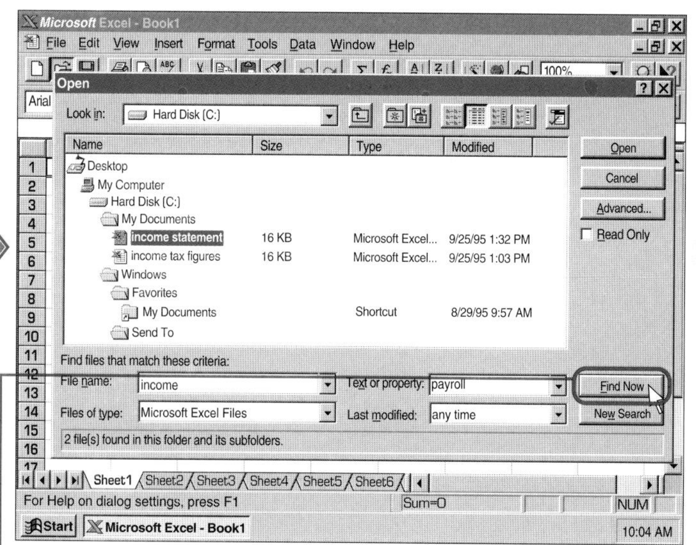

8 To complete the search, move the mouse over **Find Now** and then press the left button.

Excel remembers the names of the last four workbooks you opened. To open one of these workbooks, refer to page 45.

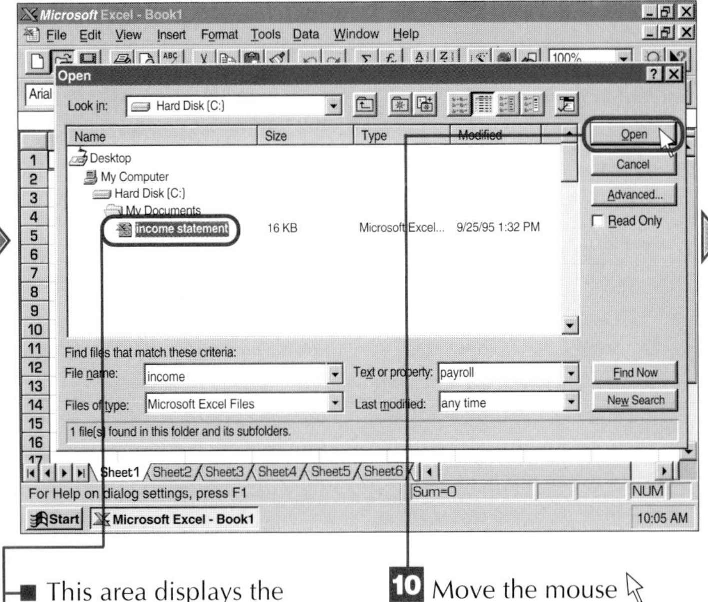

■ This area displays the names of the workbooks Excel found.

9 Move the mouse over the name of the workbook you want to open and then press the left button.

10 Move the mouse over **Open** and then press the left button.

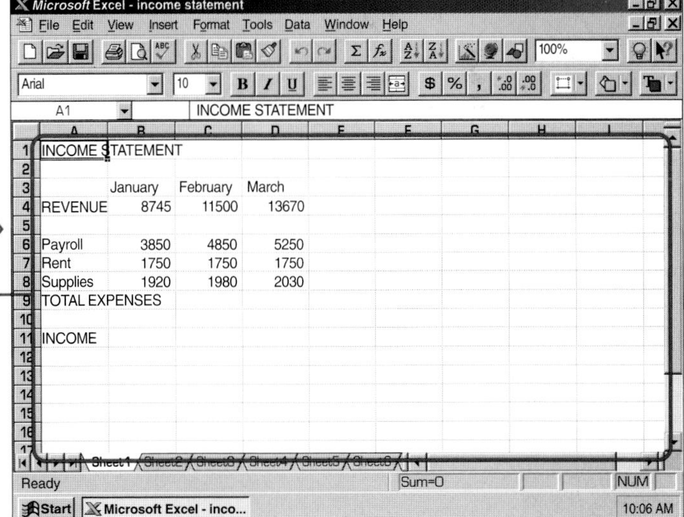

■ Excel opens the workbook and displays it on your screen. You can now review and make changes to the workbook.

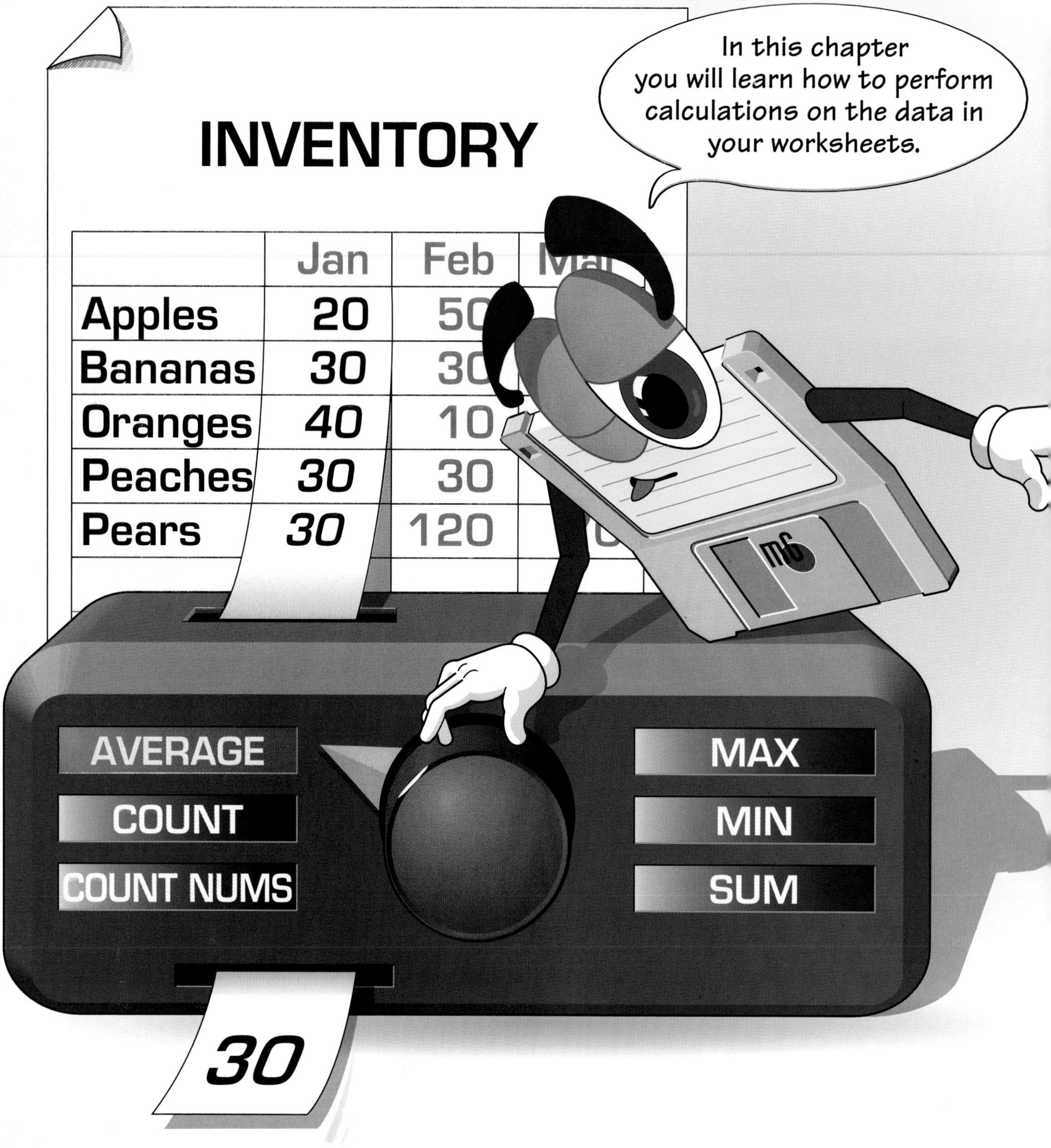

In this chapter you will learn how to perform calculations on the data in your worksheets.

INVENTORY

	Jan	Feb
Apples	20	50
Bananas	30	30
Oranges	40	10
Peaches	30	30
Pears	30	120

AVERAGE
COUNT
COUNT NUMS
MAX
MIN
SUM

30

CHAPTER 4

USING FORMULAS AND FUNCTIONS

Formulas

Enter a Formula

Functions

Enter a Function

Using AutoCalculate

Add Numbers

Errors in Formulas

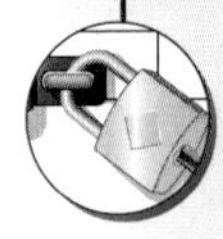
Copy Formulas

Inventory
Apples
Bananas
Kiwis
Mangoes
Oranges
Total
10
5
20
10
30
75

FORMULAS

You can enter formulas to perform calculations on your worksheet data.
6 /98.08 - 45.76

INTRODUCTION TO FORMULAS

■ A formula always begins with an equal sign (=).

■ When entering formulas, use cell references whenever possible (example: **=A1+A2**). Try not to use actual data (example: **=10+20**). This way, if your data changes, Excel will automatically redo the calculations for you.

Microsoft Excel - Book1

File Edit View Insert Format Tools Data Window Help

Arial 10 100%

I16

	A	B	C	D	E	F	G	H
1	10		10		10			
2	20		20		20			
3	30		30		30			
4	40		40		40			
5								
6	1230		320		63			
7								

This cell contains the formula:

=A1+A2+A3*A4

=10+20+30*40

=1230

This cell contains the formula:

=C1*C3-C2+C4

=10*30-20+40

=320

This cell contains the formula:

=E3/E1+E2+E4

=30/10+20+40

=63

You use operators to calculate your data. Excel performs calculations in the following order:

1. Exponentiation (^)
2. Multiplication (*) and Division (/)
3. Addition (+) and Subtraction (-)

■ If you use parentheses ( ) in your formula, Excel will calculate the data in the parentheses first.

This cell contains the formula:

=A1+(A2+A3)*A4

=10+(20+30)*40

=2010

This cell contains the formula:

=C1*(C3-C2)+C4

=10*(30-20)+40

=140

This cell contains the formula:

=E3/(E1+E2)+E4

=30/(10+20)+40

=41

ENTER A FORMULA

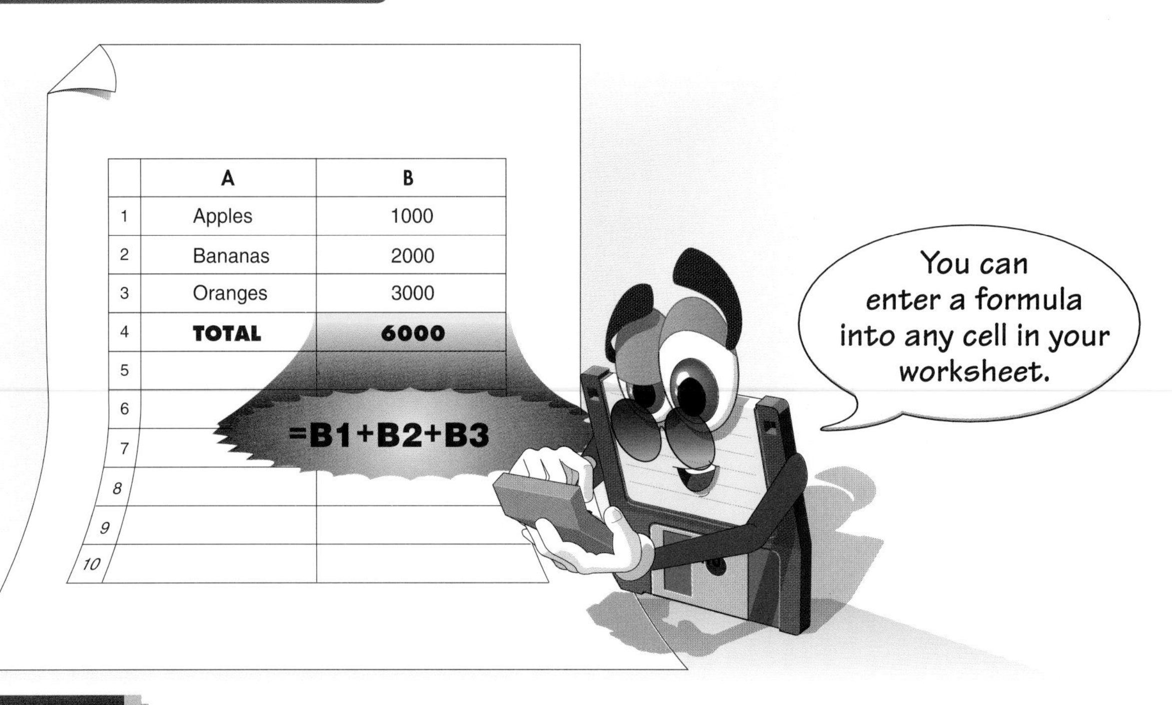

A
B
1 Apples 1000
2 Bananas 2000
3 Oranges 3000
4 TOTAL 6000
=B1+B2+B3
You can enter a formula into any cell in your worksheet.

ENTER A FORMULA

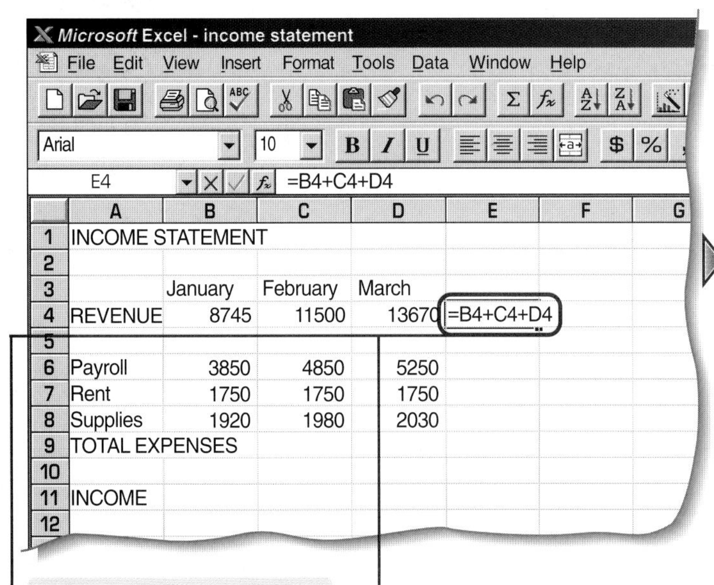

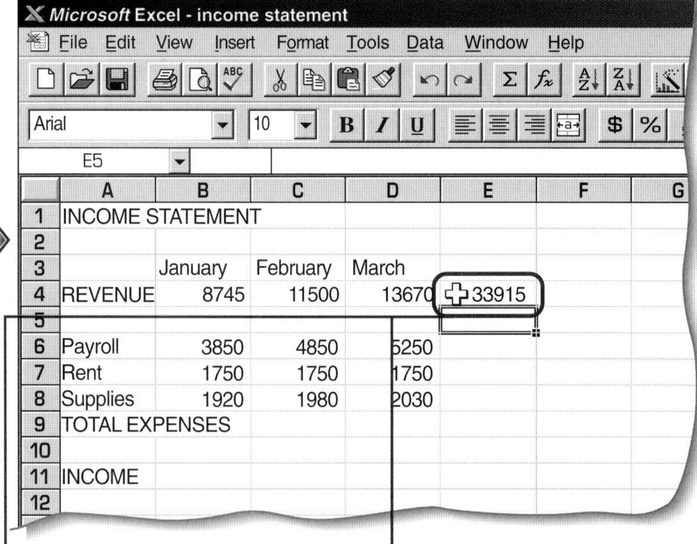

1 Move the mouse over the cell where you want to enter a formula and then press the left button.

2 Type an equal sign (=) to begin the formula.

3 Type the calculation you want to perform and then press **Enter** on your keyboard.

■ The result of the calculation appears in the cell.

4 To view the formula you entered, move the mouse over the cell containing the formula and then press the left button.

Tip

If an error message appears in a cell, you must correct the error.

Note: For information on error messages, refer to page 68.

Microsoft Excel - income statement

File Edit View Insert Format Tools Data Window Help

E4 =B4+C4+D4

	A	B	C	D	E	F	G
1	INCOME STATEMENT						
2							
3		January	February	March			
4	REVENUE	8745	11500	13670	33915		
5							
6	Payroll	3850	4850	5250			
7	Rent	1750	1750	1750			
8	Supplies	1920	1980	2030			
9	TOTAL EXPENSES						
10							
11	INCOME						
12							

■ The formula for the cell appears in the formula bar.

AUTOMATIC RECALCULATION

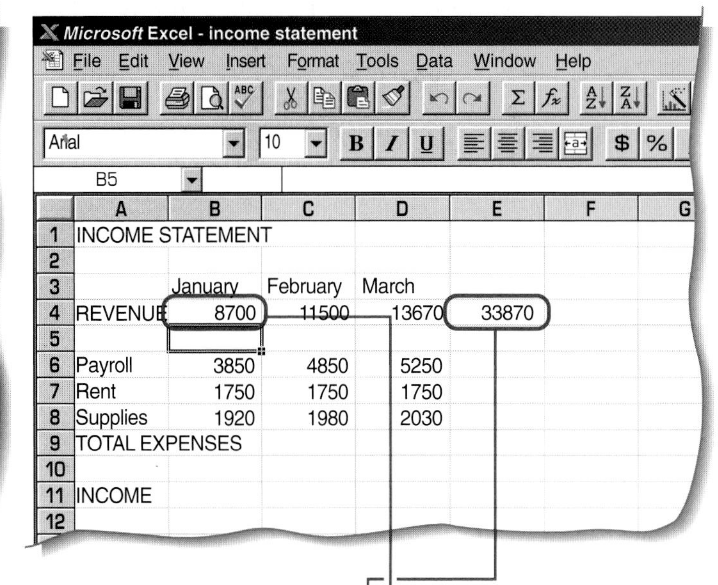

If you change a number used in a formula, Excel will automatically calculate a new result.

■ In this example, the number in cell B4 was changed to 8700.

■ The cell containing the formula automatically displays the new result.

FUNCTIONS

A function is a ready-to-use formula. Excel offers over 200 functions to help you perform specialized calculations on your worksheet data.
Functions
AVERAGE
MAX
ROUND

INTRODUCTION TO FUNCTIONS

■ A function always begins with an equal sign (=).

■ The data Excel will use to calculate the function is enclosed in parentheses ( ).

Microsoft Excel - Book1

File Edit View Insert Format Tools Data Window Help

	A	B	C	D	E	F	G	H
1	10		10		10			
2	20		20		20			
3	30		30		30			
4	40		40		40			
5								
6	25		4		40			
7								

Average

Calculates the average value of a list of numbers.

This cell contains the function:

=AVERAGE(A1:A4)

=(A1+A2+A3+A4)/4

=(10+20+30+40)/4

=25

Count

Displays the number of values in a list.

This cell contains the function:

=COUNT(C1:C4)

=4

Max

Finds the largest value in a list of numbers.

This cell contains the function:

=MAX(E1:E4)

=40

Tip

When there is a comma (,) between cell references in a function, Excel uses each cell to perform the calculation.

For example, =SUM(A1,A3) is the same as the formula =A1+A3.

When there is a colon (:) between cell references in a function, Excel uses the displayed cells and all cells between them to perform the calculation.

For example, =SUM(A1:A3) is the same as the formula =A1+A2+A3.

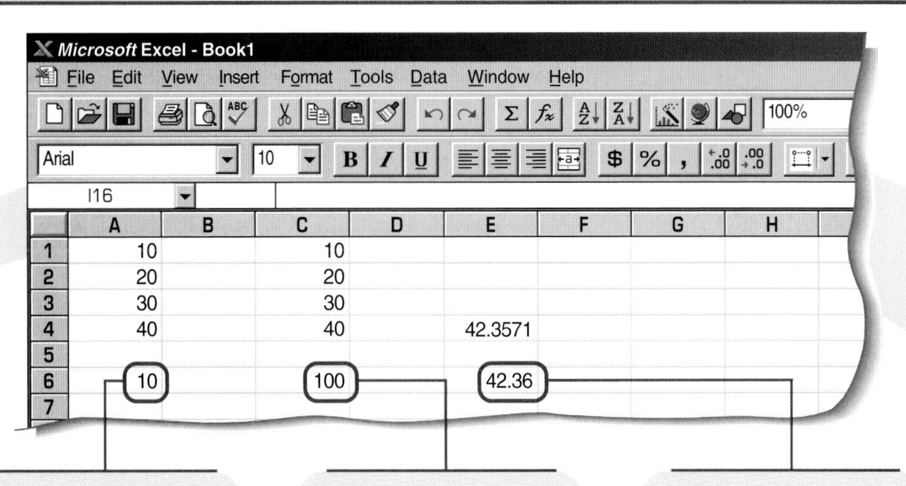

Min

Finds the smallest value in a list of numbers.

This cell contains the function:

=MIN(A1:A4)

=10

Sum

Adds a list of numbers.

This cell contains the function:

=SUM(C1:C4)

=C1+C2+C3+C4

=10+20+30+40

=100

Round

Rounds a value to a specific number of digits.

This cell contains the function:

=ROUND(E4,2)

=42.36

ENTER A FUNCTION

The Function Wizard helps you perform calculations without typing long, complex formulas.

ENTER A FUNCTION

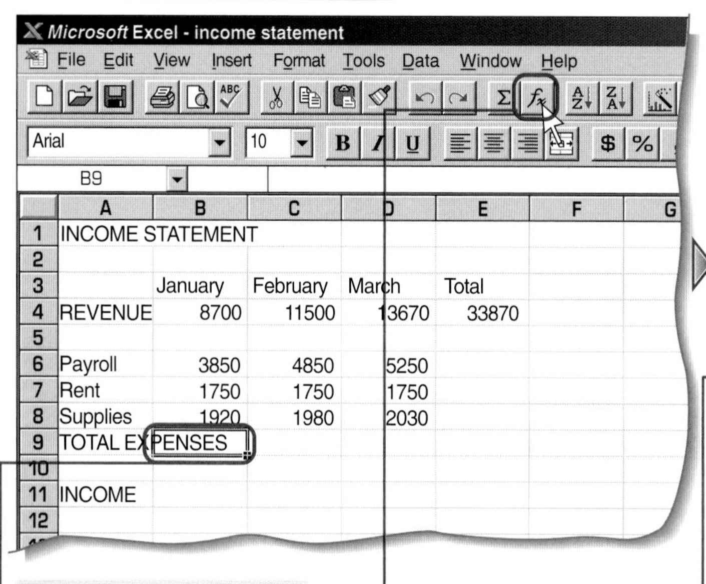

1 Move the mouse over the cell where you want to enter a function and then press the left button.

2 Move the mouse over the function button and then press the left button.

■ The **Function Wizard** dialog box appears.

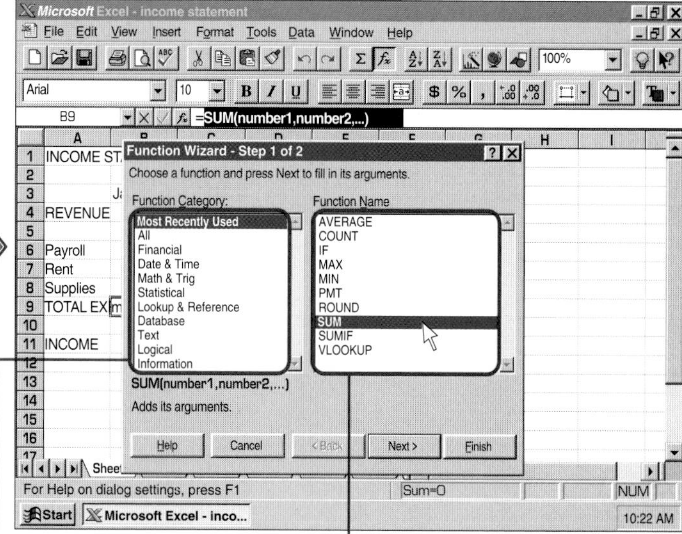

3 Move the mouse over the category that contains the function you want to use and then press the left button.

*Note: If you do not know which category contains the function you want to use, select **All**. This will display a list of all the functions.*

■ This area displays the functions in the category you selected.

4 Move the mouse over the function you want to use and then press the left button.

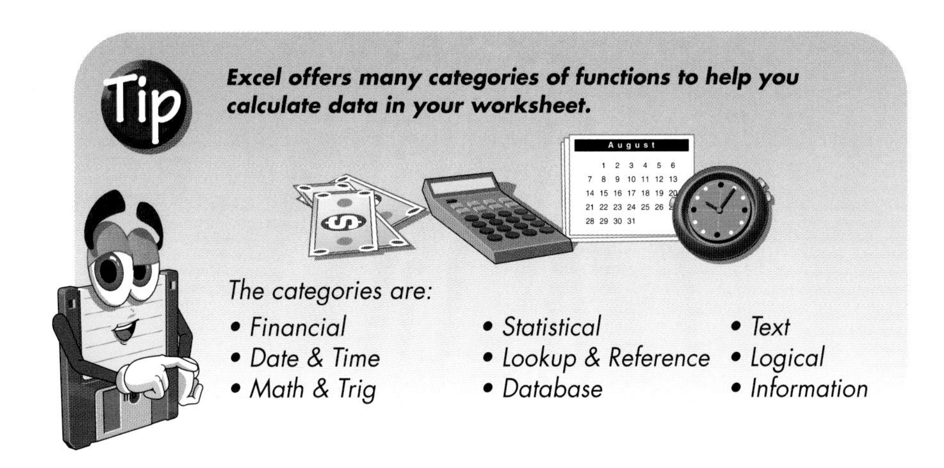

Excel offers many categories of functions to help you calculate data in your worksheet.

The categories are:

- *Financial*
- *Date & Time*
- *Math & Trig*
- *Statistical*
- *Lookup & Reference*
- *Database*
- *Text*
- *Logical*
- *Information*

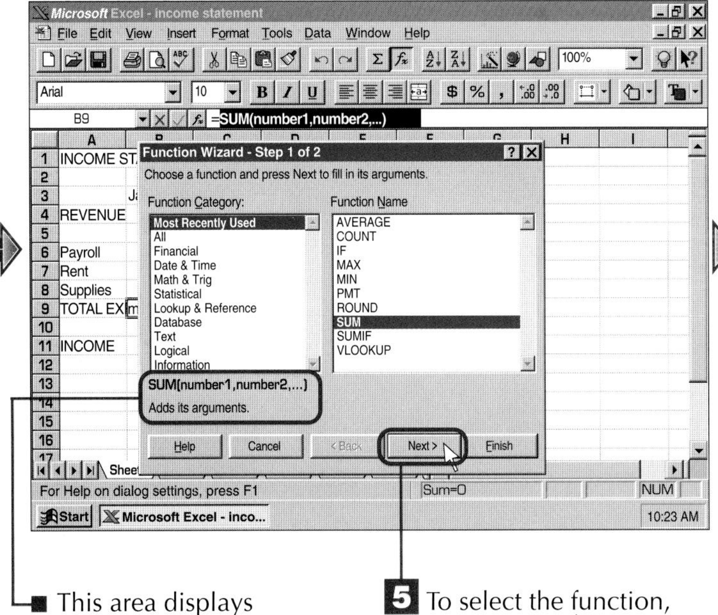

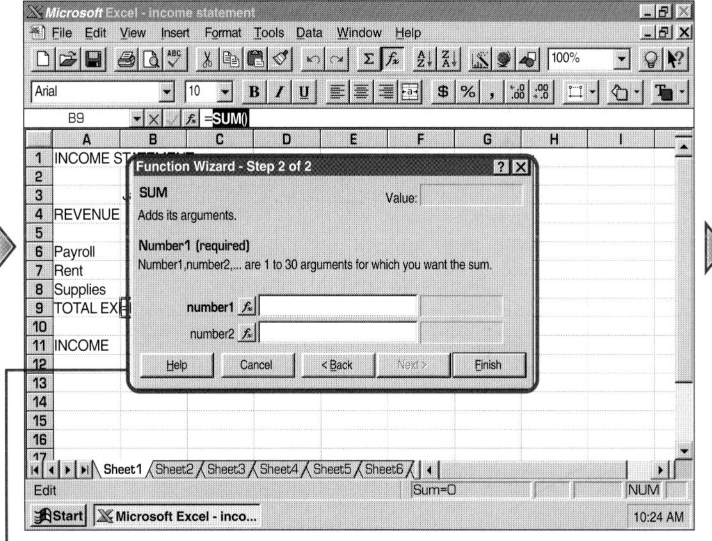

■ This area displays a description of the function you selected.

Note: Arguments are numbers in your worksheet that are used to perform the calculation.

5 To select the function, move the mouse over **Next** and then press the left button.

■ A dialog box appears. The text in the dialog box depends on the function you selected.

CONTINUED

ENTER A FUNCTION

When entering a function, you must tell Excel which numbers you want to use in the calculations.
A
B
1
Apples
10
2
Bananas
+ 20
3
Oranges
+ 30
4
Total

ENTER A FUNCTION (CONTINUED)

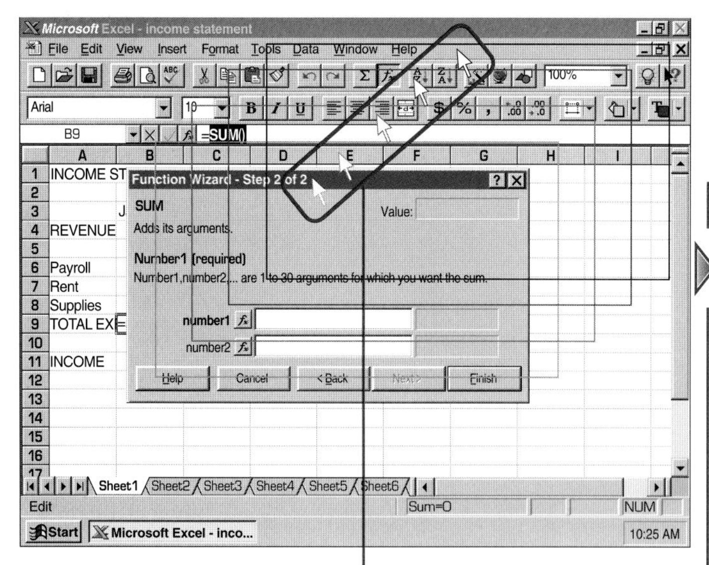

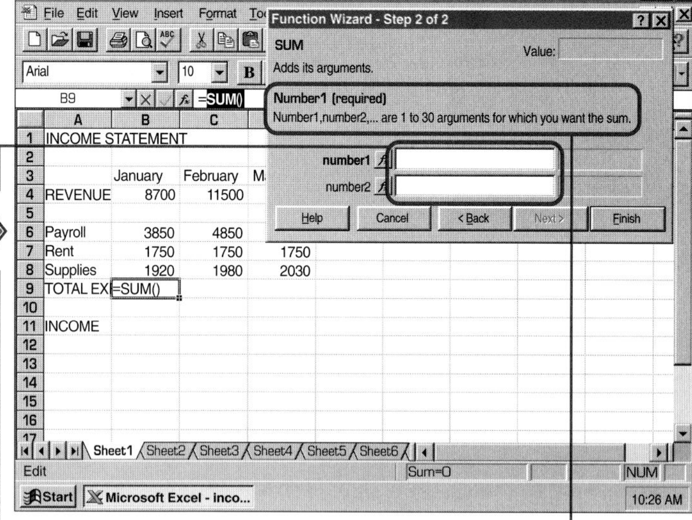

■ If the dialog box covers data you want to use in the calculation, you can move it to another location on your screen.

6 To move the dialog box, position the mouse over the title bar.

7 Press and hold down the left button as you move the mouse to where you want to place the box. Then release the button.

■ This area displays blank boxes where you enter the numbers you want to use in the calculation.

8 To enter the first number, move the mouse over the first blank box and then press the left button.

■ This area describes the number you must enter.

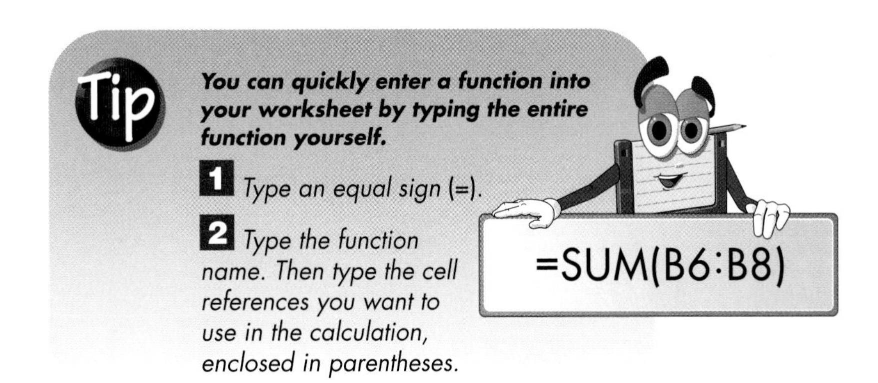

Tip

You can quickly enter a function into your worksheet by typing the entire function yourself.

1 *Type an equal sign (=).*

2 *Type the function name. Then type the cell references you want to use in the calculation, enclosed in parentheses.*

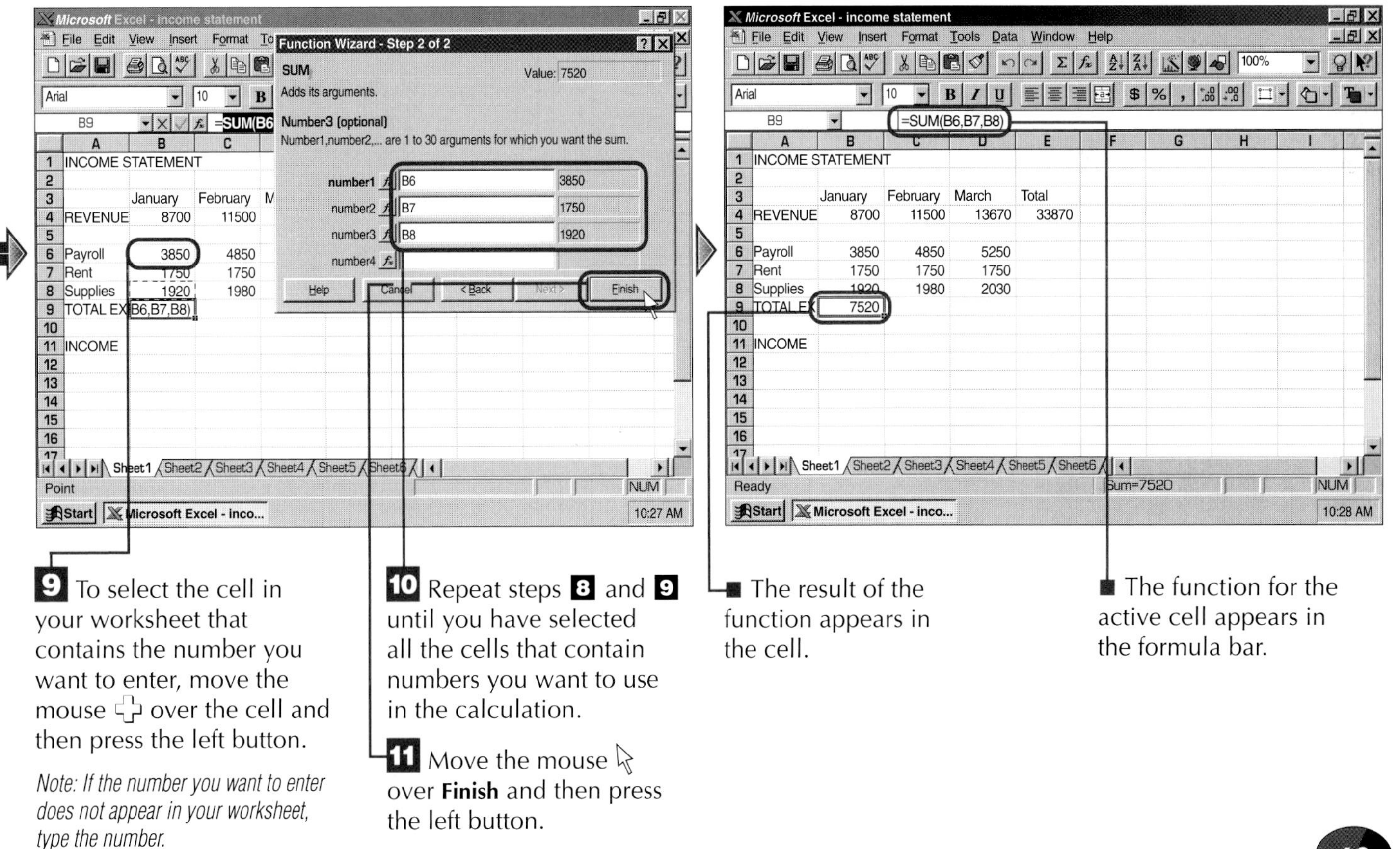

9 To select the cell in your worksheet that contains the number you want to enter, move the mouse over the cell and then press the left button.

Note: If the number you want to enter does not appear in your worksheet, type the number.

10 Repeat steps **8** and **9** until you have selected all the cells that contain numbers you want to use in the calculation.

11 Move the mouse over **Finish** and then press the left button.

■ The result of the function appears in the cell.

■ The function for the active cell appears in the formula bar.

USING AUTOCALCULATE

You can quickly check the result of a calculation without entering a formula into your worksheet.

USING AUTOCALCULATE

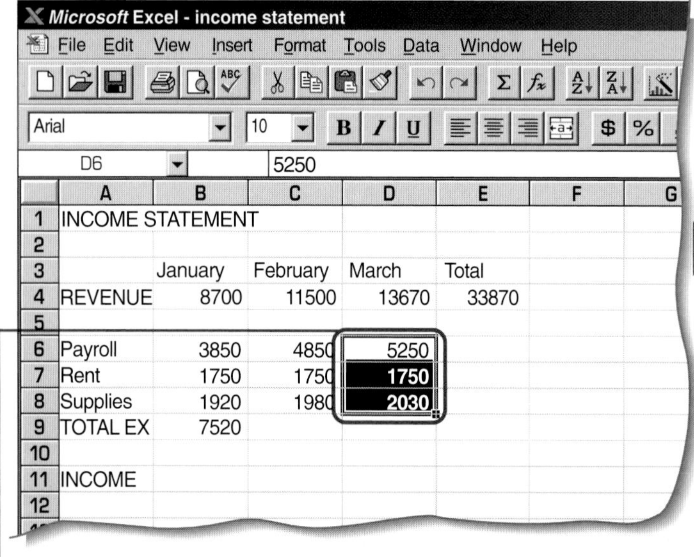

1 Select the cells containing the numbers you want to include in the calculation.

Note: To select cells, refer to page 12.

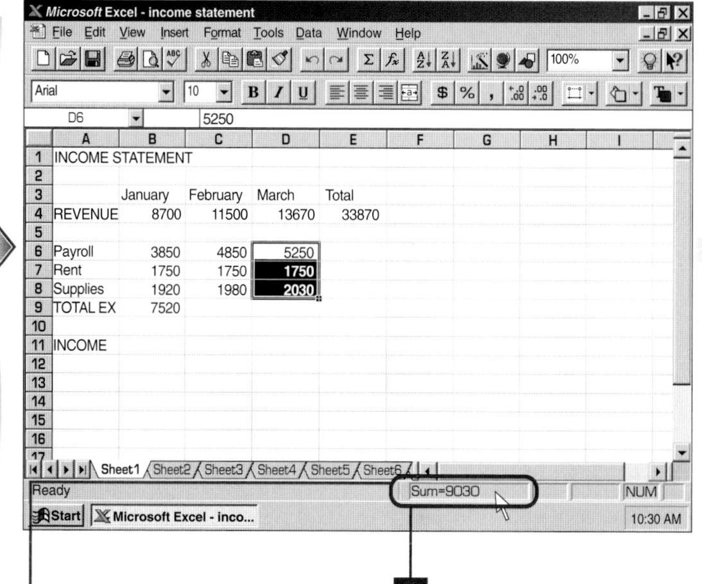

■ This area automatically displays the sum of the cells you selected.

2 To display the result for a different calculation, move the mouse over this area and then press the **right** button.

Tip

The AutoCalculate feature offers six calculations.

Average

Calculates the average value of the list of numbers.

Count

Displays the number of items in the list, including text.

Count Nums

Displays the number of values in the list.

Max

Displays the largest value in the list.

Min

Displays the smallest value in the list.

Sum

Adds the list of numbers.

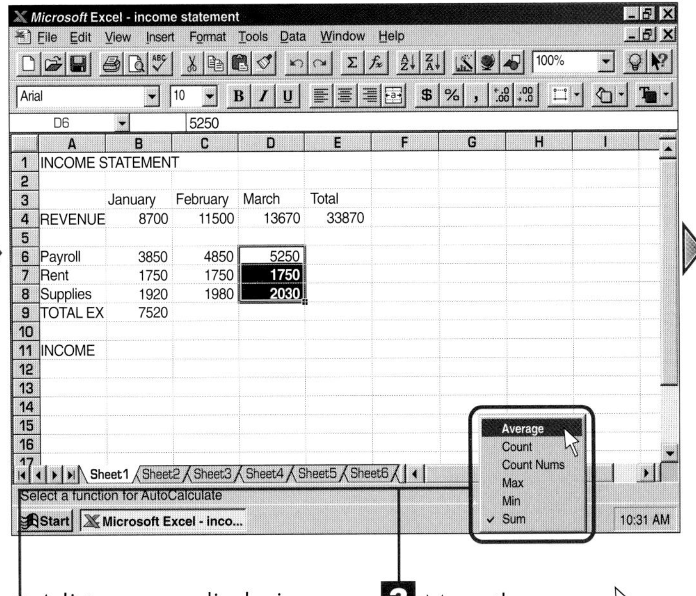

■ A list appears, displaying the calculations you can perform.

3 Move the mouse over the calculation you want to perform and then press the left button.

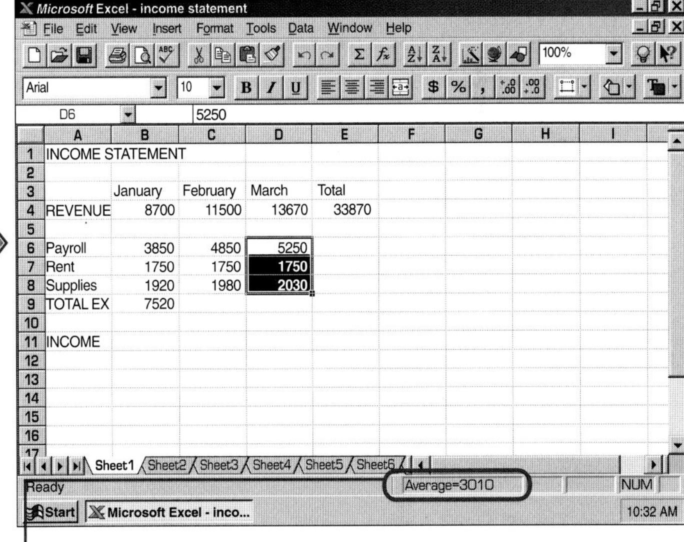

■ This area displays the result for the new calculation.

ADD NUMBERS

You can quickly add a list of numbers in your worksheet.

ADD A LIST OF NUMBERS

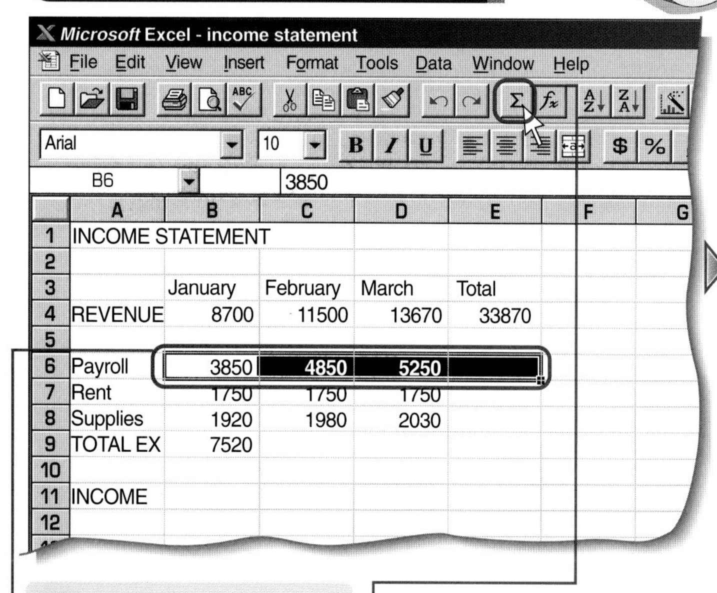

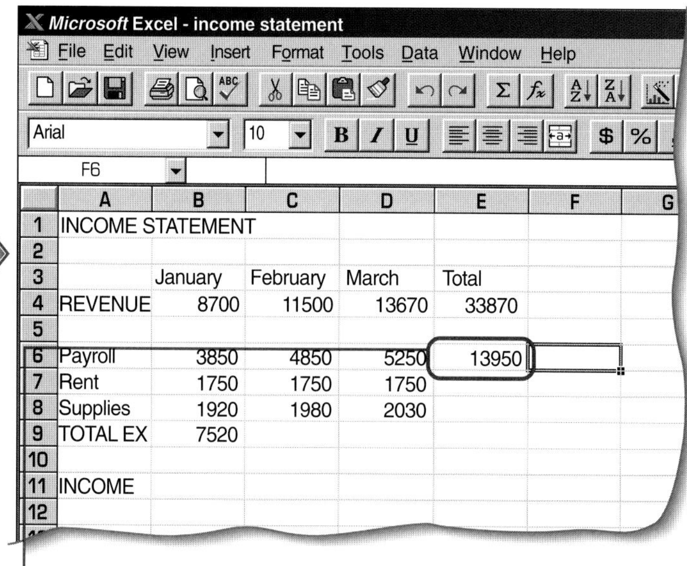

1 Select the cells containing the numbers you want to add, including a blank cell for the result.

Note: To select cells, refer to page 12.

2 Move the mouse over Σ and then press the left button.

■ The result appears.

Note: To deselect cells, move the mouse over any cell and then press the left button.

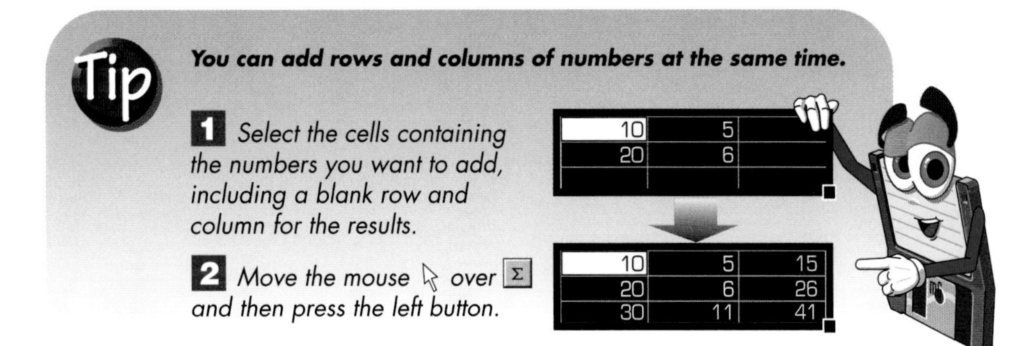

Tip

You can add rows and columns of numbers at the same time.

1 Select the cells containing the numbers you want to add, including a blank row and column for the results.

2 Move the mouse over Σ and then press the left button.

ADD SEVERAL LISTS OF NUMBERS

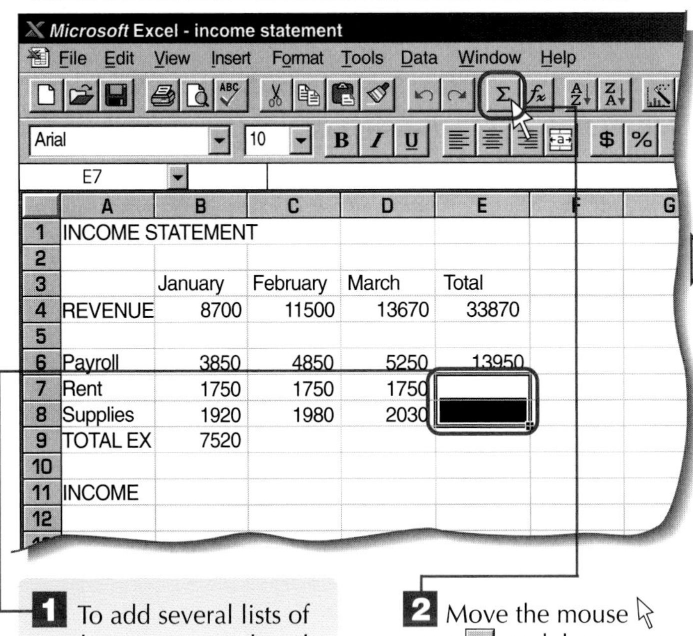

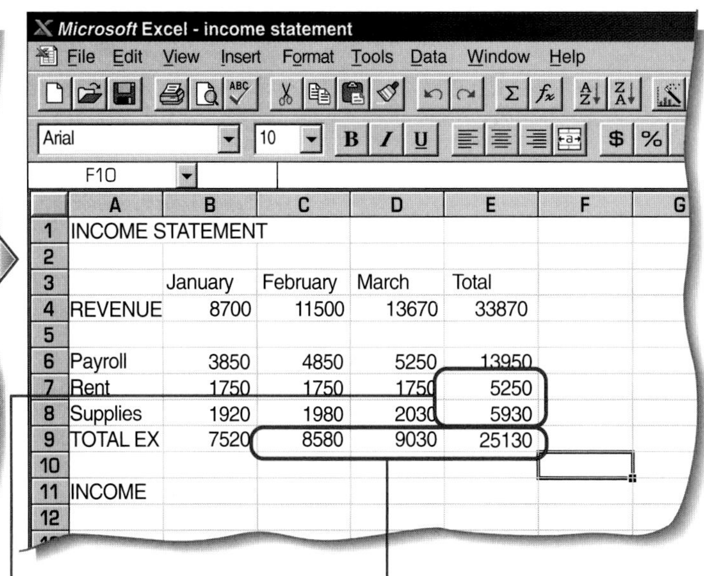

1 To add several lists of numbers at once, select the cells you want to display the results.

Note: To select cells, refer to page 12.

2 Move the mouse over Σ and then press the left button.

■ The results appear.

■ You can repeat steps 1 and 2 to add other lists of numbers in your worksheet.

Note: To deselect cells, move the mouse over any cell and then press the left button.

ERRORS IN FORMULAS

ERROR
An error message appears when Excel cannot properly calculate a formula.

COMMON ERRORS IN FORMULAS

	A	B	C	D	E	F	G
1	50		10		10		9924
2			20		20		5521
3			30		January		
4	#DIV/0!		#NAME?		#VALUE!		#####
5							

The formula divides a number by zero.

Note: Excel considers a blank cell to contain the zero value.

This cell contains the formula:

=A1/A2

=50/0

The formula contains a function name or cell reference Excel does not recognize.

This cell contains the formula:

=SUMM(C1:C3)

Note: SUM (*not* SUMM) *is the correct spelling.*

A cell used in the formula contains data that Excel cannot use in the calculation, such as text.

This cell contains the formula:

=E1+E2+E3

The column is not wide enough to display the result of the calculation.

Note: To display the result, refer to page 80 to change the column width.

Tip
Errors in formulas are often the result of typing mistakes.
You can correct an error by editing the cell containing the error.
Note: To edit data, refer to page 26.
Eraser

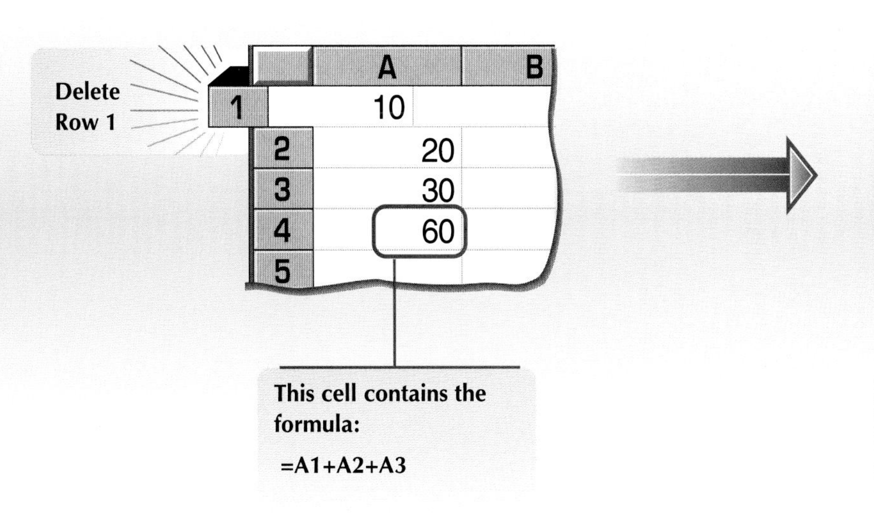

Delete Row 1
A
B
1
10
2
20
3
30
4
60
5
A
B
1
20
2
30
3
#REF!
4
5

This cell contains the formula:

=A1+A2+A3

The formula refers to a cell that is not valid.

In this example, a cell used in the formula was deleted.

COPY FORMULAS

After entering a formula into your worksheet, you can save time by copying the formula to other cells. Excel will automatically change the cell references in the new formulas.

A cell reference that changes when copied is called a relative reference.

COPY FORMULAS (USING RELATIVE REFERENCES)

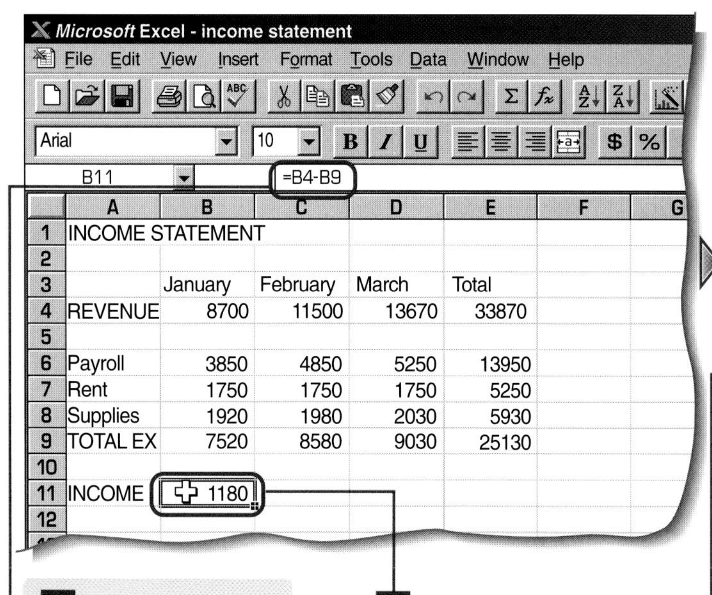

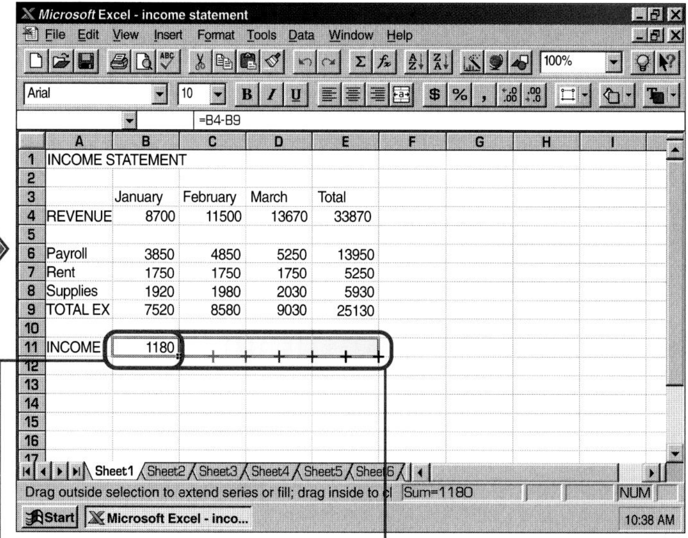

1 Enter the formula you want to copy to other cells.

Note: To calculate INCOME, enter ***=B4-B9*** *in cell* ***B11****.*

2 Move the mouse ✚ over the cell containing the formula you want to copy and then press the left button.

3 Move the mouse ✚ over the bottom right corner of the cell and ✚ changes to +.

4 Press and hold down the left button as you move the mouse + over the cells you want to receive a copy of the formula.

When you copy a formula, Excel automatically changes the cell references in the formula.

	A	B	C
1	10	20	5
2	20	30	10
3	30	40	20
4	60	90	35
5			

=A1+A2+A3

This cell contains the formula =A1+A2+A3

=B1+B2+B3 **=C1+C2+C3**

If you copy the formula to other cells in the worksheet, the cell references in the new formulas automatically change.

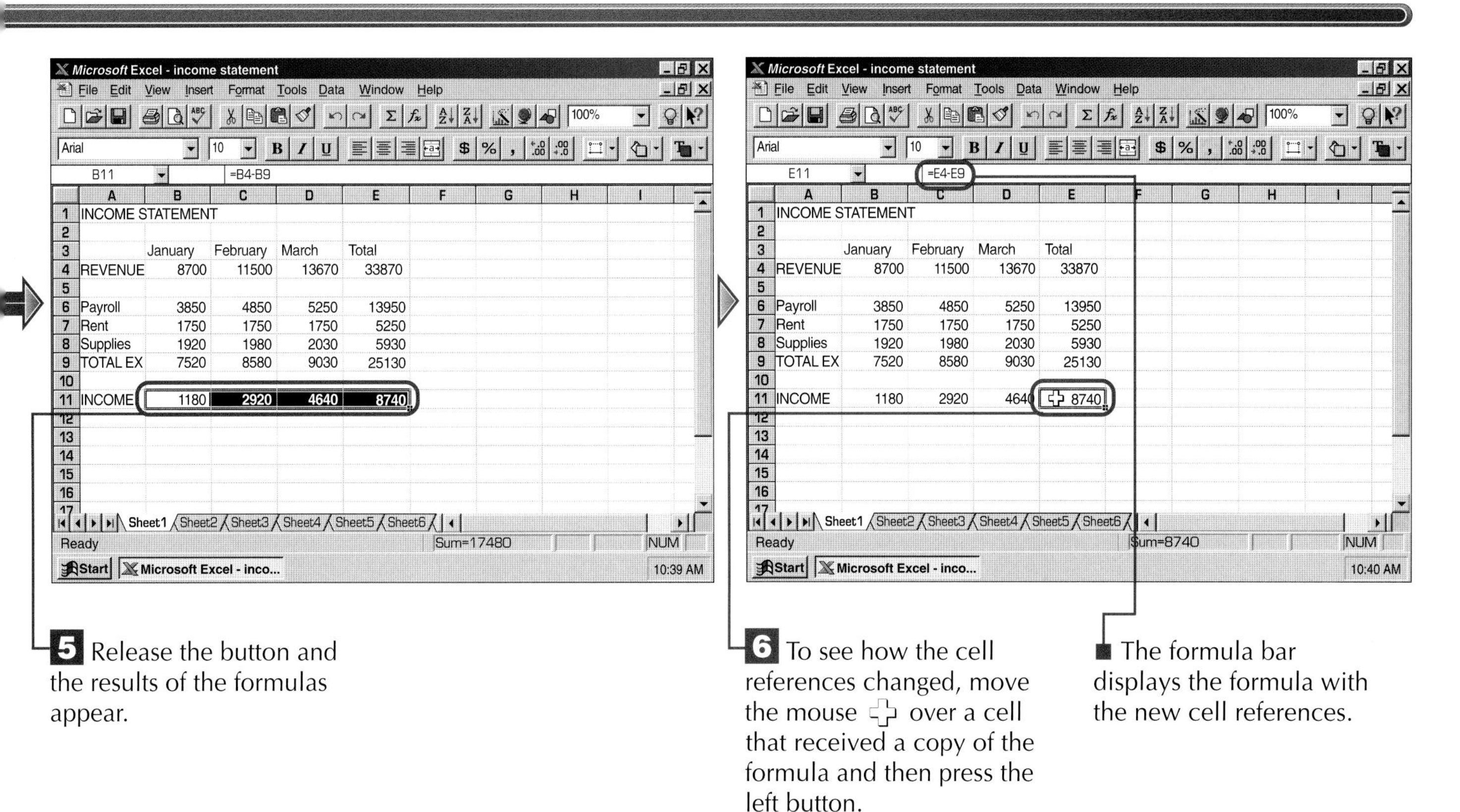

5 Release the button and the results of the formulas appear.

6 To see how the cell references changed, move the mouse over a cell that received a copy of the formula and then press the left button.

■ The formula bar displays the formula with the new cell references.

COPY FORMULAS

Commissions
Rick Susan Greg
SALES 100 200 300
COMMISSION 20 40 60
Commission Rate
0.2

To save time, you can copy a formula to other cells in your worksheet. If you do not want Excel to change a cell reference when copying the formula, you must lock the cell.

A locked cell is called an absolute reference.

COPY FORMULAS (USING ABSOLUTE REFERENCES)

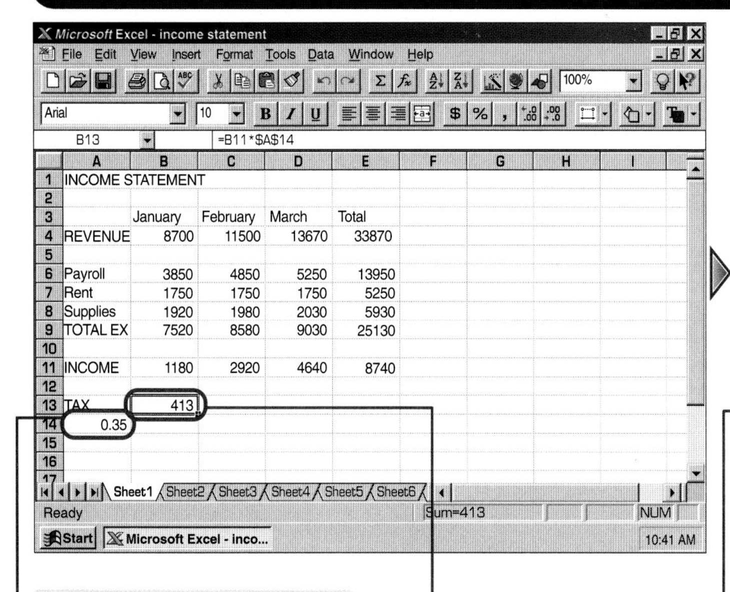

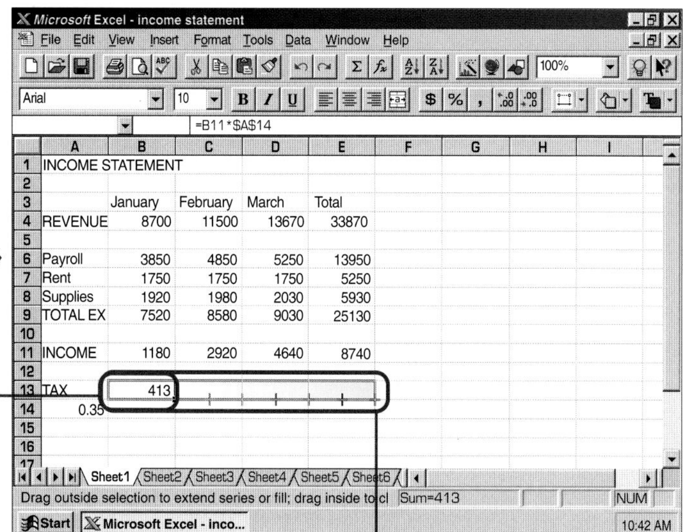

1 Enter the data you want to remain the same in all your formulas.

2 Enter the formula you want to copy to other cells.

*Note: To calculate TAX, enter **=B11*A14** in cell **B13**. To lock a cell reference, refer to the information at the top of page 73.*

3 Move the mouse ✥ over the cell containing the formula you want to copy and then press the left button.

4 Move the mouse ✥ over the bottom right corner of the cell and ✥ changes to +.

5 Press and hold down the left button as you move the mouse + over the cells you want to receive a copy of the formula.

To lock a cell reference and make it absolute, type a dollar sign ($) before both the column letter and row number (example: A7).

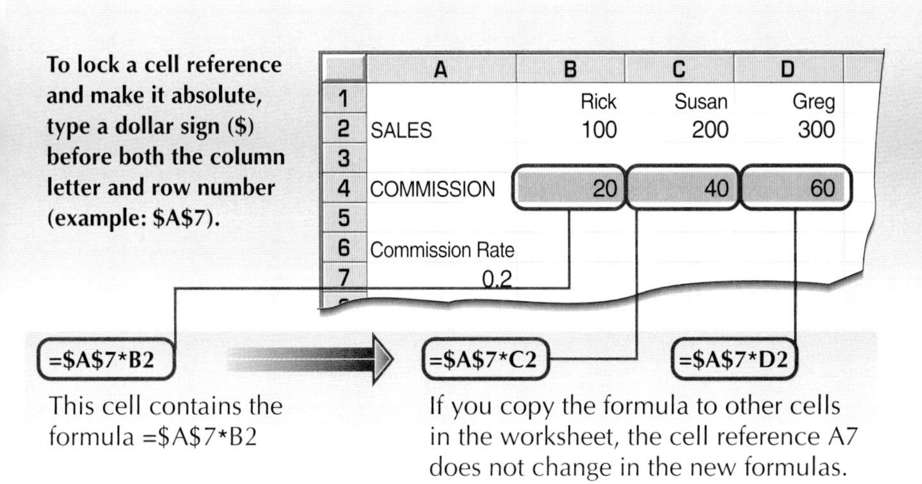

This cell contains the formula =A7*B2

If you copy the formula to other cells in the worksheet, the cell reference A7 does not change in the new formulas.

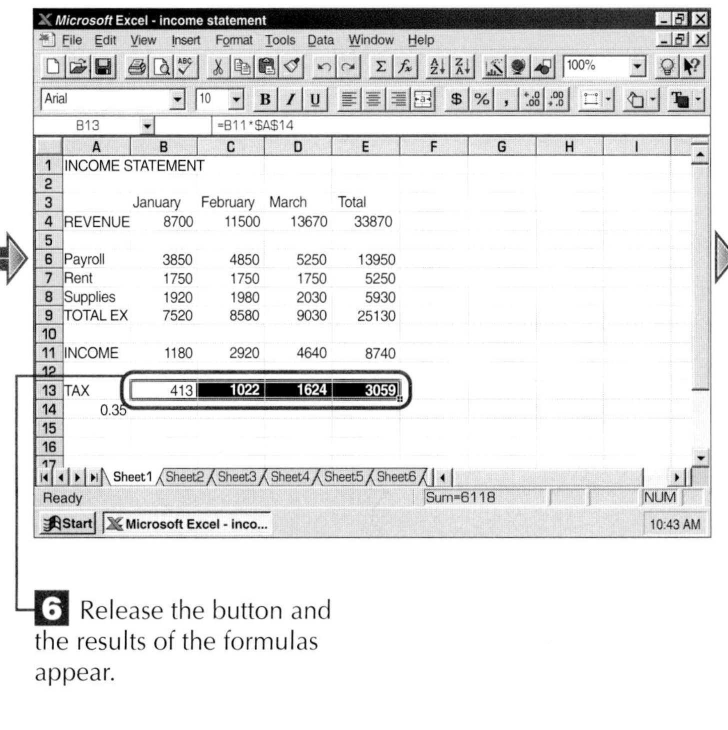

6 Release the button and the results of the formulas appear.

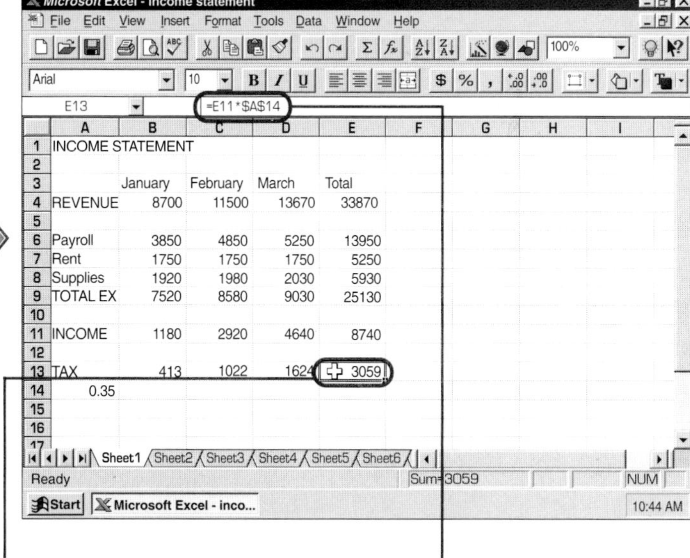

7 To see how the cell references changed, move the mouse over a cell that received a copy of the formula and then press the left button.

■ The absolute reference (example: **A14**) in the formula did not change. The relative reference (example: **E11**) in the formula did change.

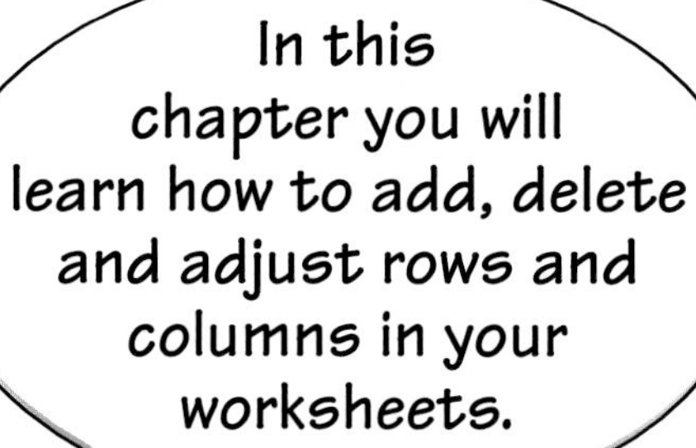
In this chapter you will learn how to add, delete and adjust rows and columns in your worksheets.

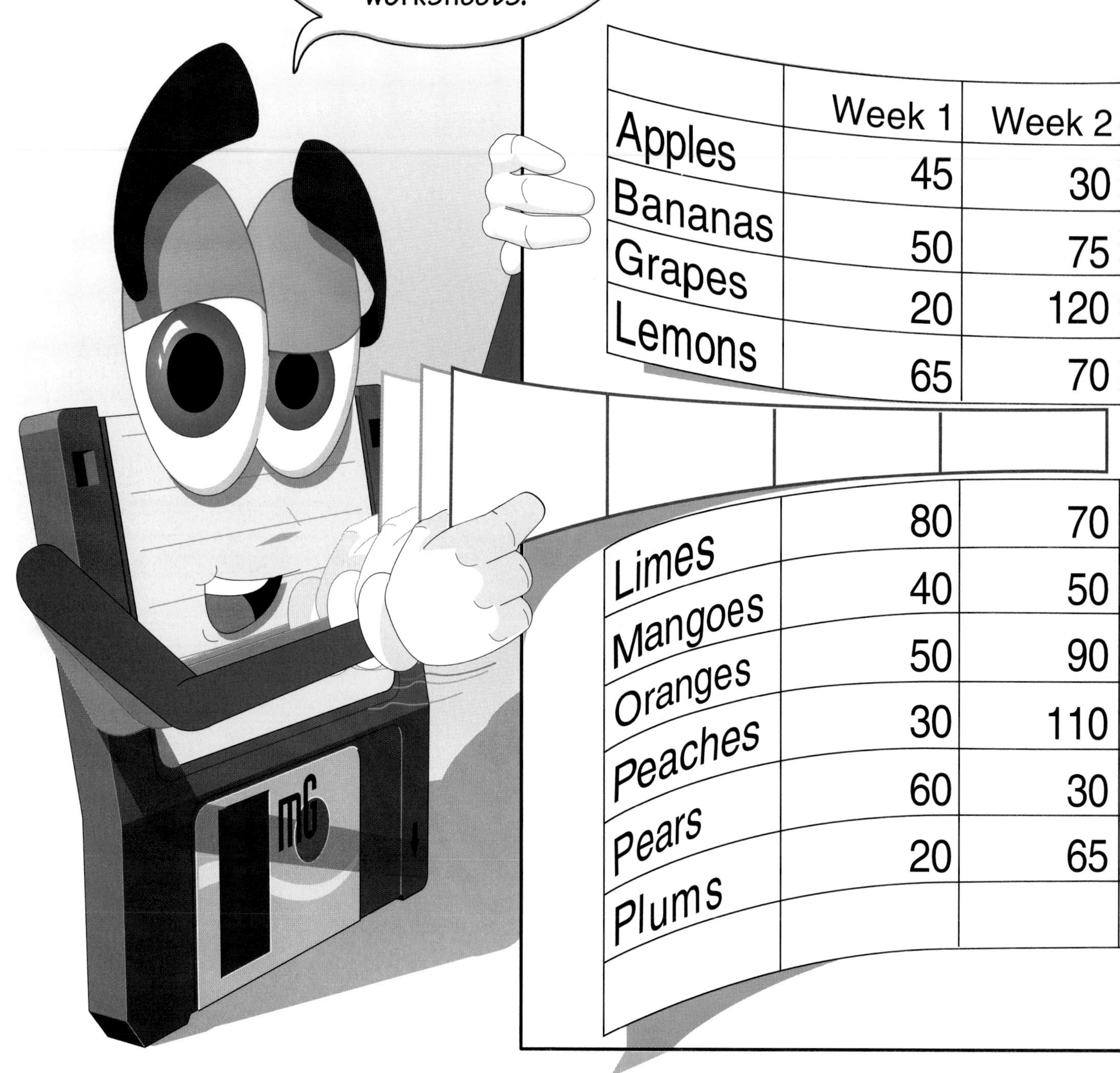
Week 1
Week 2
Apples
45
30
Bananas
50
75
Grapes
20
120
Lemons
65
70
80
70
Limes
40
50
Mangoes
50
90
Oranges
30
110
Peaches
60
30
Pears
20
65
Plums
mG

WORKING WITH ROWS AND COLUMNS

Insert a Row or Column

Delete a Row or Column

Change Column Width

Change Row Height

INSERT A ROW OR COLUMN

You can add a row or column to your worksheet if you want to insert additional data.

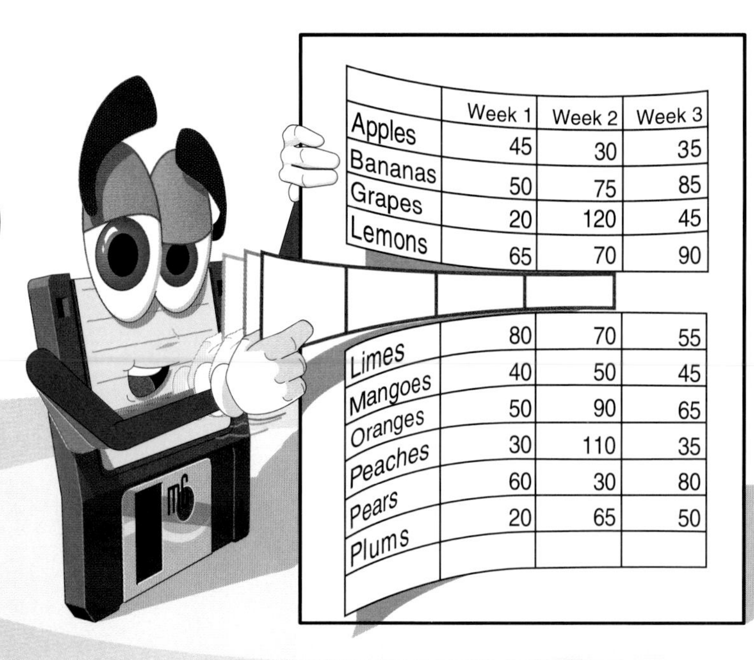

INSERT A ROW

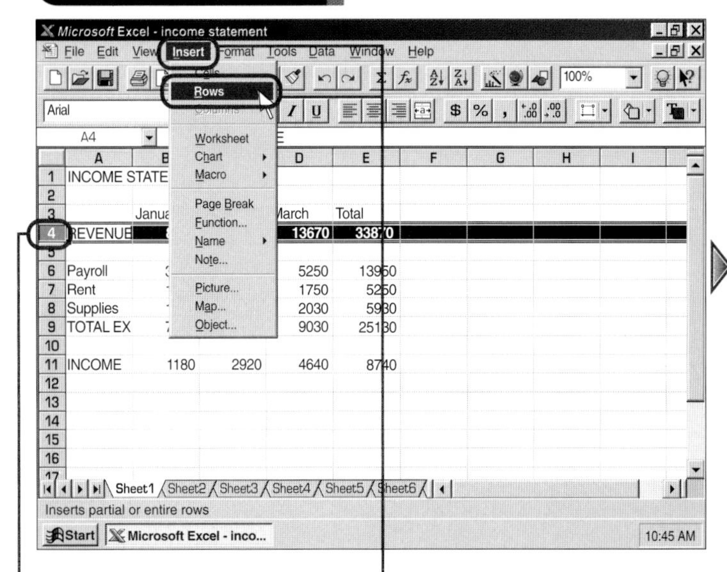

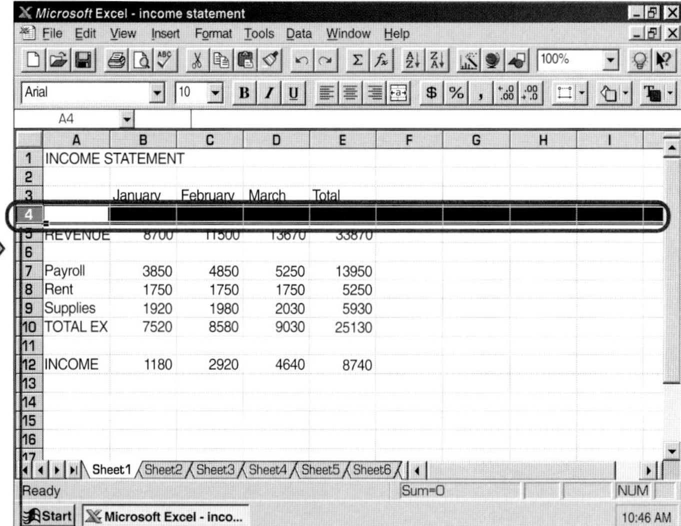

1 Select a row. Excel will insert a row above the row you select.

Note: To select a row, refer to page 13.

2 Move the mouse over **Insert** and then press the left button.

3 Move the mouse over **Rows** and then press the left button.

■ The new row appears and all the rows that follow shift downward.

- **Insert a Row or Column**
- Delete a Row or Column
- Change Column Width
- Change Row Height

Tip

When you insert a row or column, Excel automatically adjusts any formulas affected by the insertion.

Insert Column Here

=A1+A2

=B1+B2

INSERT A COLUMN

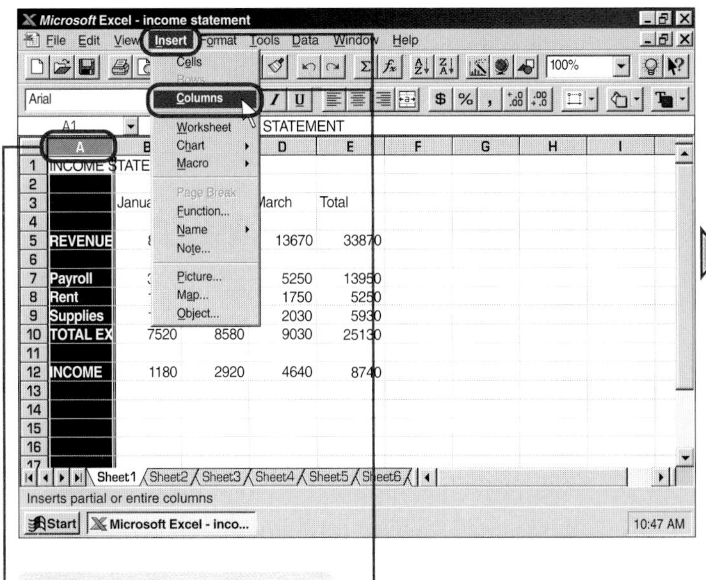

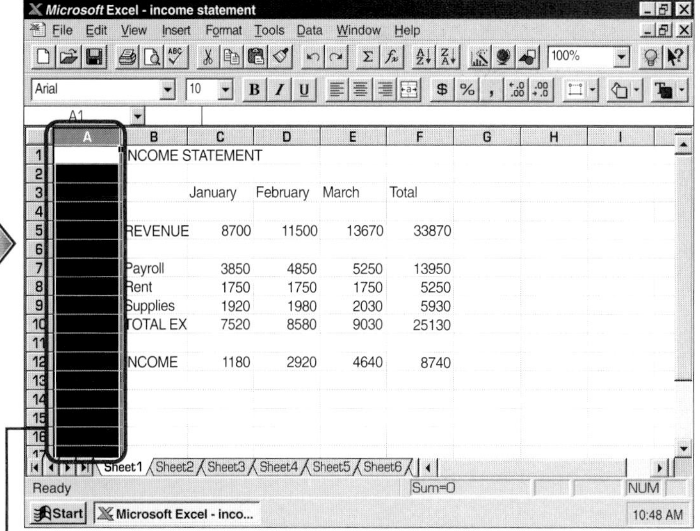

1 Select a column. Excel will insert a column to the left of the column you select.

Note: To select a column, refer to page 12.

2 Move the mouse over **Insert** and then press the left button.

3 Move the mouse over **Columns** and then press the left button.

■ The new column appears and all the columns that follow shift to the right.

DELETE A ROW OR COLUMN

You can delete a row or column from your worksheet to remove cells you no longer need.

DELETE A ROW

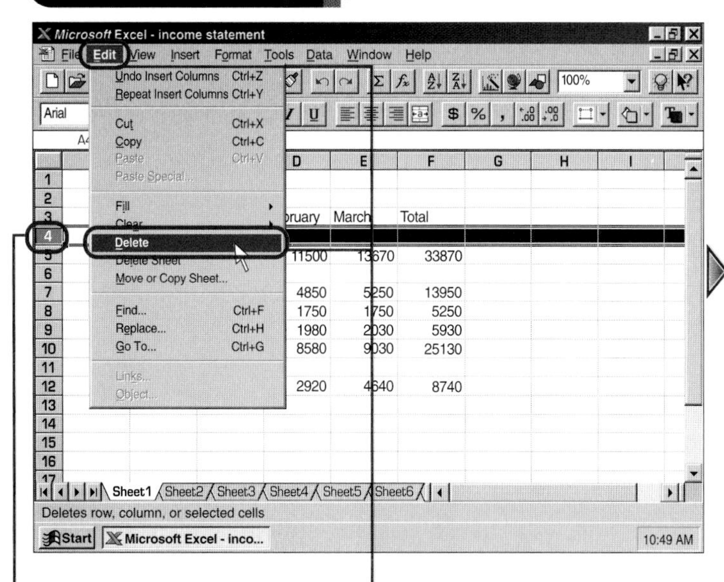

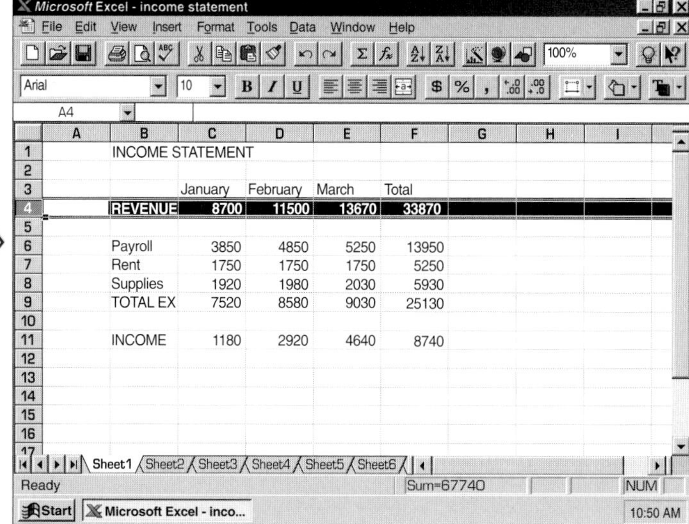

1 Select the row you want to delete.

Note: To select a row, refer to page 13.

2 Move the mouse over **Edit** and then press the left button.

3 Move the mouse over **Delete** and then press the left button.

■ The row disappears and all the rows that follow shift upward.

- Insert a Row or Column
- **Delete a Row or Column**
- Change Column Width
- Change Row Height

If #REF! appears in a cell in your worksheet, you have deleted data needed to calculate a formula.

To immediately cancel the deletion, move the mouse over [undo button] at the top of your screen and then press the left button.

DELETE A COLUMN

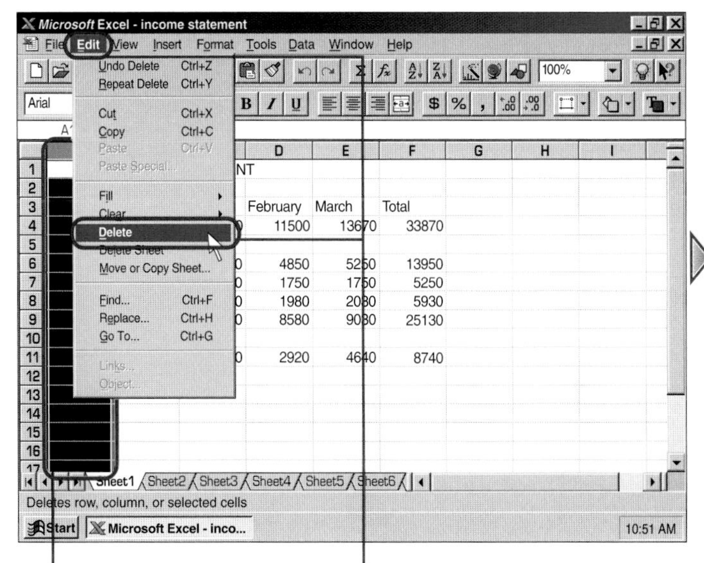

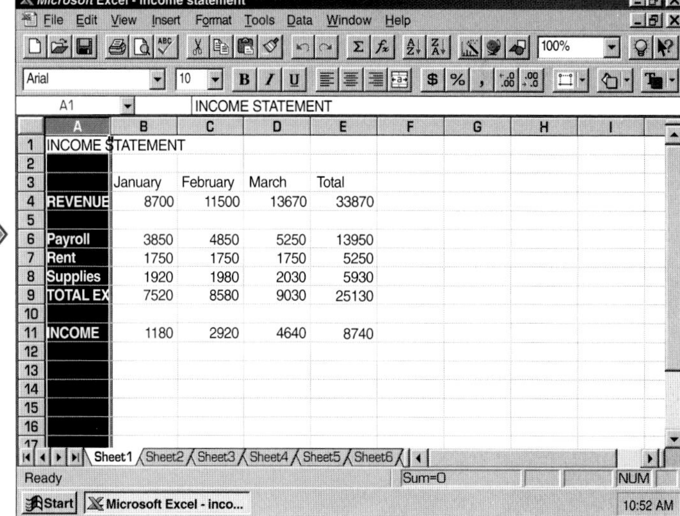

1 Select the column you want to delete.

Note: To select a column, refer to page 12.

2 Move the mouse over **Edit** and then press the left button.

3 Move the mouse over **Delete** and then press the left button.

■ The column disappears and all the columns that follow shift to the left.

CHANGE COLUMN WIDTH

You can improve the appearance of your worksheet and display hidden data by changing the width of columns.

CHANGE COLUMN WIDTH

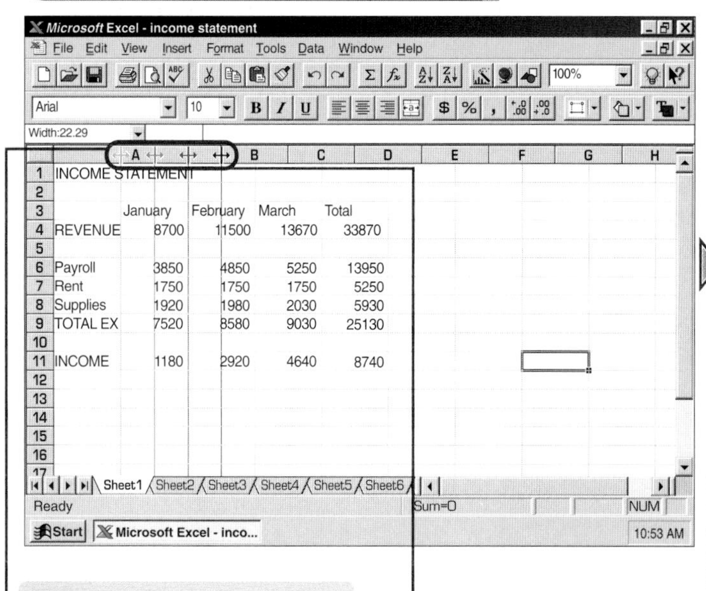

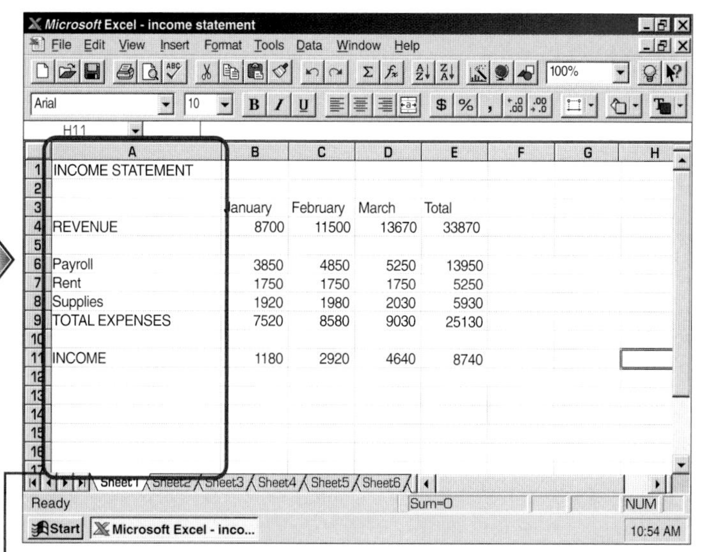

1 To change the width of a column, move the mouse ✥ over the right edge of the column heading (✥ changes to ↔).

2 Press and hold down the left button as you move the edge of the column to a new position.

■ A line indicates the new column width.

3 Release the left button and the new column width appears.

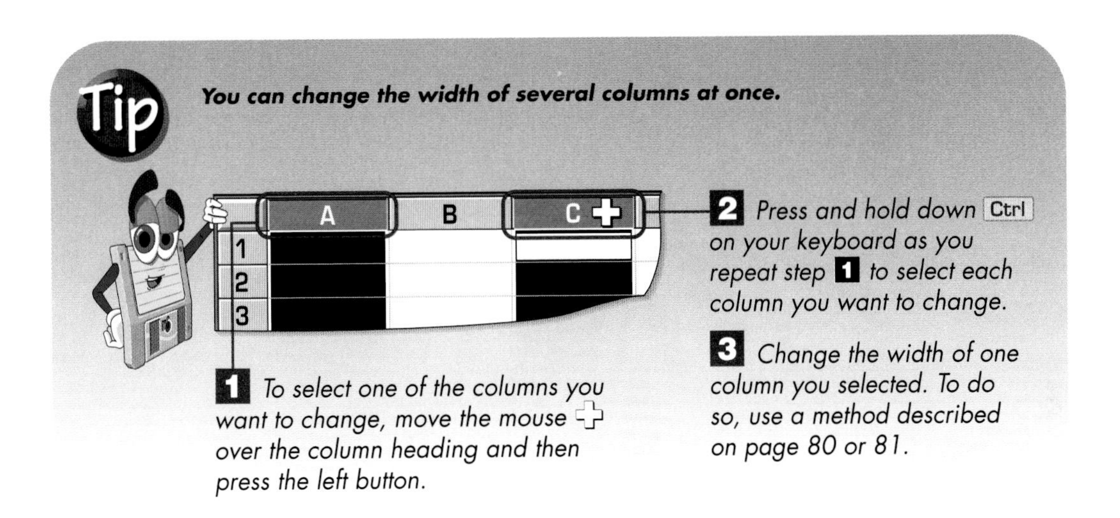

You can change the width of several columns at once.

1 To select one of the columns you want to change, move the mouse over the column heading and then press the left button.

2 Press and hold down Ctrl on your keyboard as you repeat step 1 to select each column you want to change.

3 Change the width of one column you selected. To do so, use a method described on page 80 or 81.

CHANGE COLUMN WIDTH AUTOMATICALLY

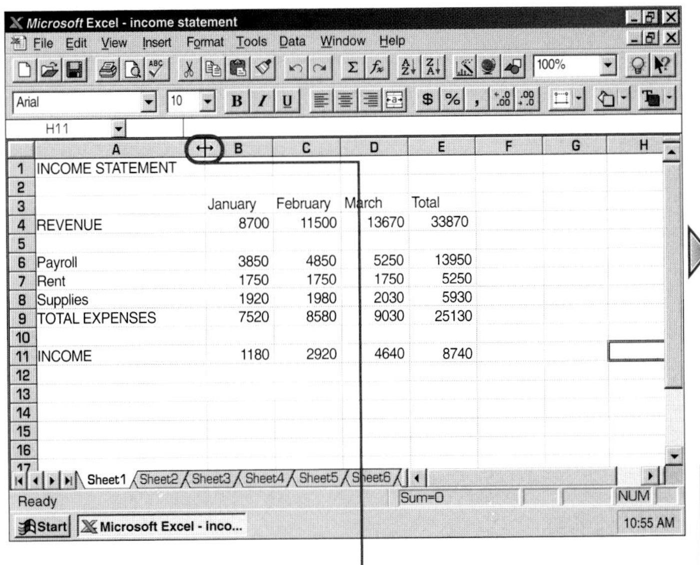

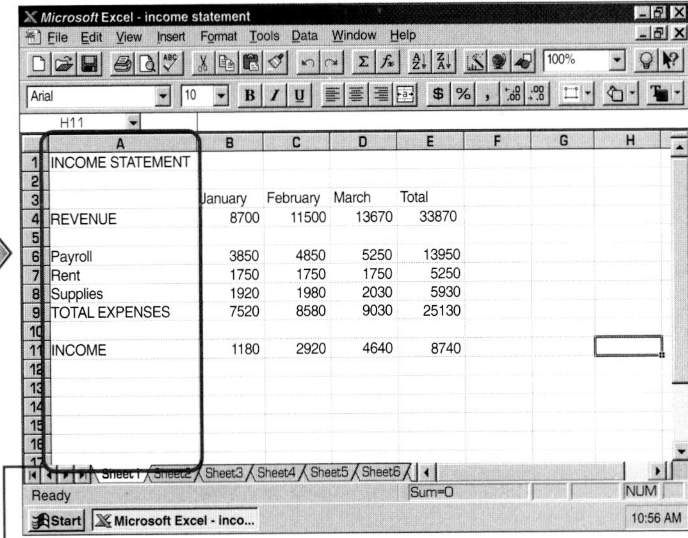

You can have Excel change a column width to fit the longest item in the column.

1 Move the mouse over the right edge of the column heading (changes to ✚) and then quickly press the left button twice.

■ The column width changes to fit the longest item in the column.

You can change the height of a row. This is useful if you want to add space between the rows of data in your worksheet.

CHANGE ROW HEIGHT

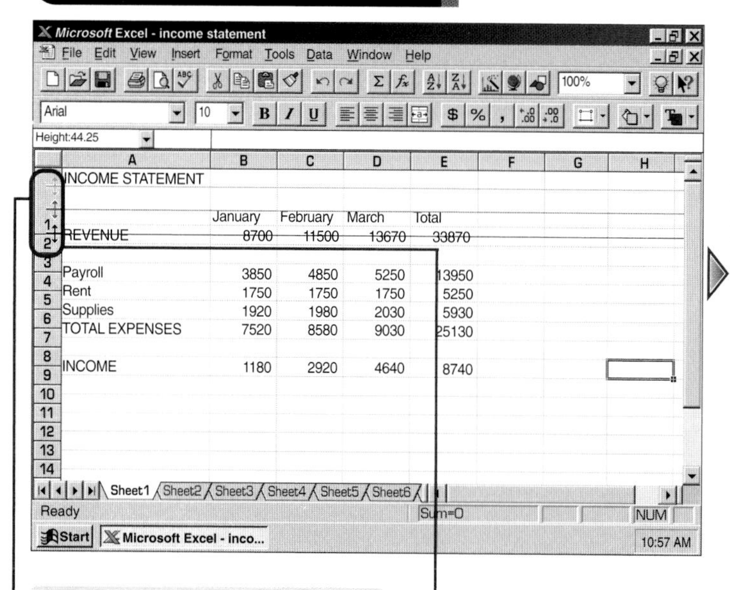

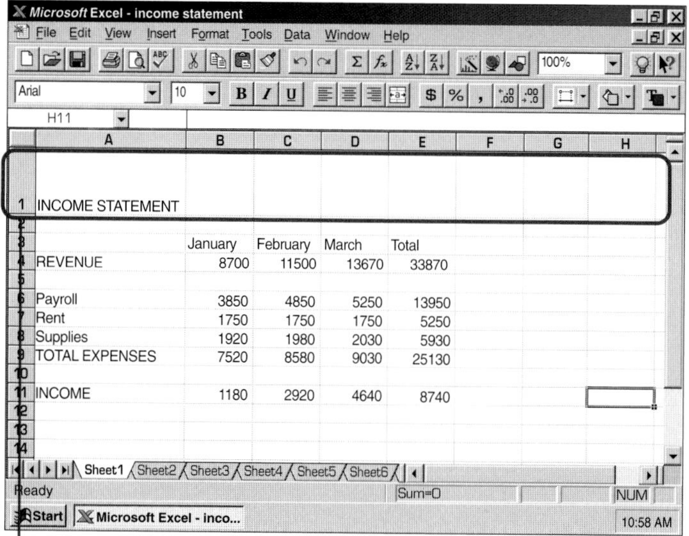

1 To change the height of a row, move the mouse ✥ over the bottom edge of the row heading (✥ changes to ‡).

2 Press and hold down the left button as you move the edge of the row to a new position.

■ A line indicates the new row height.

3 Release the left button and the new row height appears.

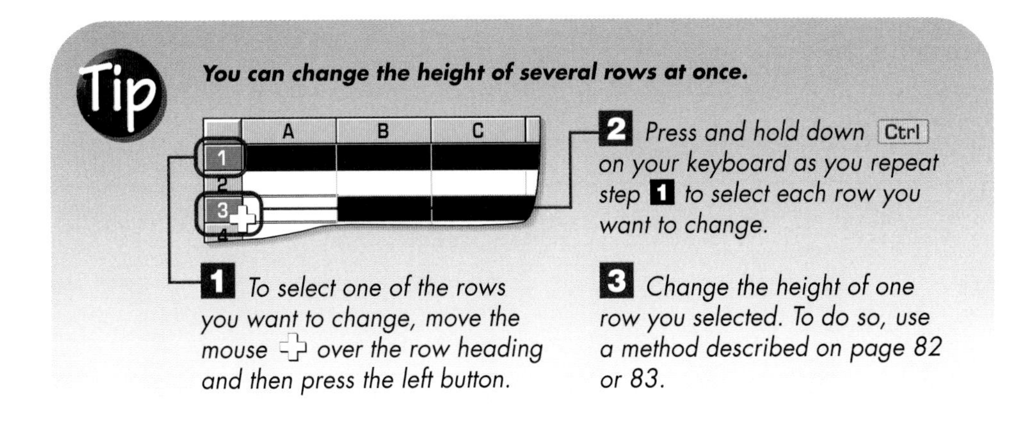

You can change the height of several rows at once.

1 To select one of the rows you want to change, move the mouse over the row heading and then press the left button.

2 Press and hold down Ctrl on your keyboard as you repeat step 1 to select each row you want to change.

3 Change the height of one row you selected. To do so, use a method described on page 82 or 83.

CHANGE ROW HEIGHT AUTOMATICALLY

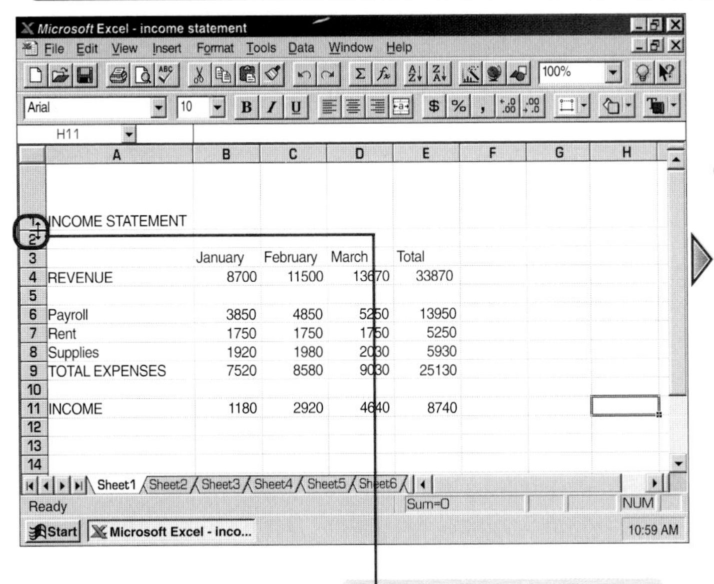

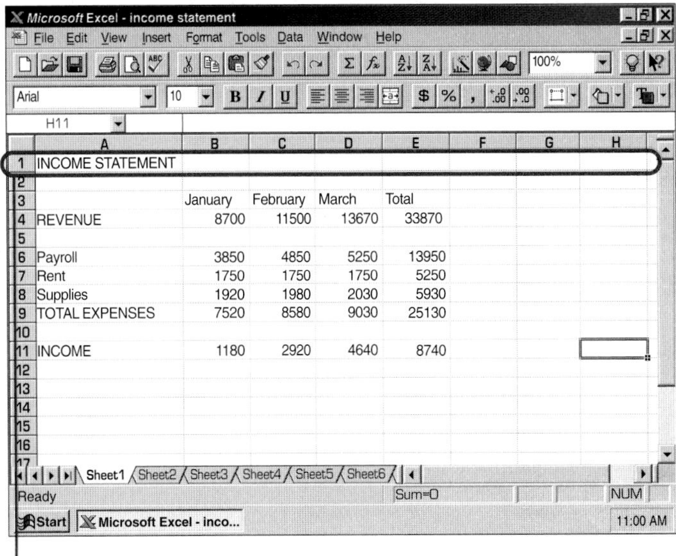

You can have Excel change a row height to fit the tallest item in the row.

1 Move the mouse over the bottom edge of the row heading (changes to ‡) and then quickly press the left button twice.

■ The row height changes to fit the tallest item in the row.

In this chapter
you will learn how to chang
the appearance of data i
your worksheets.
Sales
Apples
Peaches
27
31
88

FORMAT YOUR WORKSHEETS

CHANGE DATA ALIGNMENT

CENTER DATA ACROSS COLUMNS

Data
Left Align
Data
Center
Data
Right Align
You can change the position of data in each cell of your worksheet.

CHANGE DATA ALIGNMENT

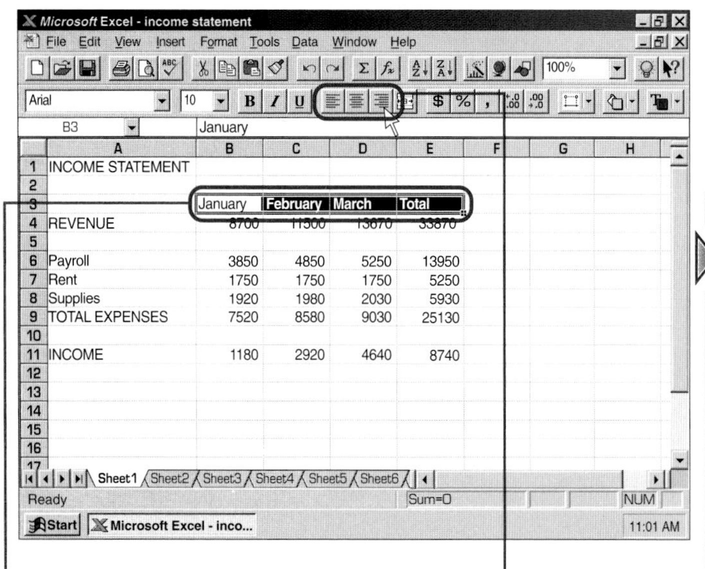

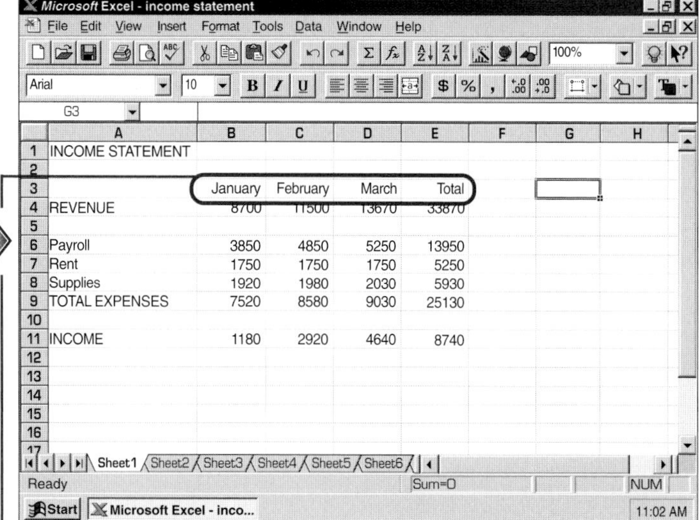

1 Select the cells containing the data you want to align differently.

Note: To select cells, refer to page 12.

2 Move the mouse over one of the following options and then press the left button.

- Left align data
- Center data
- Right align data

■ The data displays the alignment you selected.

Note: To deselect cells, move the mouse over any cell and then press the left button.

- **Change Data Alignment**
- **Center Data Across Columns**
- Bold, Italic and Underline
- Change Appearance of Numbers
- Change Fonts
- Wrap Text in a Cell
- Add Borders
- Add Color
- Using Format Painter
- Clear Formats
- Format a Worksheet Automatically

You can center data across columns in your worksheet. This is useful for centering titles over your data.

CENTER DATA ACROSS COLUMNS

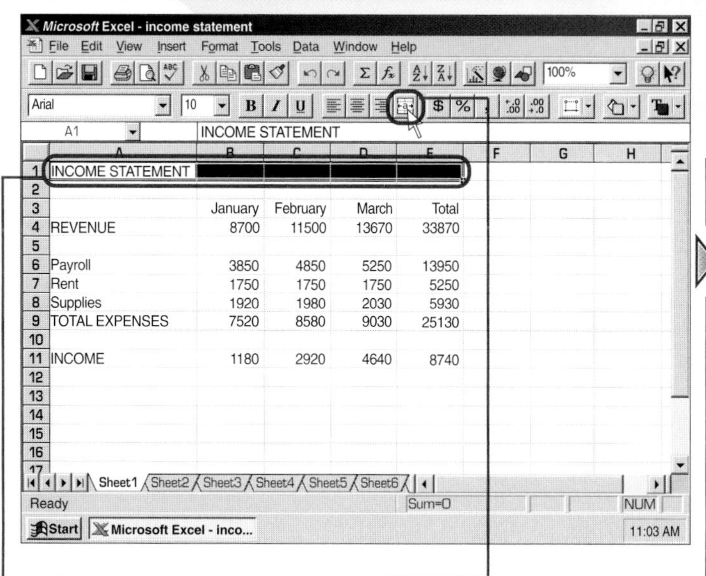

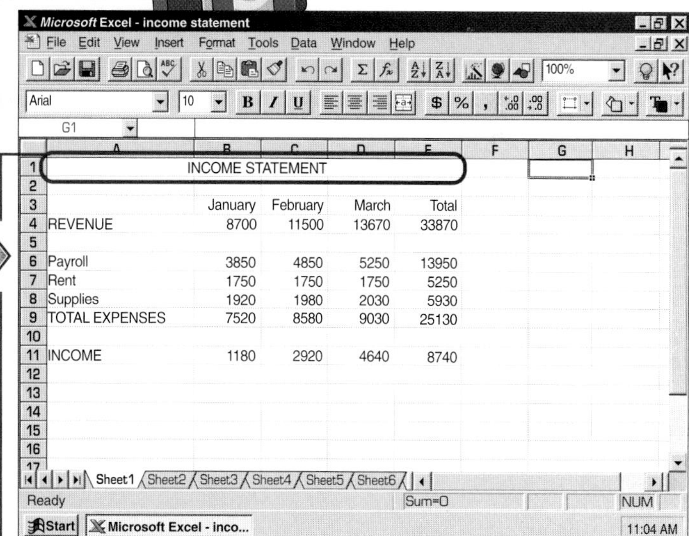

1 Select the cells you want to center the data between.

Note: The first cell you select should contain the data you want to center.

2 Move the mouse over the Center Across Columns button and then press the left button.

■ Excel centers the data between the cells you selected.

Note: To deselect cells, move the mouse over any cell and then press the left button.

BOLD, ITALIC AND UNDERLINE

CHANGE APPEARANCE OF NUMBERS

You can use the Bold, Italic and Underline features to emphasize data in your worksheet.

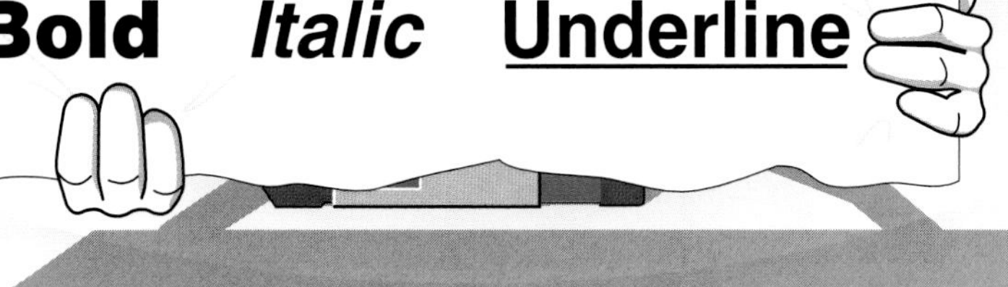

BOLD, ITALIC AND UNDERLINE

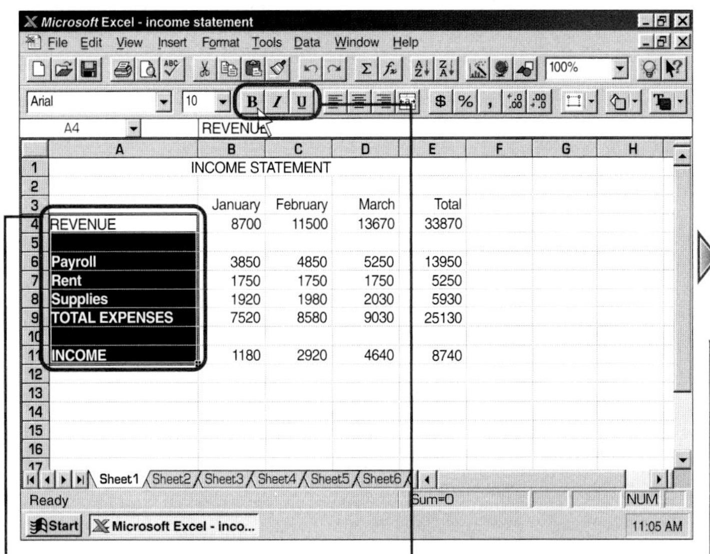

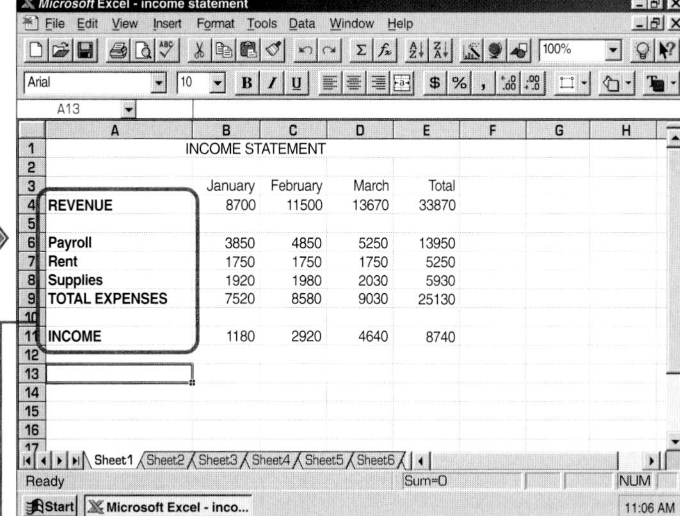

1 Select the cells containing the data you want to change.

Note: To select cells, refer to page 12.

2 Move the mouse over one of the following options and then press the left button.

- B Bold data
- I Italicize data
- U Underline data

■ The data displays the style you selected.

Note: To deselect cells, move the mouse over any cell and then press the left button.

■ To remove a bold, italic or underline style, repeat steps **1** and **2**.

You can quickly change the appearance of numbers in your worksheet without retyping the numbers.

Option		Example
$	Change to a dollar value	72 → $72.00
%	Change to a percentage	0.35 → 35%
,	Add a comma and display two decimal places	2683 → 2,683.00
+.0 .00	Add one decimal place	52.3 → 52.30
.00 →.0	Delete one decimal place	49.27 → 49.3

QUICKLY CHANGE APPEARANCE OF NUMBERS

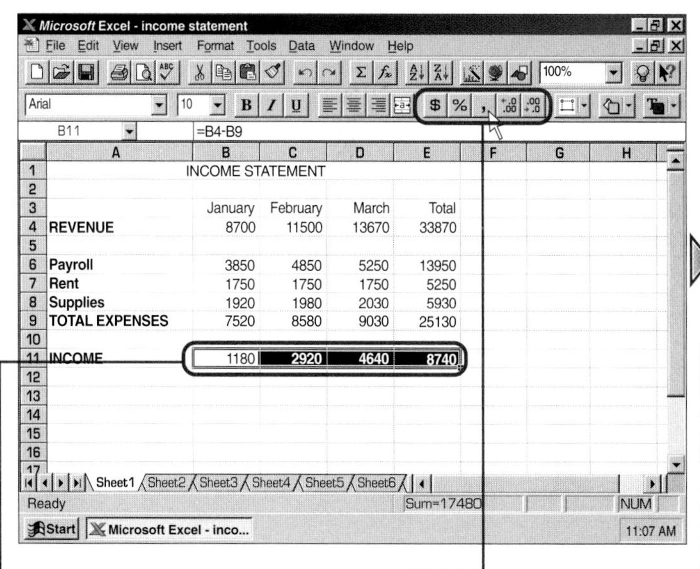

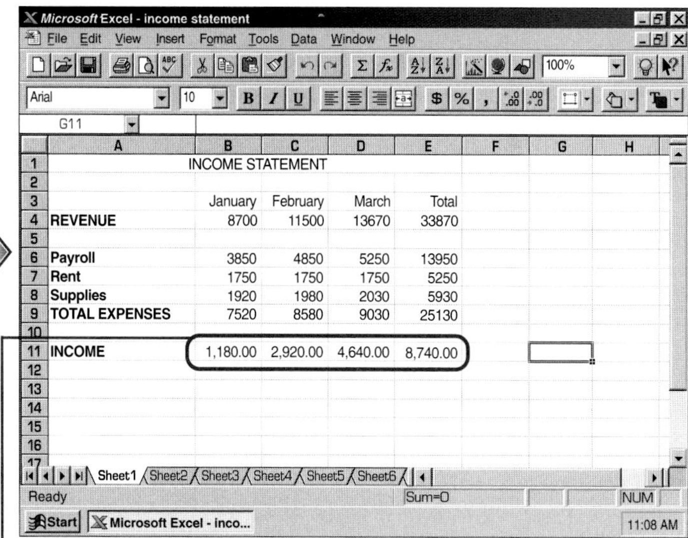

1 Select the cells containing the numbers you want to change.

Note: To select cells, refer to page 12.

2 Move the mouse over one of the number options and then press the left button.

■ The numbers display the style you selected.

Note: To deselect cells, move the mouse over any cell and then press the left button.

Note: If number signs (#) appear in a cell, the column is not wide enough to display the entire number. To change the column width, refer to page 80.

CHANGE APPEARANCE OF NUMBERS

Excel offers many different ways that you can display the numbers in your worksheet to make them easier to read and identify.

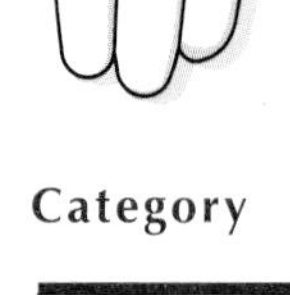

Category	Example
Currency	$1,037.80
Date	19-Jan-96
Time	11:33 AM
Percentage	35.00%
Fraction	22 3/4
Scientific	1.04E+04

To quickly change the appearance of numbers, refer to page 89.

CHANGE APPEARANCE OF NUMBERS

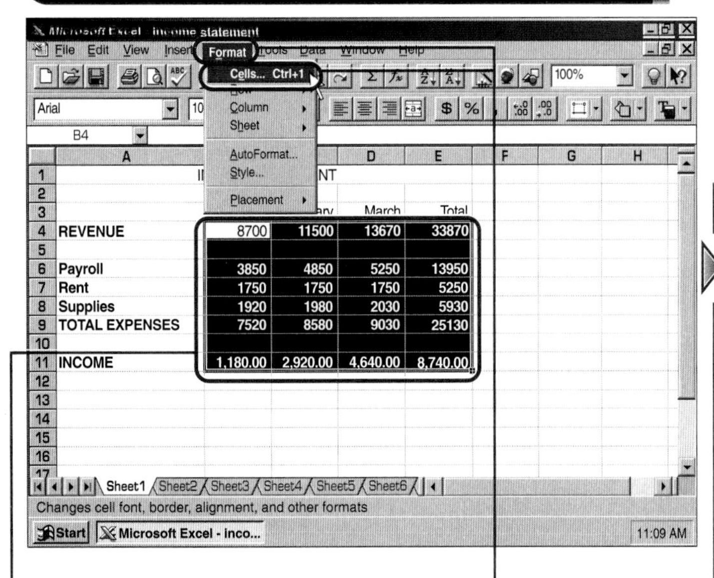

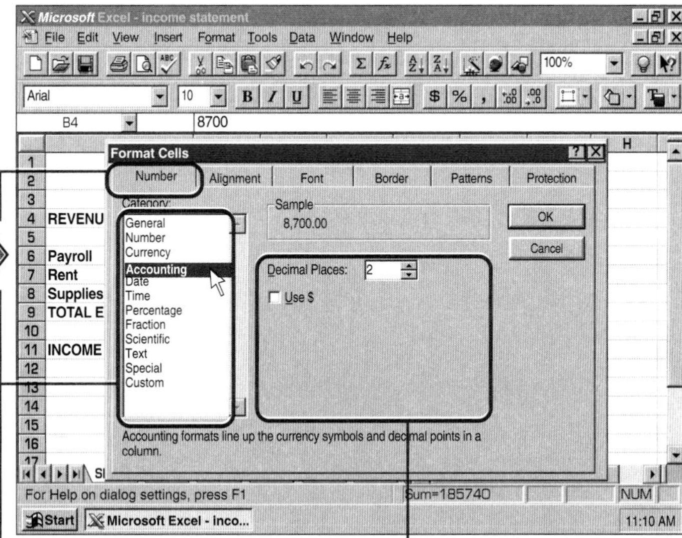

1 Select the cells containing the numbers you want to change.

Note: To select cells, refer to page 12.

2 Move the mouse over **Format** and then press the left button.

3 Move the mouse over **Cells** and then press the left button.

4 Move the mouse over the **Number** tab and then press the left button.

5 Move the mouse over the category that identifies the numbers in your worksheet and then press the left button.

■ This area displays all the options for the category you selected.

Note: Each category displays a different set of options.

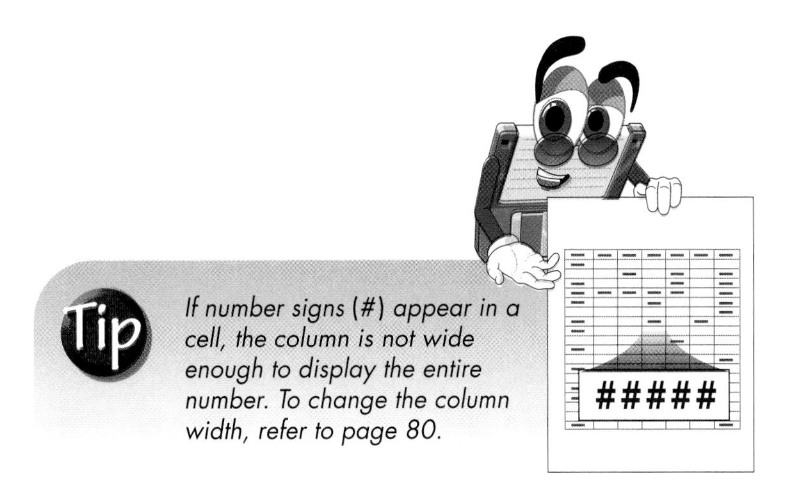

Tip *If number signs (#) appear in a cell, the column is not wide enough to display the entire number. To change the column width, refer to page 80.*

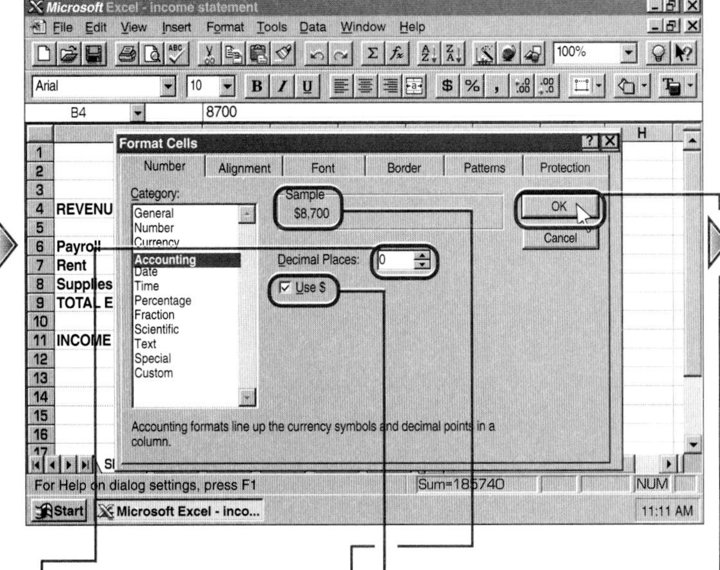

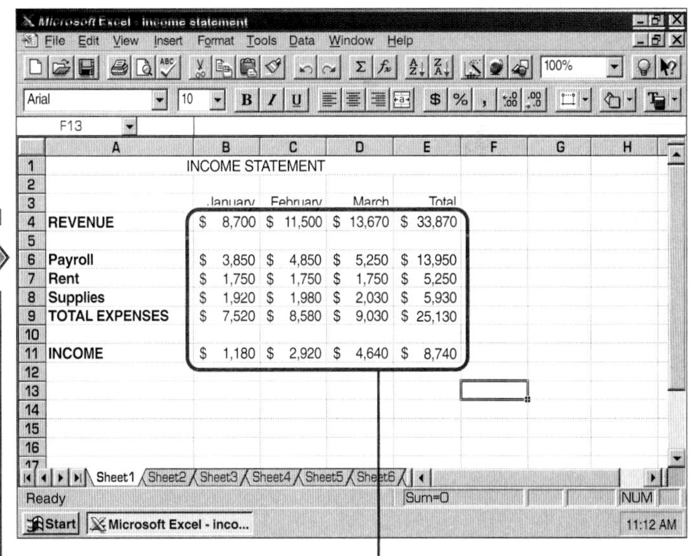

6 To change the number of displayed decimal places in this example, move the mouse over ▼ or ▲ and then press the left button. Repeat this step until the number of decimal places you want to display appears.

7 To display a dollar sign ($) in this example, move the mouse over **Use $** and then press the left button (☐ changes to ☑).

■ This area displays how the numbers will appear in your worksheet.

8 Move the mouse over **OK** and then press the left button.

■ The numbers display the changes.

Note: To deselect cells, move the mouse over any cell and then press the left button.

CHANGE FONTS

You can enhance the appearance of your worksheet by changing the font of data.
Arial
Times
Courier

CHANGE FONT OF DATA

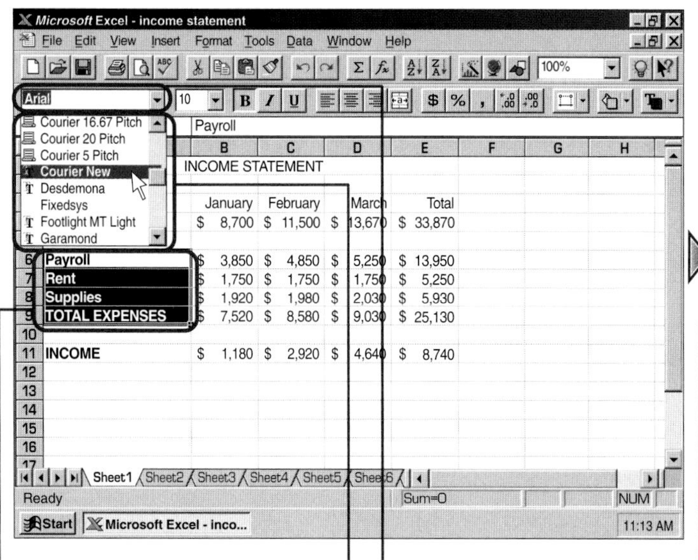

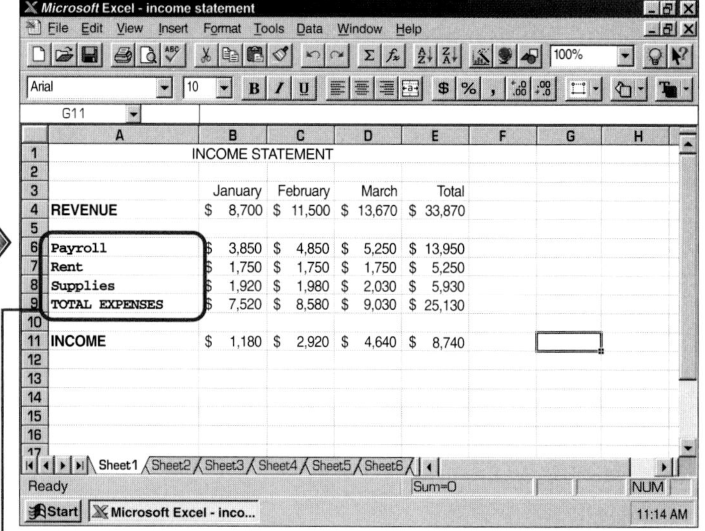

1 Select the cells containing the data you want to change.

Note: To select cells, refer to page 12.

2 To display a list of the available fonts, move the mouse over ▾ in this area and then press the left button.

3 Move the mouse over the font you want to use and then press the left button.

■ The data displays the font you selected.

Note: To deselect cells, move the mouse over any cell and then press the left button.

You can increase or decrease the size of data in your worksheet.
8 point
12 point
14 point
18 point
24 point
Excel measures the size of data in points. There are approximately 72 points in one inch.

CHANGE SIZE OF DATA

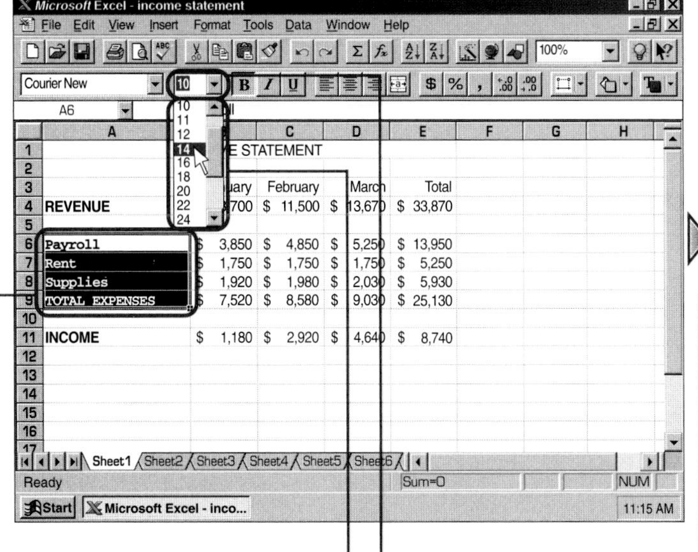

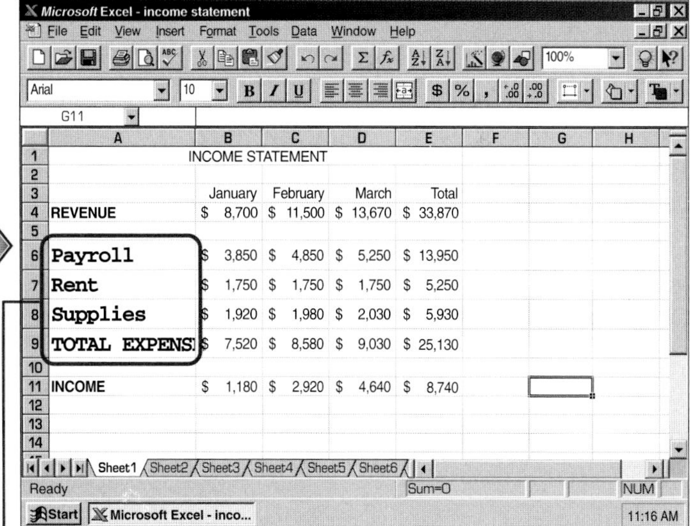

1 Select the cells containing the data you want to change.

Note: To select cells, refer to page 12.

2 To display a list of the available sizes, move the mouse over ▼ in this area and then press the left button.

3 Move the mouse over the size you want to use and then press the left button.

■ The data displays the size you selected.

Note: To deselect cells, move the mouse over any cell and then press the left button.

CHANGE FONTS

You can change the font and size of data in your worksheet at the same time.

CHANGE FONT AND SIZE OF DATA

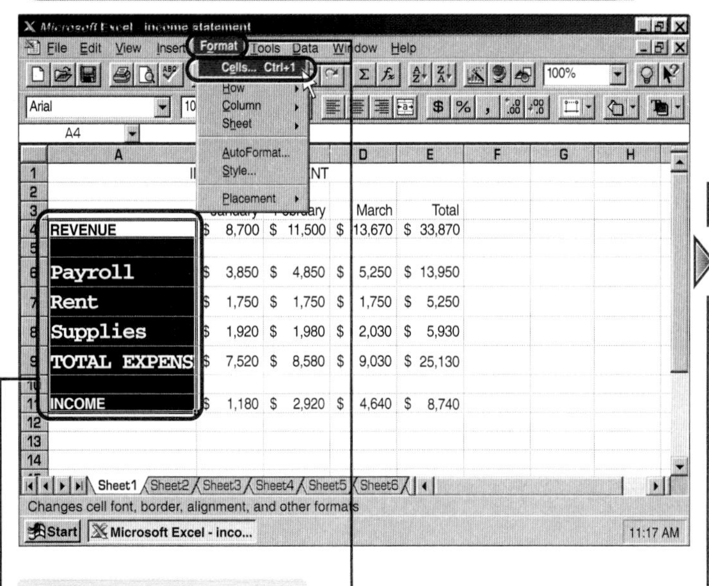

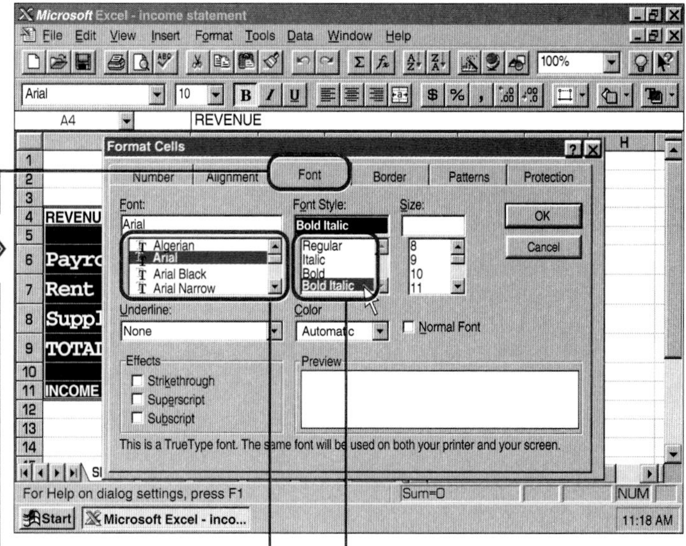

1 Select the cells containing the data you want to change.

Note: To select cells, refer to page 12.

2 Move the mouse over **Format** and then press the left button.

3 Move the mouse over **Cells** and then press the left button.

4 Move the mouse over the **Font** tab and then press the left button.

Note: To view options in the dialog box, use the scroll bars. For more information, refer to page 14.

5 To change the font of the data, move the mouse over the font you want to use and then press the left button.

6 To change the style of the data, move the mouse over the style you want to use and then press the left button.

Tip *The fonts available on your computer may be different from the fonts on other computers. The available fonts depend on your printer and the setup of your computer.*

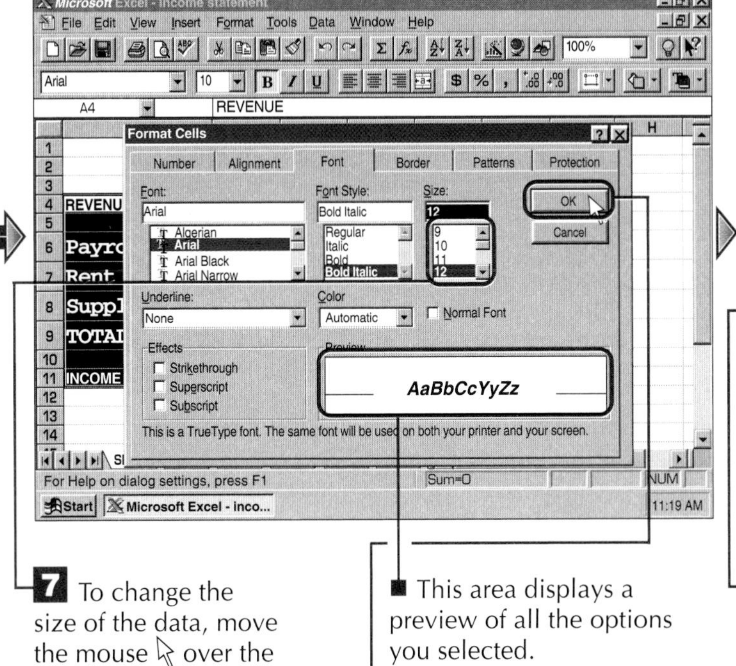

7 To change the size of the data, move the mouse over the size you want to use and then press the left button.

■ This area displays a preview of all the options you selected.

8 To confirm your changes, move the mouse over **OK** and then press the left button.

INCOME STATEMENT

	January	February	March	Total
REVENUE	$ 8,700	$ 11,500	$ 13,670	$ 33,870
Payroll	$ 3,850	$ 4,850	$ 5,250	$ 13,950
Rent	$ 1,750	$ 1,750	$ 1,750	$ 5,250
Supplies	$ 1,920	$ 1,980	$ 2,030	$ 5,930
TOTAL EXPENSE	$ 7,520	$ 8,580	$ 9,030	$ 25,130
INCOME	$ 1,180	$ 2,920	$ 4,640	$ 8,740

■ The data displays the changes.

Note: To deselect cells, move the mouse over any cell and then press the left button.

WRAP TEXT IN A CELL

Month of Jan
Month of Feb
Apples
Peaches
Pears
Plums
Total
You can display a long line of text in one cell by wrapping the text.

WRAP TEXT IN A CELL

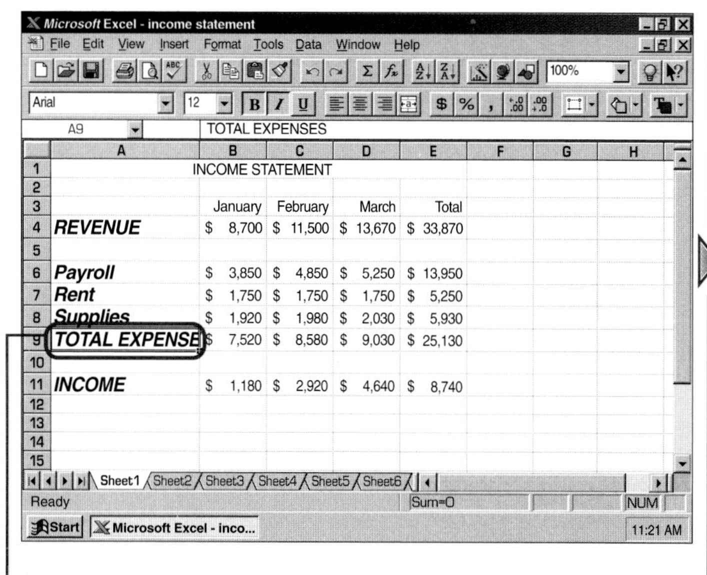

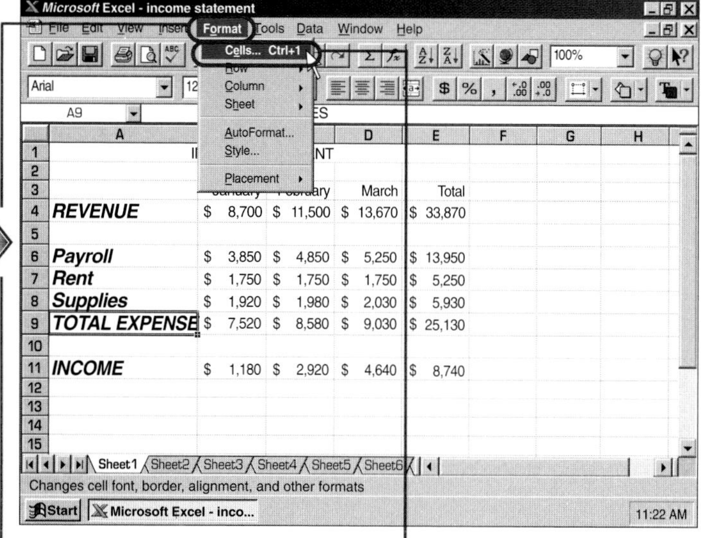

1 Select the cell(s) containing the text you want to wrap.

Note: To select cells, refer to page 12.

2 Move the mouse over **Format** and then press the left button.

3 Move the mouse over **Cells** and then press the left button.

■ The **Format Cells** dialog box appears.

You can also wrap text in a cell as you type the text.

■ *When you want to begin a new line of text, press and hold down* Alt *and then press* Enter *on your keyboard. Then release both keys.*

Note: If the wrapped text does not appear the way you want, adjust the column width. To change a column width, refer to page 80.

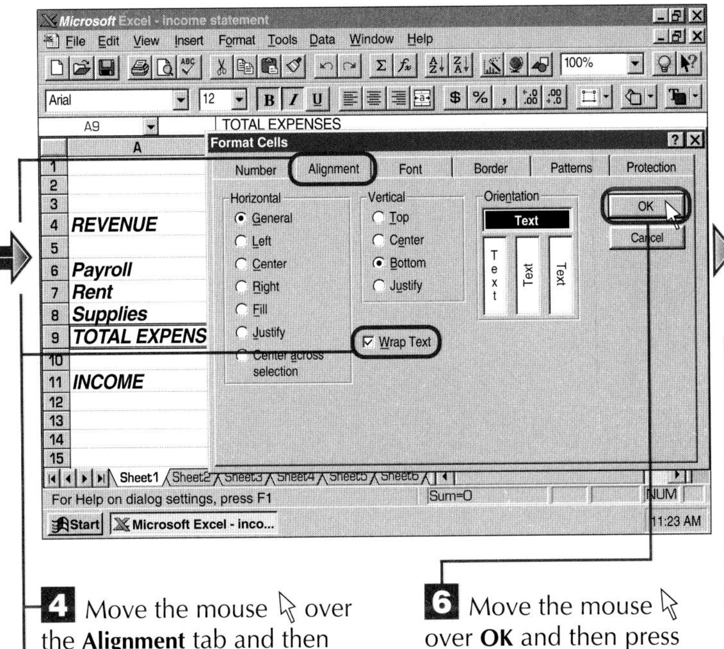

Microsoft Excel - income statement

	A	B	C	D	E
1		INCOME STATEMENT			
2					
3		January	February	March	Total
4	REVENUE	$ 8,700	$ 11,500	$ 13,670	$ 33,870
5					
6	Payroll	$ 3,850	$ 4,850	$ 5,250	$ 13,950
7	Rent	$ 1,750	$ 1,750	$ 1,750	$ 5,250
8	Supplies	$ 1,920	$ 1,980	$ 2,030	$ 5,930
9	TOTAL EXPENSES	$ 7,520	$ 8,580	$ 9,030	$ 25,130
10					
11	INCOME	$ 1,180	$ 2,920	$ 4,640	$ 8,740

4 Move the mouse over the **Alignment** tab and then press the left button.

5 Move the mouse over **Wrap Text** and then press the left button (☐ changes to ☑).

6 Move the mouse over **OK** and then press the left button.

■ Excel wraps the text in the cell(s) you selected.

■ The row height automatically changes to fit the wrapped text.

ADD BORDERS

You can add borders to emphasize a section of your worksheet. Borders help you separate headings from the rest of your data.

ADD BORDERS

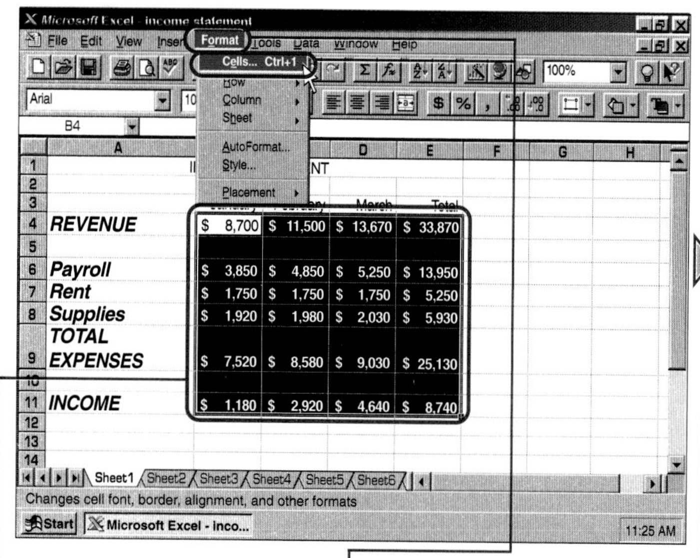

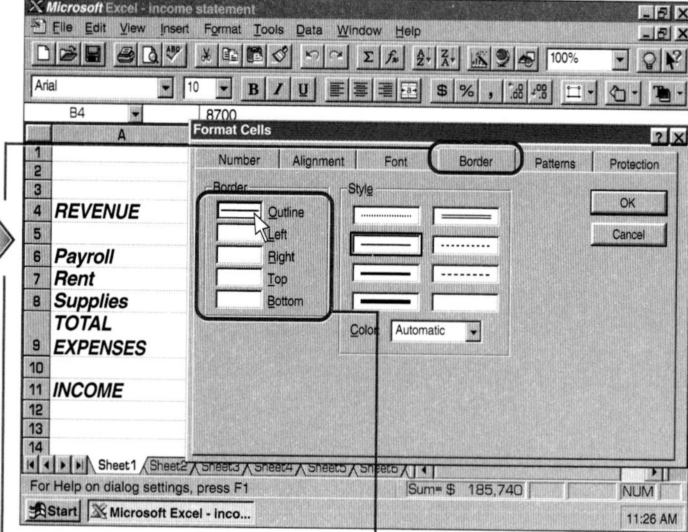

1 Select the cells you want to display borders.

Note: To select cells, refer to page 12.

2 Move the mouse over **Format** and then press the left button.

3 Move the mouse over **Cells** and then press the left button.

■ The **Format Cells** dialog box appears.

4 Move the mouse over the **Border** tab and then press the left button.

5 To select a border you want to add, move the mouse over one of these options and then press the left button.

■ A line appears in the area beside the border you selected.

- Change Data Alignment
- Center Data Across Columns
- Bold, Italic and Underline
- Change Appearance of Numbers
- Change Fonts
- Wrap Text in a Cell
- **Add Borders**
- Add Color
- Using Format Painter
- Clear Formats
- Format a Worksheet Automatically

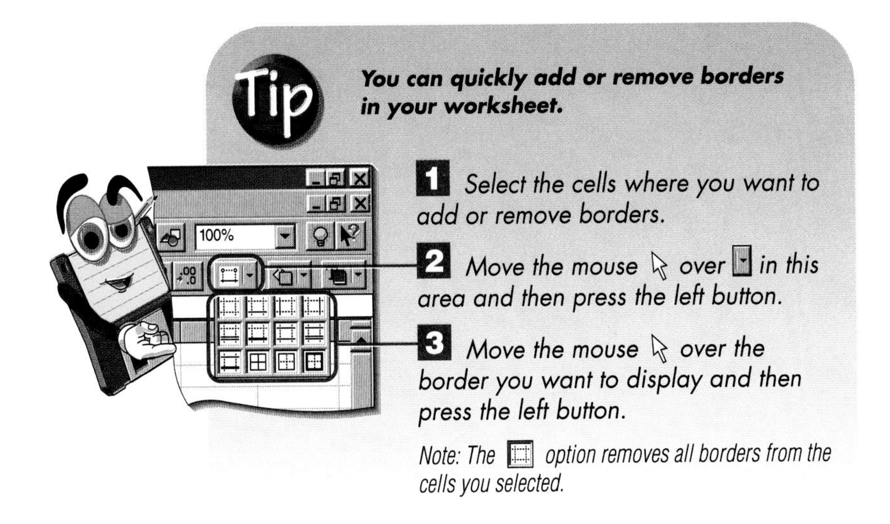

Tip ***You can quickly add or remove borders in your worksheet.***

1 Select the cells where you want to add or remove borders.

2 Move the mouse over ▾ in this area and then press the left button.

3 Move the mouse over the border you want to display and then press the left button.

Note: The option removes all borders from the cells you selected.

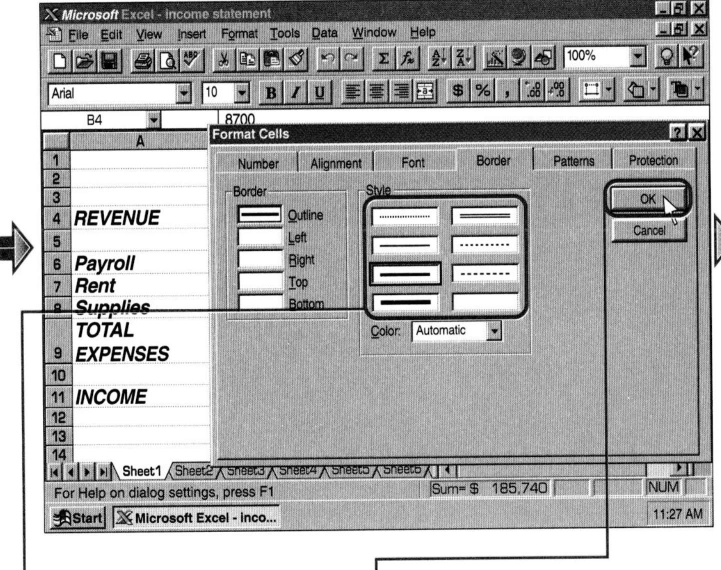

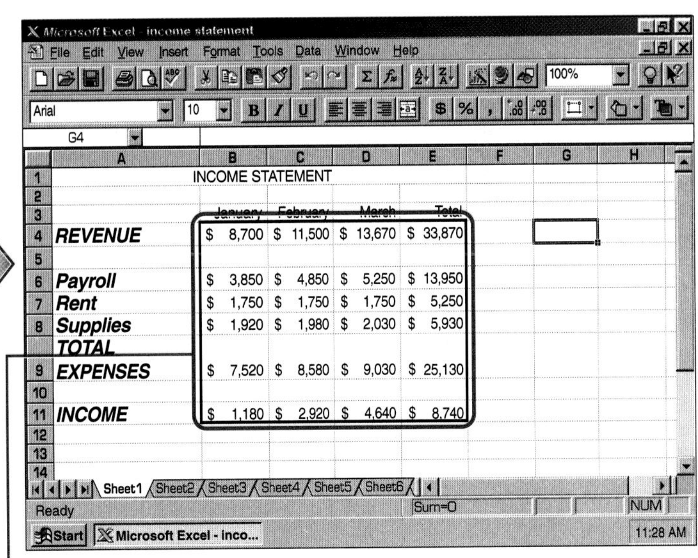

6 To select a line style for the border, move the mouse over one of these options and then press the left button.

7 Repeat steps **5** and **6** for each border you want to add.

8 Move the mouse over **OK** and then press the left button.

■ The cells display the borders you selected.

Note: To deselect cells, move the mouse over any cell and then press the left button.

Note: To remove borders from your worksheet, refer to the ***Tip*** *above.*

ADD COLOR

CHANGE CELL COLOR

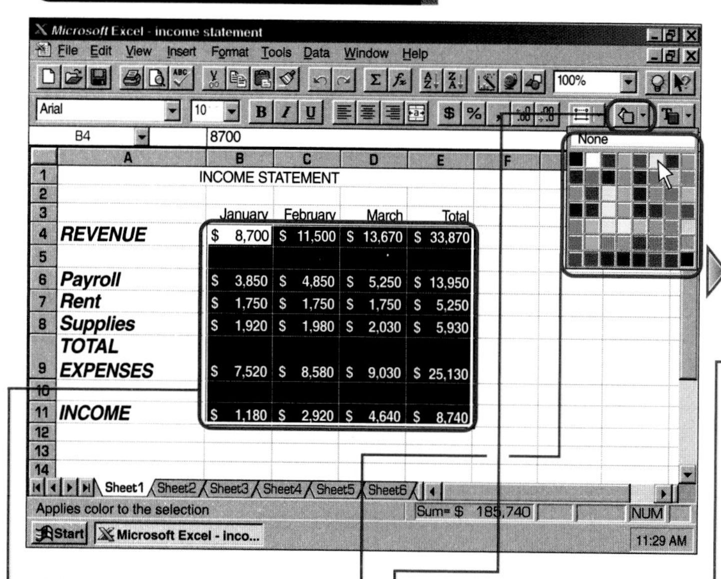

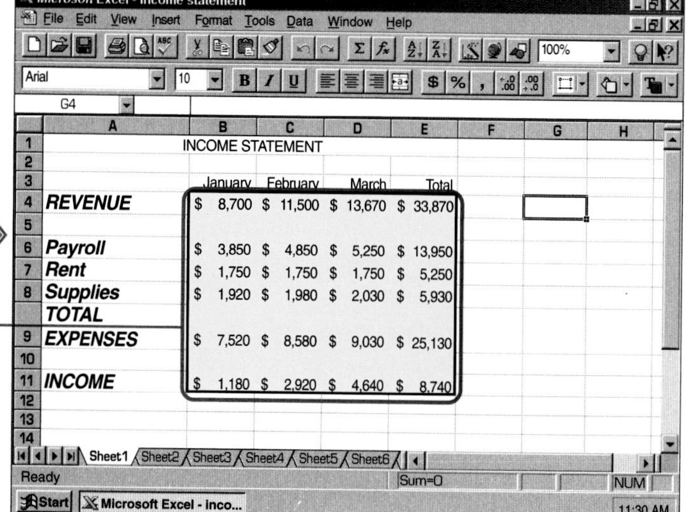

1 Select the cells you want to display color.

Note: To select cells, refer to page 12.

2 Move the mouse over ▾ in this area and then press the left button.

3 Move the mouse over the color you want to use and then press the left button.

■ The cells display the color you selected.

Note: To deselect cells, move the mouse over any cell and then press the left button.

■ The data in colored cells may be hard to read if you print the worksheet on a black-and-white printer. To ensure the worksheet prints clearly, refer to page 116.

- Change Data Alignment
- Center Data Across Columns
- Bold, Italic and Underline
- Change Appearance of Numbers
- Change Fonts
- Wrap Text in a Cell
- Add Borders
- **Add Color**
- Using Format Painter
- Clear Formats
- Format a Worksheet Automatically

These buttons display the last colors you added to your worksheet. You can quickly add these colors to other cells.

1 Select the cells where you want to add color.

2 Move the mouse over one of the following options and then press the left button.

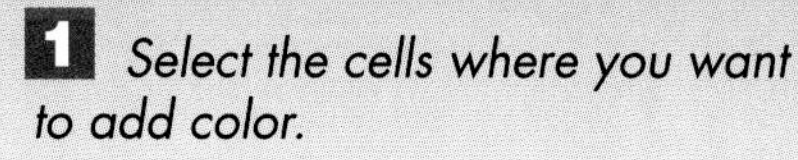

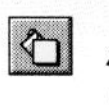 *Adds color in button to cells.*

 *Adds color in button to data in cells.*

CHANGE DATA COLOR

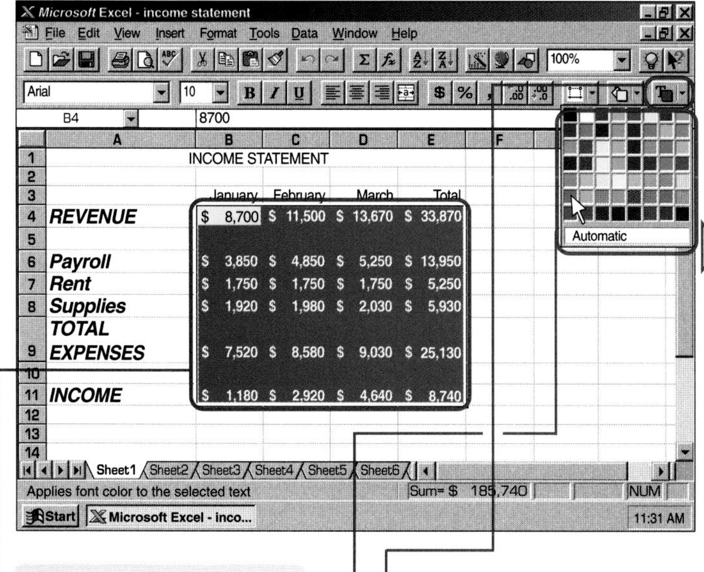

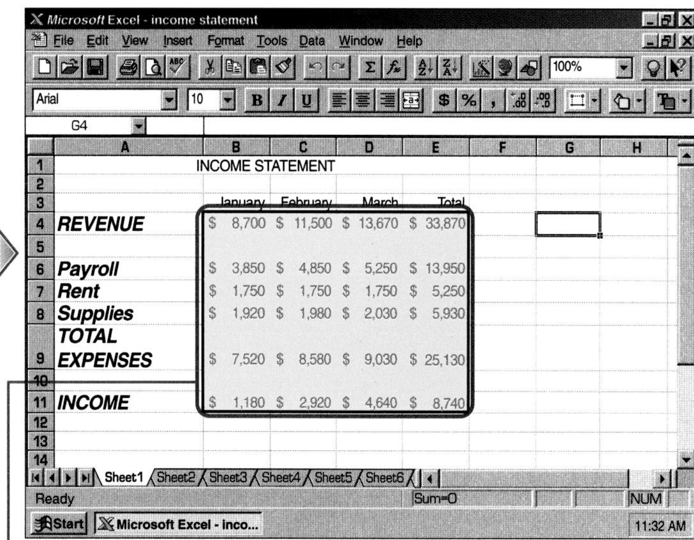

1 Select the cells containing the data you want to display color.

Note: To select cells, refer to page 12.

2 Move the mouse over ▾ in this area and then press the left button.

3 Move the mouse over the color you want to use and then press the left button.

■ The data displays the color you selected.

Note: To deselect cells, move the mouse over any cell and then press the left button.

USING FORMAT PAINTER

If you like the appearance of a cell in your worksheet, you can make other cells look exactly the same.

USING FORMAT PAINTER

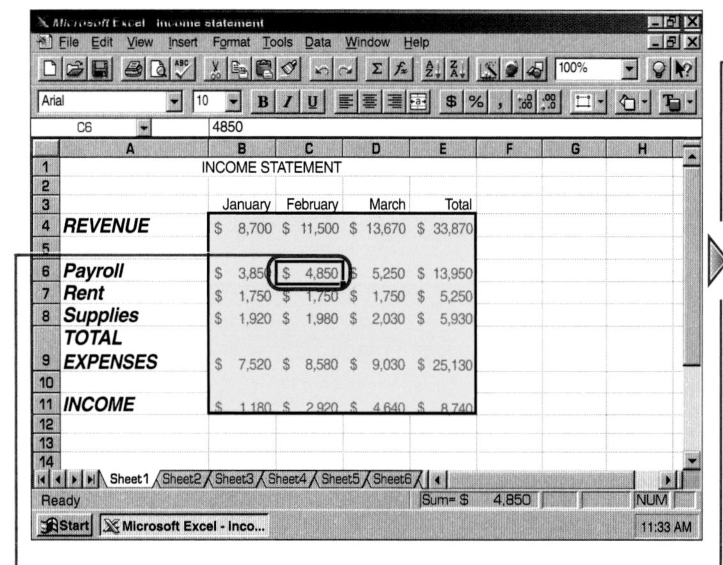

1 Select a cell displaying the formats you like.

Note: To select a cell, refer to page 12.

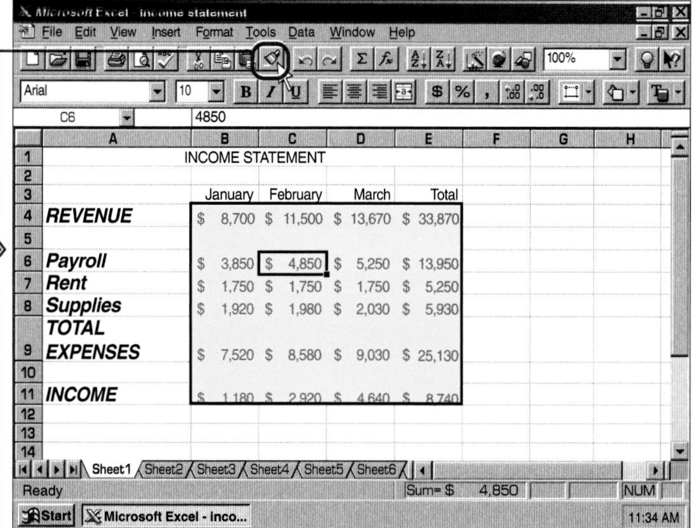

2 Move the mouse over the Format Painter button and then press the left button (the mouse pointer changes to a paintbrush pointer).

Tip

You can use the AutoFormat feature to instantly give your entire worksheet a consistent look.

Note: For more information on the AutoFormat feature, *refer to page 106.*

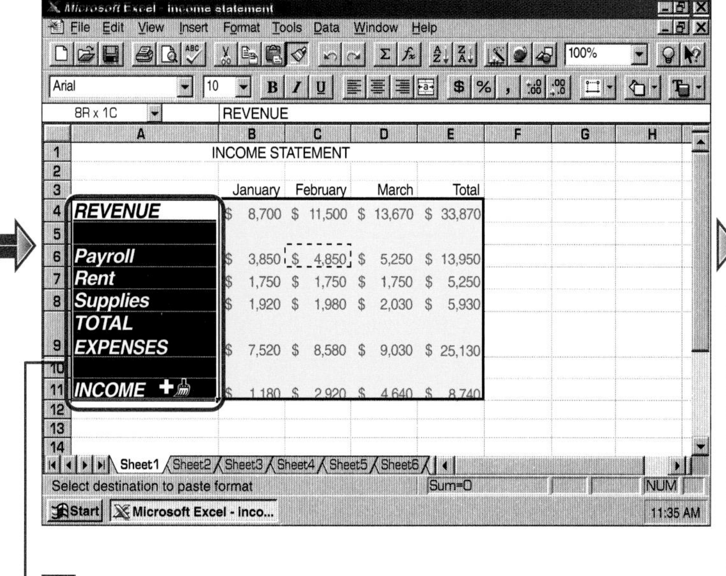

3 Select the cells you want to display the formats.

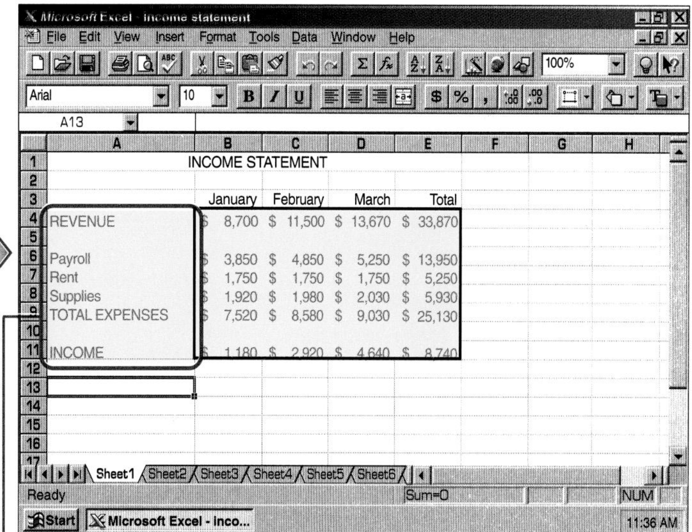

■ When you release the left button, the cells display the formats.

Note: To deselect cells, move the mouse over any cell and then press the left button.

CLEAR FORMATS

You can quickly remove all the formats you applied to cells in your worksheet.

CLEAR FORMATS

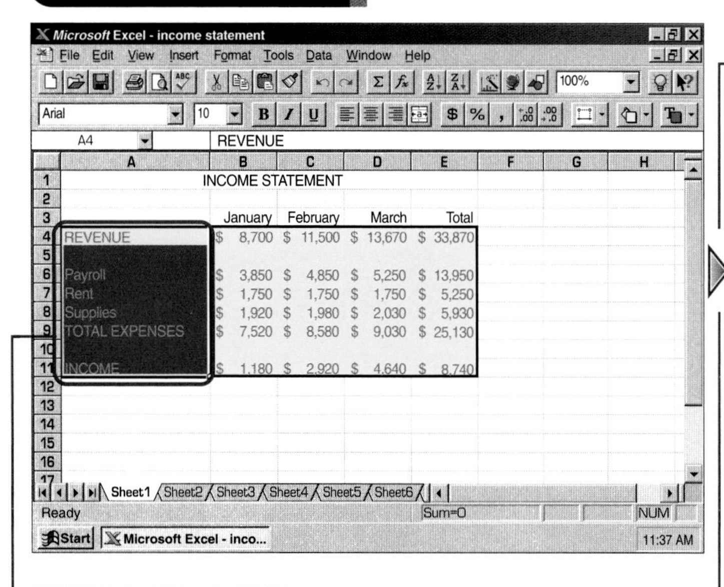

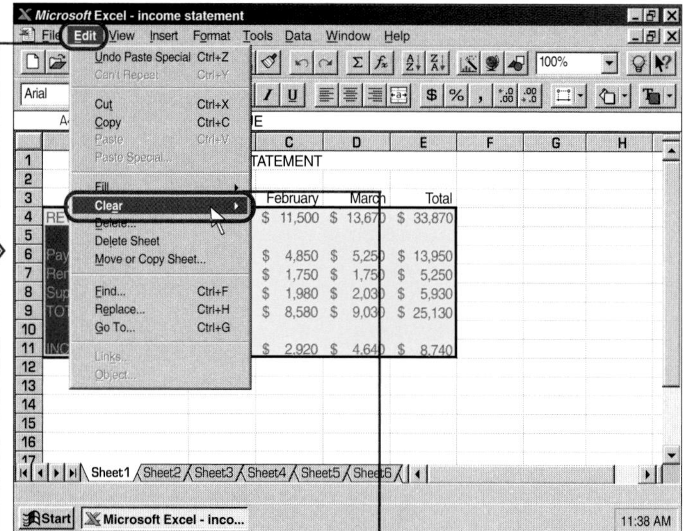

1 Select the cells displaying the formats you want to remove.

Note: To select cells, refer to page 12.

2 Move the mouse over **Edit** and then press the left button.

3 Move the mouse over **Clear**.

You can quickly remove formats and data at the same time.

■ *Perform steps 1 to 4 starting on page 104, selecting **All** in step 4.*

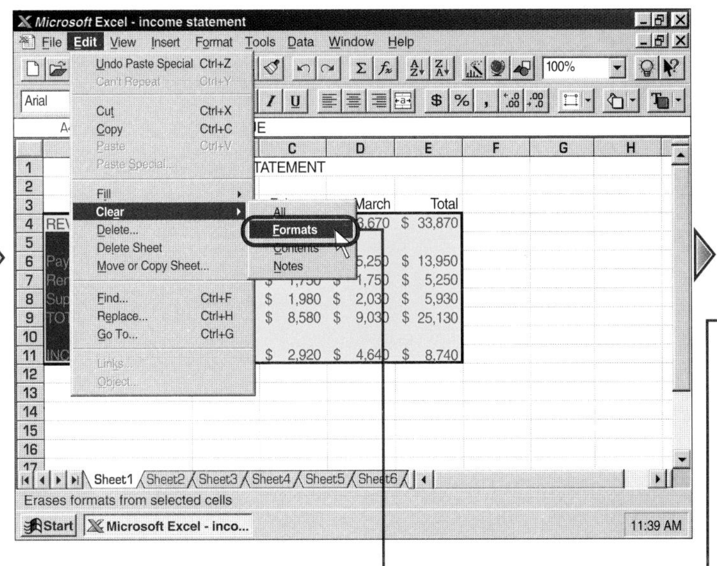

■ A new menu appears.

4 Move the mouse over **Formats** and then press the left button.

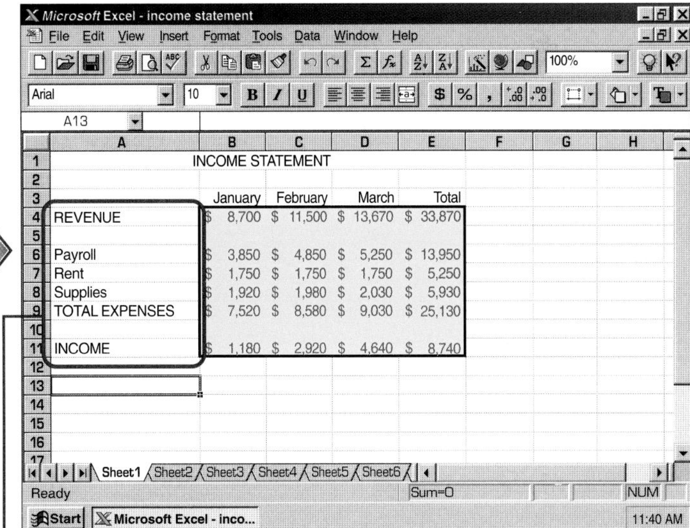

■ All the formats disappear from the cells you selected.

Note: The data in the cells remains unchanged.

Note: To deselect cells, move the mouse over any cell and then press the left button.

FORMAT A WORKSHEET AUTOMATICALLY

FORMAT A WORKSHEET AUTOMATICALLY

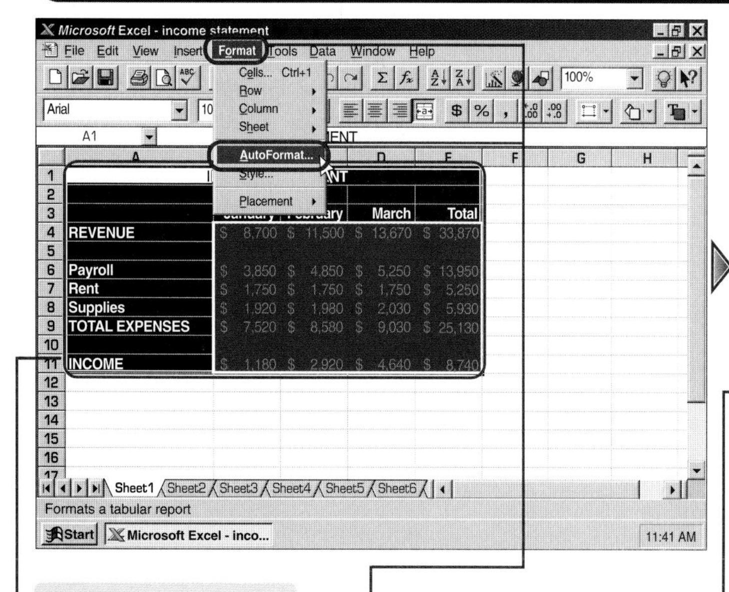

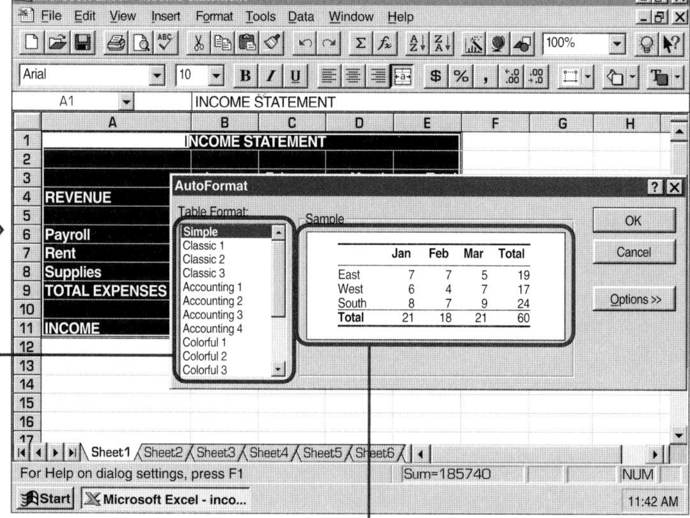

1 Select the cells you want to change.

Note: To select cells, refer to page 12.

2 Move the mouse over **Format** and then press the left button.

3 Move the mouse over **AutoFormat** and then press the left button.

■ The **AutoFormat** dialog box appears.

■ This area displays a list of the available designs.

■ This area displays a sample of the highlighted design.

- Change Data Alignment
- Center Data Across Columns
- Bold, Italic and Underline
- Change Appearance of Numbers
- Change Fonts
- Wrap Text in a Cell
- Add Borders
- Add Color
- Using Format Painter
- Clear Formats
- **Format a Worksheet Automatically**

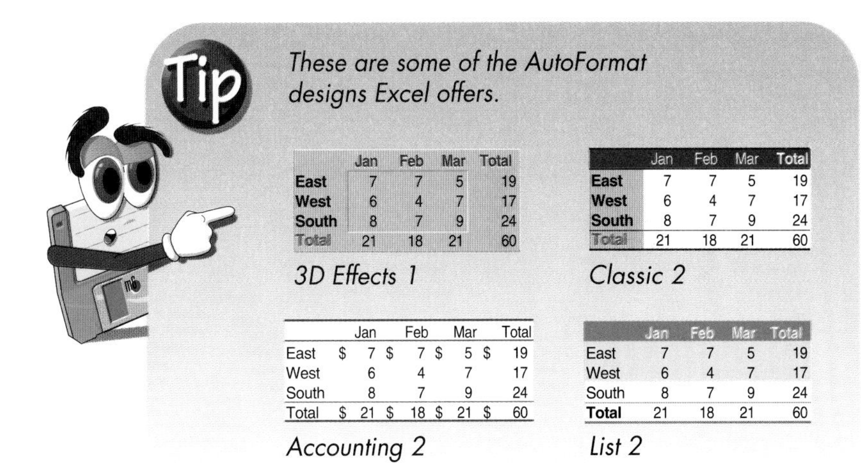

Tip
These are some of the AutoFormat designs Excel offers.
3D Effects 1
Classic 2
Accounting 2
List 2

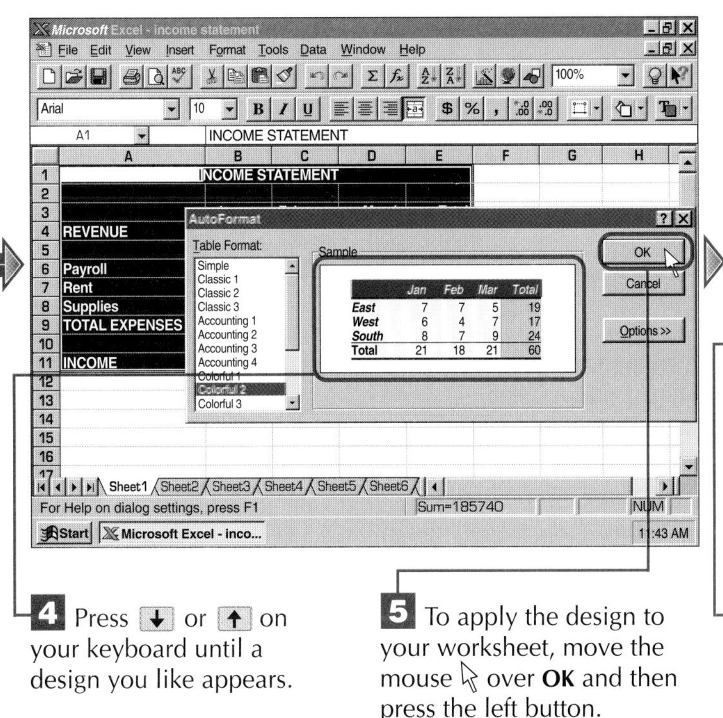

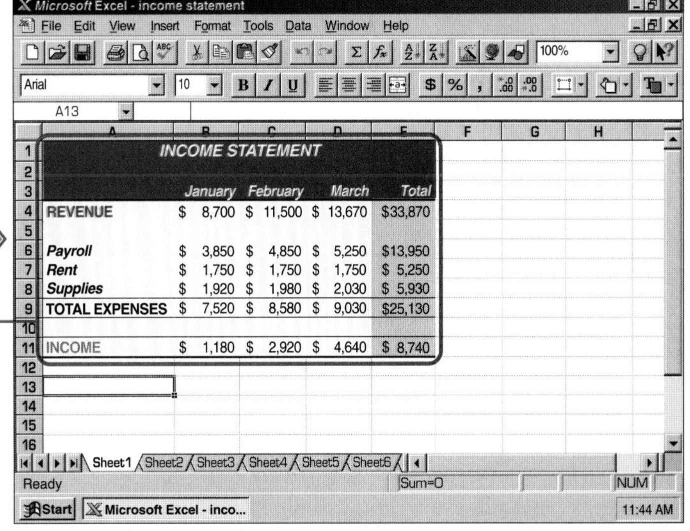

4 Press ↓ or ↑ on your keyboard until a design you like appears.

5 To apply the design to your worksheet, move the mouse over **OK** and then press the left button.

■ The cells display the design you selected.

Note: To deselect cells, move the mouse over any cell and then press the left button.

Remove AutoFormat

Perform steps **1** to **5**, selecting **None** in step **4**.

In this chapter you will learn how to print your worksheets and change the way your worksheets appear on a printed page.

INCOME STATEMENT				
	January	February	March	Total
REVENUE	$ 8,700	$ 11,500	$ 13,670	$33,870
Payroll	$ 3,850	$ 4,850	$ 5,250	$13,950
Rent	$ 1,750	$ 1,750	$ 1,750	$ 5,250
Supplies	$ 1,920	$ 1,980	$ 2,030	$ 5,930
TOTAL EXPENSES	$ 7,520	$ 8,580	$ 9,030	$25,130
INCOME	$ 1,180	$ 2,920	$ 4,640	$ 8,740

PRINT YOUR WORKSHEETS

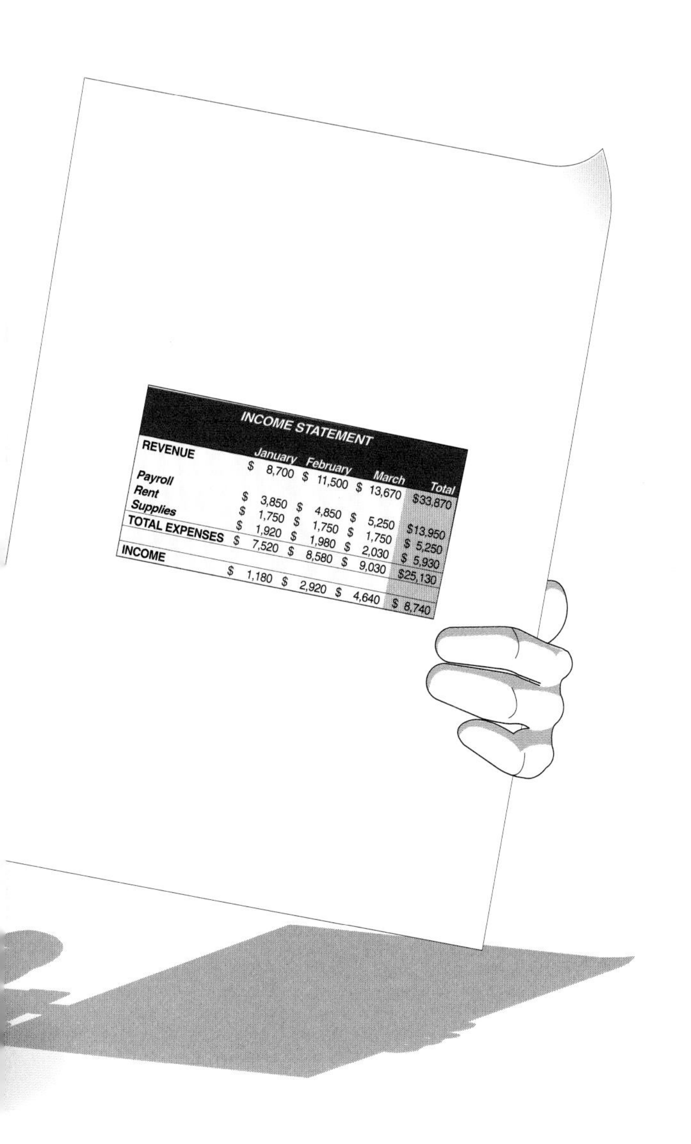

INCOME STATEMENT	January	February	March	Total
REVENUE	$ 8,700	$ 11,500	$ 13,670	$33,870
Payroll	$ 3,850	$ 4,850	$ 5,250	$13,950
Rent	$ 1,750	$ 1,750	$ 1,750	$ 5,250
Supplies	$ 1,920	$ 1,980	$ 2,030	$ 5,930
TOTAL EXPENSES	$ 7,520	$ 8,580	$ 9,030	$25,130
INCOME	$ 1,180	$ 2,920	$ 4,640	$ 8,740

Preview a Worksheet

Change Margins

Print a Worksheet

Change Print Options

Insert a Page Break

Center Data on a Page

Change Page Orientation

Change Scaling

Create a Header or Footer

Repeat Titles on Printed Pages

PREVIEW A WORKSHEET

You can see on the screen how your worksheet will look when printed.

PREVIEW A WORKSHEET

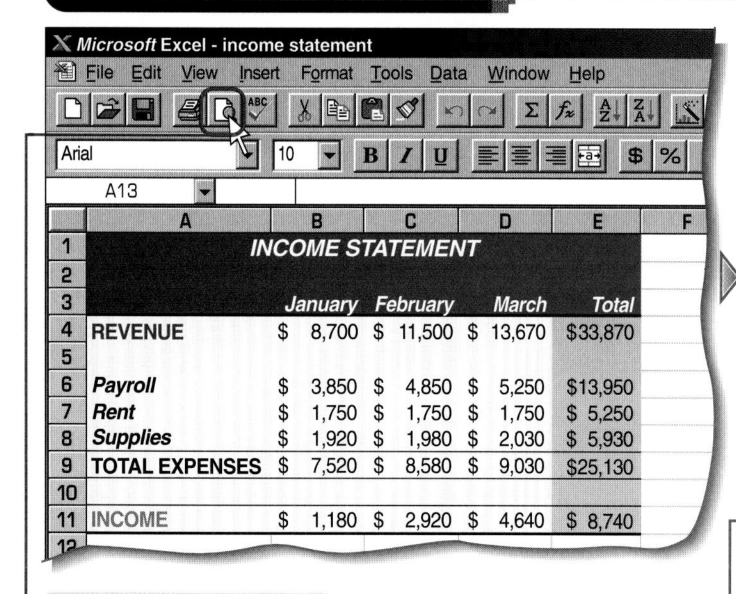

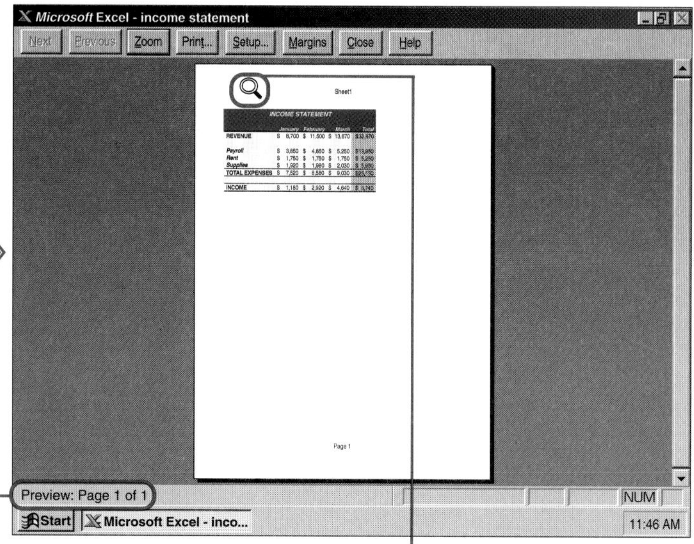

1 Move the mouse ↖ over 🔍 and then press the left button.

■ The first page of your worksheet appears.

■ This area tells you which page is displayed and the number of pages in the worksheet.

2 To magnify an area of the page, move the mouse ↖ over the area (↖ changes to 🔍) and then press the left button.

Tip ***If your worksheet contains more than one page, you can easily display another page in the Print Preview window.***

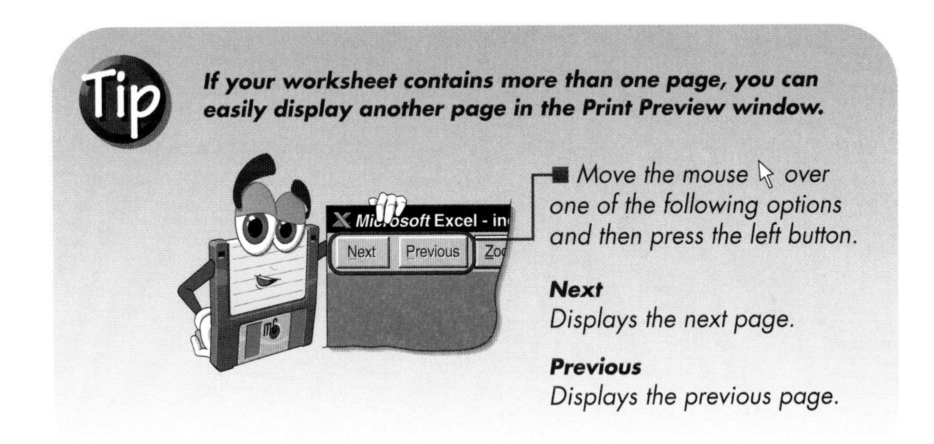

■ *Move the mouse over one of the following options and then press the left button.*

Next
Displays the next page.

Previous
Displays the previous page.

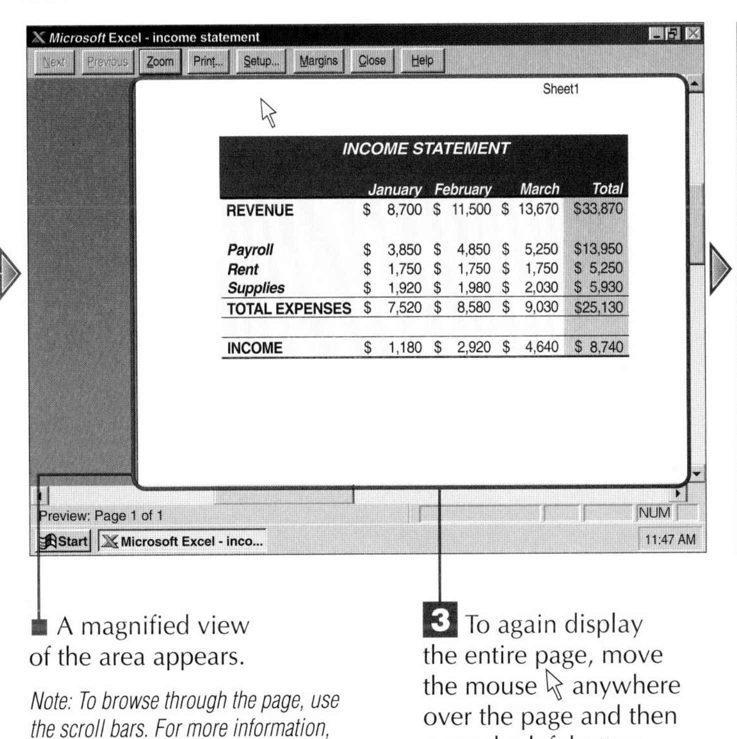

■ A magnified view of the area appears.

Note: To browse through the page, use the scroll bars. For more information, refer to page 14.

3 To again display the entire page, move the mouse anywhere over the page and then press the left button.

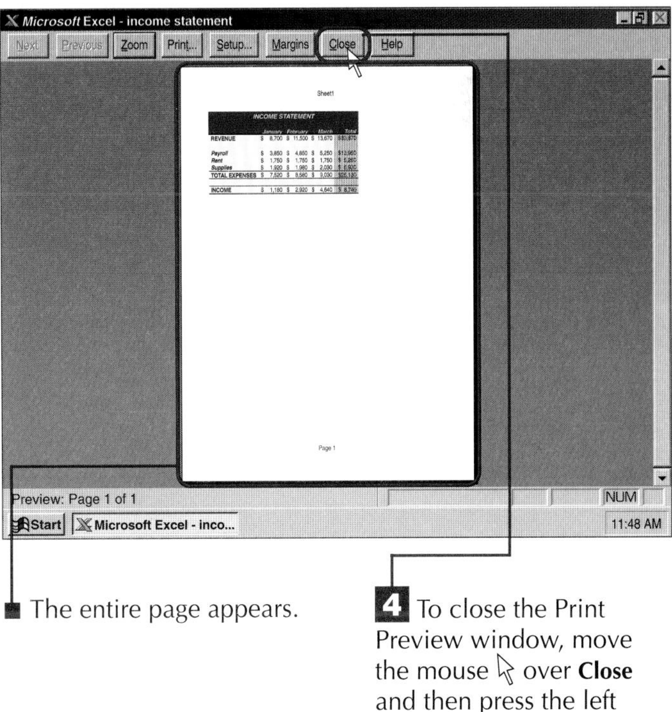

■ The entire page appears.

4 To close the Print Preview window, move the mouse over **Close** and then press the left button.

CHANGE MARGINS

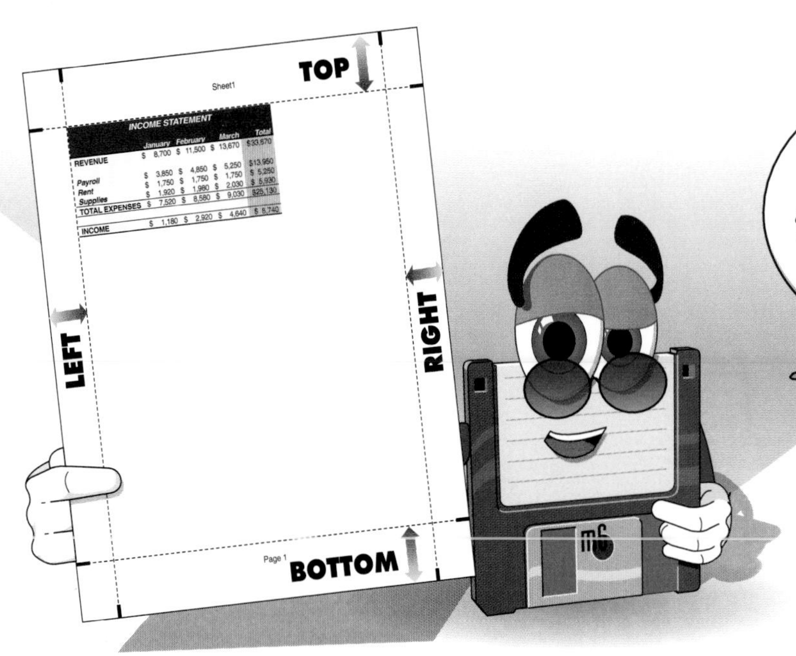

TOP
LEFT
RIGHT
BOTTOM
A margin is the amount of space between data and an edge of your paper. You can easily change the margins in your worksheet.

Excel initially sets the top and bottom margins at 1.0 inches. The left and right margins are initially set at 0.75 inches.

CHANGE MARGINS

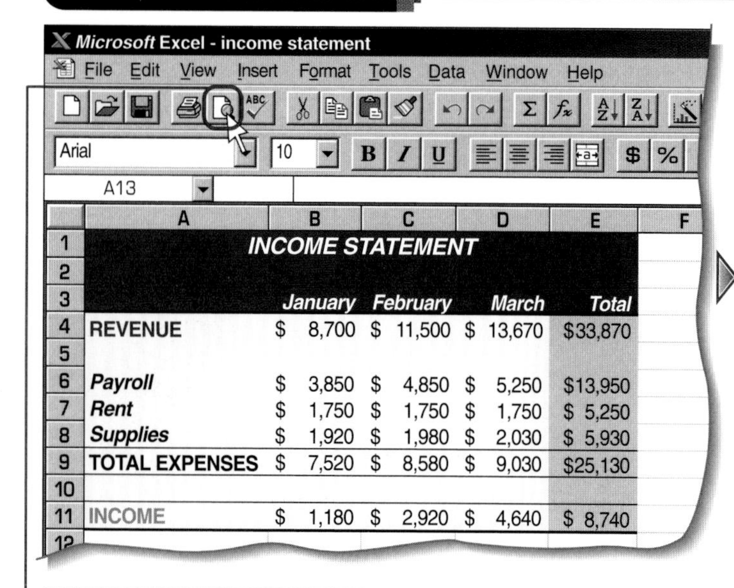

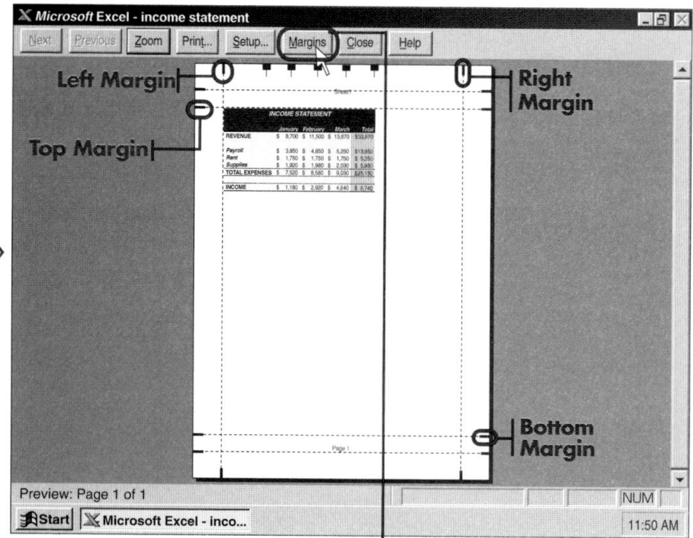

1 To display your worksheet in the Print Preview window, move the mouse over and then press the left button.

Note: For more information on using Print Preview, refer to page 110.

■ The first page of your worksheet appears.

2 If the margins do not appear on your screen, move the mouse over **Margins** and then press the left button.

Tip
Increasing the margins will fit less data on a page.
Decreasing the margins will fit more data on a page.

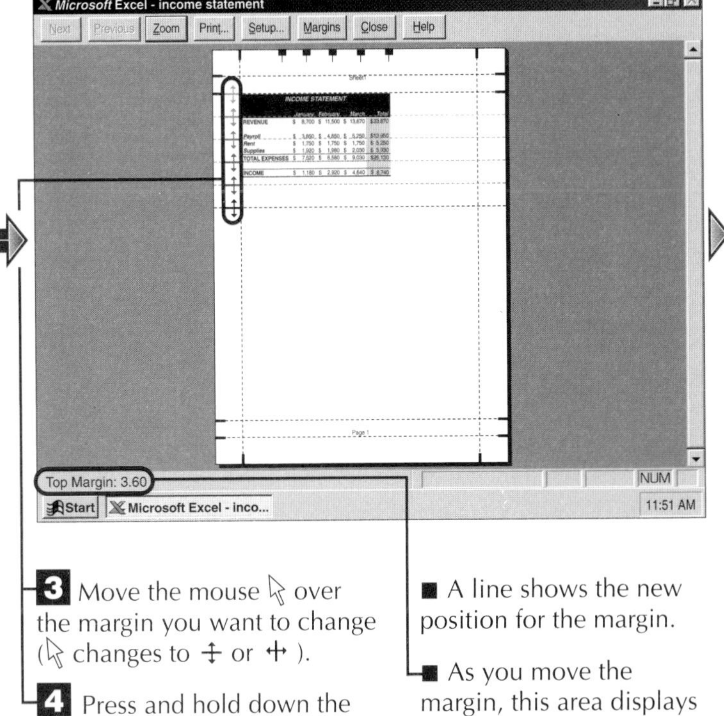

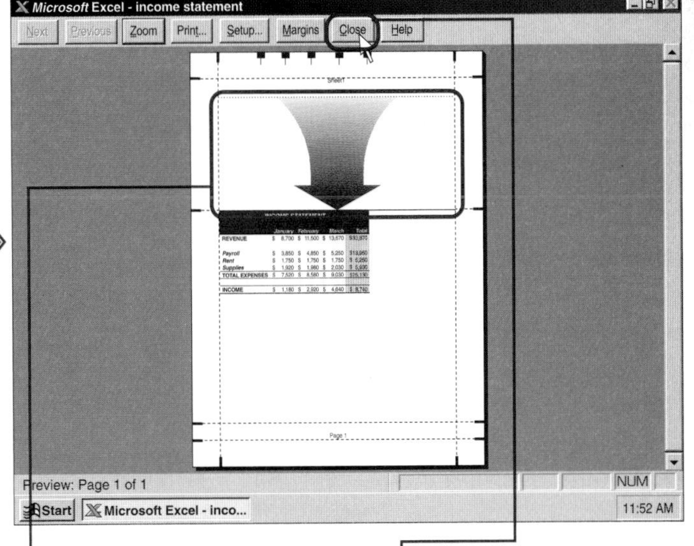

3 Move the mouse over the margin you want to change (changes to ‡ or ✢).

4 Press and hold down the left button as you move the margin to a new location.

■ A line shows the new position for the margin.

■ As you move the margin, this area displays the distance between the margin and the edge of the page.

5 Release the left button and the margin moves to the new location.

6 Repeat steps **3** to **5** for each margin you want to change.

7 To close the Print Preview window, move the mouse over **Close** and then press the left button.

PRINT A WORKSHEET

You can produce a paper copy of the worksheet displayed on your screen.

PRINT A WORKSHEET

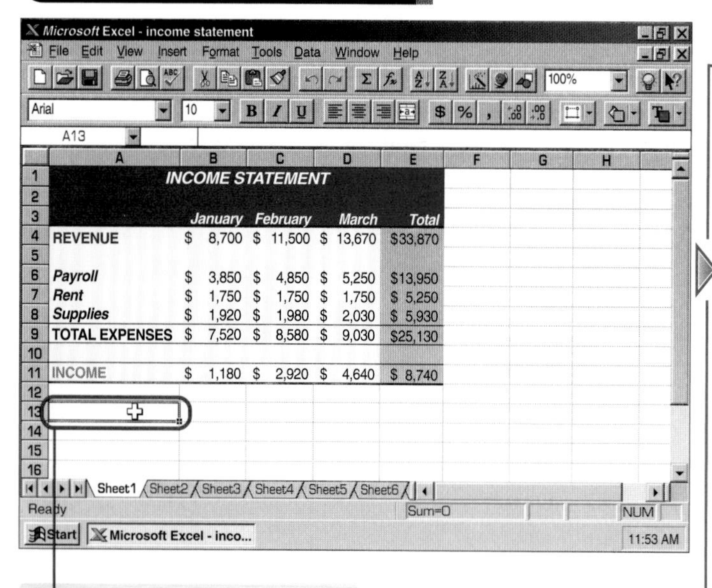

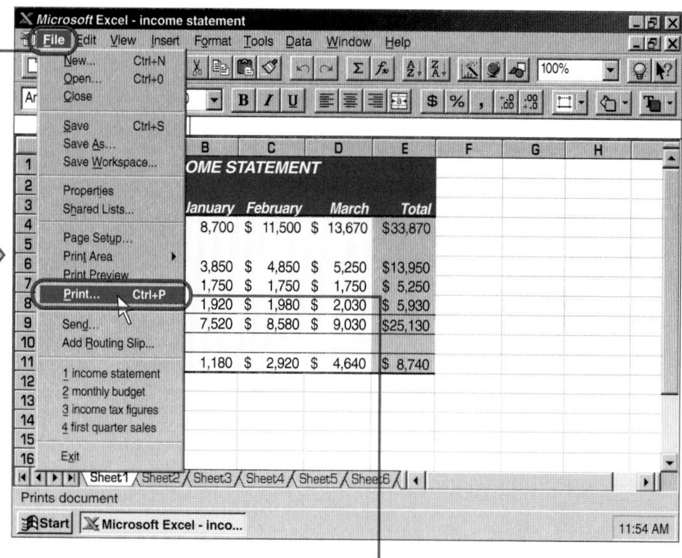

1 Move the mouse over any cell in the worksheet you want to print and then press the left button.

■ To only print data in specific cells, select the cells you want to print.

Note: To select cells, refer to page 12.

2 Move the mouse over **File** and then press the left button.

3 Move the mouse over **Print** and then press the left button.

■ The **Print** dialog box appears.

Excel automatically places the worksheet name and page number on each printed page.

Note: To change or remove this information, refer to page 124 to create a header or footer.

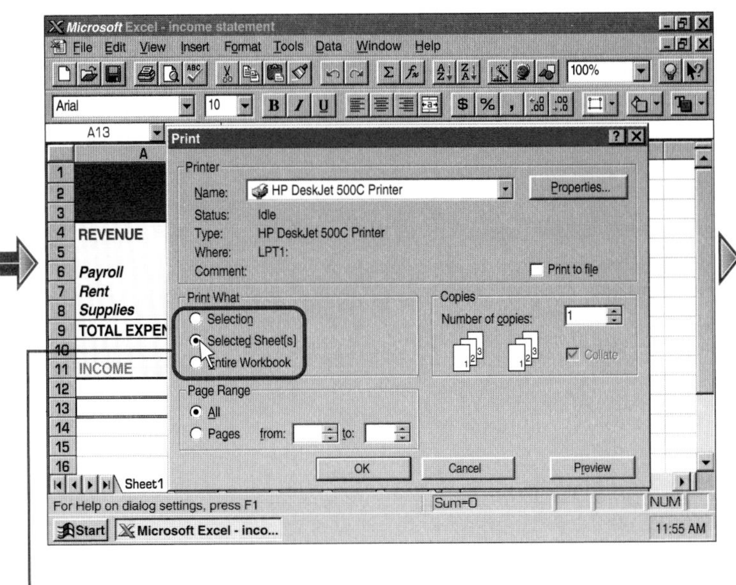

4 Move the mouse over the print option you want to use and then press the left button (○ changes to ◉).

Selection - Prints the data in the cells you selected.

Selected Sheet(s) - Prints the entire worksheet.

Entire Workbook - Prints all the worksheets in the workbook.

Note: For information on using the worksheets in a workbook, refer to pages 140-151.

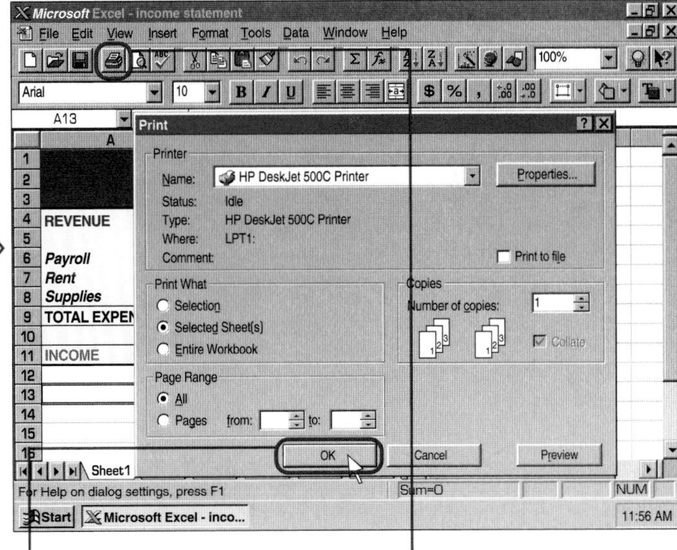

5 Move the mouse over **OK** and then press the left button.

Note: Excel offers several print options to change the way your worksheet appears on a printed page. For more information, refer to page 116.

You can quickly print your entire worksheet.

■ Move the mouse over 🖨 and then press the left button.

CHANGE PRINT OPTIONS

You can change the way your worksheet appears on a printed page.

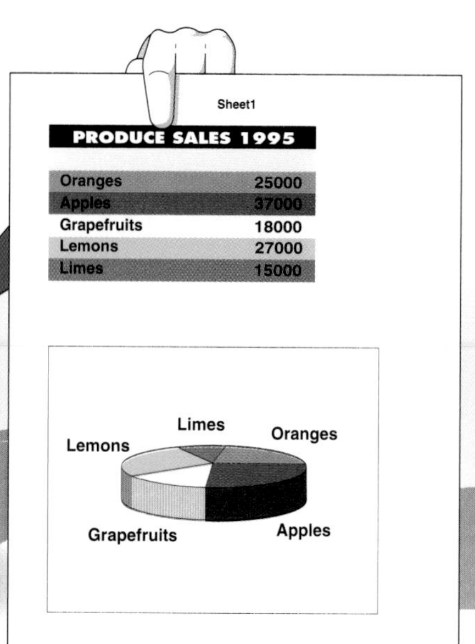

CHANGE PRINT OPTIONS

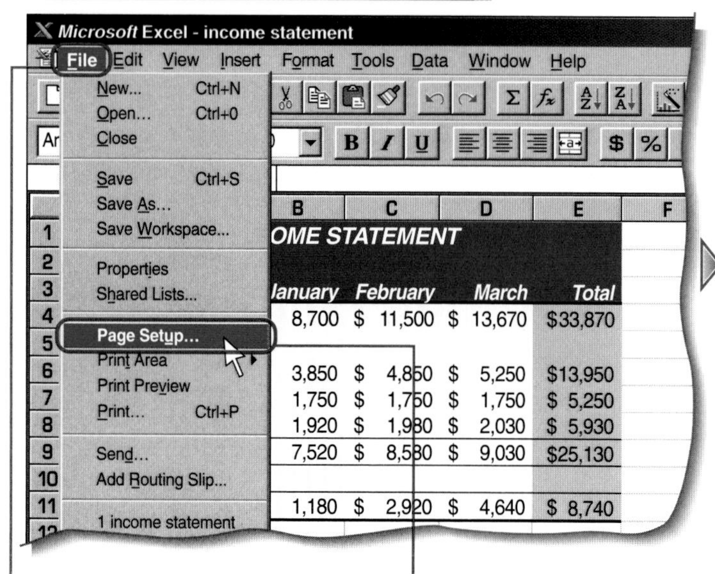

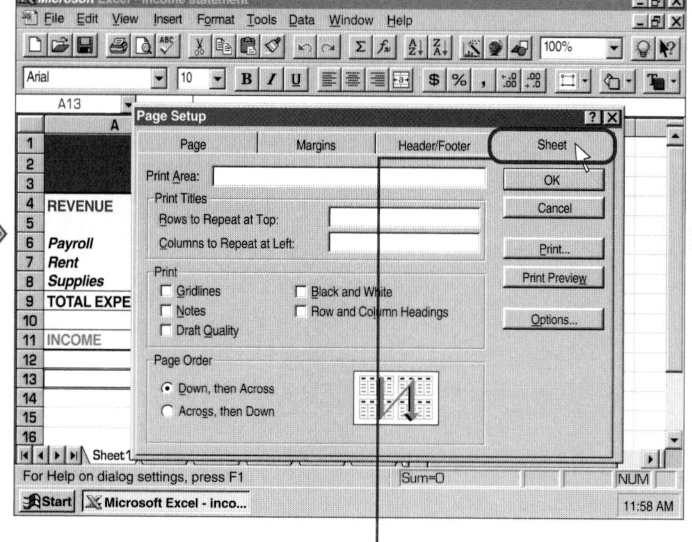

1 Move the mouse over **File** and then press the left button.

2 Move the mouse over **Page Setup** and then press the left button.

■ The **Page Setup** dialog box appears.

3 Move the mouse over the **Sheet** tab and then press the left button.

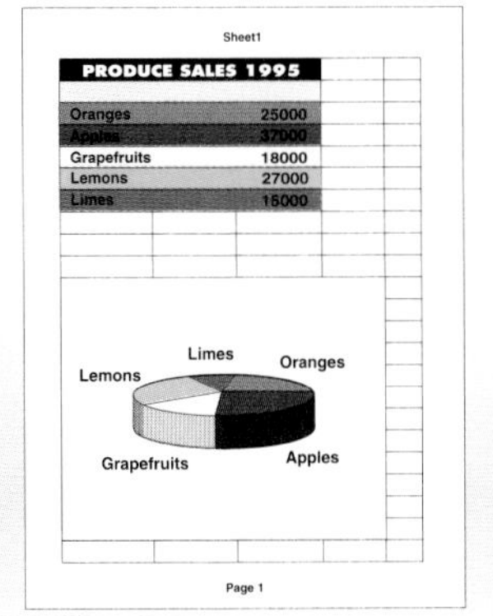

Gridlines - Prints lines to separate the cells in your worksheet.

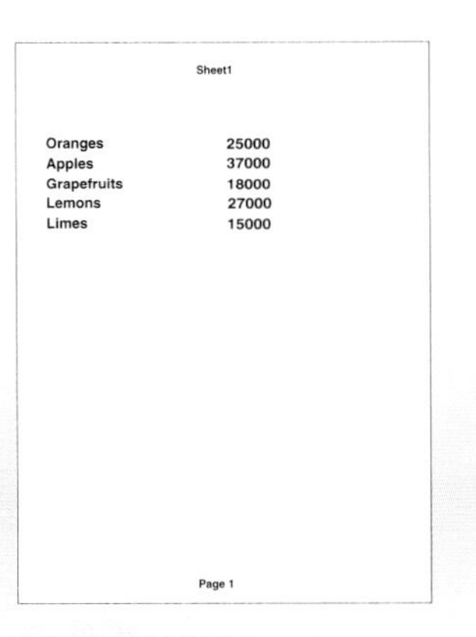

Draft Quality - Does not print gridlines or most graphics to reduce printing time.

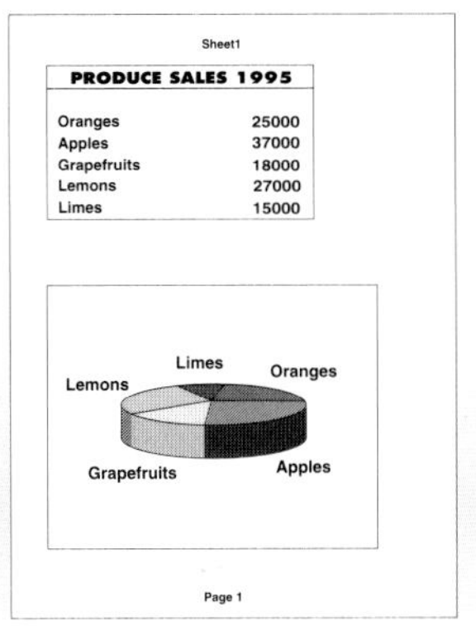

Black and White - Prints the worksheet in black and white. A colored worksheet printed on a black-and-white printer may be difficult to read.

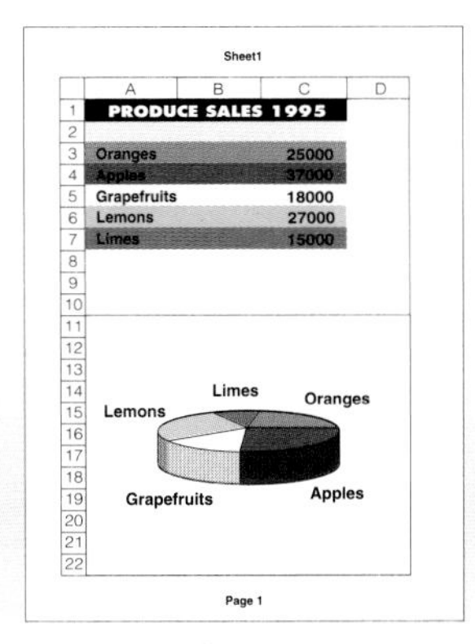

Row and Column Headings - Prints the row and column headings as they appear on your screen.

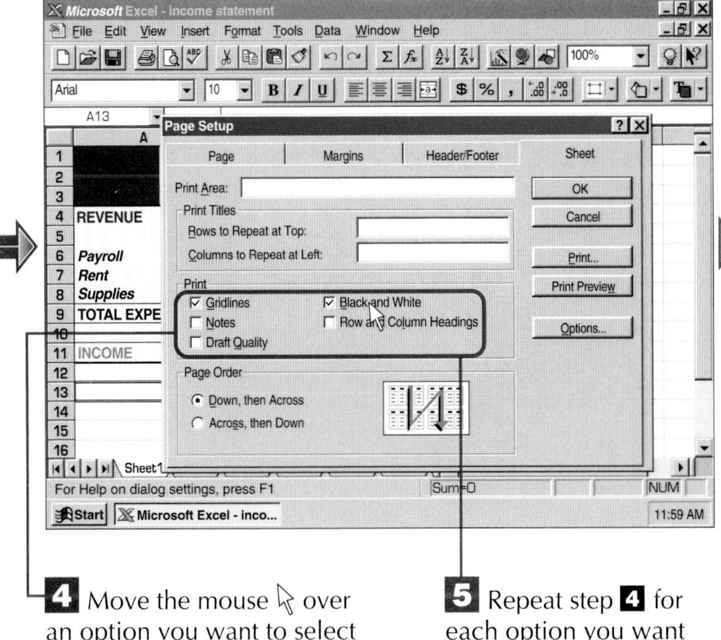

4 Move the mouse over an option you want to select and then press the left button.

☑ The option is on.

☐ The option is off.

5 Repeat step **4** for each option you want to select.

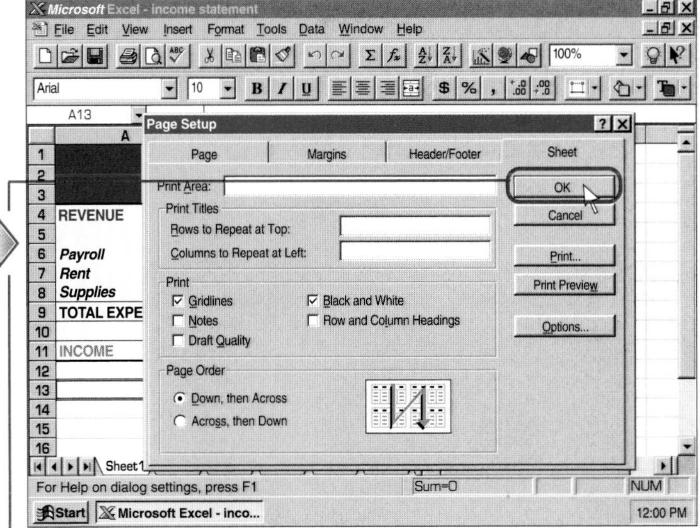

6 Move the mouse over **OK** and then press the left button.

Note: The print options you select only change the way the worksheet appears on a printed page. The options do not affect the way the worksheet appears on your screen.

INSERT A PAGE BREAK

If you want to start a new page at a specific place in your worksheet, you can add a page break. A page break defines where one page ends and another begins.

INSERT A PAGE BREAK

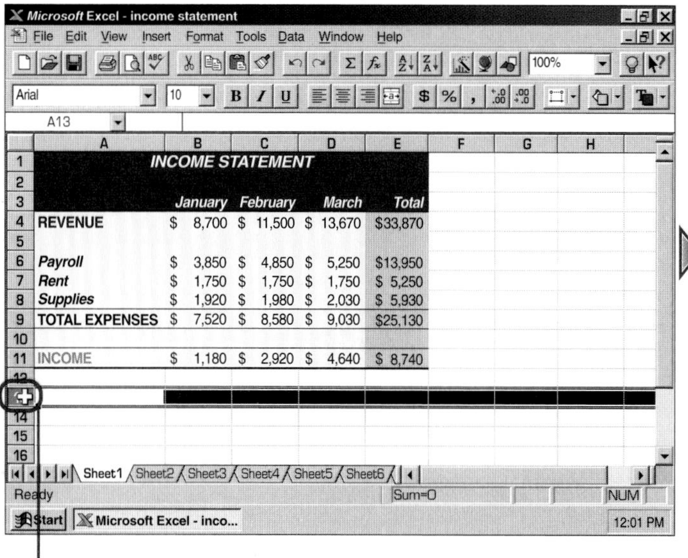

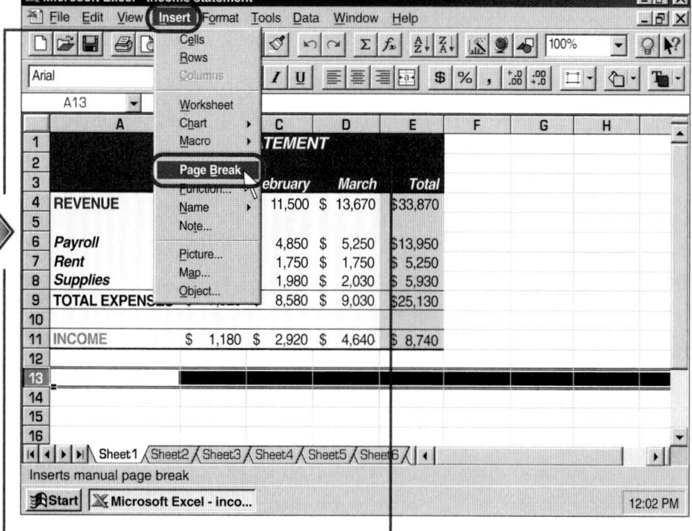

1 Select the row or column you want to appear at the beginning of the new page.

Note: To select a row or column, refer to page 12.

2 Move the mouse over **Insert** and then press the left button.

3 Move the mouse over **Page Break** and then press the left button.

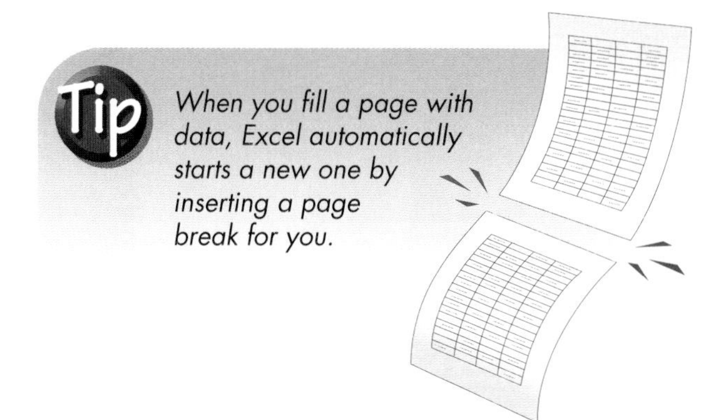

Tip
When you fill a page with data, Excel automatically starts a new one by inserting a page break for you.

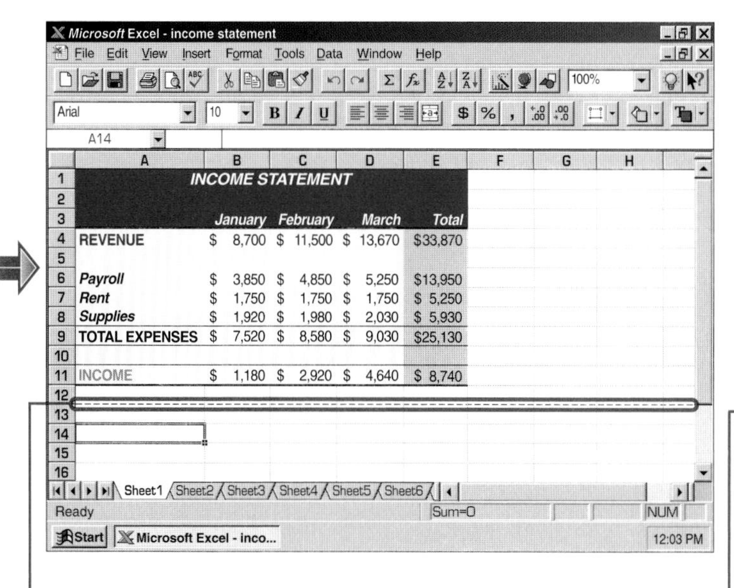

■ A line appears on your screen. This line defines where one page ends and another begins.

■ The page break line will not appear when you print your worksheet.

Note: To deselect the row or column, move the mouse over any cell and then press the left button.

REMOVE A PAGE BREAK

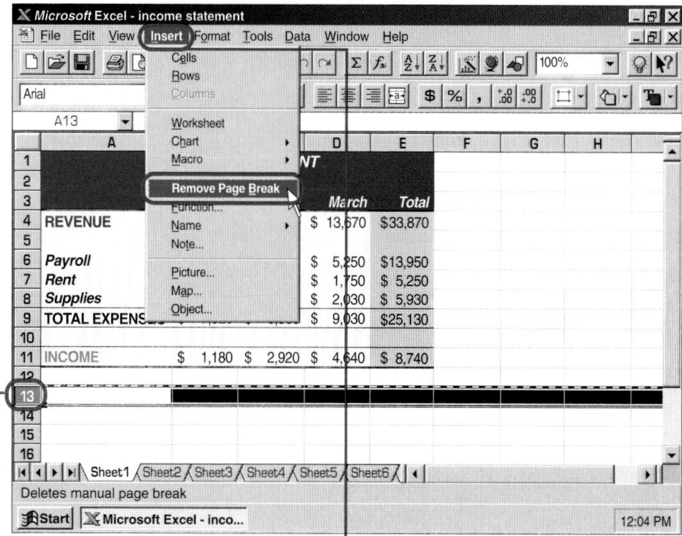

1 Select the row directly below or the column directly to the right of the page break line.

Note: To select a row or column, refer to page 12.

2 Move the mouse over **Insert** and then press the left button.

3 Move the mouse over **Remove Page Break** and then press the left button.

CENTER DATA ON A PAGE

CHANGE PAGE ORIENTATION

You can center data horizontally and vertically on a page.
Horizontally
Vertically

CENTER DATA ON A PAGE

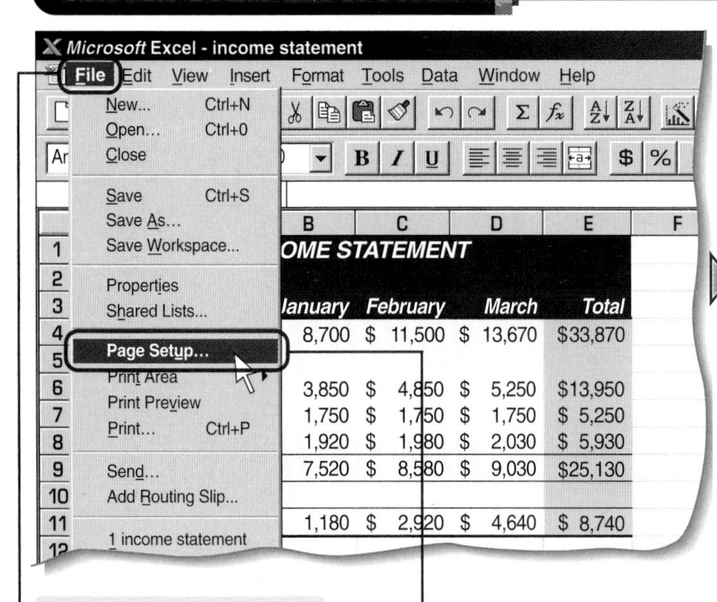

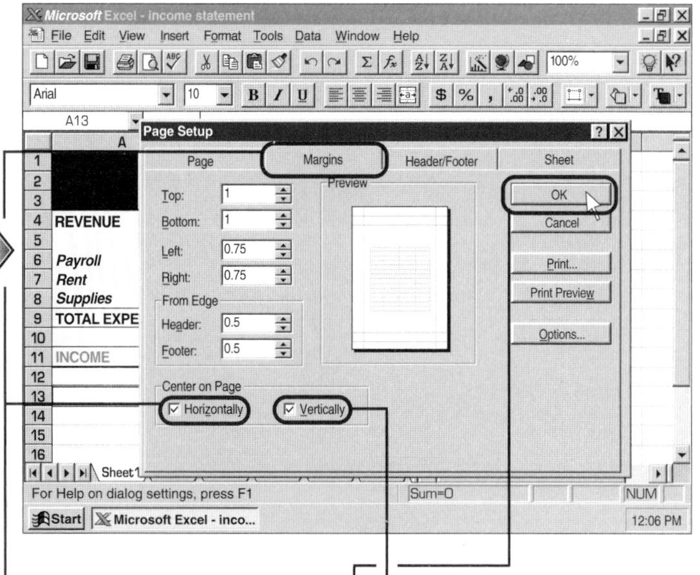

1 Move the mouse over **File** and then press the left button.

2 Move the mouse over **Page Setup** and then press the left button.

■ The **Page Setup** dialog box appears.

3 Move the mouse over the **Margins** tab and then press the left button.

4 To center the data horizontally, move the mouse over **Horizontally** and then press the left button (☐ changes to ☑).

5 To center the data vertically, move the mouse over **Vertically** and then press the left button (☐ changes to ☑).

6 Move the mouse over **OK** and then press the left button.

- Preview a Worksheet
- Change Margins
- Print a Worksheet
- Change Print Options
- Insert a Page Break
- **Center Data on a Page**
- **Change Page Orientation**
- Change Scaling
- Create a Header or Footer
- Repeat Titles on Printed Pages

If your worksheet is too wide to fit on one page, you can change its orientation.
Portrait
Landscape

CHANGE PAGE ORIENTATION

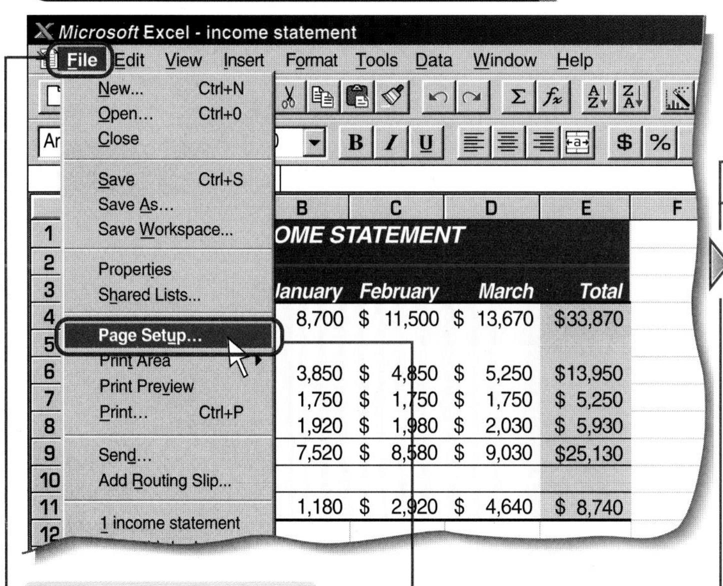

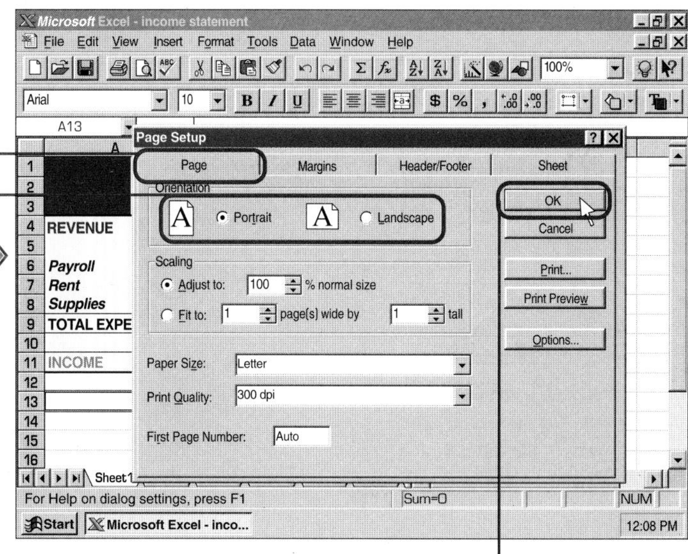

1 Move the mouse over **File** and then press the left button.

2 Move the mouse over **Page Setup** and then press the left button.

■ The **Page Setup** dialog box appears.

3 Move the mouse over the **Page** tab and then press the left button.

4 Move the mouse over the orientation you want to use and then press the left button (○ changes to ◉).

5 Move the mouse over **OK** and then press the left button.

CHANGE SCALING

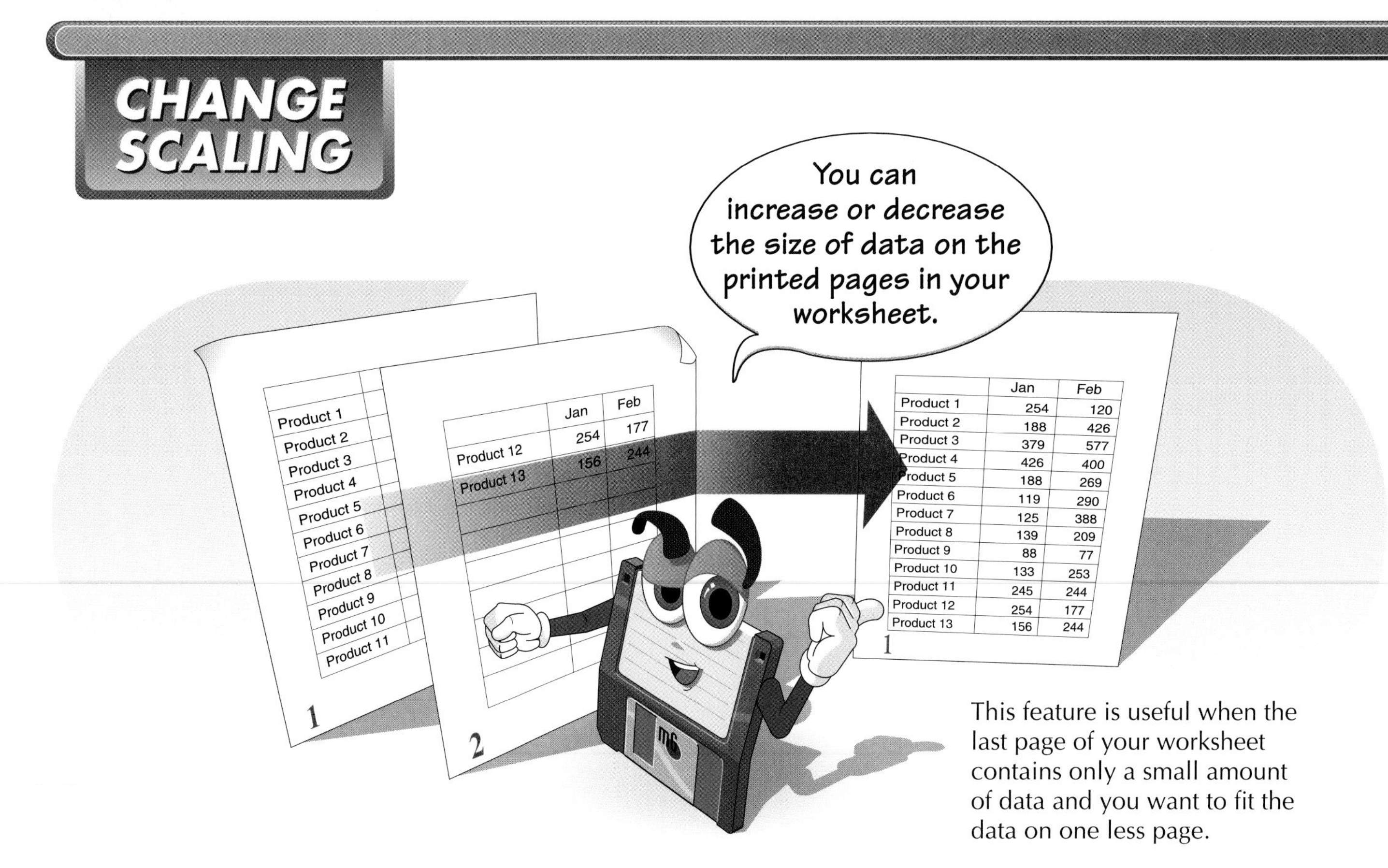

You can increase or decrease the size of data on the printed pages in your worksheet.

This feature is useful when the last page of your worksheet contains only a small amount of data and you want to fit the data on one less page.

CHANGE SCALING

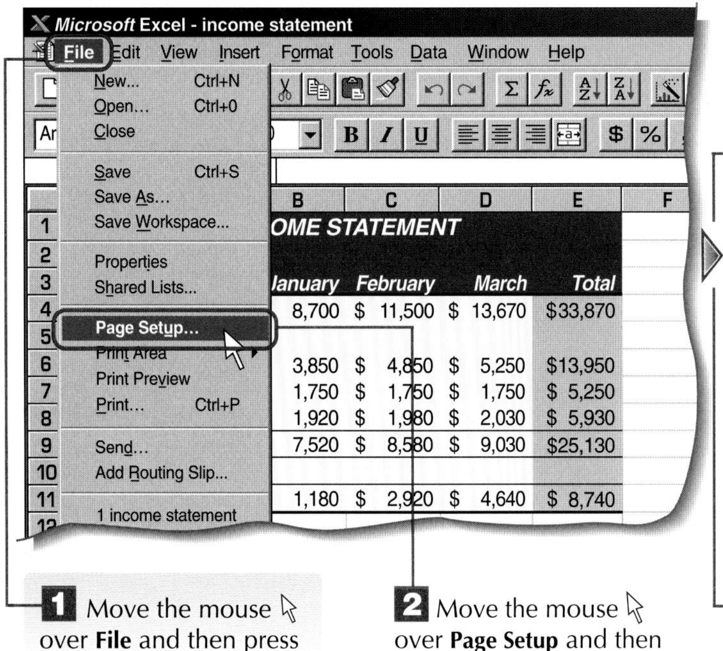

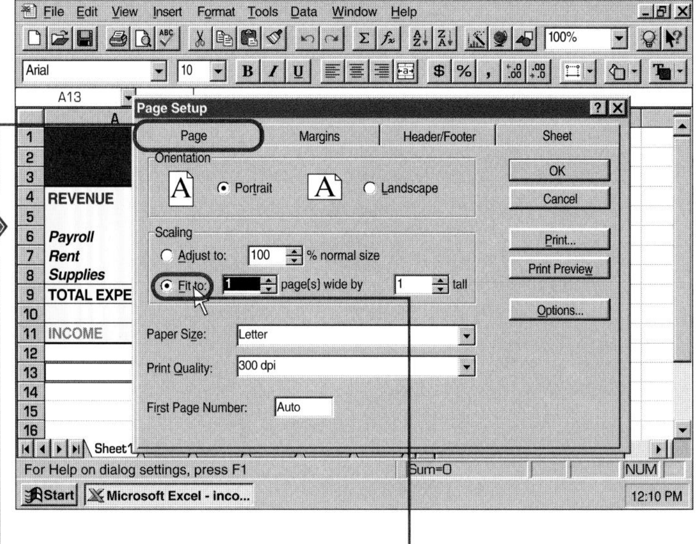

1 Move the mouse ⇖ over **File** and then press the left button.

2 Move the mouse ⇖ over **Page Setup** and then press the left button.

■ The **Page Setup** dialog box appears.

3 Move the mouse ⇖ over the **Page** tab and then press the left button.

4 Move the mouse ⇖ over **Fit to:** and then press the left button (○ changes to ◉).

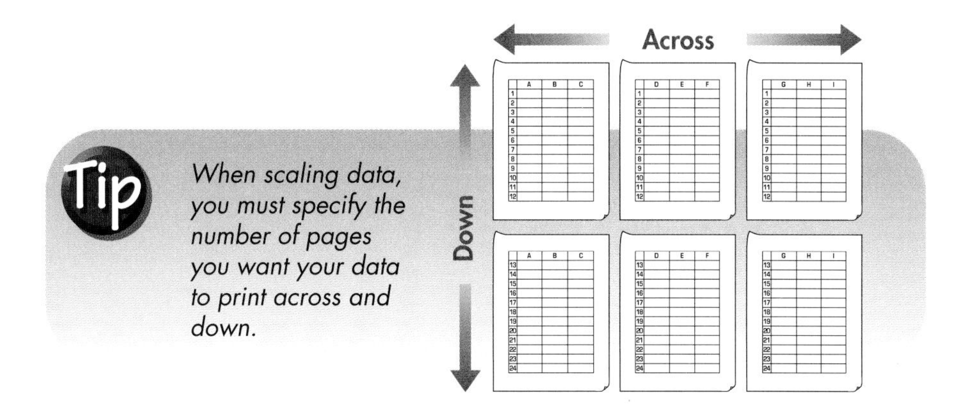

Tip
When scaling data, you must specify the number of pages you want your data to print across and down.
Across
Down

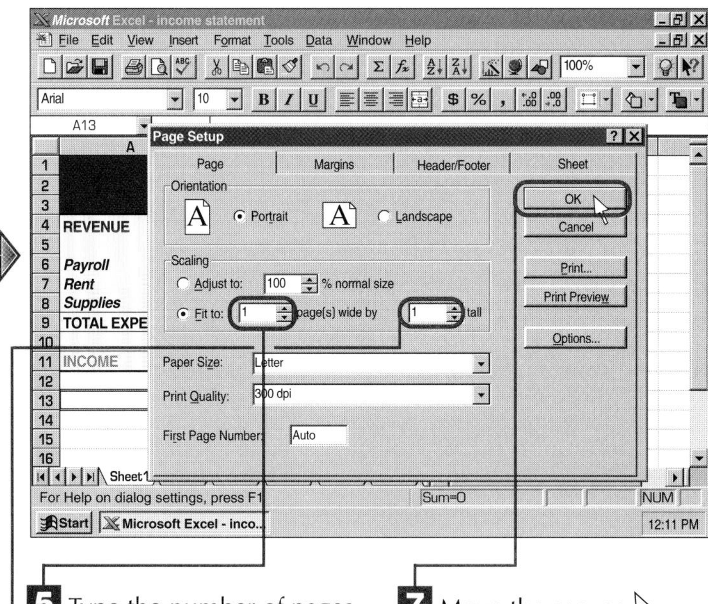

5 Type the number of pages you want your data to print across and then press Tab on your keyboard.

6 Type the number of pages you want your data to print down.

7 Move the mouse over **OK** and then press the left button.

Note: Changing the scaling does not affect the way your data appears on the screen. To increase or decrease the display of data on your screen, refer to page 130.

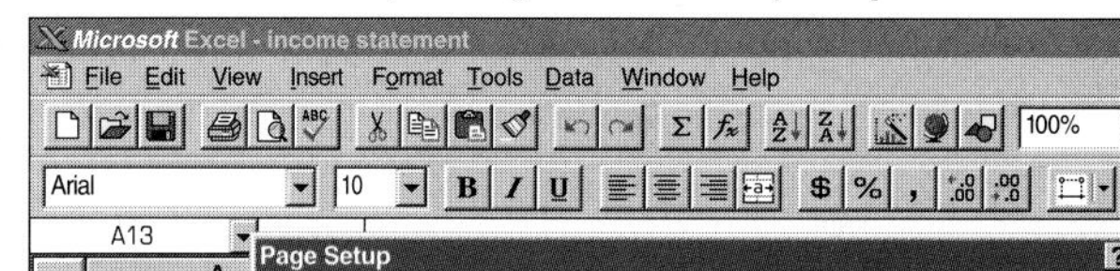

You can manually change the size of your printed data.

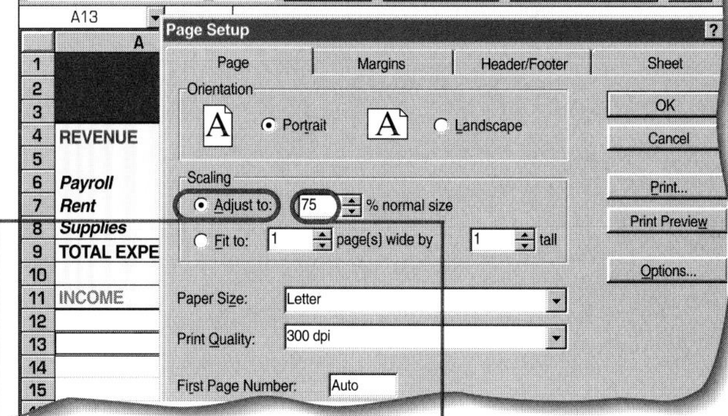

1 To display the **Page Setup** dialog box, perform steps **1** to **3** on page 122.

2 Move the mouse over **Adjust to:** and then press the left button (○ changes to ◉).

3 Type the percentage you want to use and then press Enter on your keyboard.

Note: A percentage over 100 will increase the size of the printed data. A percentage under 100 will decrease the size of the printed data.

CREATE A HEADER OR FOOTER

Headers and footers print information at the top and bottom of each page.
Sheet1
Page 1

■ **Header**
Excel initially prints the name of the worksheet at the top of each page.

■ **Footer**
Excel initially prints the page number at the bottom of each page.

CREATE A HEADER OR FOOTER

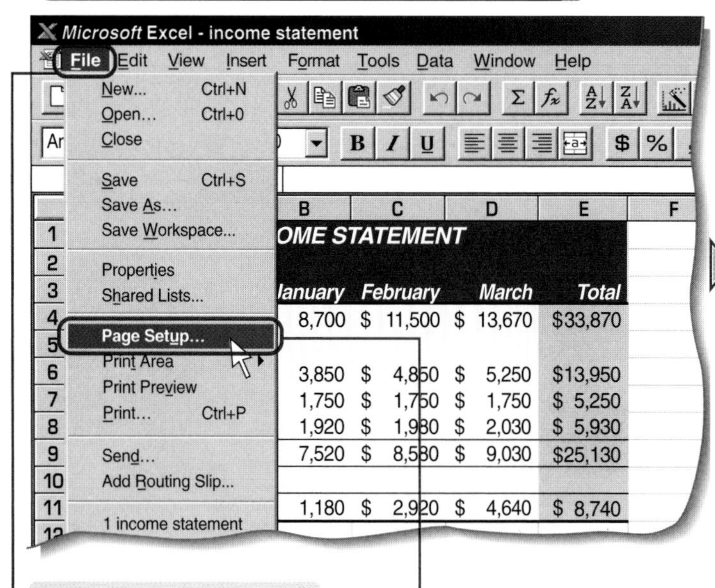

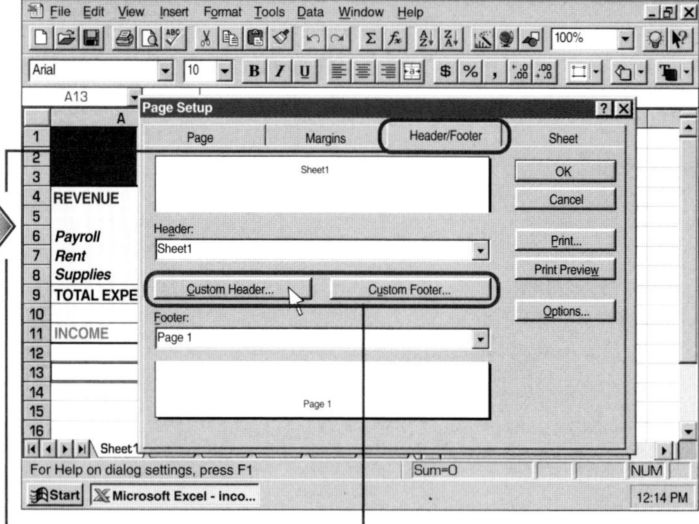

1 Move the mouse over **File** and then press the left button.

2 Move the mouse over **Page Setup** and then press the left button.

■ The **Page Setup** dialog box appears.

3 Move the mouse over the **Header/Footer** tab and then press the left button.

4 Move the mouse over one of the following options and then press the left button.

Custom Header
Creates a header.

Custom Footer
Creates a footer.

When you are typing text for a header or footer in step 7 below, you can have Excel insert additional information for you.

■ *Move the mouse over one of the options and then press the left button.*

 *Inserts page number.*

Inserts total number of pages.

Inserts current date.

 *Inserts current time.*

 *Inserts workbook name.*

 *Inserts worksheet name.*

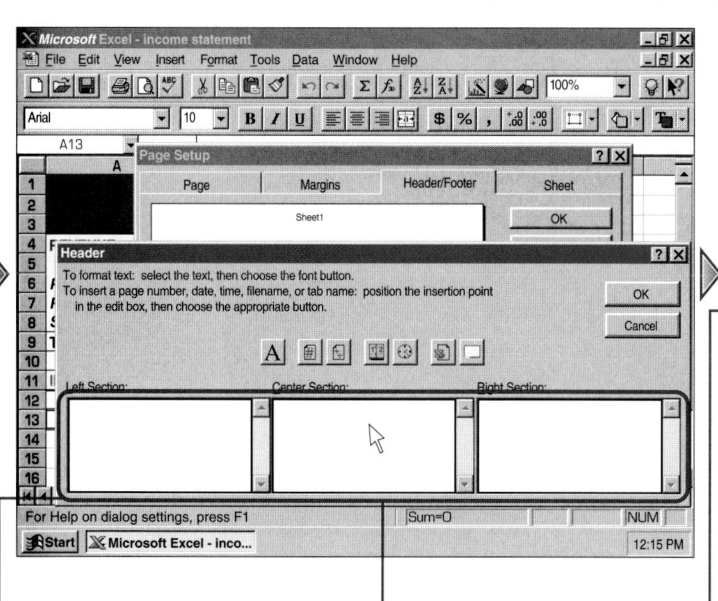

■ A dialog box appears.

5 To remove the existing header or footer, move the mouse over the text and then press the left button. Press Backspace or Delete on your keyboard until the text disappears.

6 Move the mouse over the area for the section of the page where you want to display a header or footer and then press the left button.

Note: If you do not want a header or footer to appear in your worksheet, skip to step 8.

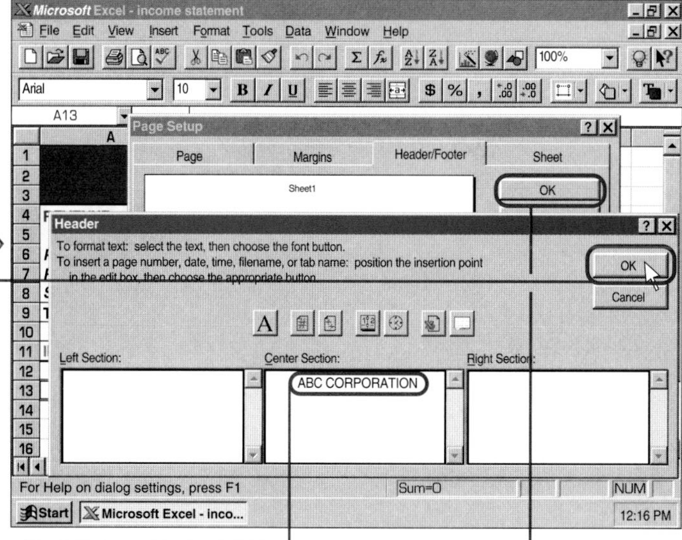

7 Type the header or footer text.

8 Move the mouse over **OK** and then press the left button.

9 To close the **Page Setup** dialog box, move the mouse over **OK** and then press the left button.

REPEAT TITLES ON PRINTED PAGES

You can repeat a row or column of titles on each printed page. This helps you review data in worksheets that print on more than one page.

REPEAT TITLES ON PRINTED PAGES

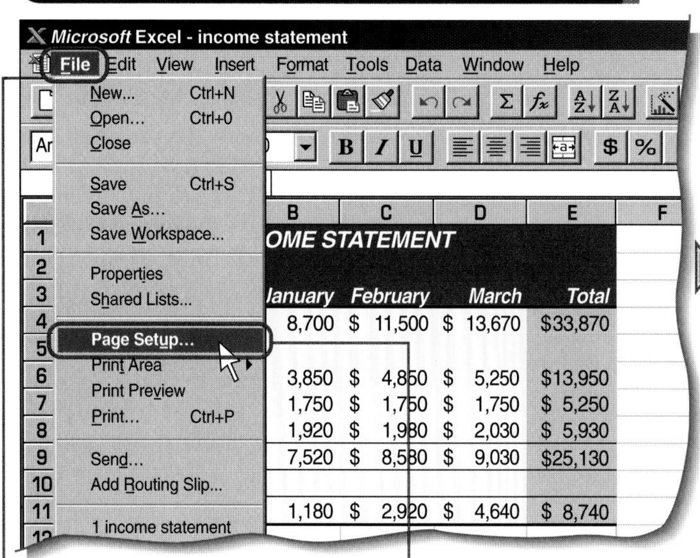

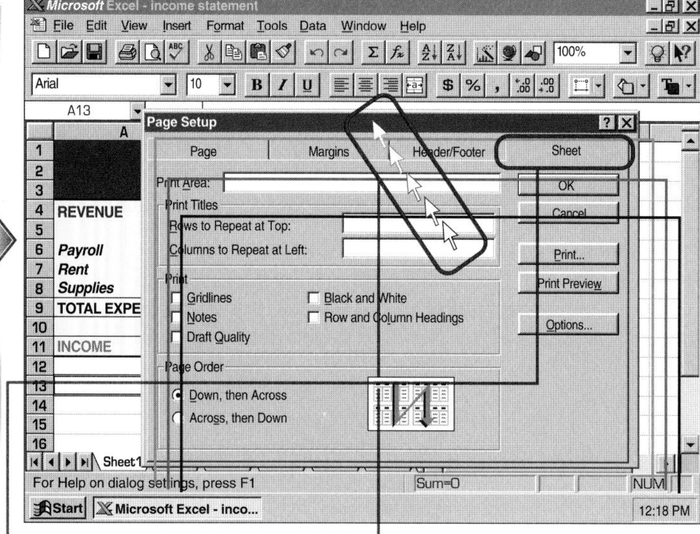

1 Move the mouse over **File** and then press the left button.

2 Move the mouse over **Page Setup** and then press the left button.

■ The **Page Setup** dialog box appears.

3 Move the mouse over the **Sheet** tab and then press the left button.

■ If the dialog box covers the row or column containing the titles you want to repeat, you can move the dialog box to a new location.

4 To move the dialog box, position the mouse over the title bar.

5 Press and hold down the left button as you move the dialog box to a new location on your screen. Then release the button.

You can use the Print Preview feature to view the titles before printing.

Note: For more information, refer to page 110.

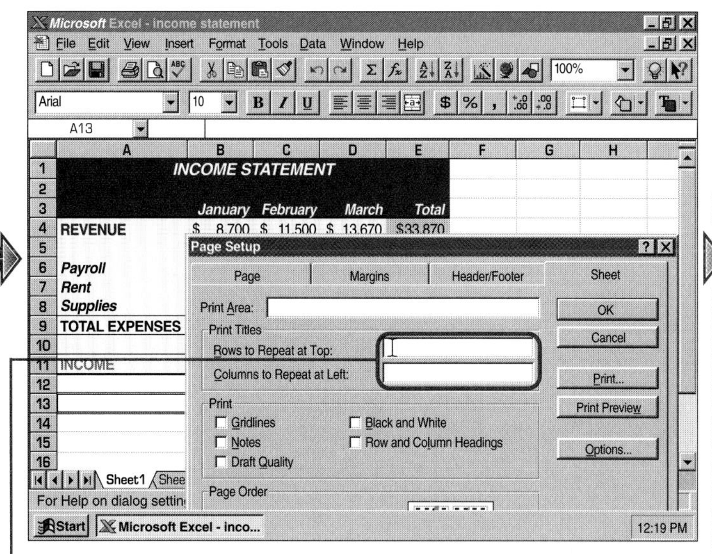

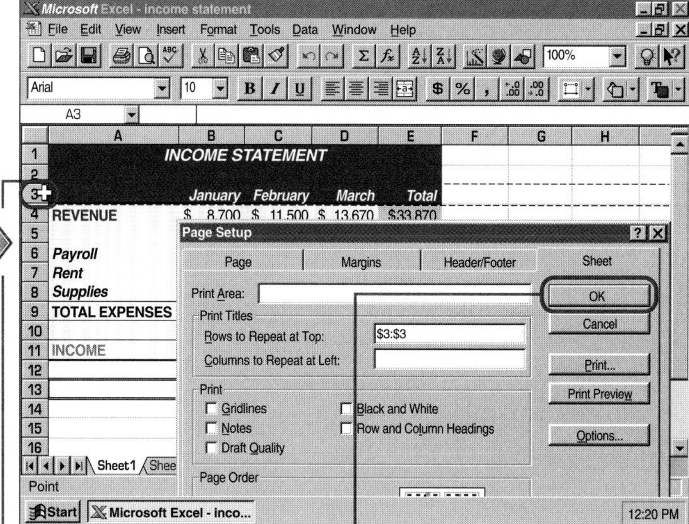

6 Move the mouse I over the box beside the type of title you want to repeat and then press the left button.

Rows to Repeat at Top: Repeats titles across the top of each page.

Columns to Repeat at Left: Repeats titles down the left edge of each page.

7 Select the row or column containing the titles you want to repeat.

Note: To select a row or column, refer to page 12.

8 Move the mouse over **OK** and then press the left button.

In this chapter you will learn how to change the way your worksheets appear on the screen.
Microsoft Excel - income statement
File Edit View Insert Format Tools Data Window
Arial
10
A13
A B C D
INCOME STATEMENT
January February March
REVENUE $ 8,700 $ 11,500 $ 13,670
Payroll $ 3,850 $ 4,850 $ 5,250
$ 1,750 $ 1,750 $ 1,750
$ 1,920 $ 1,980 $ 2,030
$ 7,520 $ 8,580 $ 9,030
$ 1,180 $ 2,920 $ 4,640
Drawing
Sheet4 Sheet5

CHANGE YOUR SCREEN DISPLAY

Zoom In or Out

Display Full Screen

Display or Hide a Toolbar

Freeze Rows and Columns

Split the Screen

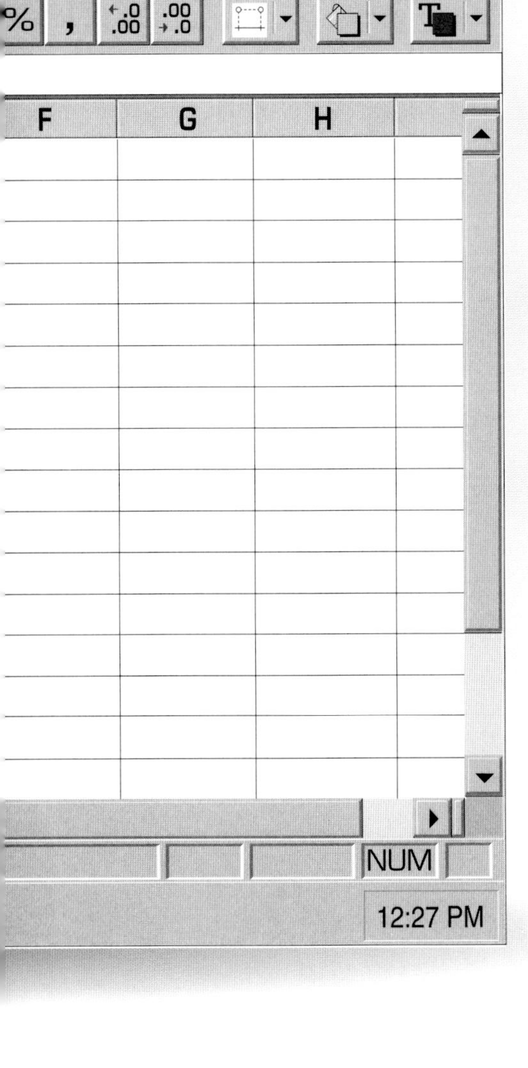

ZOOM IN OR OUT

DISPLAY FULL SCREEN

You can enlarge or reduce the display of data on your screen.

■ Magnifying the worksheet allows you to read small data.

■ Reducing the worksheet allows you to display more data on your screen.

ZOOM IN OR OUT

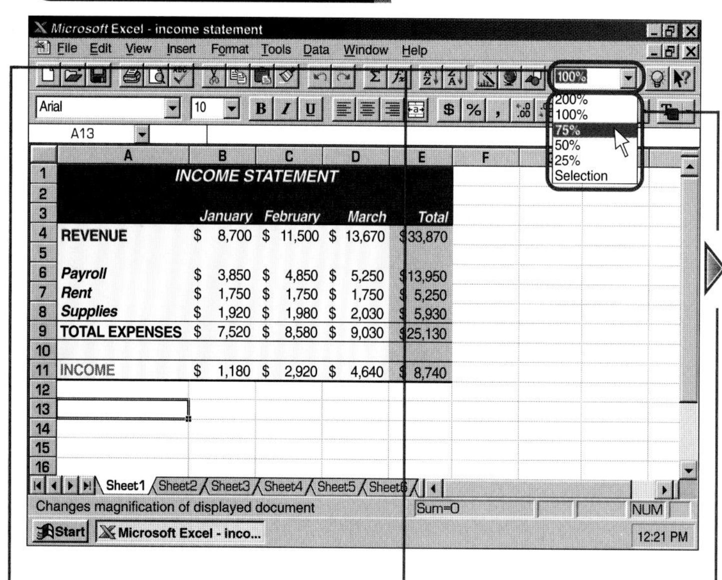

■ When you first start Excel, your worksheet appears in the 100% zoom setting.

1 To display a list of the available zoom settings, move the mouse over in this area and then press the left button.

2 Move the mouse over the zoom setting you want to use and then press the left button.

■ The worksheet appears in the new zoom setting.

■ To return to the normal zoom setting, repeat steps **1** and **2**, selecting **100%** in step **2**.

Note: Changing the zoom setting only affects the way the data appears on your screen. It does not affect the way your data appears on a printed page.

- **Zoom In or Out**
- **Display Full Screen**
- Display or Hide a Toolbar
- Freeze Rows and Columns
- Split the Screen

You can display a larger working area by hiding most parts of the Excel screen. This is useful when you are entering a lot of data into a worksheet.

DISPLAY FULL SCREEN

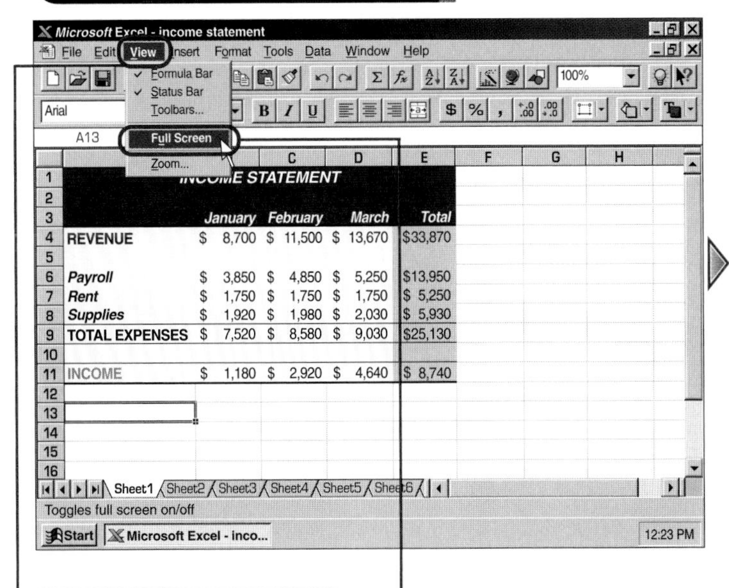

File Edit View Insert Format Tools Data Window Help — Full

	A	B	C	D	E
1	INCOME STATEMENT				
2					
3		January	February	March	Total
4	REVENUE	$ 8,700	$ 11,500	$ 13,670	$33,870
5					
6	Payroll	$ 3,850	$ 4,850	$ 5,250	$13,950
7	Rent	$ 1,750	$ 1,750	$ 1,750	$ 5,250
8	Supplies	$ 1,920	$ 1,980	$ 2,030	$ 5,930
9	TOTAL EXPENSES	$ 7,520	$ 8,580	$ 9,030	$25,130
10					
11	INCOME	$ 1,180	$ 2,920	$ 4,640	$ 8,740

Sheet1 Sheet2 Sheet3 Sheet4 Sheet5 Sheet6

1 Move the mouse over **View** and then press the left button.

2 Move the mouse over **Full Screen** and then press the left button.

■ Excel hides parts of the screen to provide a larger working area.

■ To return to the original view, repeat steps **1** and **2**.

DISPLAY OR HIDE A TOOLBAR

Excel offers several toolbars that you can display or hide at any time. Each toolbar contains a series of buttons that let you quickly select commands.

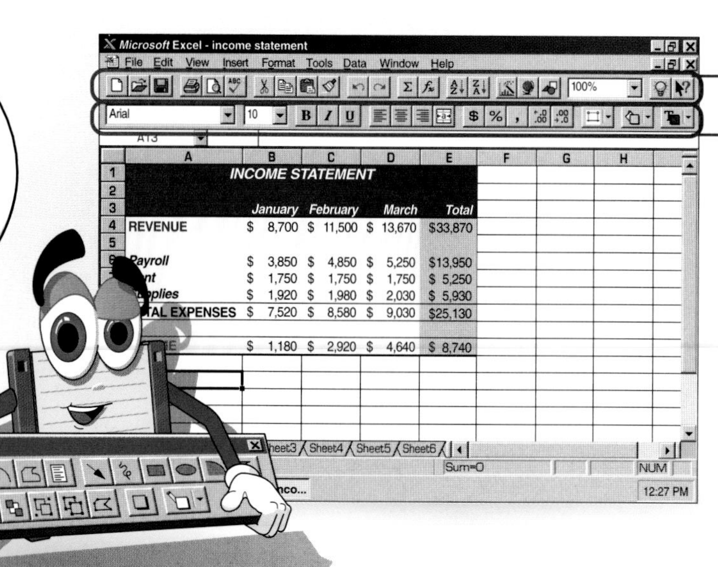

Standard

Formatting

When you first start Excel, the Standard and Formatting toolbars appear on your screen.

DISPLAY OR HIDE A TOOLBAR

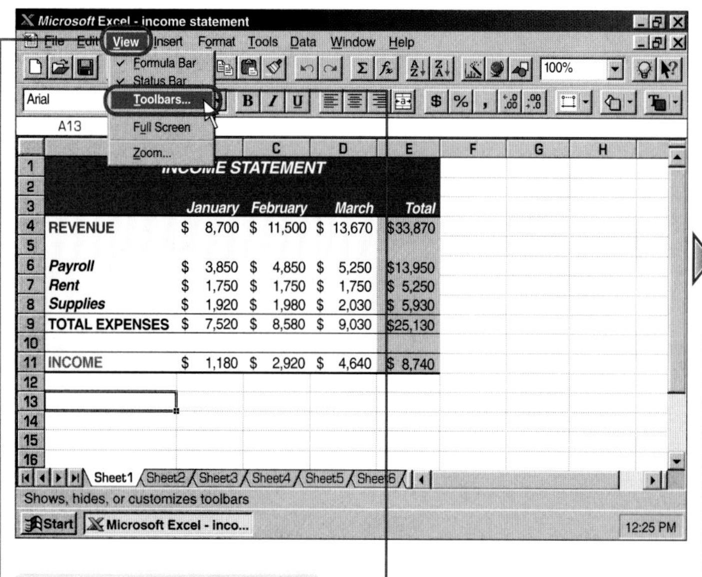

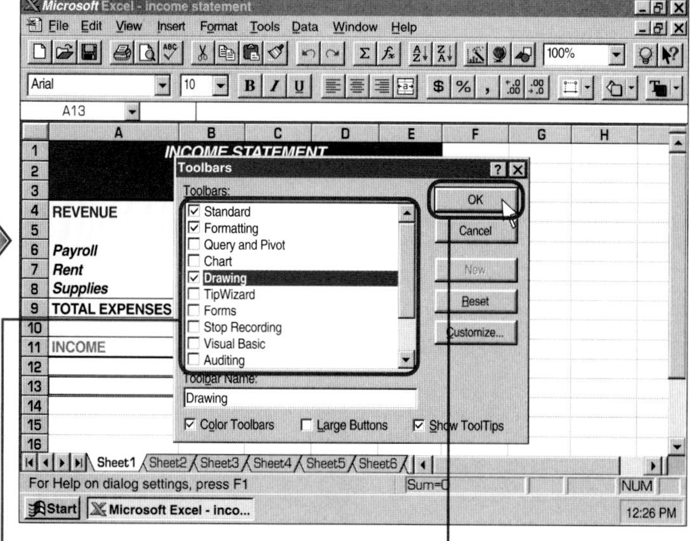

1 Move the mouse over **View** and then press the left button.

2 Move the mouse over **Toolbars** and then press the left button.

■ The **Toolbars** dialog box appears.

3 Move the mouse over the toolbar you want to display or hide and then press the left button.

☑ The toolbar will appear on your screen.

☐ The toolbar will not appear on your screen.

4 Move the mouse over **OK** and then press the left button.

- Zoom In or Out
- Display Full Screen
- **Display or Hide a Toolbar**
- Freeze Rows and Columns
- Split the Screen

A screen displaying fewer toolbars provides a larger and less cluttered working area.

You can quickly display or hide a toolbar.

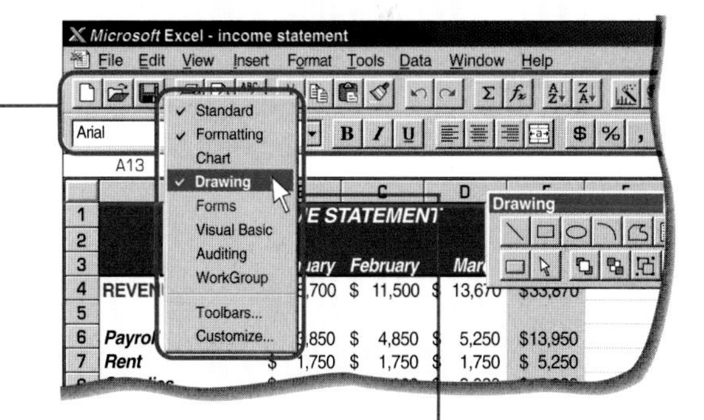

1 Move the mouse over a toolbar displayed on your screen and then press the **right** button.

- A menu appears.

2 Move the mouse over the name of the toolbar you want to display or hide and then press the left button.

Note: A check mark (✔) beside a toolbar name indicates that the toolbar is currently displayed on your screen.

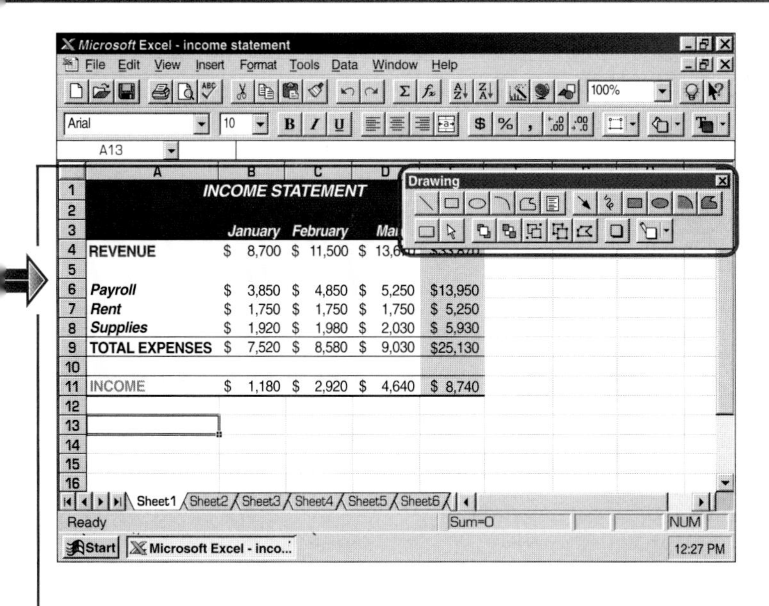

- Excel displays or hides the toolbar you selected.

FREEZE ROWS AND COLUMNS

You can freeze rows and columns in your worksheet so they will not move. This lets you keep headings on the screen as you move through data in a large worksheet.

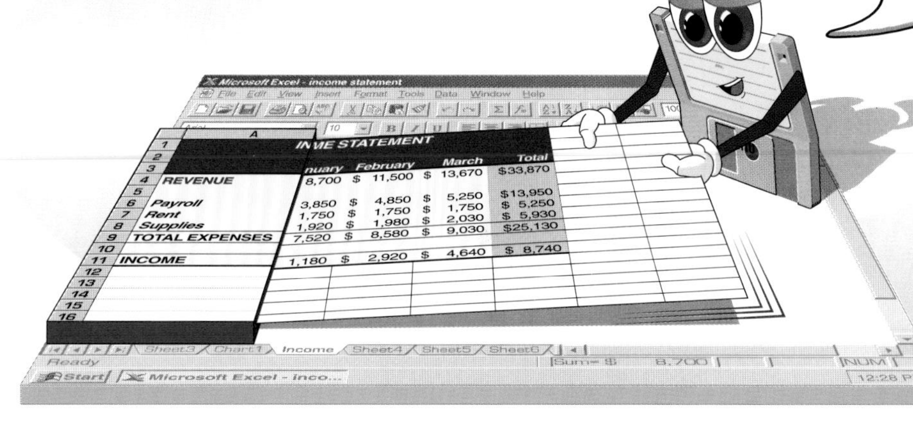

FREEZE ROWS AND COLUMNS

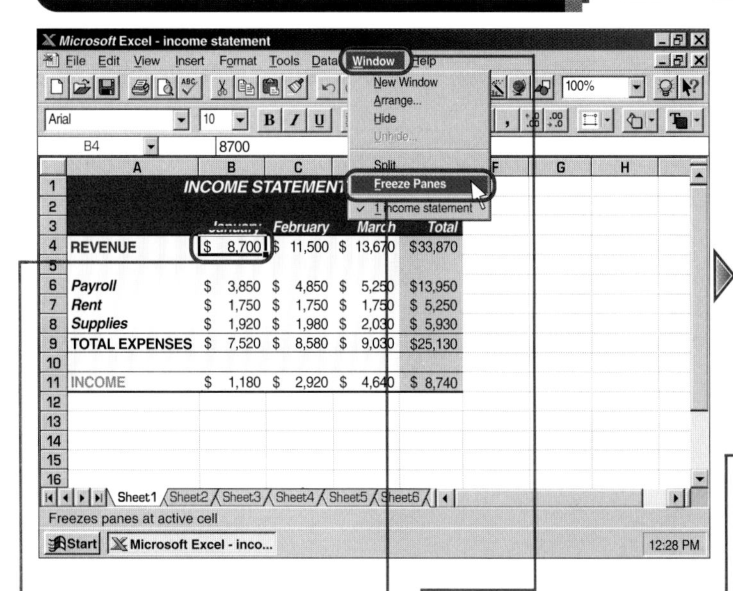

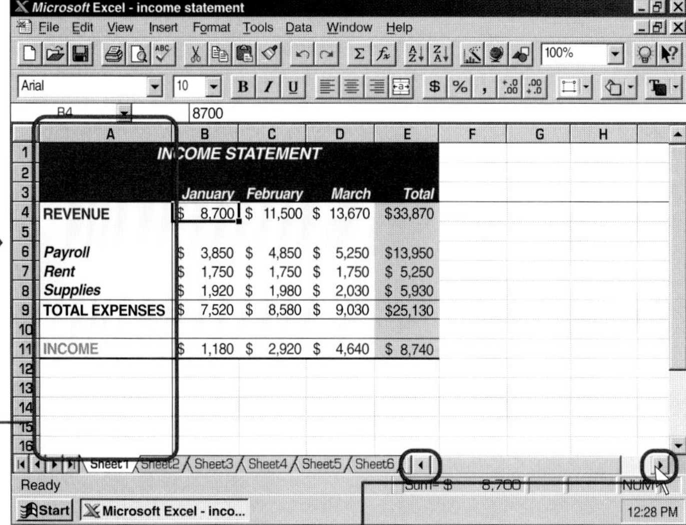

1 Select a cell. Excel will freeze the rows above and the columns to the left of the cell you select.

Note: To select a cell, refer to page 12.

2 Move the mouse over **Window** and then press the left button.

3 Move the mouse over **Freeze Panes** and then press the left button.

■ The columns to the left of the vertical line are frozen. These columns will not move when you scroll through the worksheet.

■ The columns to the right of the vertical line are not frozen.

4 To shift these columns, move the mouse over ◄ or ► and then press the left button.

- Zoom In or Out
- Display Full Screen
- Display or Hide a Toolbar
- **Freeze Rows and Columns**
- Split the Screen

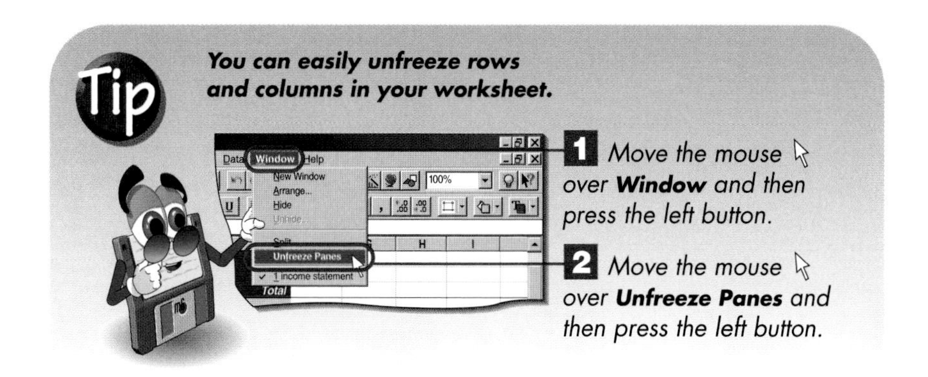

You can easily unfreeze rows and columns in your worksheet.

1 *Move the mouse over* ***Window*** *and then press the left button.*

2 *Move the mouse over* ***Unfreeze Panes*** *and then press the left button.*

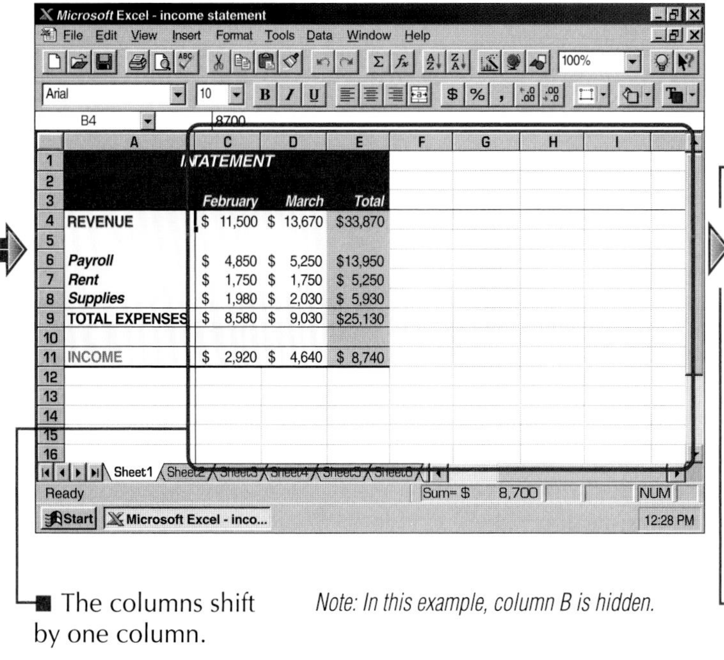

■ The columns shift by one column.

Note: In this example, column B is hidden.

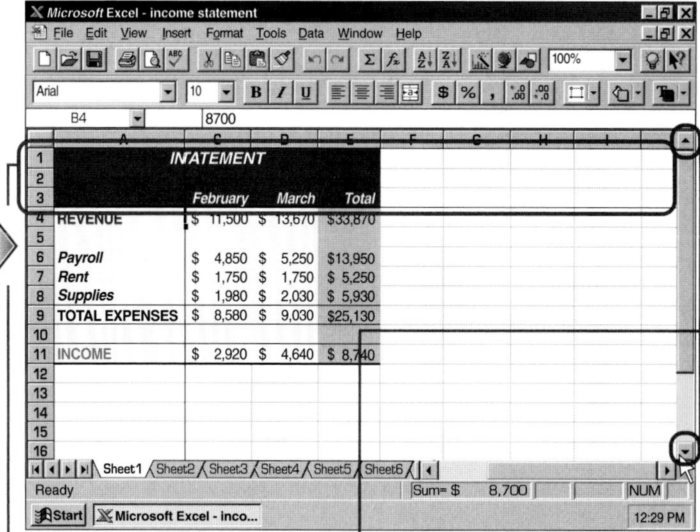

■ The rows above the horizontal line are frozen. These rows will not move when you scroll through the worksheet.

■ The rows below the horizontal line are not frozen.

5 To shift these rows, move the mouse over ▼ or ▲ and then press the left button.

SPLIT THE SCREEN

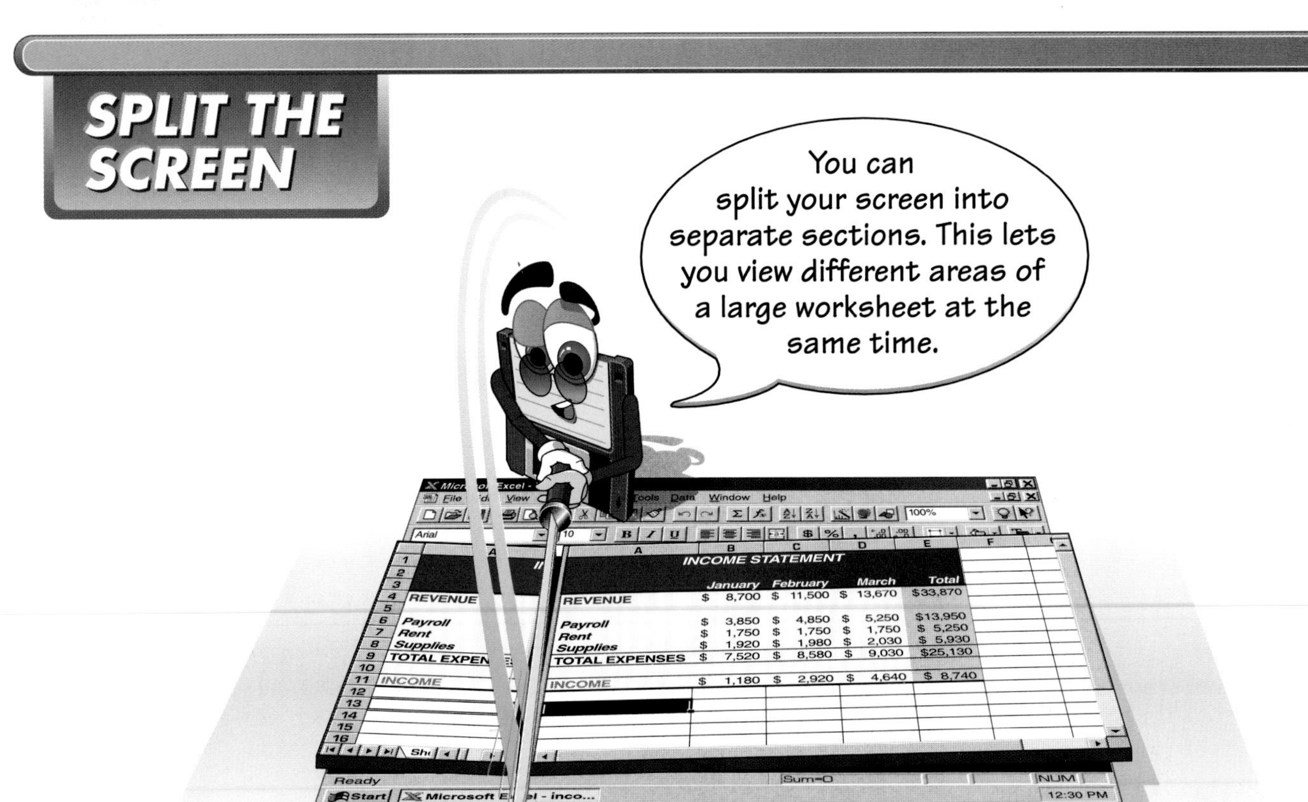

You can split your screen into separate sections. This lets you view different areas of a large worksheet at the same time.

SPLIT THE SCREEN VERTICALLY

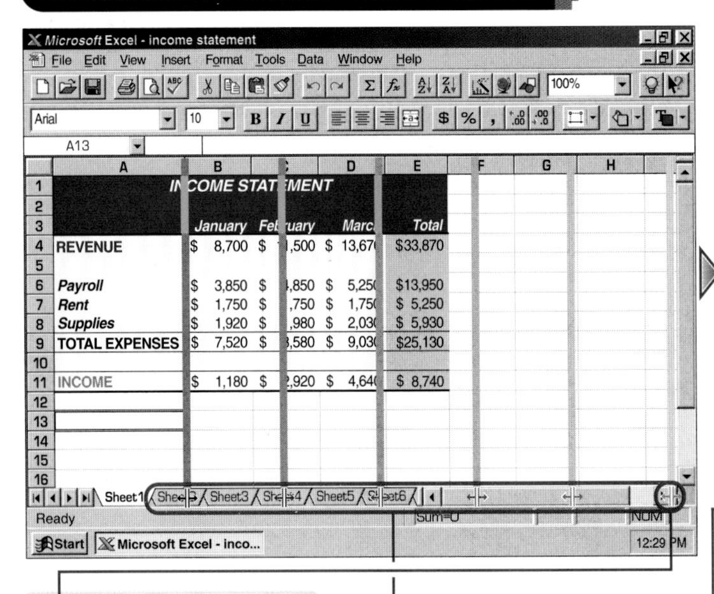

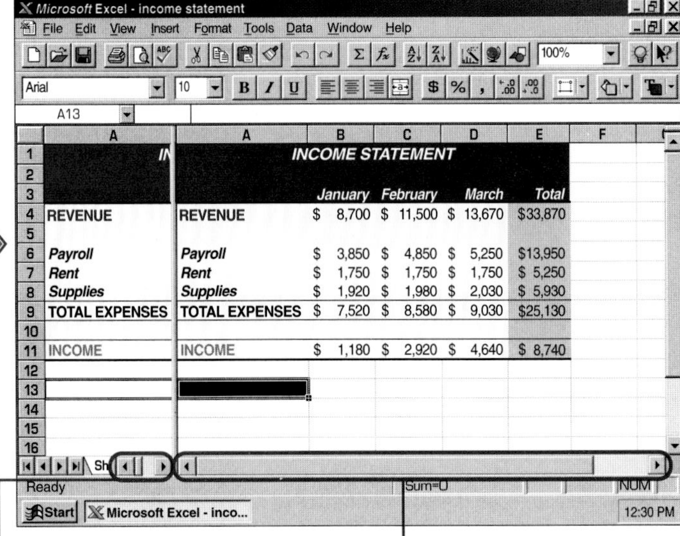

1 Move the mouse ↖ over this area and ↖ changes to ⟺.

2 Press and hold down the left button as you move the mouse ⟺ to where you want to split the screen. Then release the button.

■ The screen splits vertically into two sections.

■ To move through the columns to the left of the dividing line, move the mouse ↖ over ◀ or ▶ and then press the left button.

■ To move through the columns to the right of the dividing line, move the mouse ↖ over ◀ or ▶ and then press the left button.

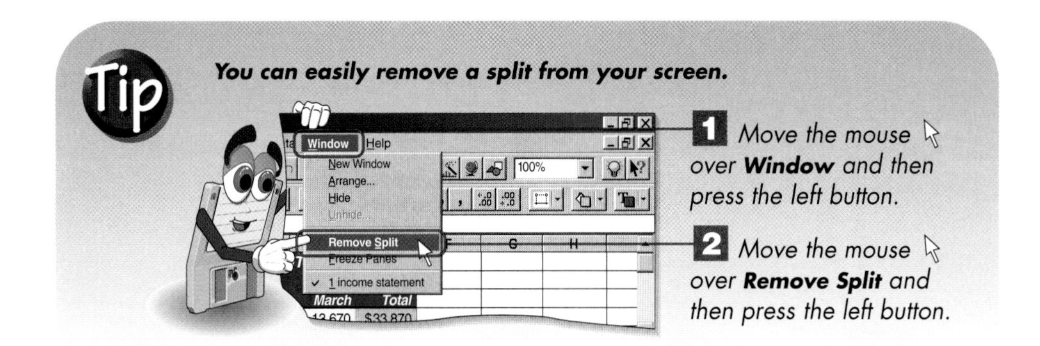

Tip ***You can easily remove a split from your screen.***

1 *Move the mouse over **Window** and then press the left button.*

2 *Move the mouse over **Remove Split** and then press the left button.*

SPLIT THE SCREEN HORIZONTALLY

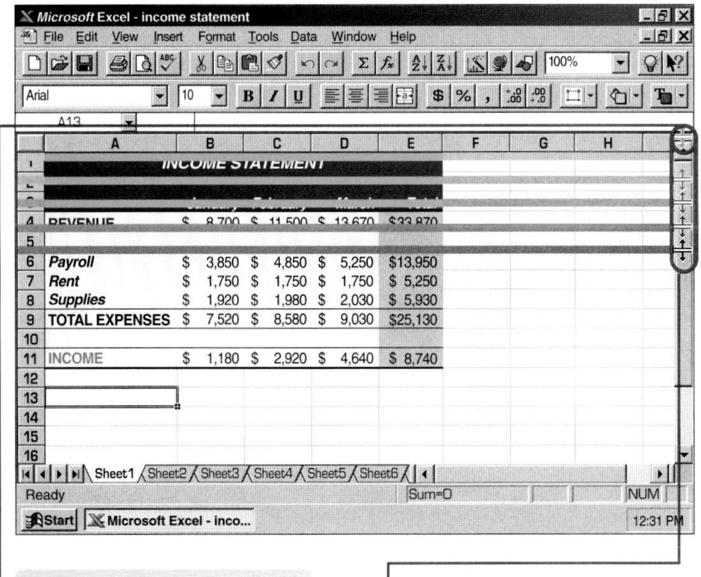

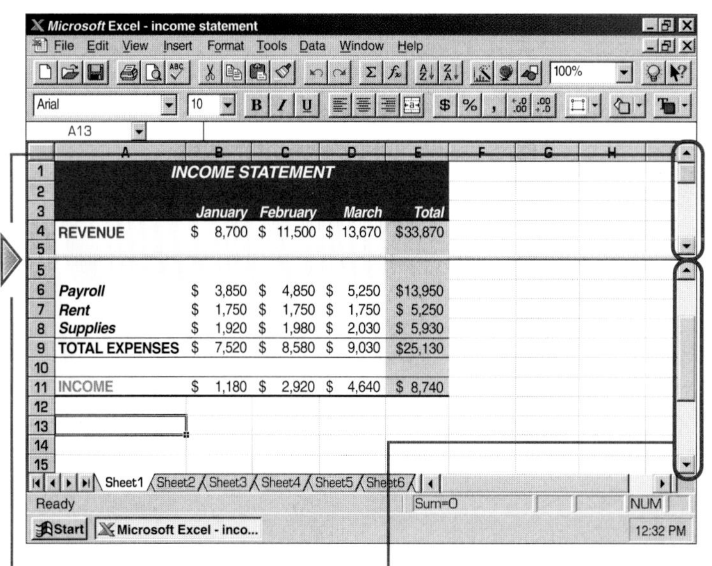

1 Move the mouse over this area and changes to ╪.

2 Press and hold down the left button as you move the mouse ╪ to where you want to split the screen. Then release the button.

■ The screen splits horizontally into two sections.

■ To move through the rows above the dividing line, move the mouse over ▲ or ▼ and then press the left button.

■ To move through the rows below the dividing line, move the mouse over ▲ or ▼ and then press the left button.

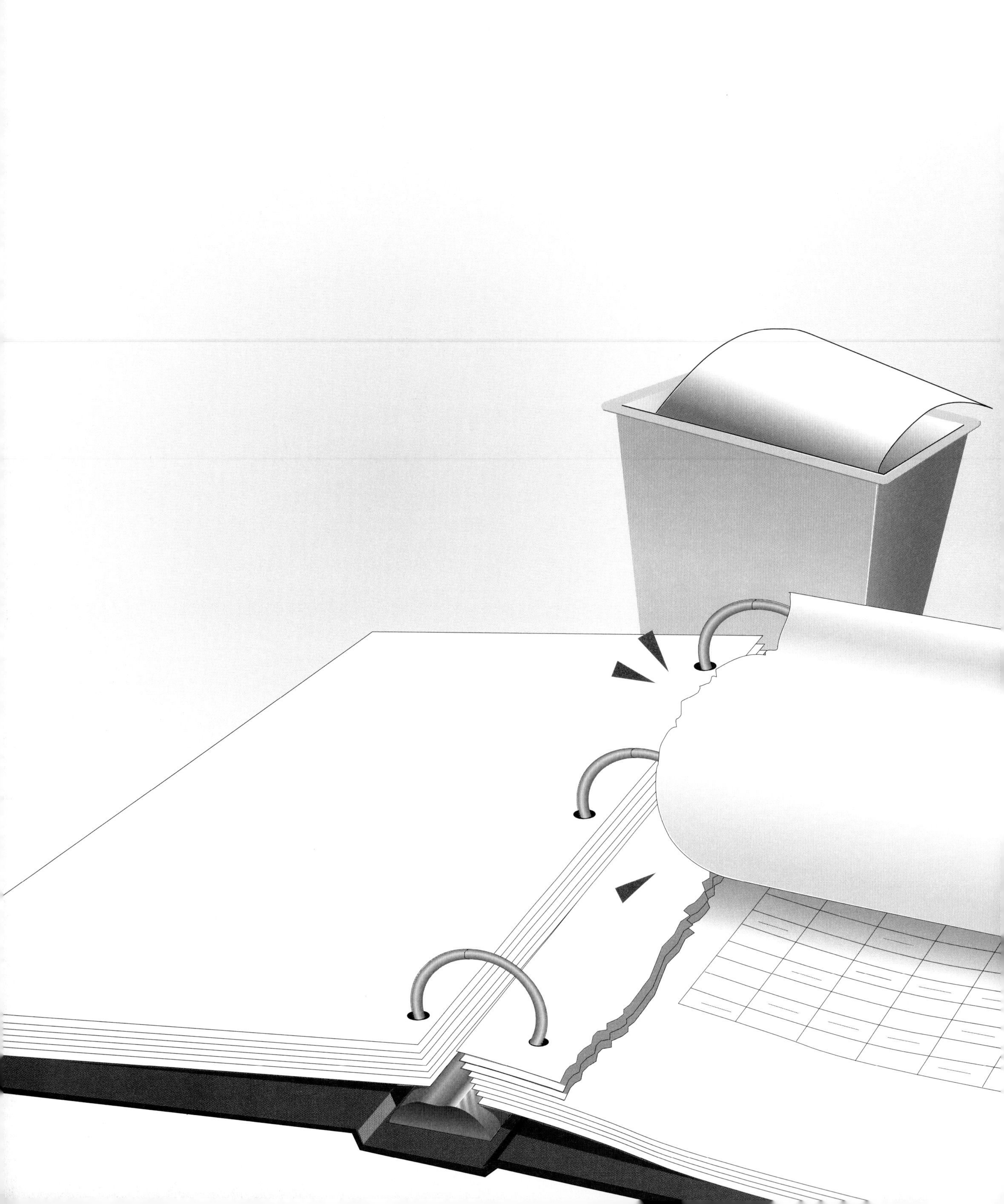

USING MULTIPLE WORKSHEETS

In this chapter you will learn how to work with more than one worksheet in a workbook.

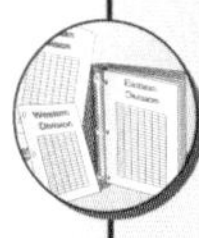

Switch Between Worksheets

Rename a Worksheet

Move a Worksheet

Copy or Move Data Between Worksheets

Link Data Across Worksheets

Enter a Formula Across Worksheets

Delete a Worksheet

SWITCH BETWEEN WORKSHEETS

The worksheet displayed on your screen is one of several sheets in a workbook. You can easily switch between the worksheets.
Sheet 1
Sheet 2
INCOME STATEMENT

SWITCH BETWEEN WORKSHEETS

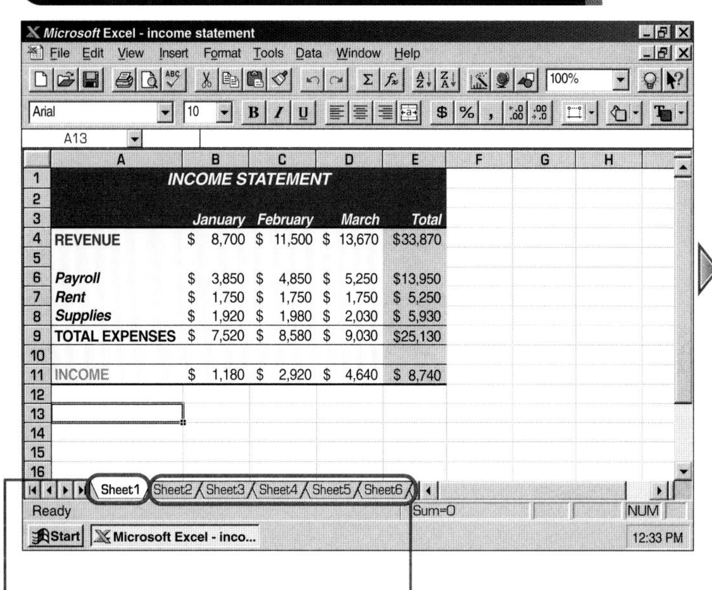

■ The worksheet displayed on your screen has a white tab. It is one of 16 worksheets in the workbook.

■ The other worksheets have gray tabs. The contents of these worksheets are hidden.

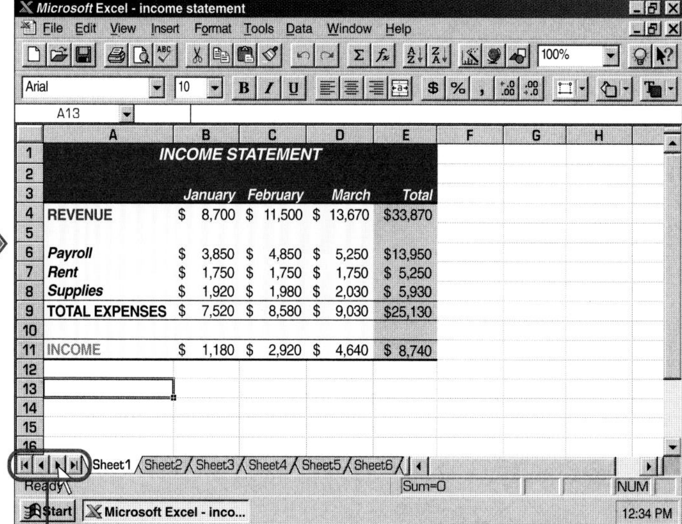

1 To browse through the worksheet tabs, move the mouse over one of the options and then press the left button.

- Displays first tab.
- Displays tab to the left.
- Displays tab to the right.
- Displays last tab.

Think of a workbook as a three-ring binder that contains several worksheets you can use to store related information. For example, you can store information for each division of a company on a separate worksheet.

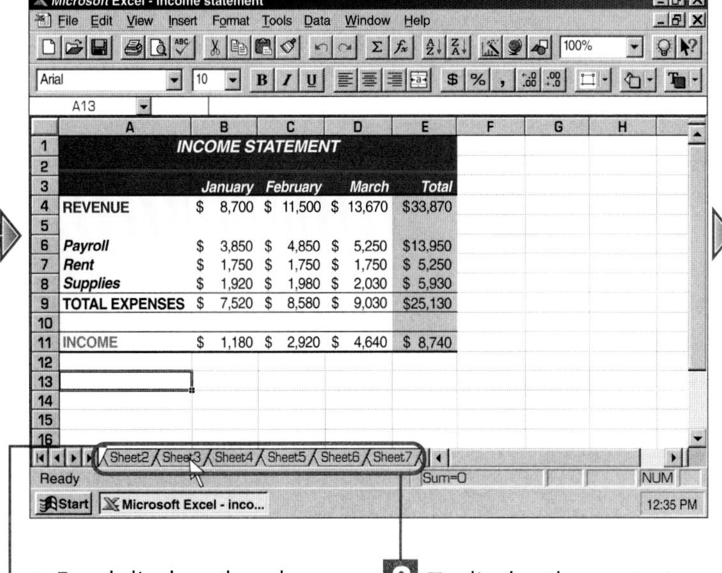

■ Excel displays the tabs for other worksheets.

2 To display the contents of a worksheet, move the mouse over the tab of the worksheet and then press the left button.

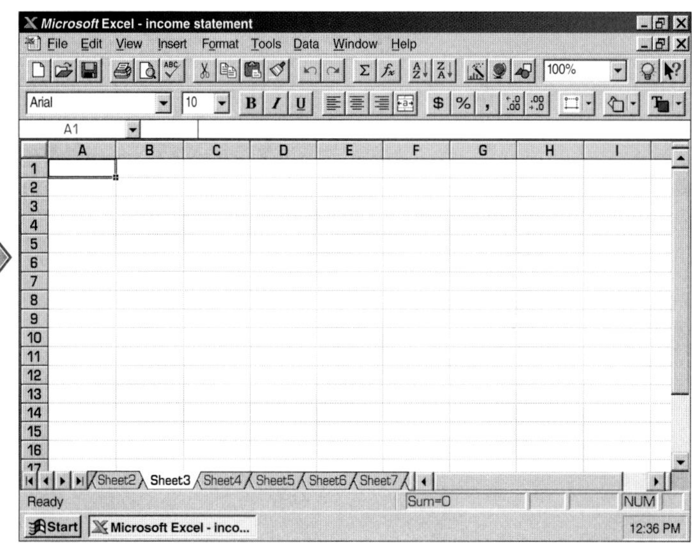

■ The contents of the worksheet appear.

RENAME A WORKSHEET

MOVE A WORKSHEET

You can give each workbook a descriptive name. This helps you remember where you stored your data.

RENAME A WORKSHEET

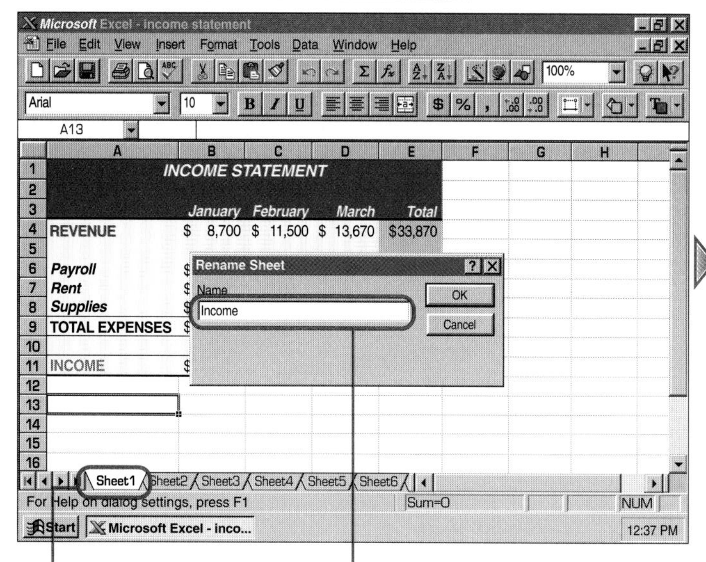

1 Move the mouse over the tab of the worksheet you want to rename and then quickly press the left button twice.

■ The **Rename Sheet** dialog box appears.

2 Type a name for the worksheet and then press **Enter** on your keyboard.

Note: A worksheet name can contain up to 31 characters, including spaces.

■ The worksheet tab displays the new name.

You can move a worksheet to a new location in your workbook. This lets you reorganize your data.

MOVE A WORKSHEET

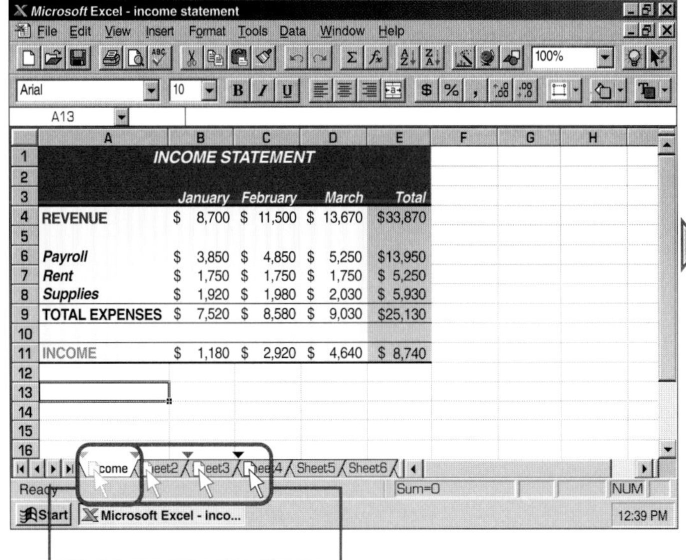

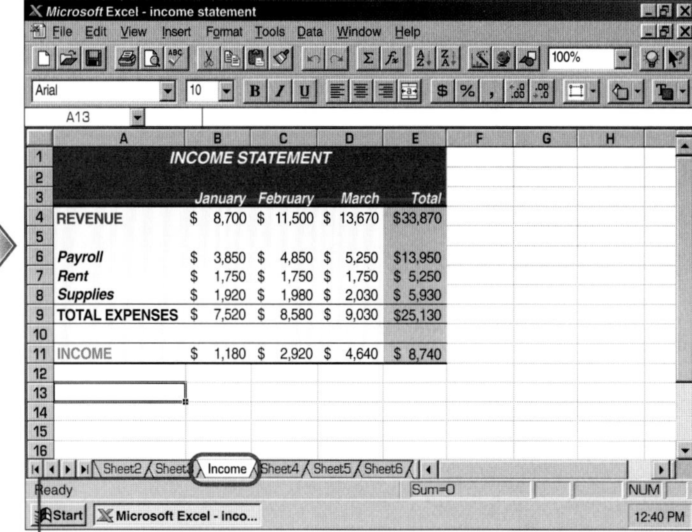

1 Move the mouse over the tab of the worksheet you want to move and then press and hold down the left button (changes to).

2 Still holding down the left button, move the mouse to where you want to place the worksheet.

■ An arrow (▾) shows where the worksheet will appear.

3 Release the left button and the worksheet appears in the new location.

COPY OR MOVE DATA BETWEEN WORKSHEETS

Copying or moving data between worksheets saves you time when you are working in one worksheet and want to use data from another.
Sheet 1
Sheet 2

COPY OR MOVE DATA BETWEEN WORKSHEETS

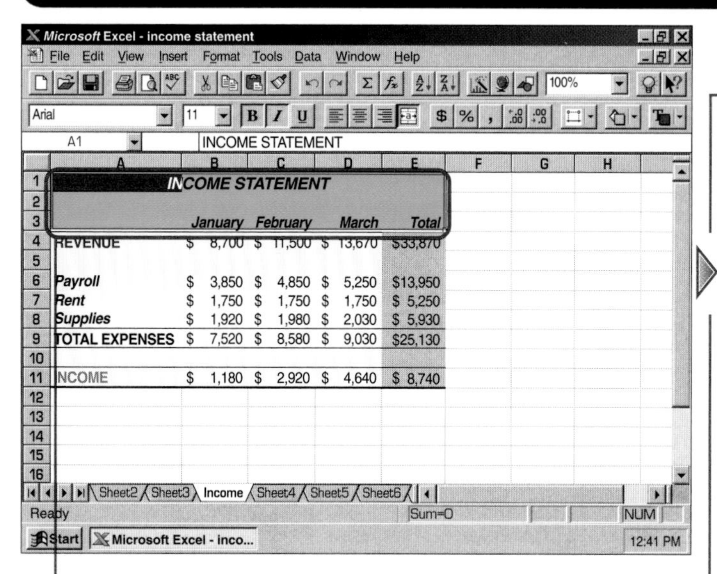

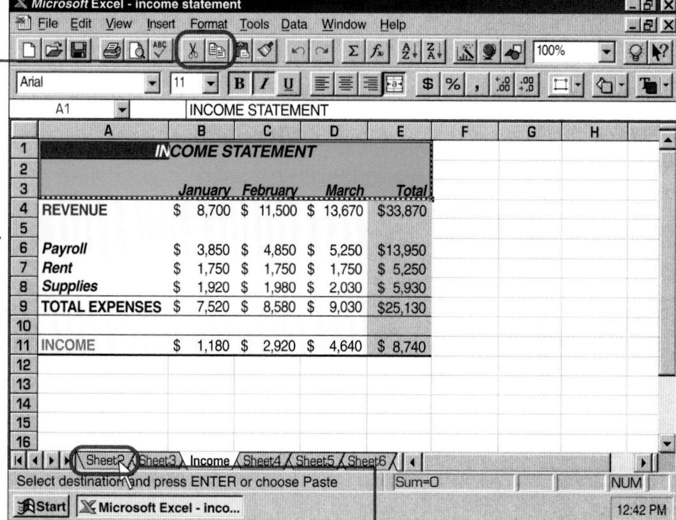

1 Select the cells containing the data you want to place in another worksheet.

Note: To select cells, refer to page 12.

2 Move the mouse over one of the following options and then press the left button.

- Moves the data.
- Copies the data.

3 Move the mouse over the tab of the worksheet where you want to place the data and then press the left button.

Tip ***The Copy and Move features both place data in a new location, but they have one distinct difference.***

Copy Data

When you copy data, the original data remains in its place.

Move Data

When you move data, the original data disappears.

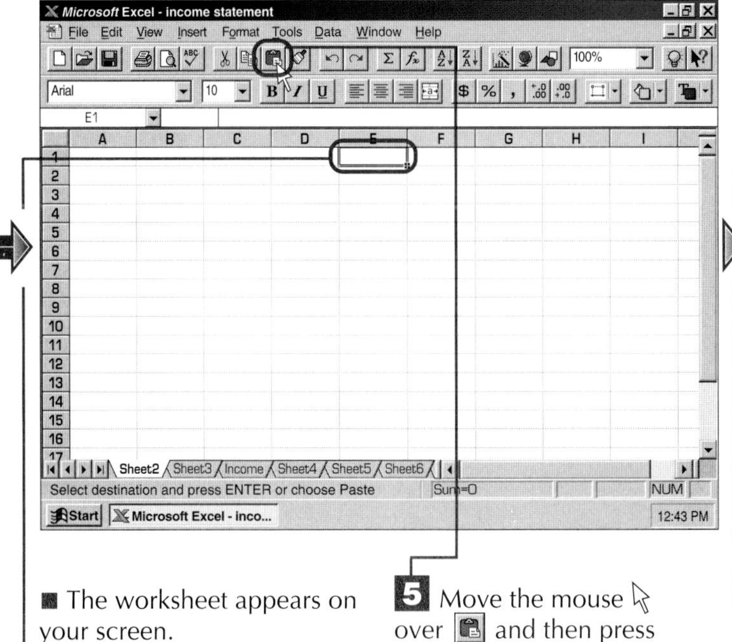

■ The worksheet appears on your screen.

4 Move the mouse over the cell where you want to place the data and then press the left button. This cell will become the top left cell of the new location.

5 Move the mouse over and then press the left button.

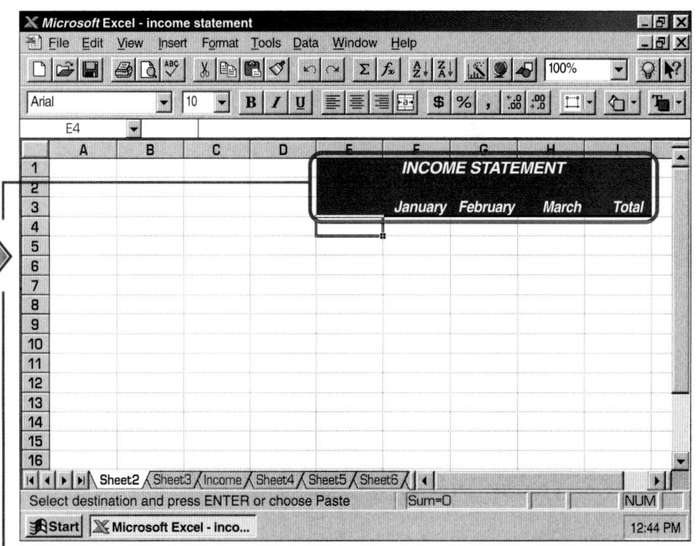

■ The data appears in the new location.

Note: To deselect cells, move the mouse over any cell and then press the left button.

Note: After you copy or move data, the data may no longer display the same column widths or row heights. To change column widths, refer to page 80; to change row heights, refer to page 82.

LINK DATA ACROSS WORKSHEETS

If you change the data in the original worksheet, the data in the linked worksheet will also change.

LINK DATA ACROSS WORKSHEETS

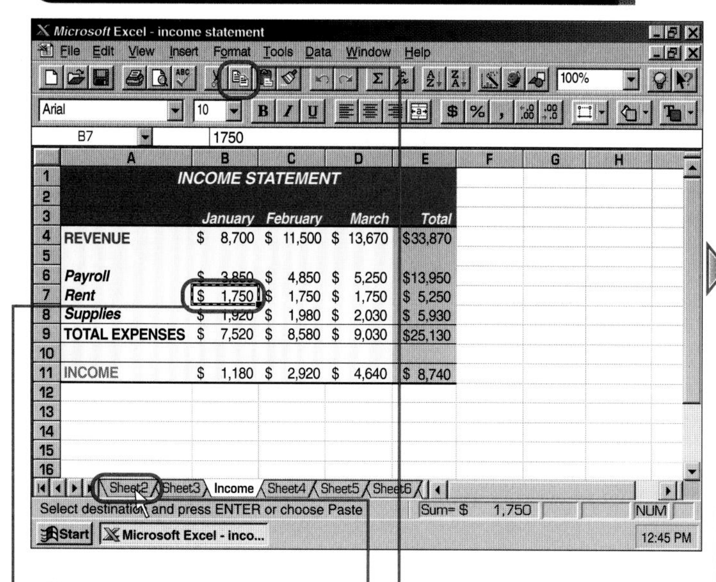

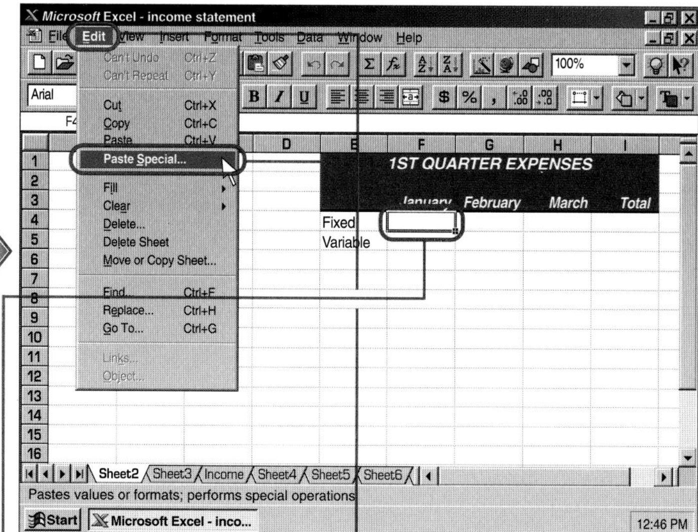

1 Move the mouse over the cell containing the data you want to link to another worksheet and then press the left button.

2 Move the mouse over and then press the left button.

3 Move the mouse over the tab of the worksheet where you want to link the data and then press the left button.

■ The worksheet appears on your screen.

4 Move the mouse over the cell where you want to place the data and then press the left button.

5 Move the mouse over **Edit** and then press the left button.

6 Move the mouse over **Paste Special** and then press the left button.

Tip

You can link information across several worksheets in a workbook. This is useful when you want the worksheets to always display the same, up-to-date information.

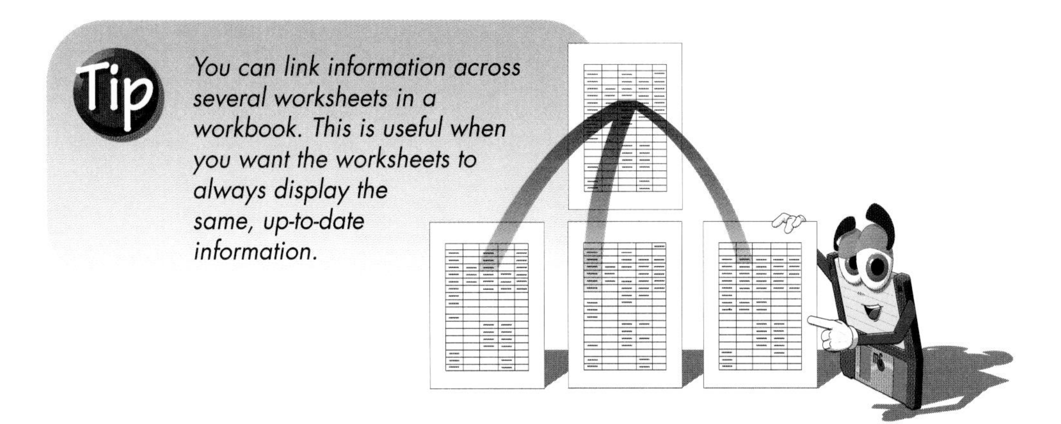

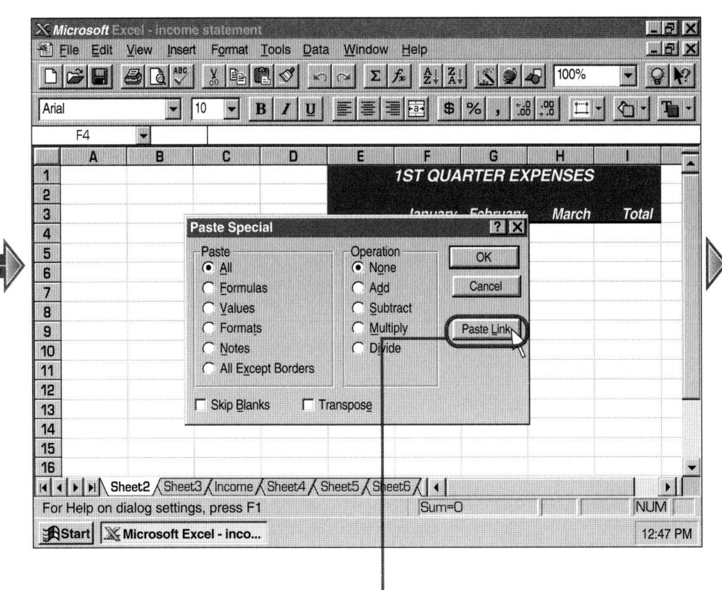

■ The **Paste Special** dialog box appears.

7 To link the data across the worksheets, move the mouse over **Paste Link** and then press the left button.

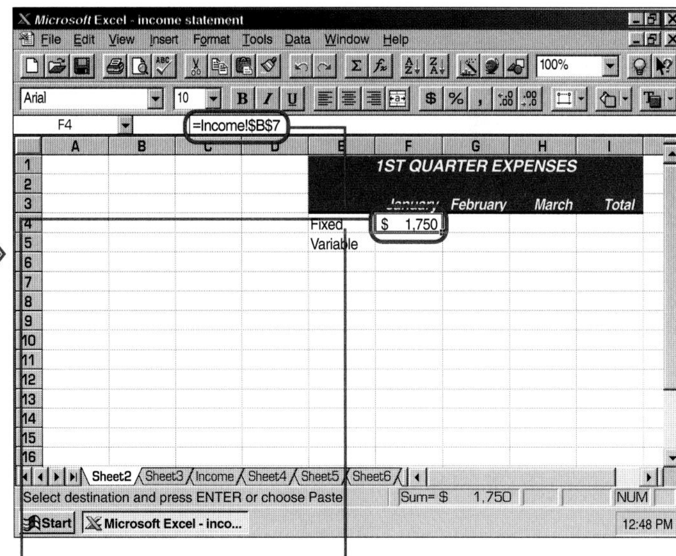

■ The data appears in the worksheet.

■ If you make changes to the data in the original worksheet, the linked data will also change.

■ The formula bar displays the worksheet name and cell reference for the linked cell.

ENTER A FORMULA ACROSS WORKSHEETS

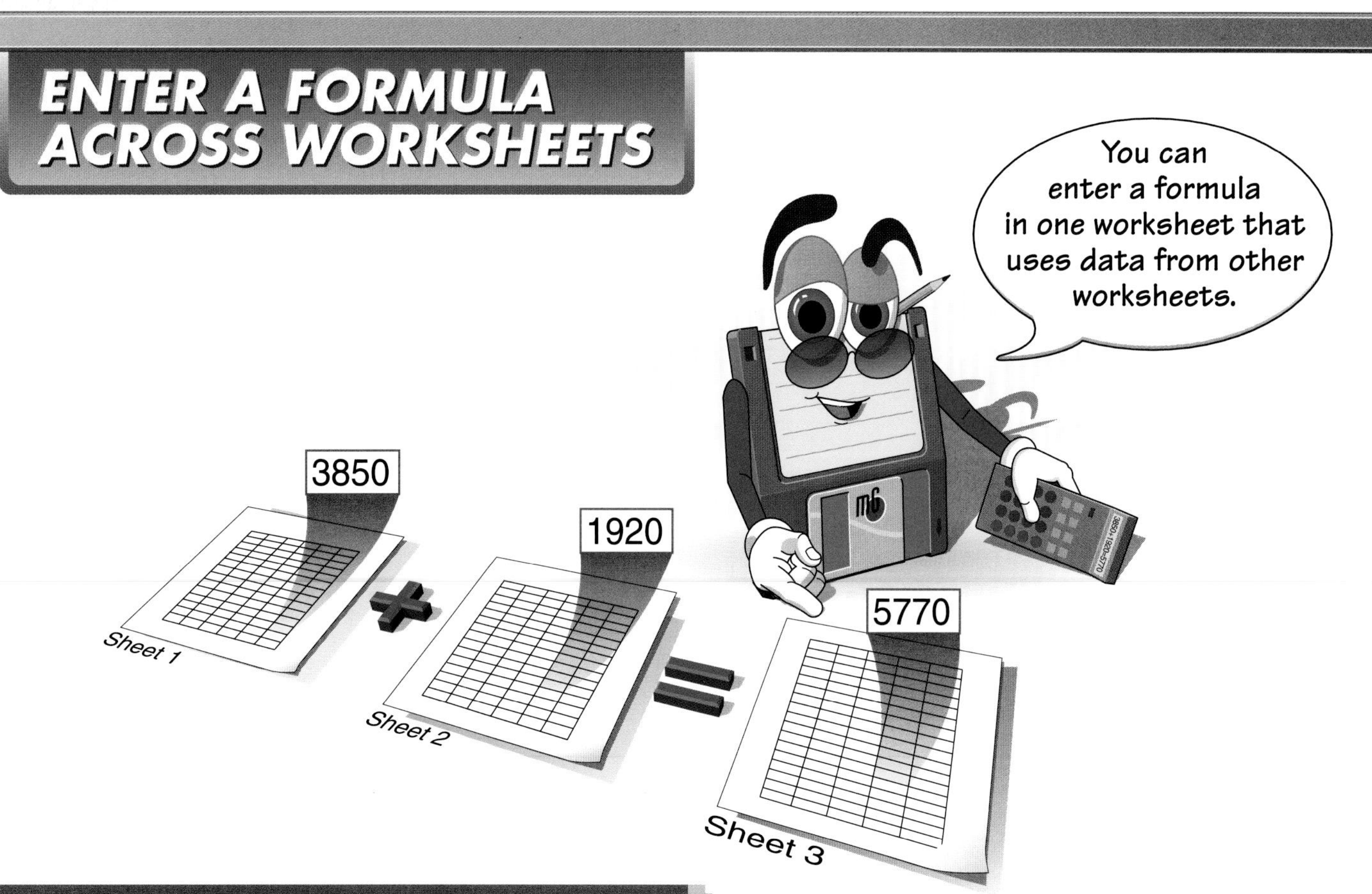

You can enter a formula in one worksheet that uses data from other worksheets.
3850
1920
5770
Sheet 1
Sheet 2
Sheet 3

ENTER A FORMULA ACROSS WORKSHEETS

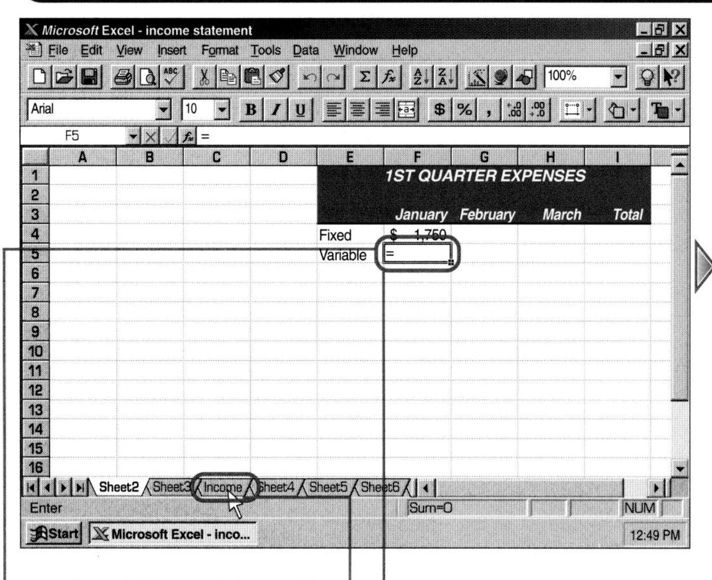

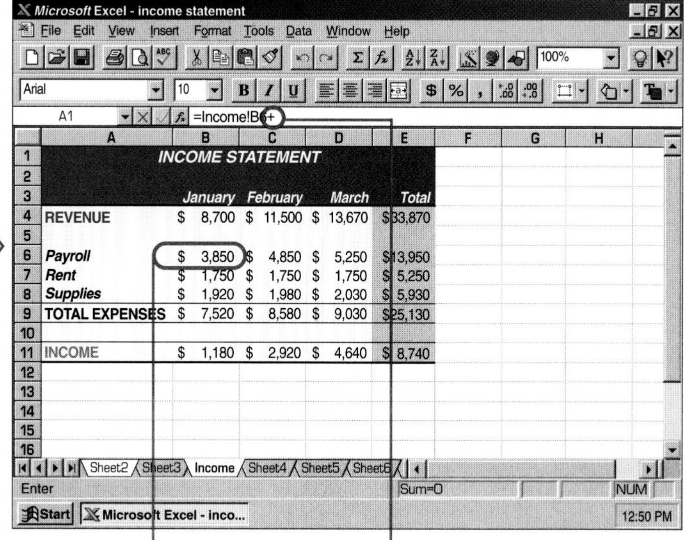

1 Move the mouse ✚ over the cell where you want to display the result of the formula and then press the left button.

2 To begin the formula, type an equal sign (=).

3 Move the mouse ↖ over the tab of the worksheet containing the data you want to use in the formula and then press the left button.

■ The worksheet appears on your screen.

4 Move the mouse ✚ over the cell containing the data and then press the left button.

5 Type an operator for the formula (example: **+**).

- Switch Between Worksheets
- Rename a Worksheet
- Move a Worksheet
- Copy or Move Data Between Worksheets
- Link Data Across Worksheets
- **Enter a Formula Across Worksheets**
- Delete a Worksheet

If you change a number used in a formula, Excel will automatically calculate a new result. This ensures that your calculations are always up-to-date.

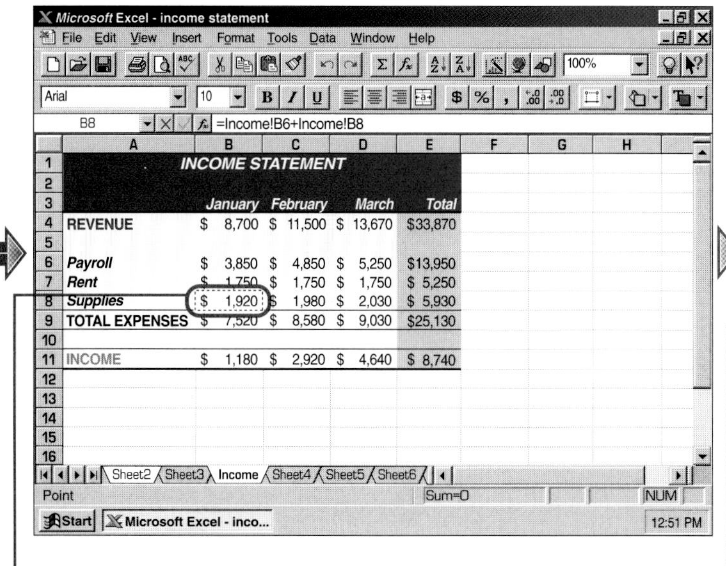

6 Repeat steps **3** to **5** until you have selected all the cells containing the data you want to use.

*Note: In this example, **Payroll** and **Supplies** for the month of January are added together.*

7 Press Enter on your keyboard to complete the formula.

■ The result of the calculation appears in the cell you selected in step **1**.

8 To view the formula you entered, move the mouse over the cell containing the formula and then press the left button.

■ The formula bar displays the worksheet name and cell reference for each cell used in the formula.

DELETE A WORKSHEET

You can permanently remove a worksheet you no longer need.

DELETE A WORKSHEET

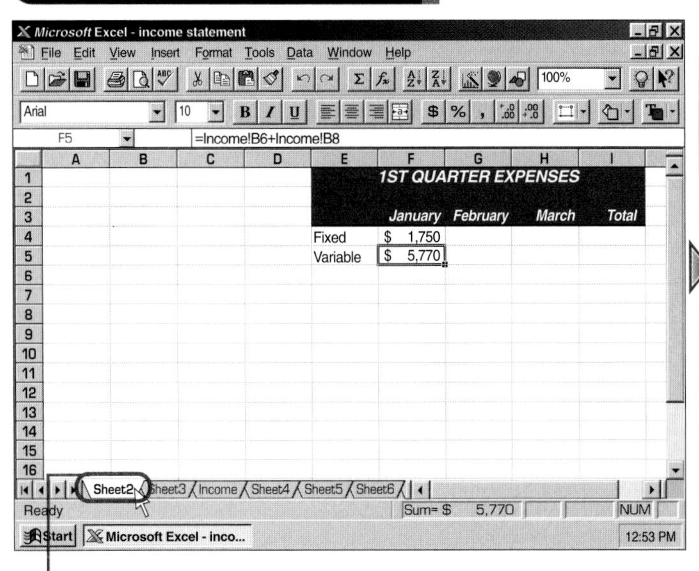

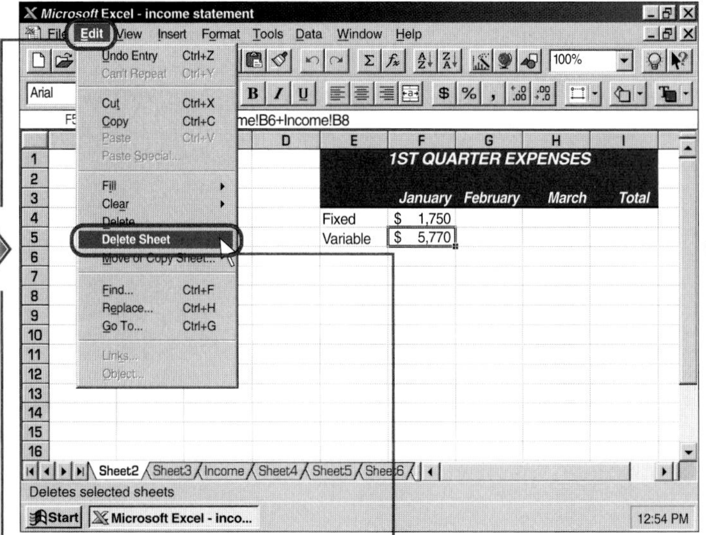

1 Move the mouse over the tab of the worksheet you want to delete and then press the left button.

■ The contents of the worksheet appear on your screen.

2 Move the mouse over **Edit** and then press the left button.

3 Move the mouse over **Delete Sheet** and then press the left button.

IMPORTANT

Do not delete a worksheet you may need in the future. Once you delete a worksheet, Excel erases the data from your computer.

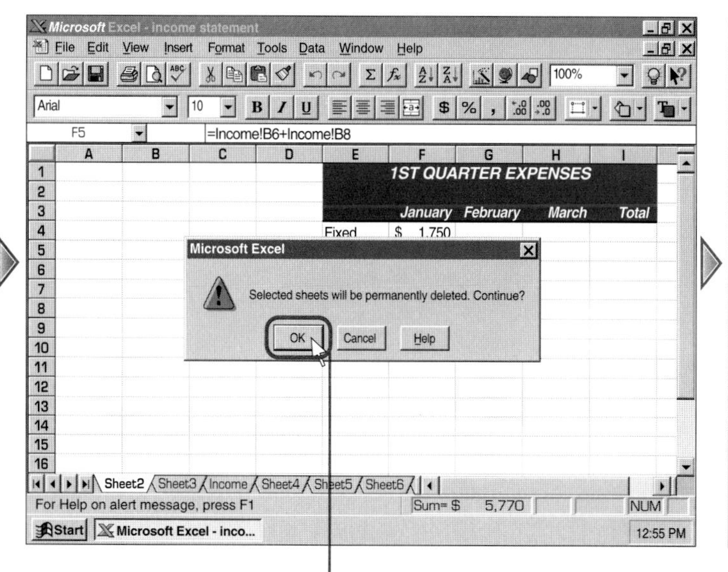

■ A dialog box appears.

4 To delete the worksheet, move the mouse over **OK** and then press the left button.

■ Excel removes the worksheet from your workbook.

■ The next worksheet in the workbook appears on your screen.

Book 1
Book 2
Book 3
Book 4
Book 5
Book 6
Book 7
Book 8
Book 9
Sheet1

USING MULTIPLE WORKBOOKS

In this chapter you will learn how to create a new workbook and use more than one workbook at a time.

Create a New Workbook

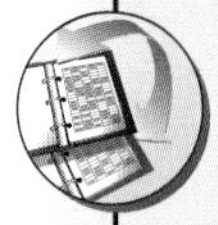

Switch Between Workbooks

Arrange Open Workbooks

Close a Workbook

Maximize a Workbook

CREATE A NEW WORKBOOK

SWITCH BETWEEN WORKBOOKS

CREATE A NEW WORKBOOK

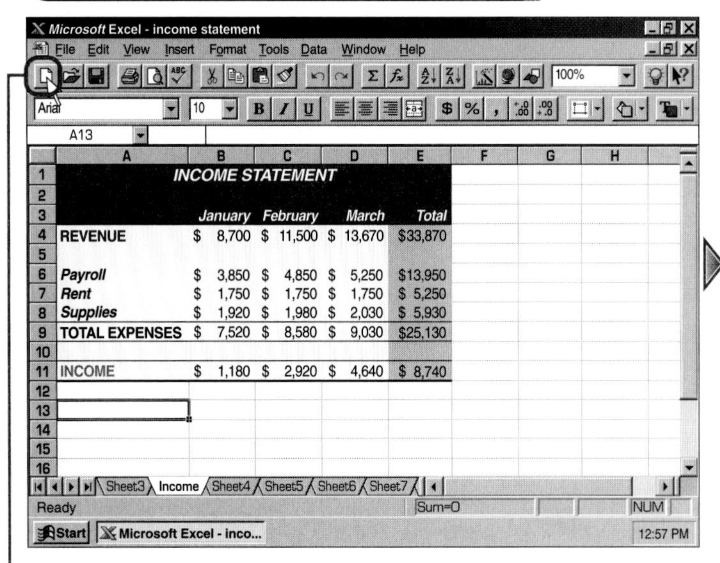

1 Move the mouse over and then press the left button.

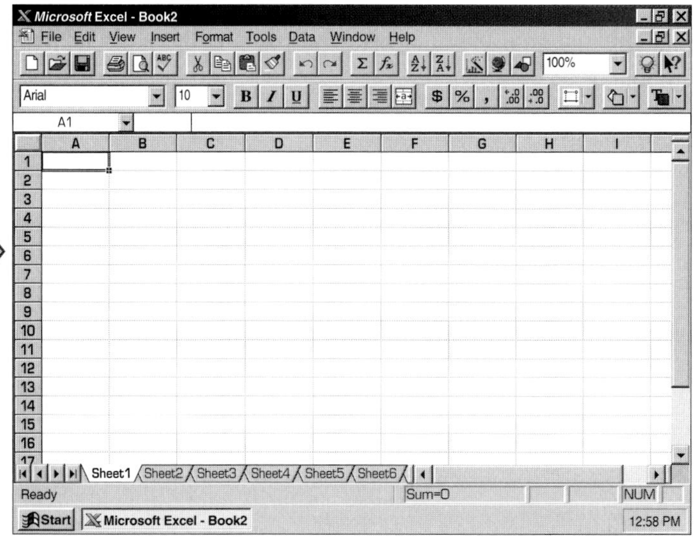

■ A new workbook appears.

Note: The previous workbook is now hidden behind the new workbook.

- **Create a New Workbook**
- **Switch Between Workbooks**
- Arrange Open Workbooks
- Close a Workbook
- Maximize a Workbook

Excel lets you have many workbooks open at once. You can easily switch between all your open workbooks.

SWITCH BETWEEN WORKBOOKS

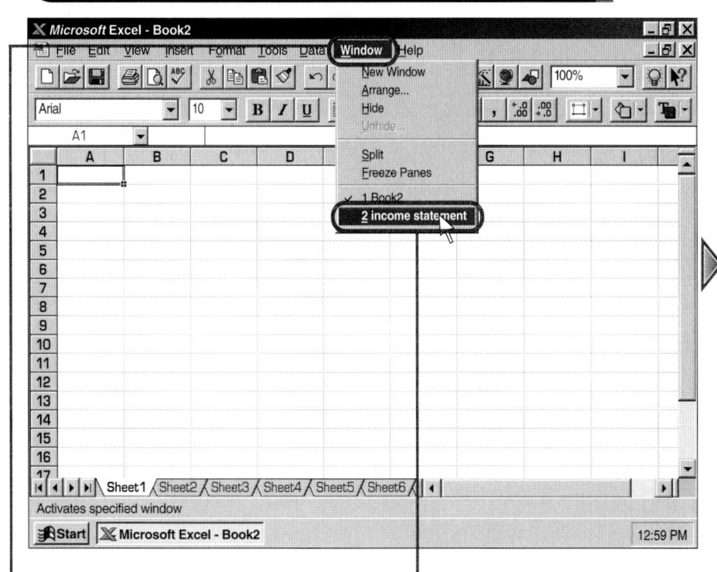

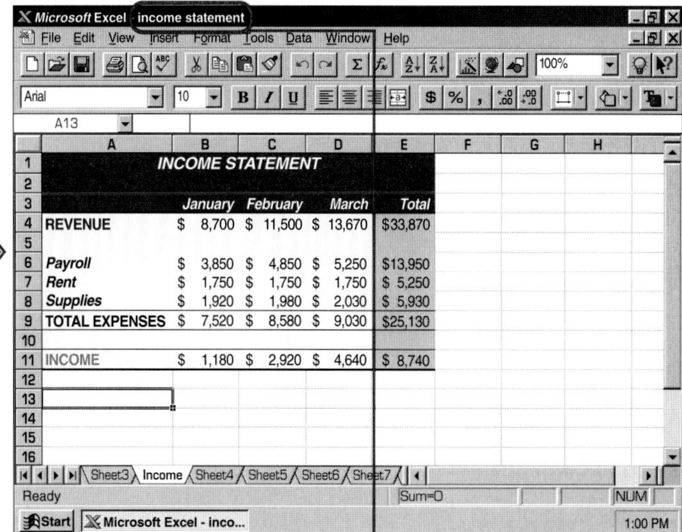

	January	February	March	Total
REVENUE	$ 8,700	$ 11,500	$ 13,670	$33,870
Payroll	$ 3,850	$ 4,850	$ 5,250	$13,950
Rent	$ 1,750	$ 1,750	$ 1,750	$ 5,250
Supplies	$ 1,920	$ 1,980	$ 2,030	$ 5,930
TOTAL EXPENSES	$ 7,520	$ 8,580	$ 9,030	$25,130
INCOME	$ 1,180	$ 2,920	$ 4,640	$ 8,740

1 To display a list of all your open workbooks, move the mouse over **Window** and then press the left button.

2 Move the mouse over the workbook you want to display and then press the left button.

Note: The workbook displayed on the screen has a check mark (✔) beside its name.

■ The workbook appears.

■ Excel displays the name of the workbook at the top of your screen.

ARRANGE OPEN WORKBOOKS

If you have several workbooks open, some of them may be hidden. Excel offers four ways to display the contents of all your open workbooks.

ARRANGE OPEN WORKBOOKS

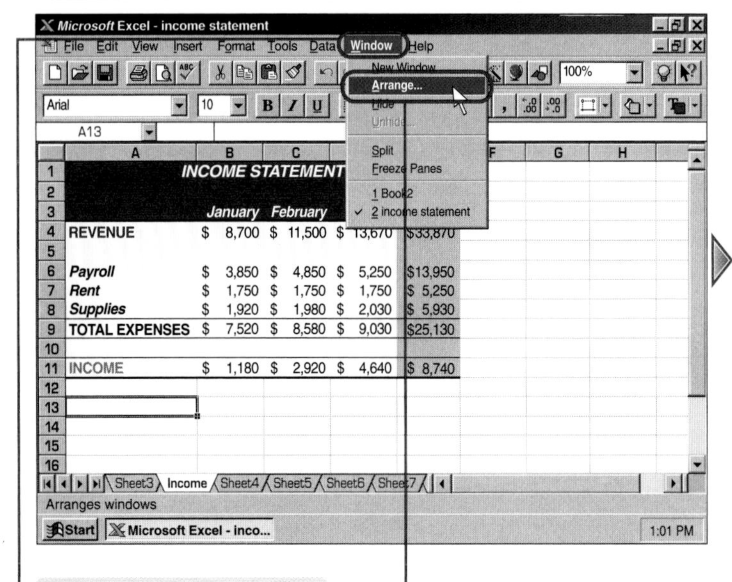

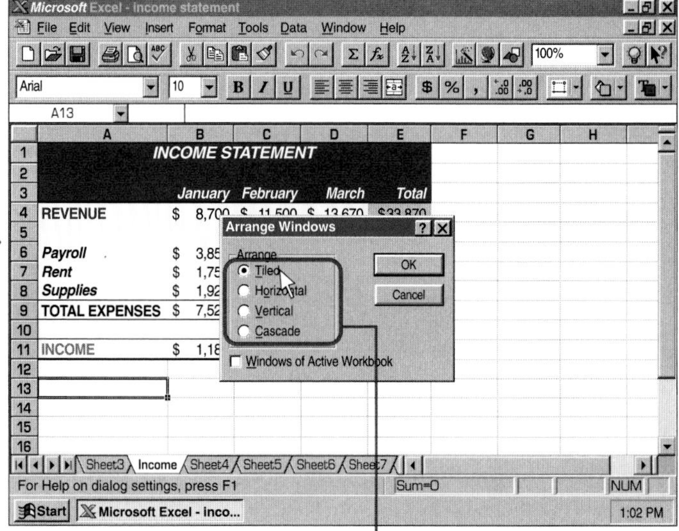

1 Move the mouse over **Window** and then press the left button.

2 Move the mouse over **Arrange** and then press the left button.

■ The **Arrange Windows** dialog box appears.

3 Move the mouse over the way you want to arrange the workbooks and then press the left button (○ changes to ◉).

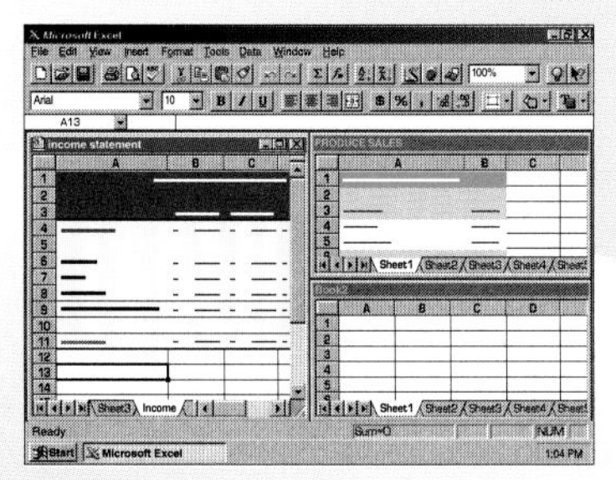

Tiled

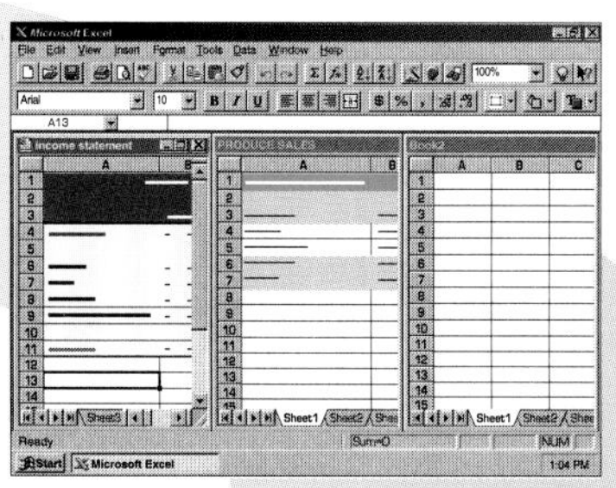

Vertical

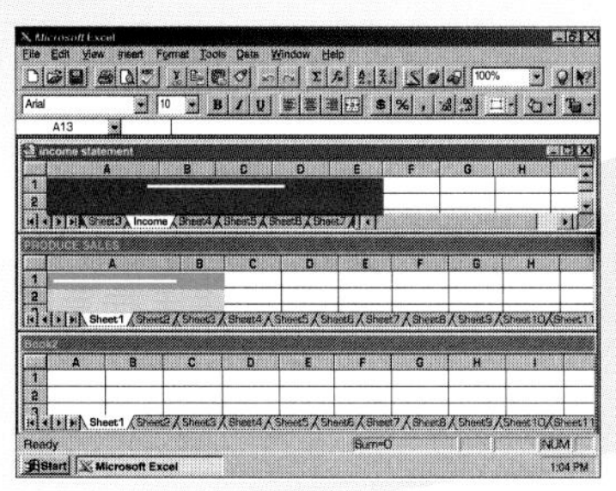

Horizontal

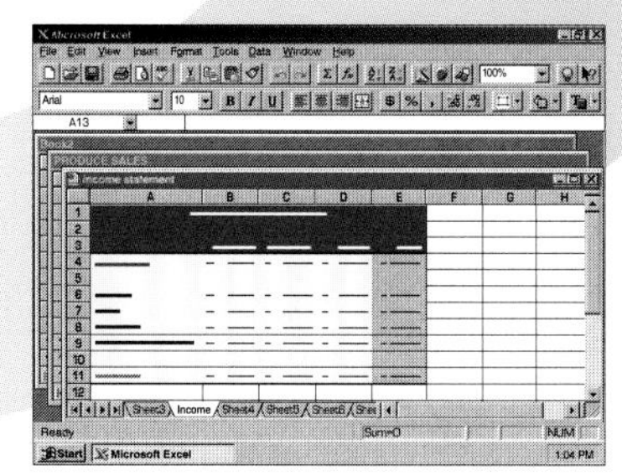

Cascade

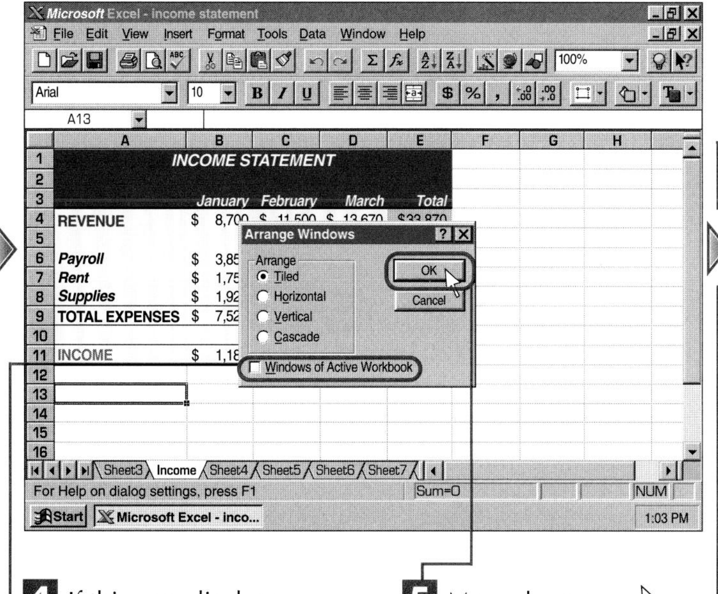

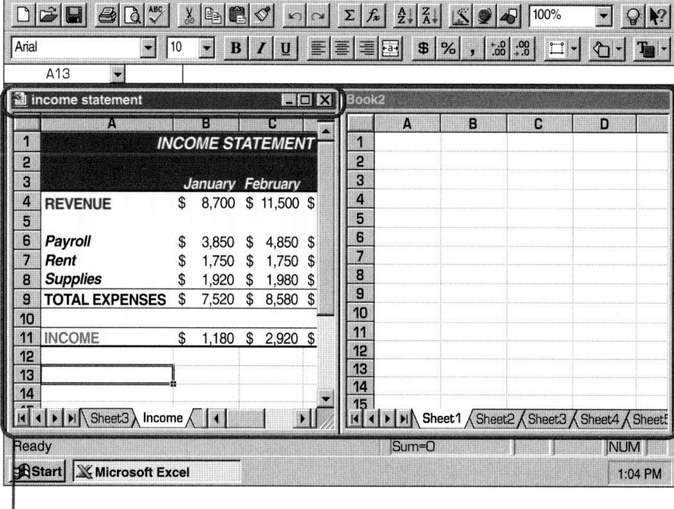

4 If this area displays a check mark (✓), move the mouse over the area and then press the left button to remove the check mark (☑ changes to ☐).

5 Move the mouse over **OK** and then press the left button.

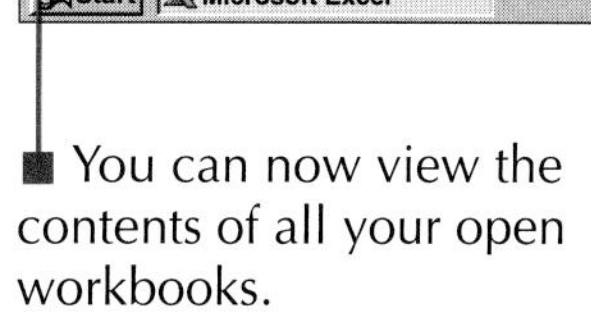

■ You can now view the contents of all your open workbooks.

■ You can only work in the current workbook, which displays a highlighted title bar.

Note: To make another workbook current, move the mouse anywhere over the workbook and then press the left button. To enlarge a workbook to fill your screen, refer to page 159.

CLOSE A WORKBOOK

MAXIMIZE A WORKBOOK

When you finish using a workbook, you can close the workbook to remove it from your screen.
Book2

CLOSE A WORKBOOK

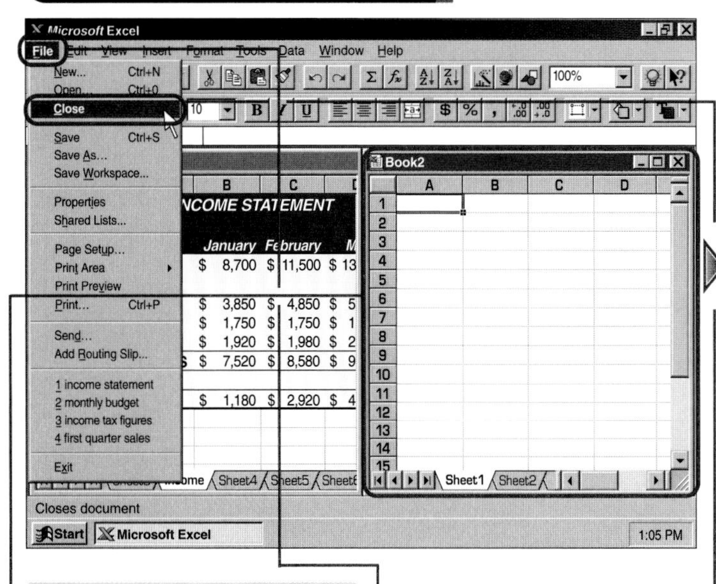

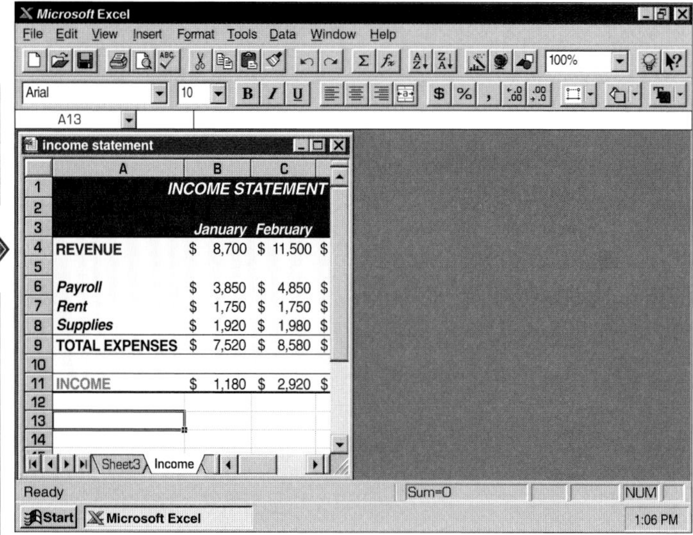

1 To select the workbook you want to close, move the mouse anywhere over the workbook and then press the left button.

2 To save the workbook before closing, refer to page 40.

3 Move the mouse over **File** and then press the left button.

4 Move the mouse over **Close** and then press the left button.

■ Excel removes the workbook from your screen.

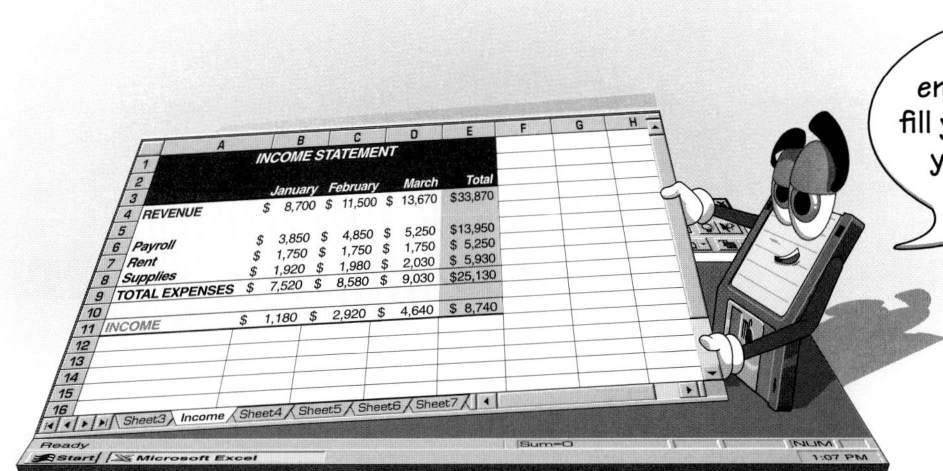

MAXIMIZE A WORKBOOK

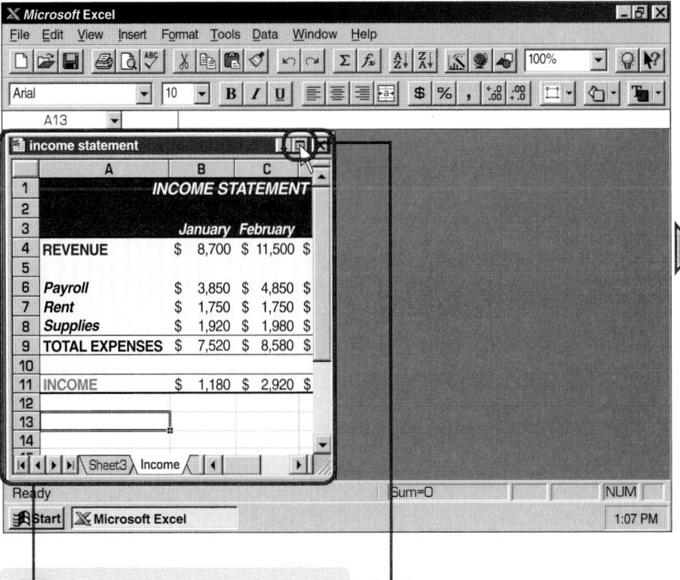

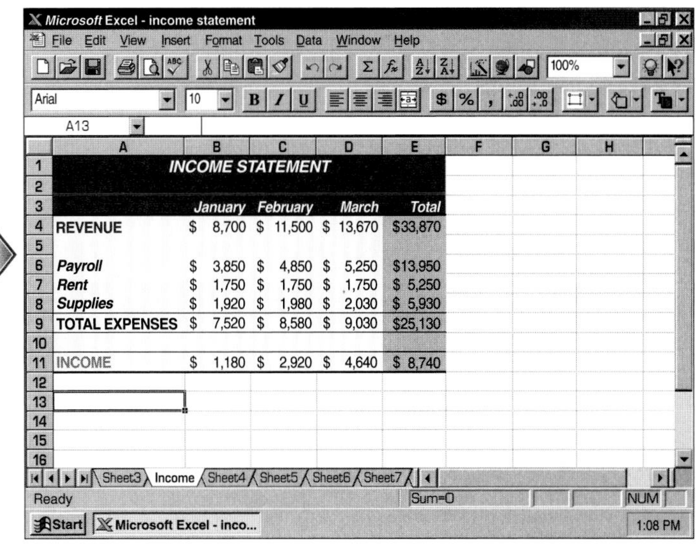

1 To select the workbook you want to fill your screen, move the mouse over any cell in the workbook and then press the left button.

2 Move the mouse over ▣ and then press the left button.

■ The workbook fills your screen.

In this chapter you will learn how to create, change and print charts.
1,750 $
Supplies
1,920 $ 1,980 $
$ 7,520 $ 8,580 $
INCOME $ 1,180 $ 2,920 $

CHAPTER 11

CHARTING DATA

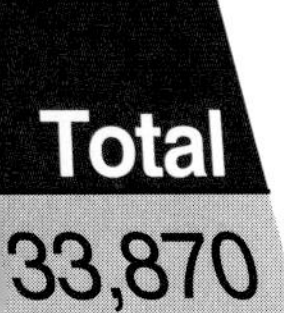

Total
33,870
$13,950
$ 5,250
$ 5,930
$25,130
$ 8,740

Introduction

Create a Chart on a Worksheet

Create a Chart on a Chart Sheet

Move and Size a Chart

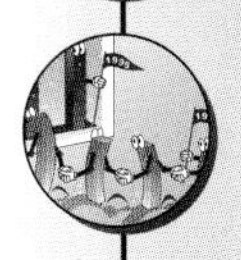

Add a Data Series to a Chart

Change Titles in a Chart

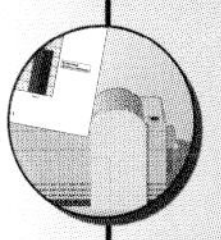

Print a Chart

Delete a Chart

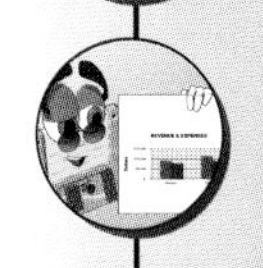

Add/Delete Gridlines or Legend

Change Chart Type

Format a Chart Automatically

Add a Text Box

INTRODUCTION

You can use a chart to visually display your worksheet data. Excel offers many different chart types.

PARTS OF A CHART

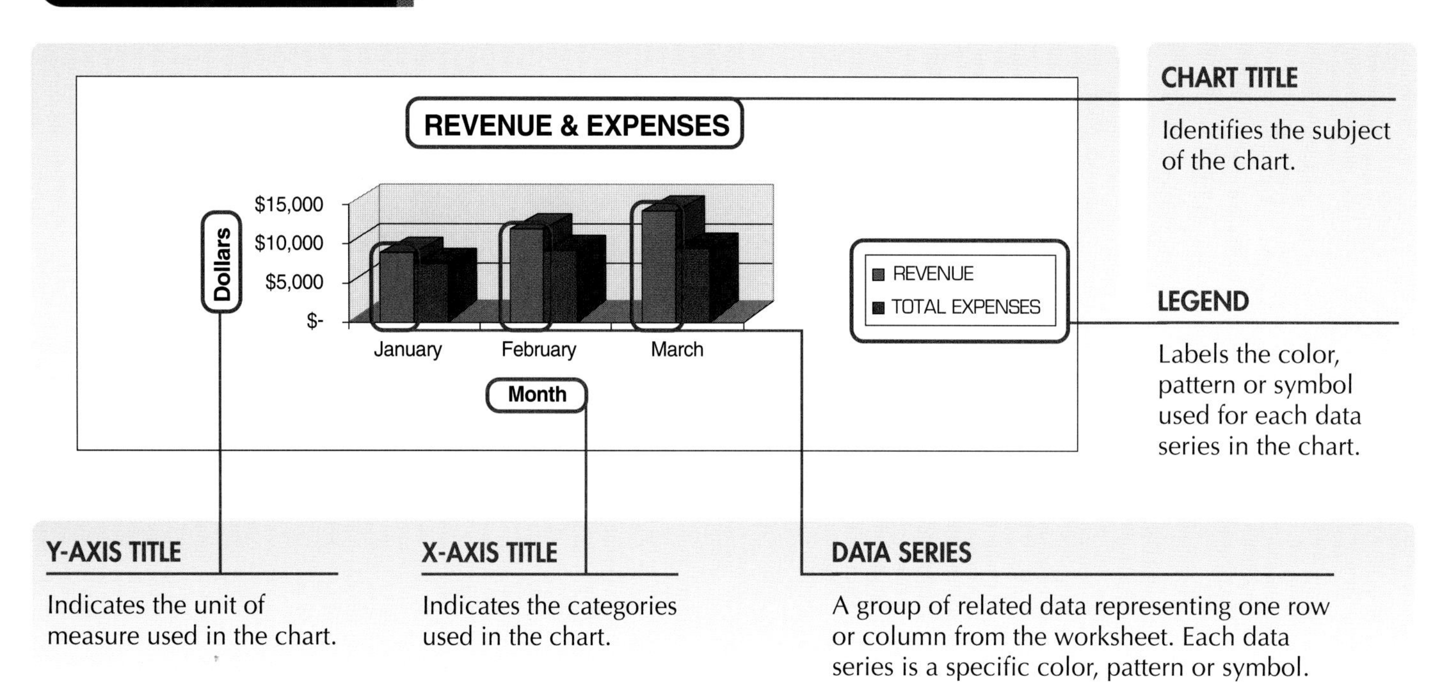

CHART TITLE

Identifies the subject of the chart.

LEGEND

Labels the color, pattern or symbol used for each data series in the chart.

Y-AXIS TITLE

Indicates the unit of measure used in the chart.

X-AXIS TITLE

Indicates the categories used in the chart.

DATA SERIES

A group of related data representing one row or column from the worksheet. Each data series is a specific color, pattern or symbol.

CHART TYPES

AREA

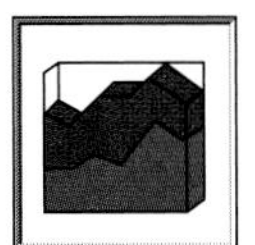

Each line represents a data series. The area below each line is filled in. This is useful for showing the amount of change in values over time (example: sales figures for the last five years).

LINE

Each line represents a data series measured at regular intervals. This is useful for showing the rate of change in values over time.

BAR

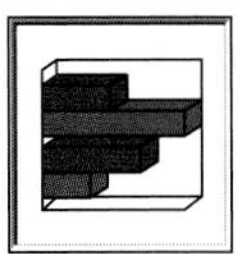

Each horizontal bar represents a value in a data series. This chart shows differences between values (example: a comparison of revenue and expenses for each month in a year).

PIE

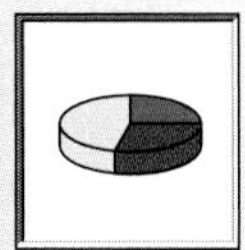

This chart shows each value in a data series as a piece of a pie. A pie chart can only display one data series at a time. This is useful for showing percentages (example: January sales as a percentage of sales for the year).

COLUMN

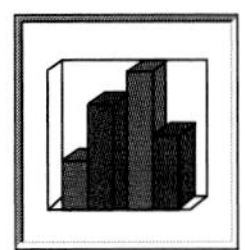

This chart is similar to a bar chart. Each vertical bar represents a value in a data series. This is useful for showing changes to values over a period of time.

RADAR

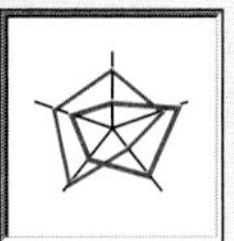

This chart represents each data series as a line around a central point (example: each axis is a month, and the distance from the center point shows the sales for the month).

DOUGHNUT

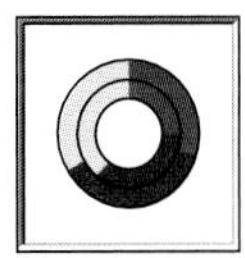

This chart is similar to a pie chart, except it can display more than one data series at a time. Each ring in the doughnut represents a data series.

XY (SCATTER)

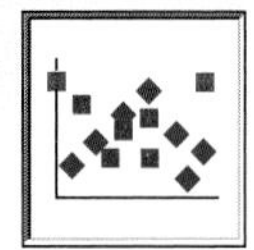

This chart shows the relationship between two or more data series measured at uneven intervals (example: relationship between education and lifetime earnings).

CREATE A CHART ON A WORKSHEET

You can create a chart directly from your worksheet data. The ChartWizard leads you through each step to create a chart.

CREATE A CHART ON A WORKSHEET

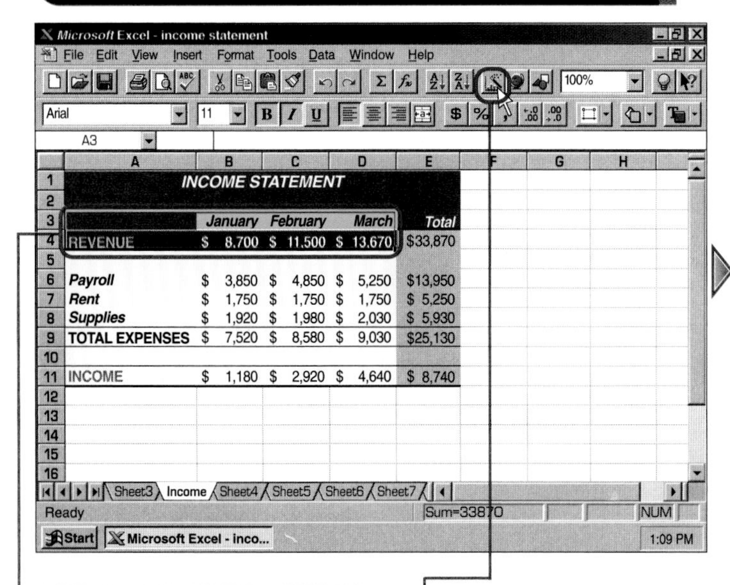

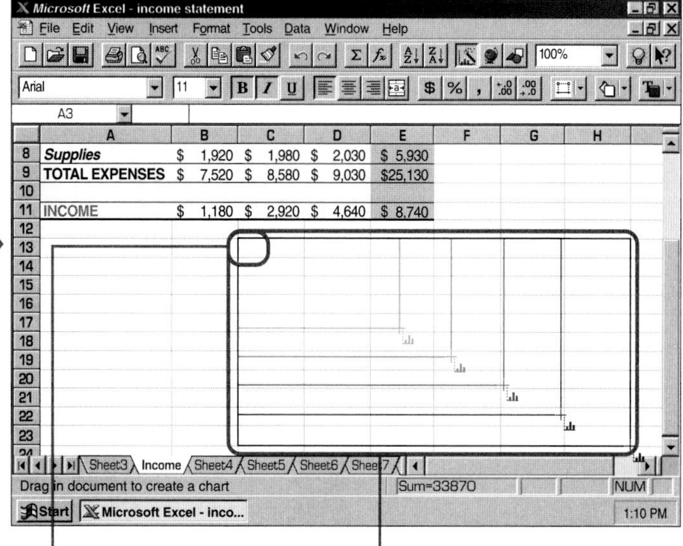

1 Select the cells containing the data you want to chart, including the row and column headings.

Note: To select cells, refer to page 12.

2 Move the mouse over the ChartWizard button and then press the left button (the mouse pointer changes shape).

3 Move the mouse to where you want the top left corner of the chart to appear.

4 Press and hold down the left button as you move the mouse until the box displays the chart size you want. Then release the button.

You can display a chart in one of two locations.

■ *To display the chart and data on the same worksheet, perform steps **1** to **14** starting on page 164.*

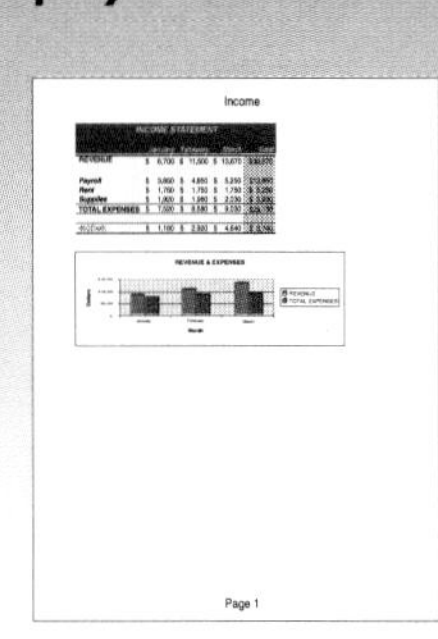

■ *To display the chart and data on separate worksheets, perform steps **1** to **6** starting on page 168.*

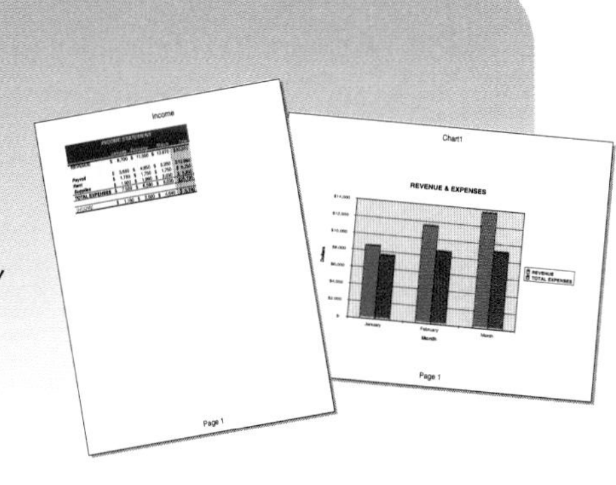

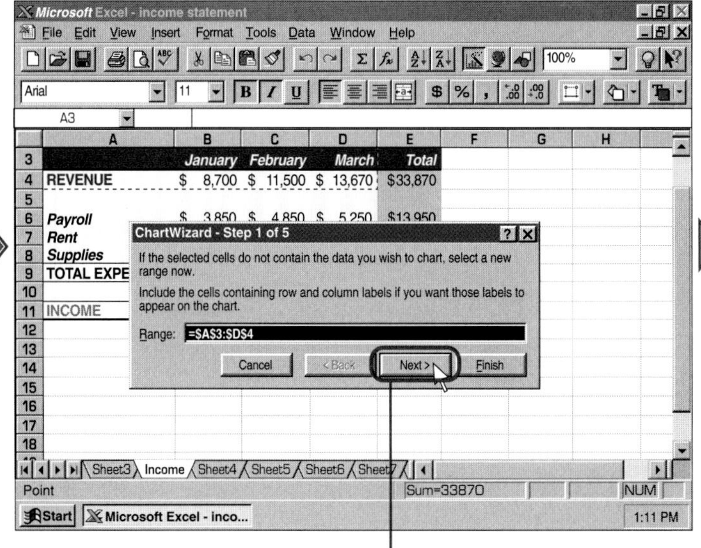

■ The **ChartWizard** dialog box appears.

5 To continue, move the mouse over **Next** and then press the left button.

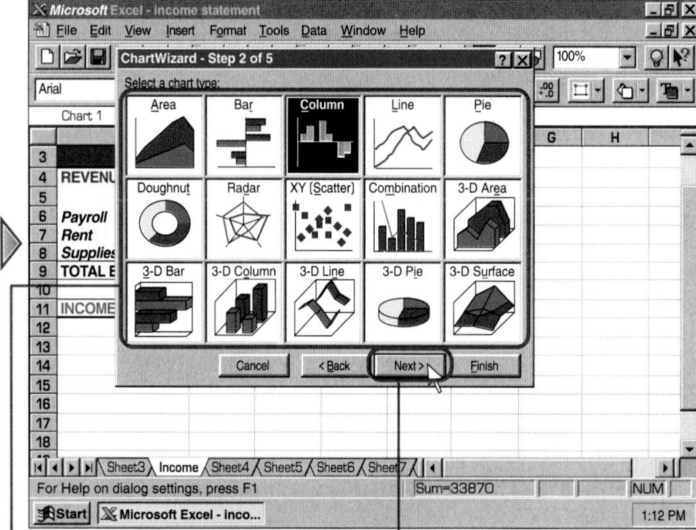

6 Move the mouse over the type of chart you want to create and then press the left button.

Note: You can easily change the chart type later on. For more information, refer to page 180.

7 To continue, move the mouse over **Next** and then press the left button.

CREATE A CHART ON A WORKSHEET

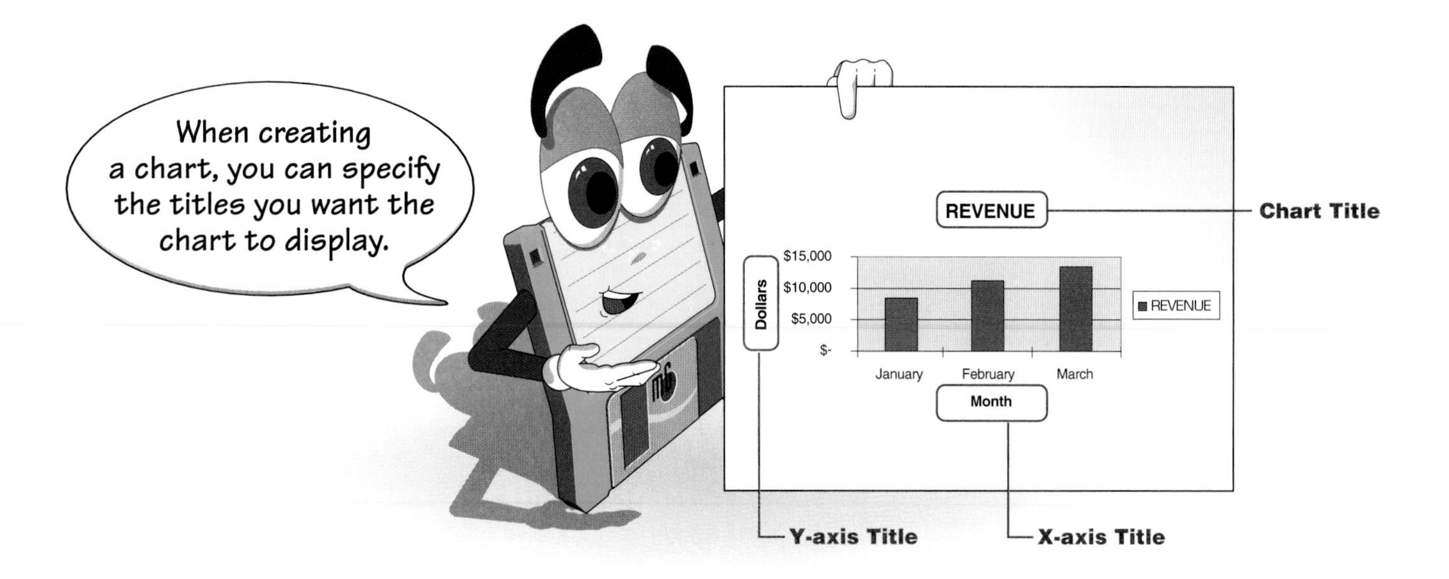

CREATE A CHART ON A WORKSHEET (CONTINUED)

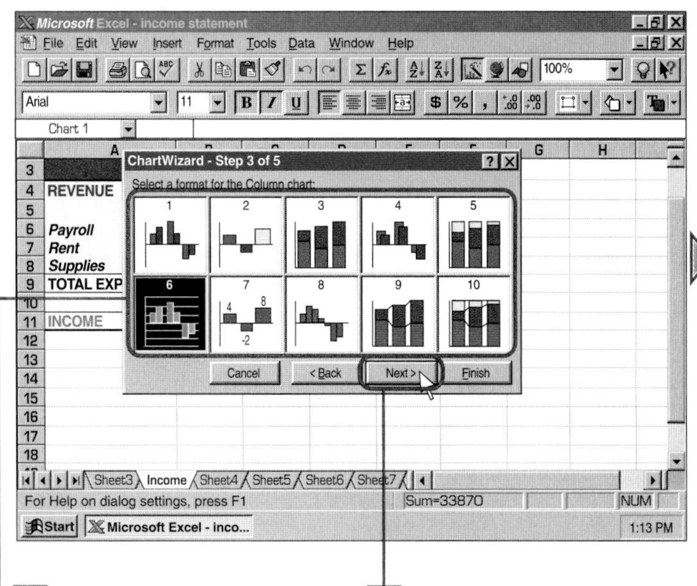

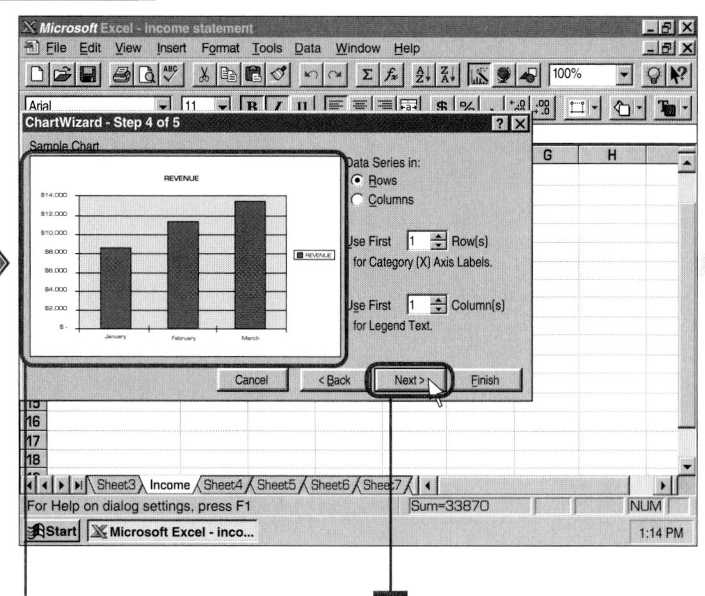

8 Move the mouse over the way you want the chart to appear and then press the left button.

Note: The available designs depend on the chart type you selected in step **6**.

9 To continue, move the mouse over **Next** and then press the left button.

■ This area displays a sample of your chart.

Note: You can return to a previous step at any time to change your selections. To do so, move the mouse over ***Back*** *and then press the left button.*

10 To continue, move the mouse over **Next** and then press the left button.

If you change the data in your worksheet, Excel will automatically update the chart to reflect the changes.

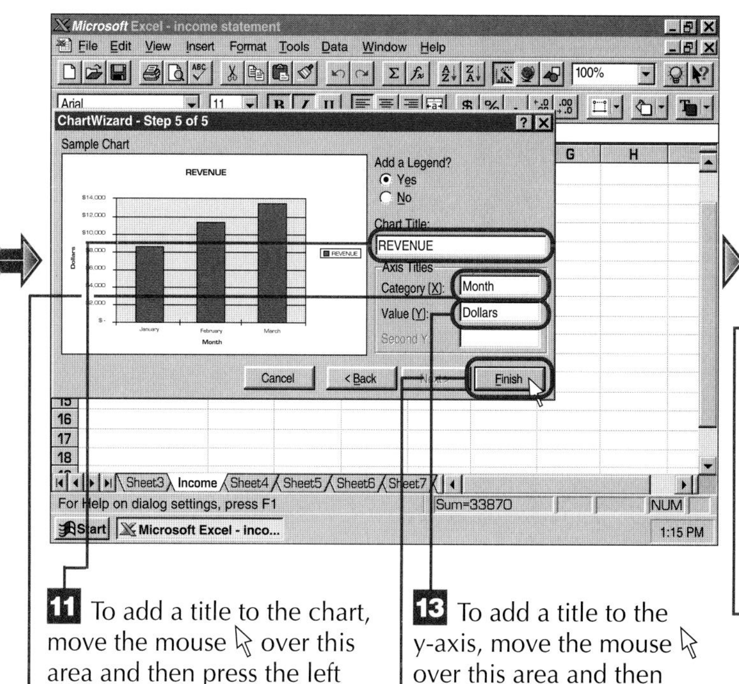

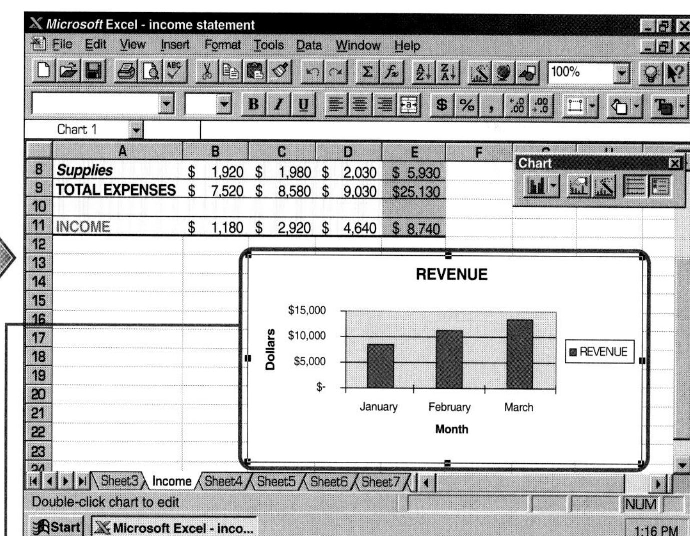

11 To add a title to the chart, move the mouse over this area and then press the left button. Then type a title.

12 To add a title to the x-axis, move the mouse over this area and then press the left button. Then type a title.

13 To add a title to the y-axis, move the mouse over this area and then press the left button. Then type a title.

14 Move the mouse over **Finish** and then press the left button.

■ The chart appears in your worksheet.

Note: To view the entire chart, use the scroll bar. For more information, refer to page 14.

CREATE A CHART ON A CHART SHEET

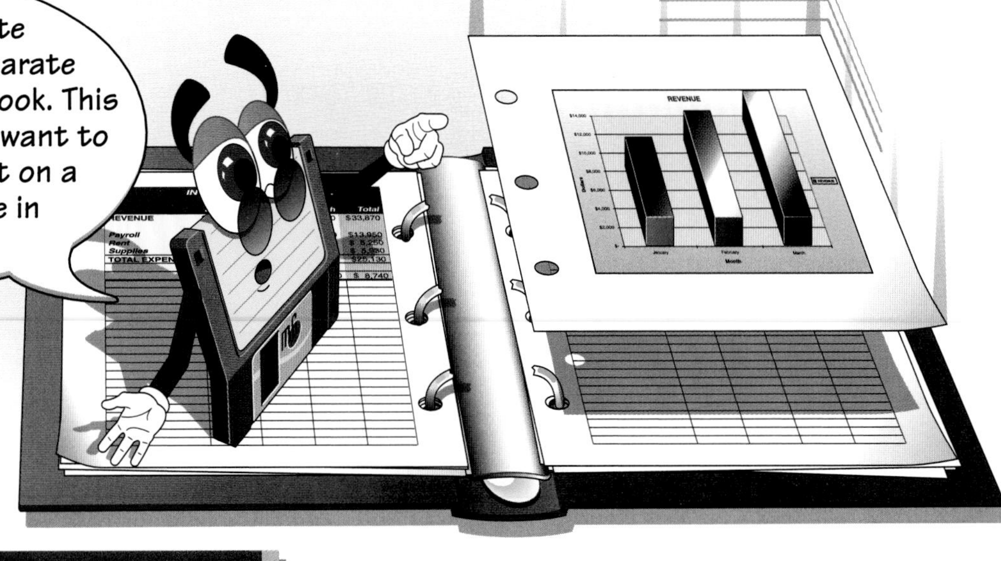

You can create a chart on a separate sheet in your workbook. This is useful when you want to display the chart on a separate page in a report.

CREATE A CHART ON A CHART SHEET

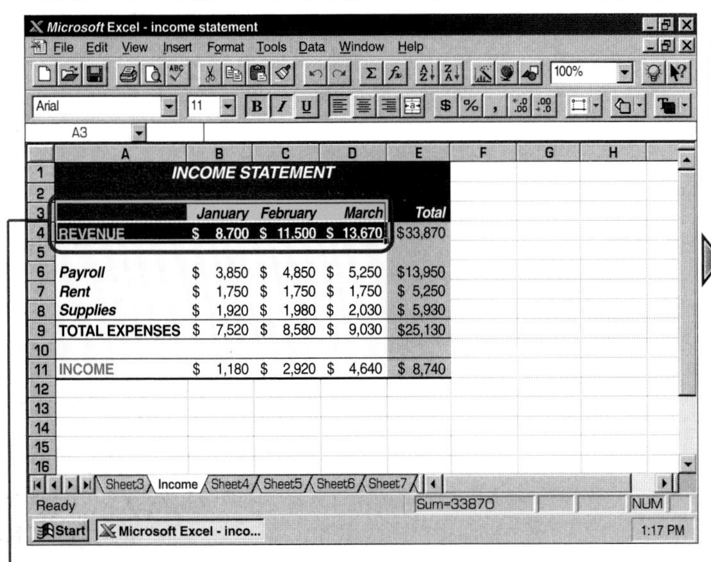

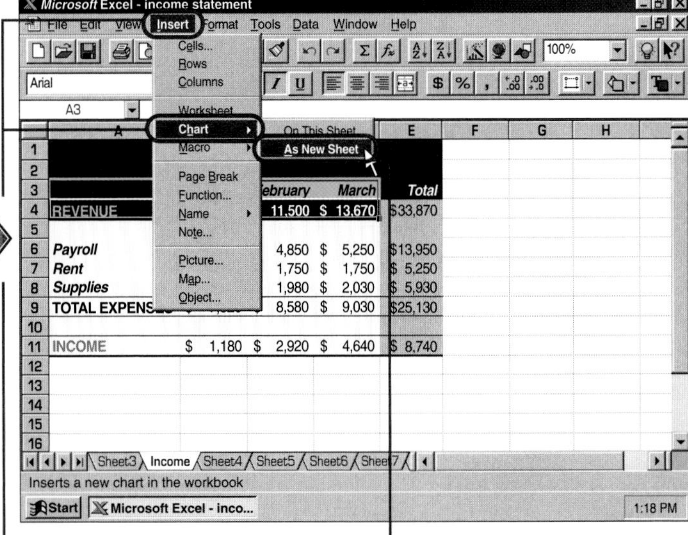

1 Select the cells containing the data you want to chart, including the row and column headings.

Note: To select cells, refer to page 12.

2 Move the mouse over **Insert** and then press the left button.

3 Move the mouse over **Chart**.

4 Move the mouse over **As New Sheet** and then press the left button.

Adding a chart sheet is like placing a new sheet of paper in a three-ring binder.

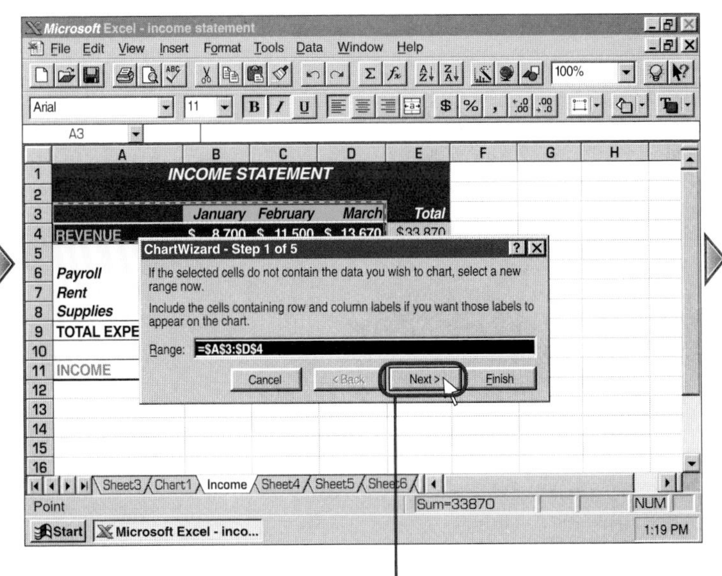

■ The **ChartWizard** dialog box appears.

5 Move the mouse over **Next** and then press the left button.

6 Perform steps **6** to **14** starting on page 165.

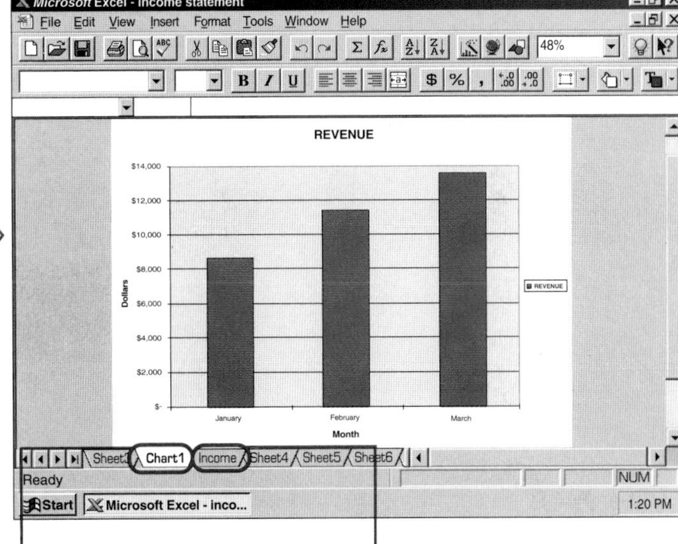

■ The chart appears on a separate sheet in the workbook.

■ To return to the worksheet containing your data, move the mouse over the worksheet tab and then press the left button.

Note: For information on using the sheets in a workbook, refer to the Using Multiple Worksheets chapter, starting on page 140.

MOVE AND SIZE A CHART

After you create a chart, you can move the chart and change its overall size.

You cannot move or size a chart on a chart sheet. For information on chart sheets, refer to page 168.

MOVE A CHART

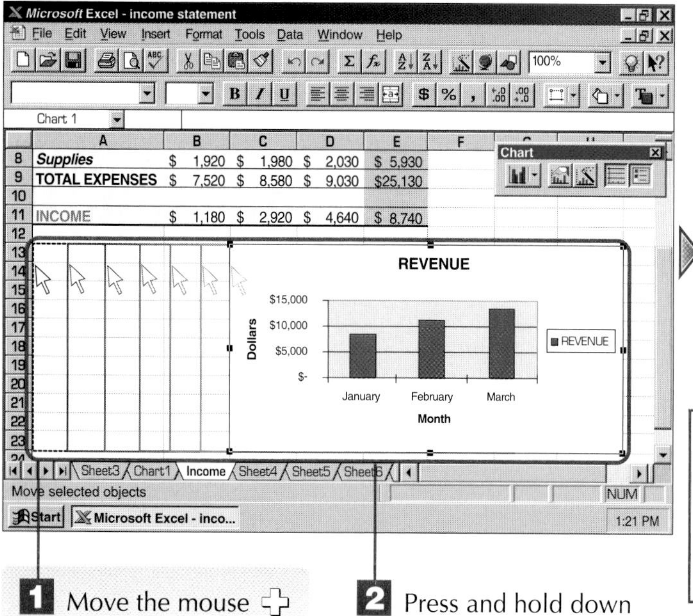

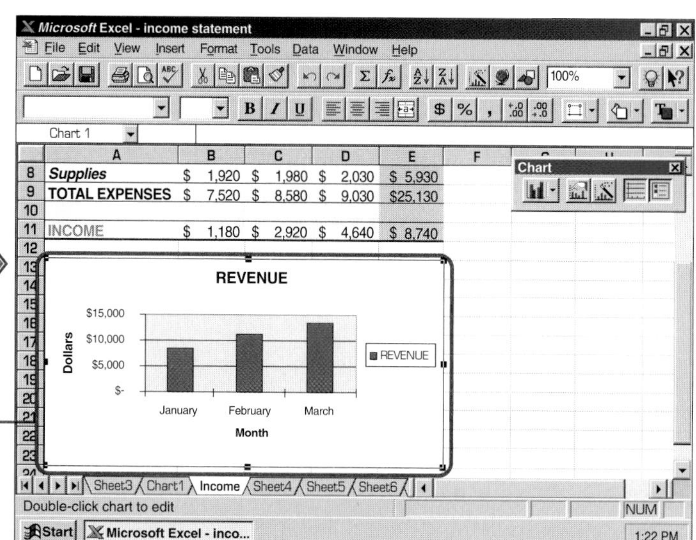

1 Move the mouse over an edge of the chart and changes to .

2 Press and hold down the left button as you move the chart to a new location.

■ A box shows the new location.

3 Release the left button and the chart appears in the new location.

Tip

You can change the size of a chart using any handle (■) around the chart.

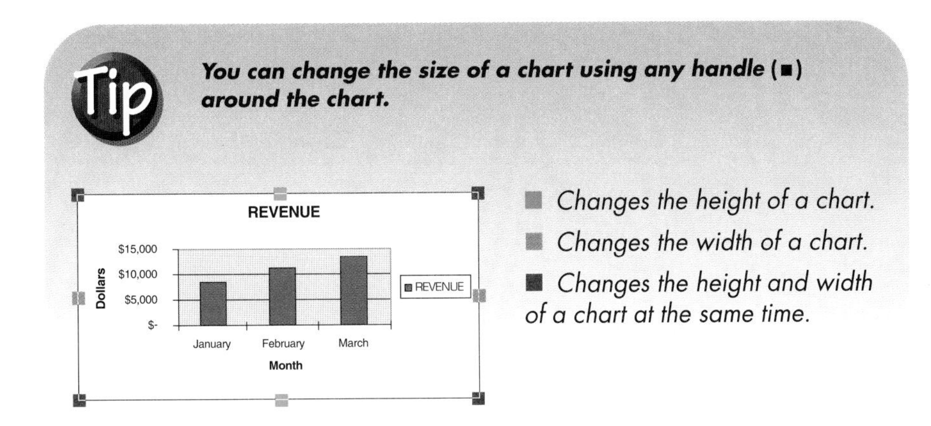

■ *Changes the height of a chart.*

■ *Changes the width of a chart.*

■ *Changes the height and width of a chart at the same time.*

SIZE A CHART

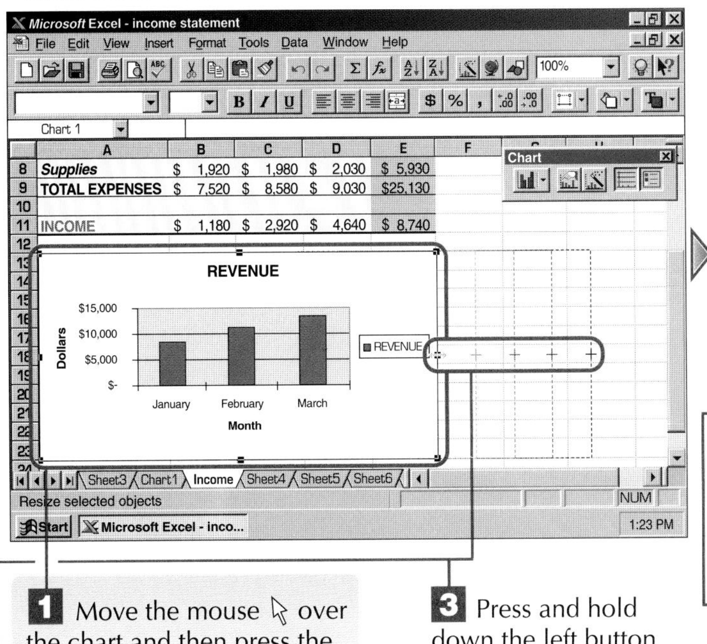

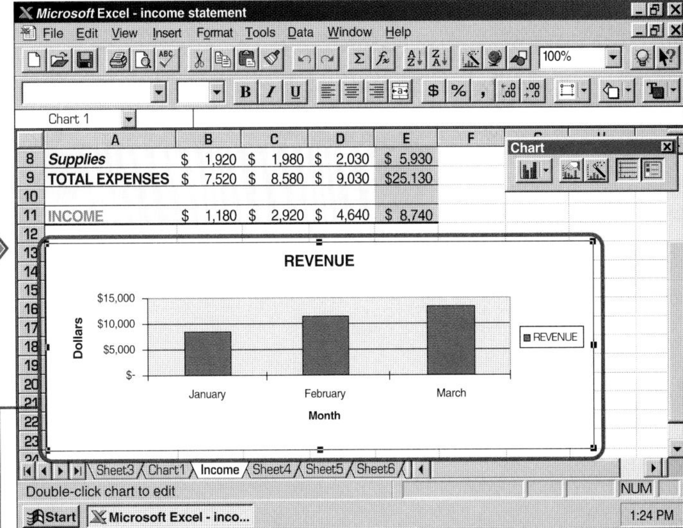

1 Move the mouse over the chart and then press the left button. Handles (■) appear around the chart.

2 Move the mouse over one of the handles (■) and changes to ↔ or ↕.

3 Press and hold down the left button as you move the edge of the chart until it is the size you want.

■ A box shows the new size.

4 Release the left button and the chart appears in the new size.

ADD A DATA SERIES TO A CHART

After you create a chart, you can easily add another data series.
1995
1996

ADD A DATA SERIES TO A CHART

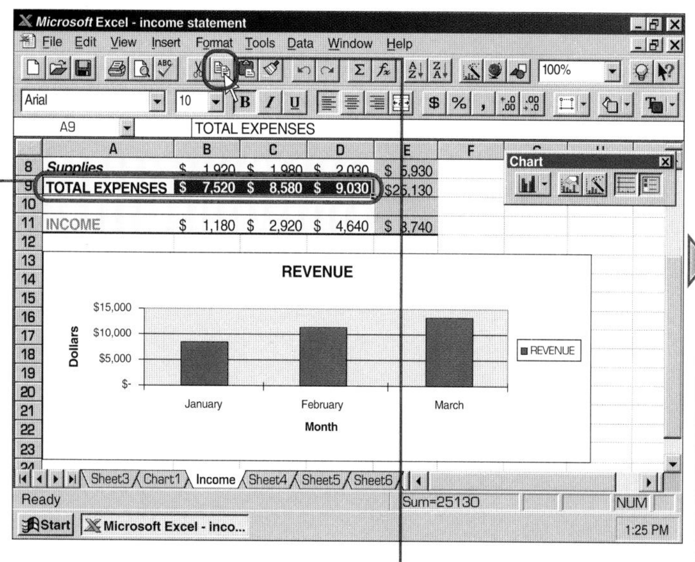

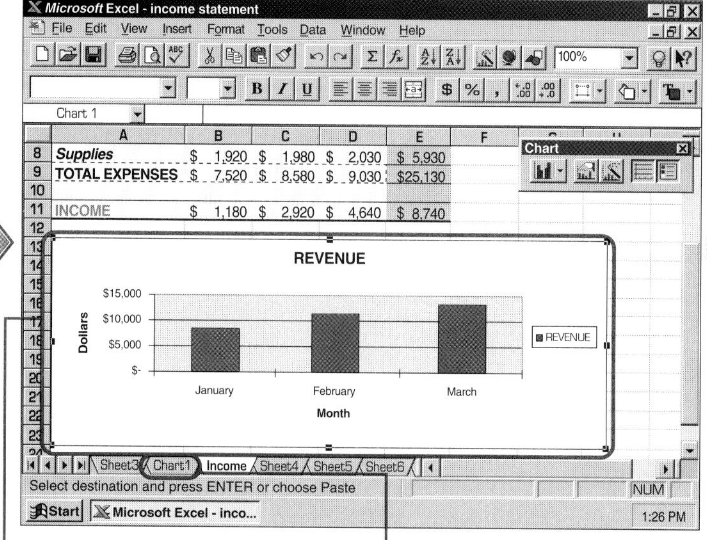

1 Select the cells containing the data you want to add to the chart, including the row or column heading.

Note: To select cells, refer to page 12.

2 To copy the data, move the mouse over the copy button and then press the left button.

3 To add the data to a chart in the worksheet, move the mouse over the chart and then press the left button.

■ To add the data to a chart on a chart sheet, move the mouse over the tab for the chart sheet and then press the left button.

Tip

A pie chart can only display one data series. You cannot add a data series to a pie chart.

Note: For information on chart types, refer to page 163.

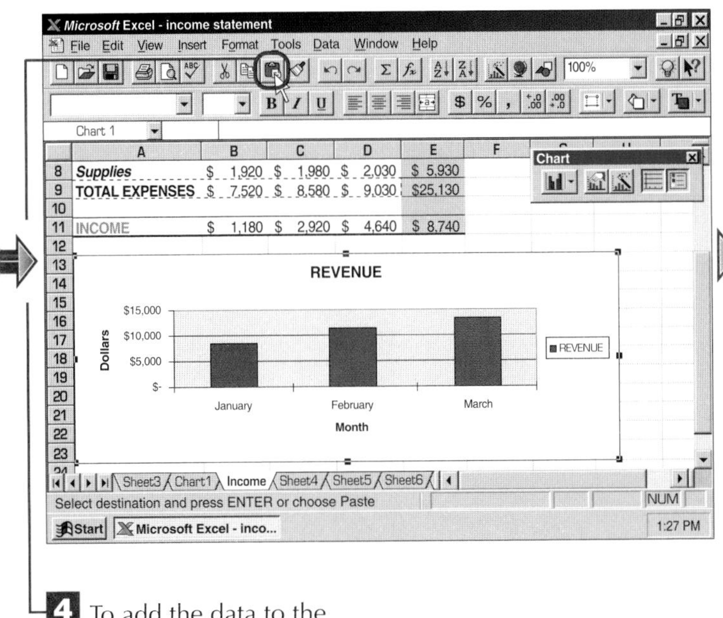

4 To add the data to the chart, move the mouse over and then press the left button.

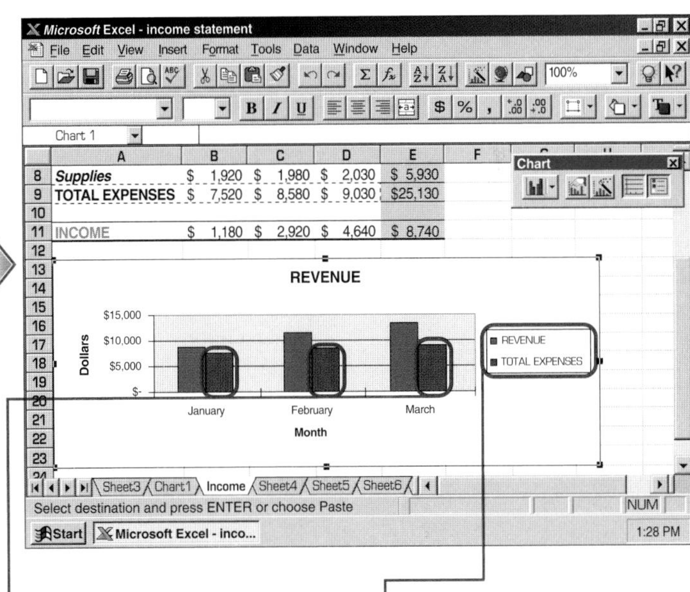

■ The chart displays the new data series.

■ When you add a data series to a chart, Excel automatically updates the legend.

CHANGE TITLES IN A CHART

You can change any title in your chart. Titles can make your data more meaningful.

CHANGE TITLES IN A CHART

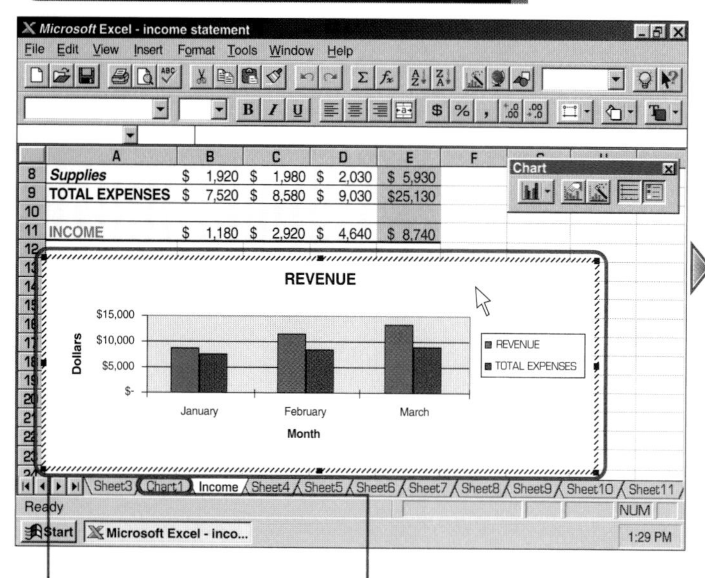

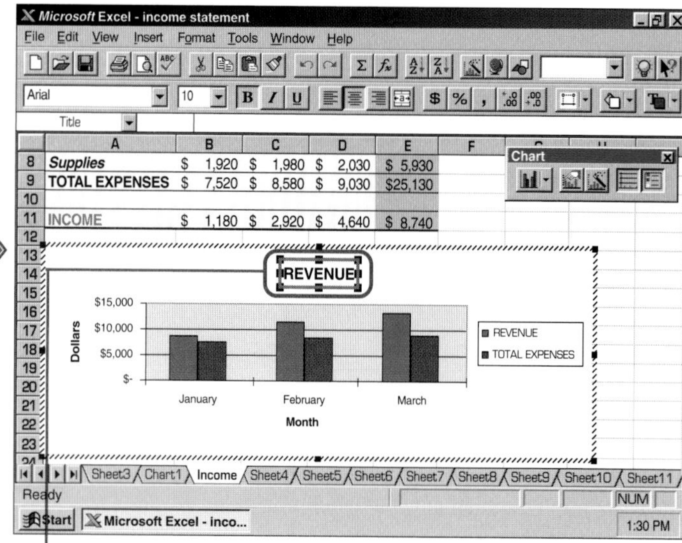

1 To change the titles for a chart in your worksheet, move the mouse over the chart and then quickly press the left button twice. A thick border appears around the chart.

■ To change the titles for a chart on a chart sheet, move the mouse over the tab for the chart sheet and then press the left button.

2 Move the mouse over the title you want to change and then press the left button. A border appears around the title.

Tip

Charts can display three different titles.

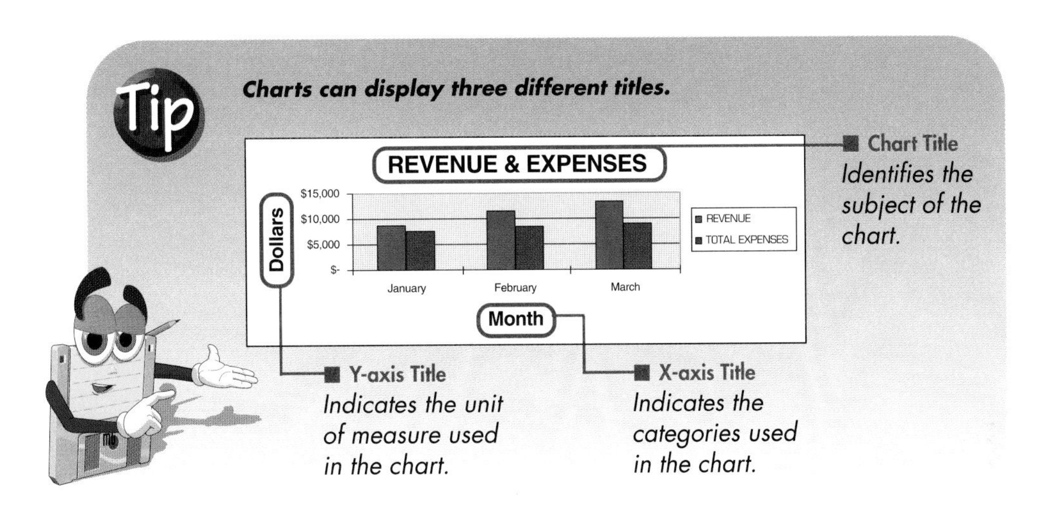

■ **Chart Title**
Identifies the subject of the chart.

■ **Y-axis Title**
Indicates the unit of measure used in the chart.

■ **X-axis Title**
Indicates the categories used in the chart.

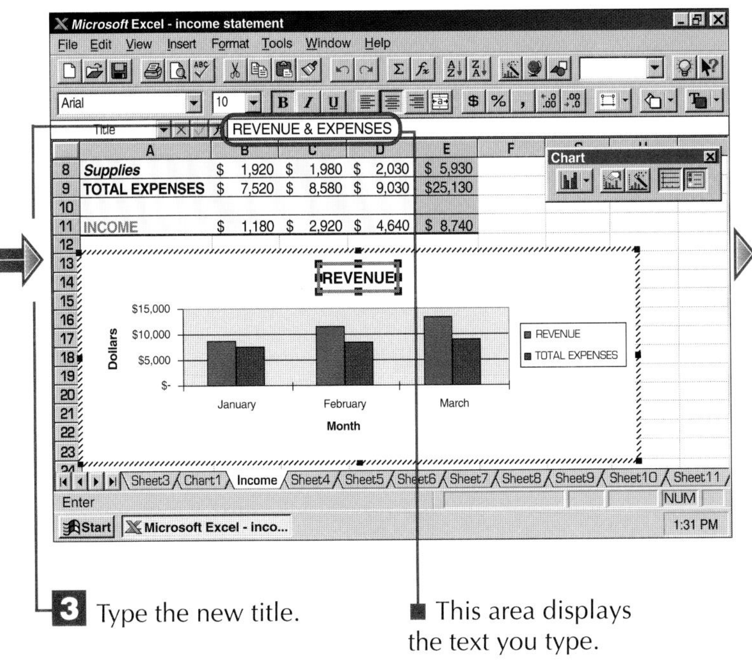

3 Type the new title.

■ This area displays the text you type.

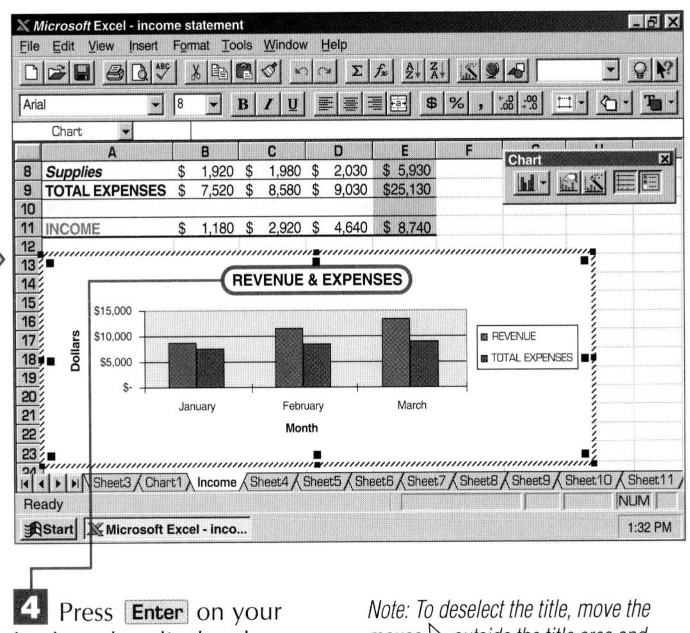

4 Press Enter on your keyboard to display the new title in the chart.

Note: To deselect the title, move the mouse outside the title area and then press the left button.

PRINT A CHART

> You can print your chart either with the worksheet data or on its own page.

PRINT A CHART WITH WORKSHEET DATA

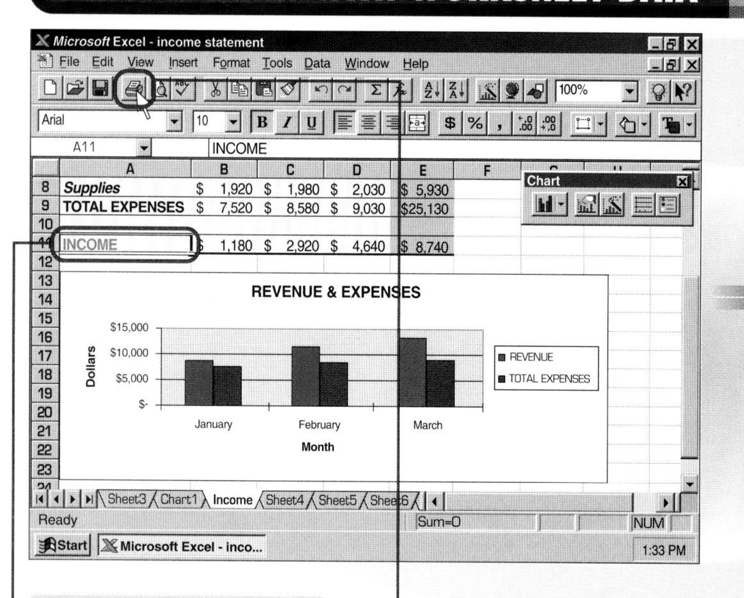

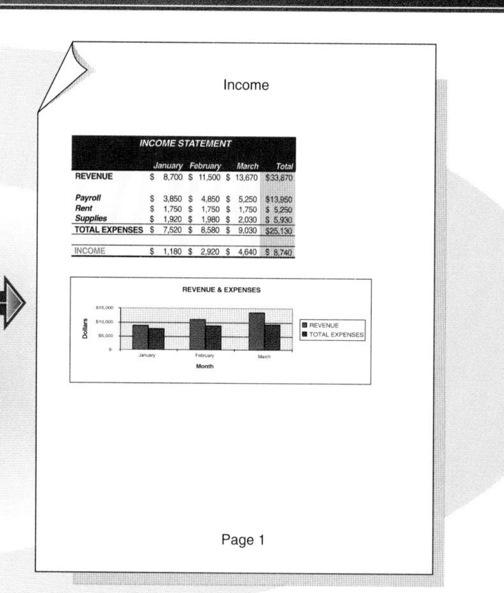

1 Move the mouse over any cell outside the chart and then press the left button.

2 Move the mouse over and then press the left button.

Note: For more information on printing, refer to the Print Your Worksheets chapter, starting on page 110.

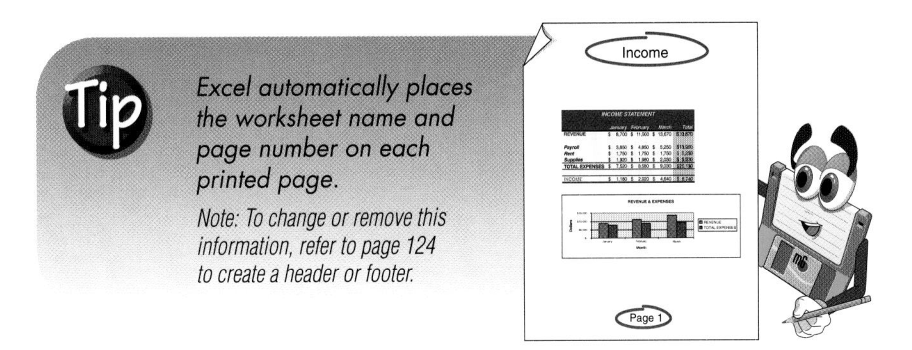

Excel automatically places the worksheet name and page number on each printed page.

Note: To change or remove this information, refer to page 124 to create a header or footer.

PRINT A CHART ON ITS OWN PAGE

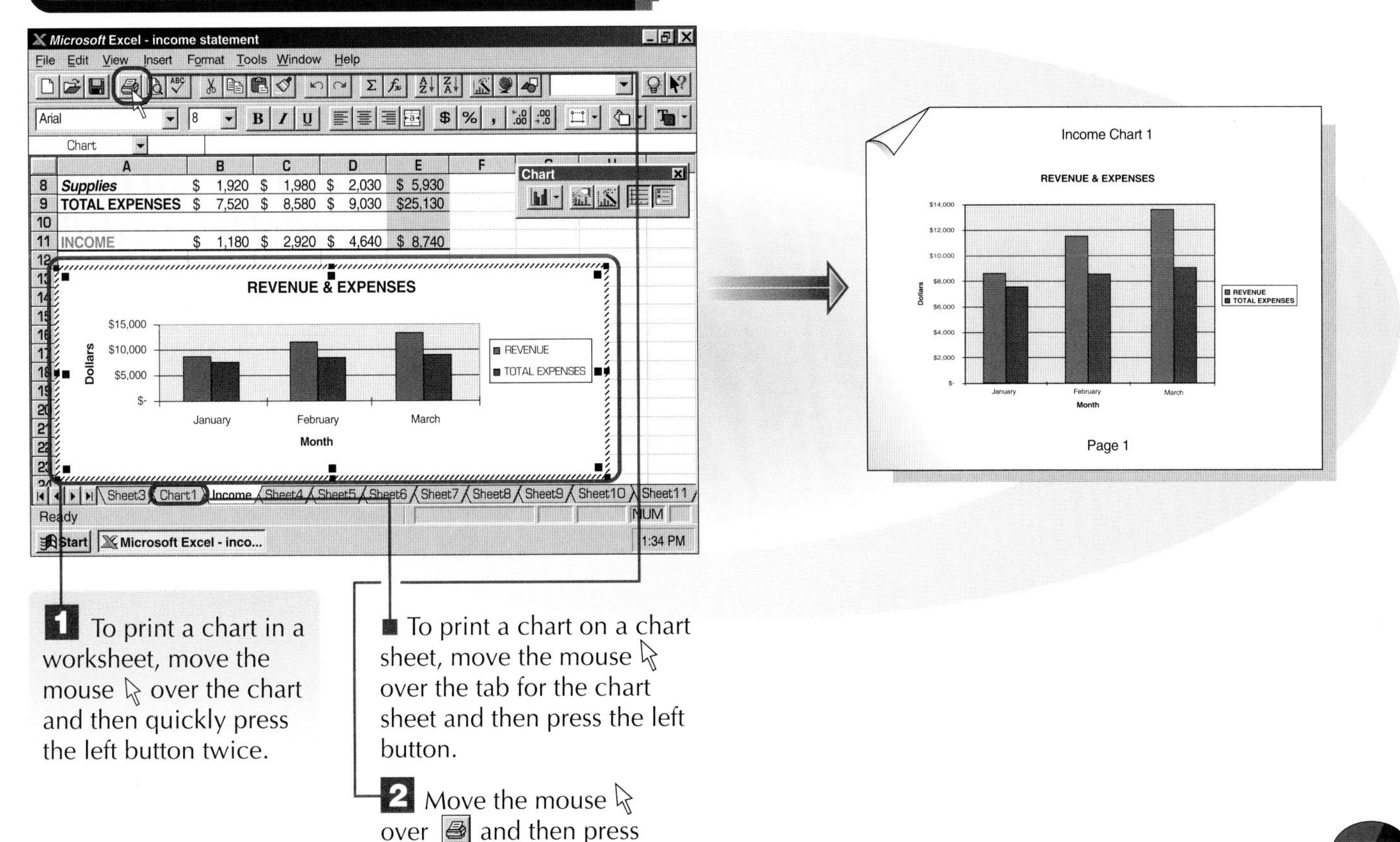

1 To print a chart in a worksheet, move the mouse over the chart and then quickly press the left button twice.

■ To print a chart on a chart sheet, move the mouse over the tab for the chart sheet and then press the left button.

2 Move the mouse over the print button and then press the left button.

DELETE A CHART

ADD/DELETE GRIDLINES OR LEGEND

You can easily delete a chart from your worksheet.

DELETE A CHART

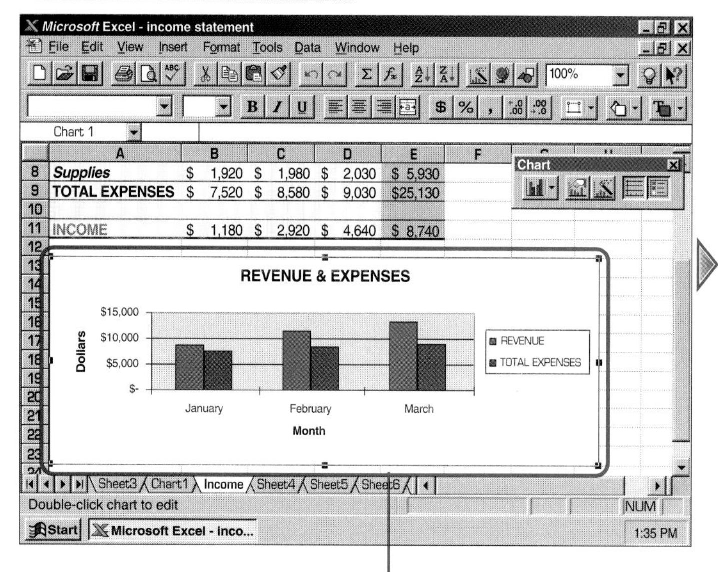

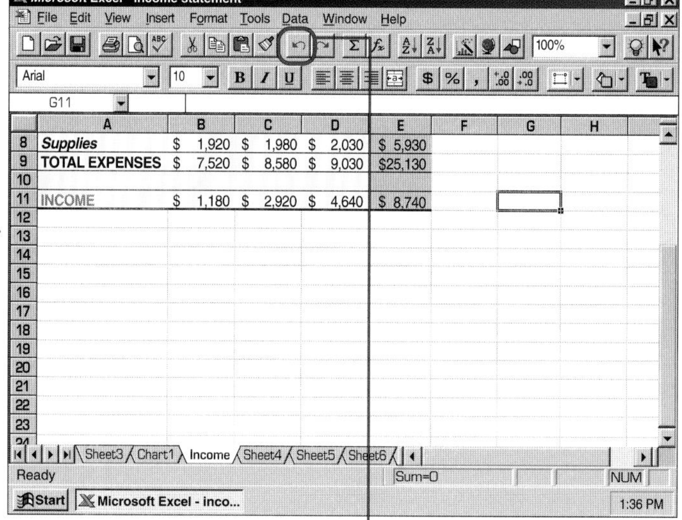

1 To deselect a chart in a worksheet, move the mouse over any cell outside the chart and then press the left button.

Note: To delete a chart on a chart sheet, refer to page 150 to delete a worksheet.

2 Move the mouse over the chart you want to delete and then press the left button.

3 Press Delete on your keyboard.

■ The chart disappears from your worksheet.

■ To reverse the change, immediately move the mouse over ↶ and then press the left button.

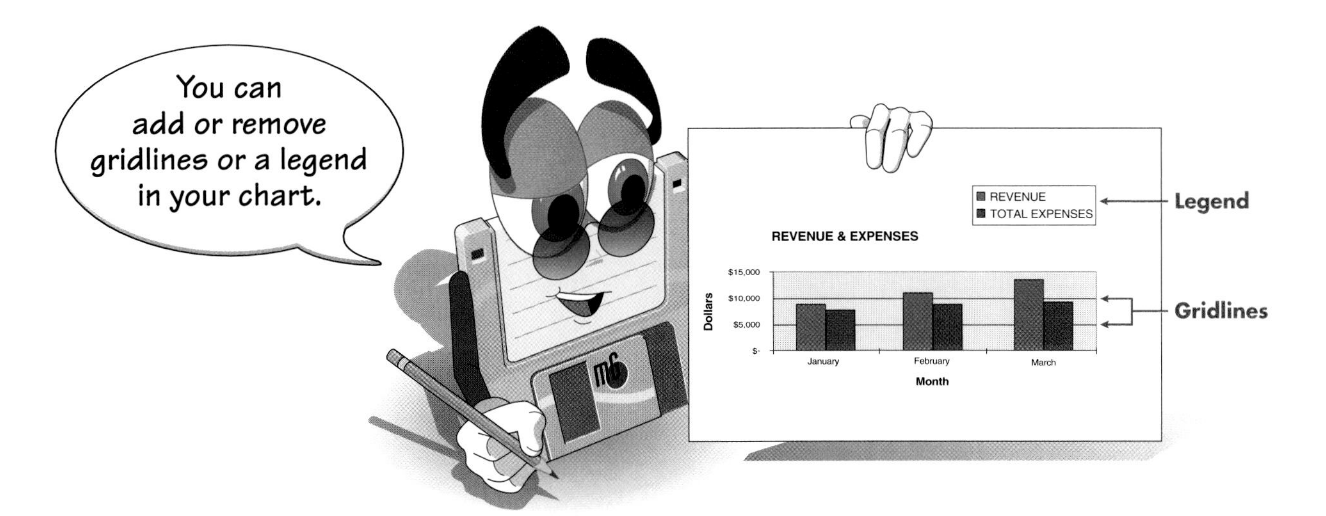

ADD/DELETE GRIDLINES OR LEGEND

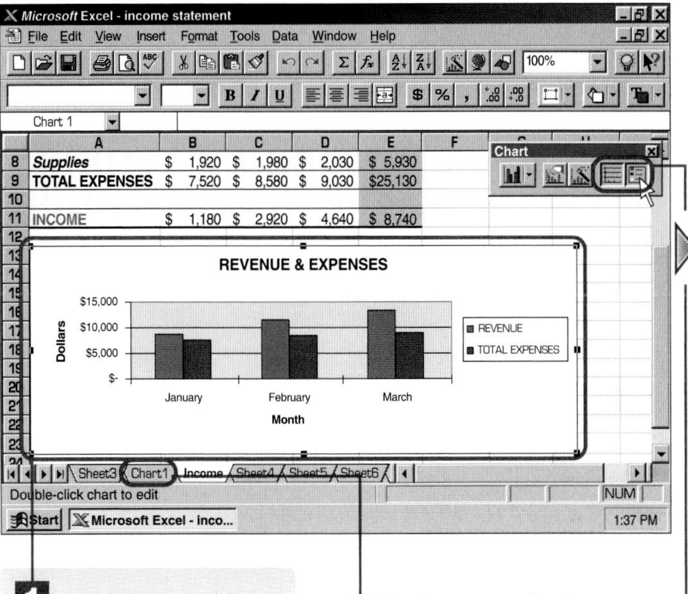

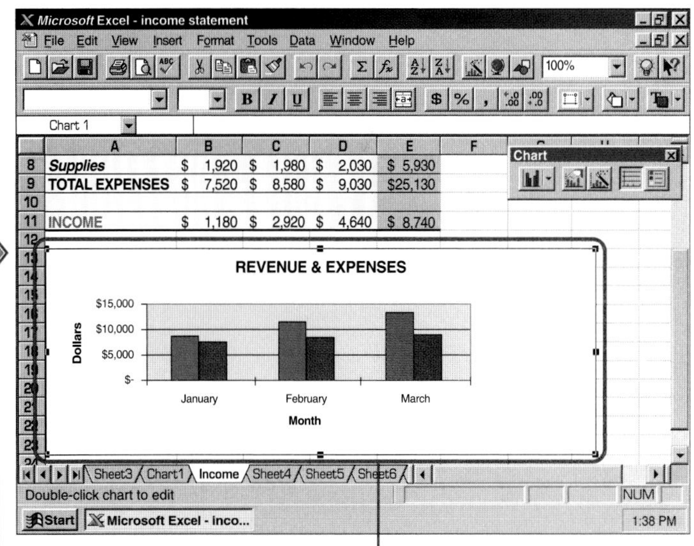

1 To change a chart in your worksheet, move the mouse over the chart and then press the left button.

■ To change a chart on a chart sheet, move the mouse over the tab for the chart sheet and then press the left button.

2 Move the mouse over an option you want to add or remove and then press the left button.

Gridlines

Legend

*Note: If the **Chart** toolbar does not appear, refer to page 132 to display the toolbar.*

■ The chart displays the changes.

CHANGE CHART TYPE

After creating a chart, you can select a new chart type that will better suit your data.

CHANGE CHART TYPE

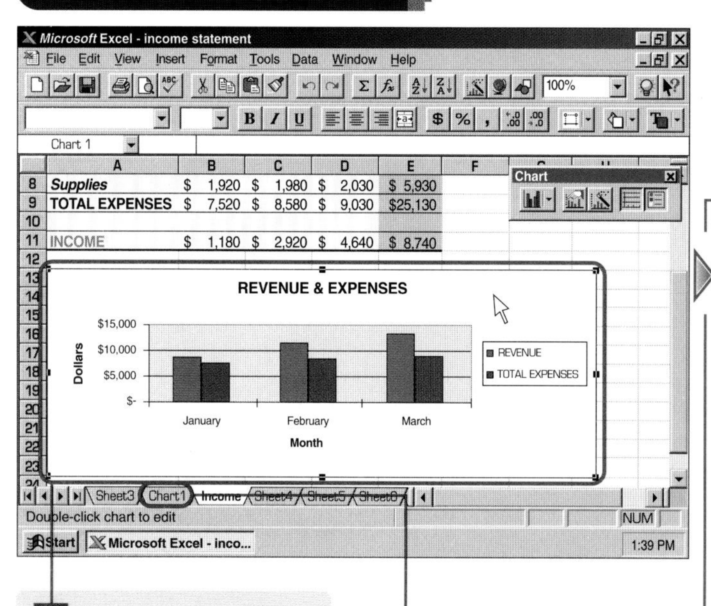

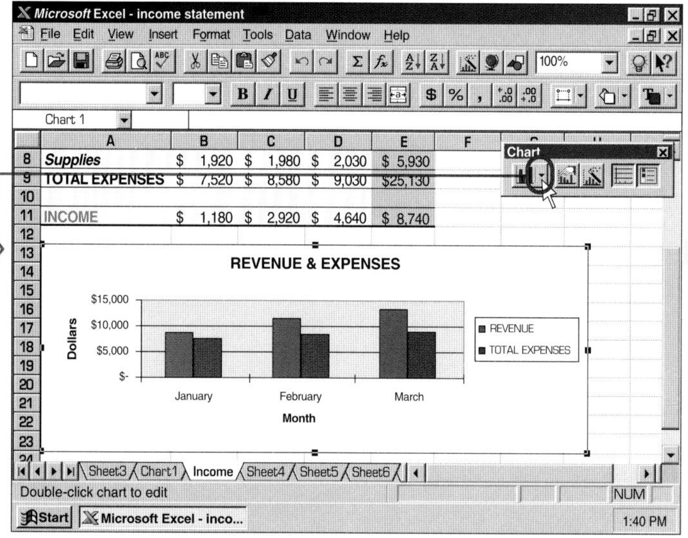

1 To change the type of chart in your worksheet, move the mouse over the chart and then press the left button.

■ To change the type of chart on a chart sheet, move the mouse over the tab for the chart sheet and then press the left button.

2 Move the mouse over ▾ on the **Chart** toolbar and then press the left button.

*Note: If the **Chart** toolbar does not appear, refer to page 132 to display the toolbar.*

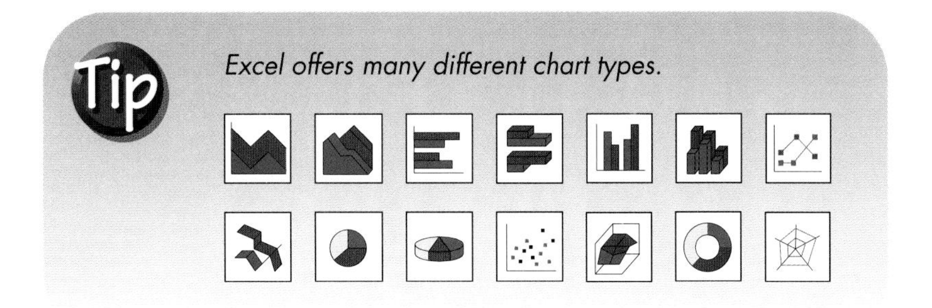

Excel offers many different chart types.

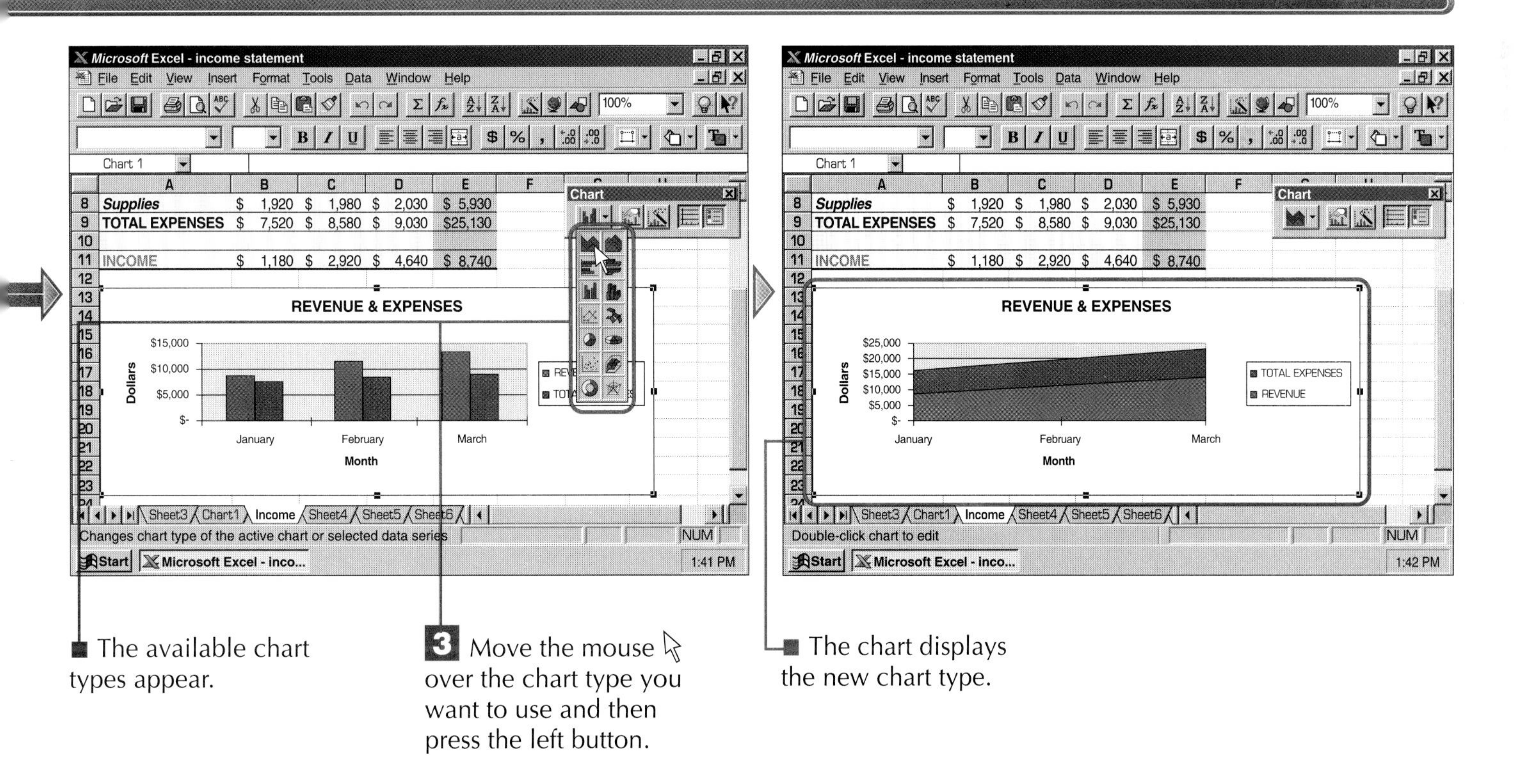

■ The available chart types appear.

3 Move the mouse over the chart type you want to use and then press the left button.

■ The chart displays the new chart type.

FORMAT A CHART AUTOMATICALLY

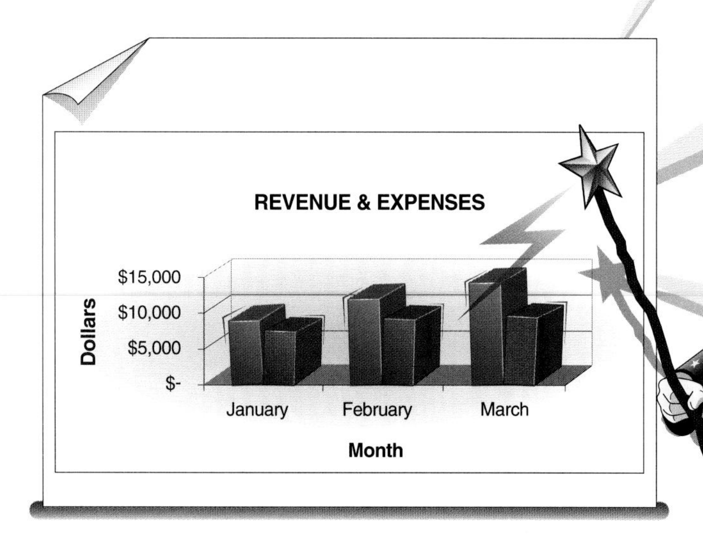

You can choose a design that suits your chart and then have Excel apply the design for you.

FORMAT A CHART AUTOMATICALLY

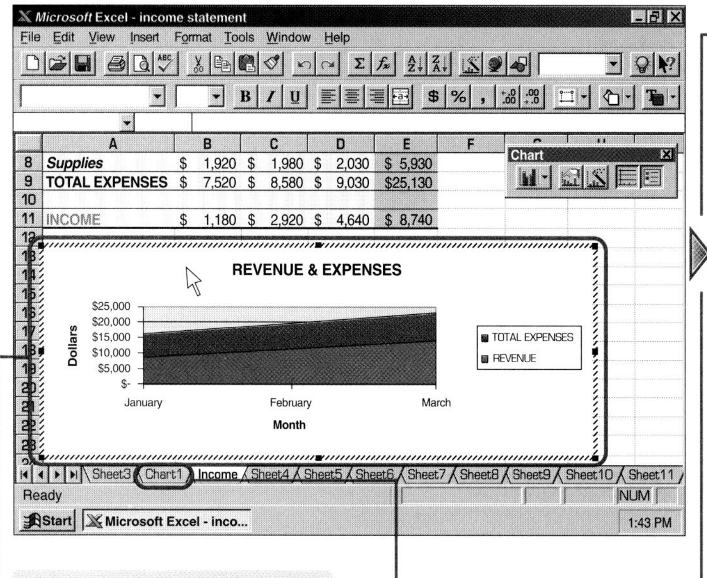

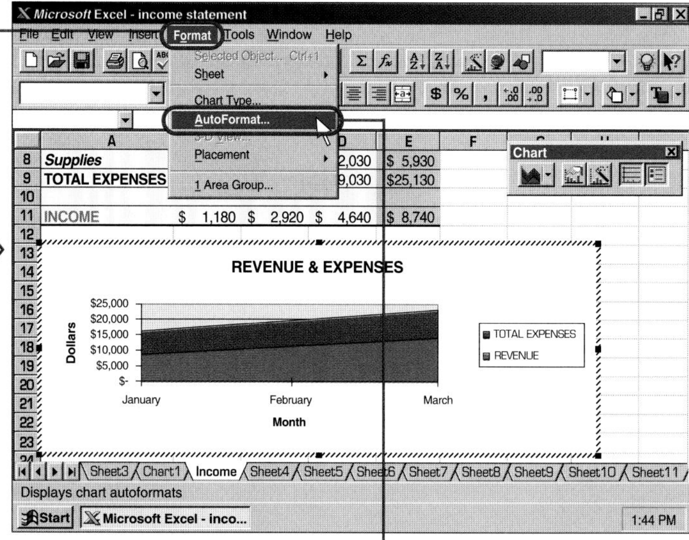

1 To format a chart in your worksheet, move the mouse over the chart and then quickly press the left button twice. A thick border appears around the chart.

■ To format a chart on a chart sheet, move the mouse over the tab for the chart sheet and then press the left button.

2 Move the mouse over **Format** and then press the left button.

3 Move the mouse over **AutoFormat** and then press the left button.

■ The **AutoFormat** dialog box appears.

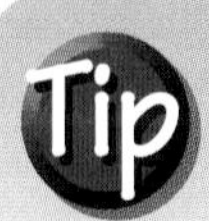

Excel offers several chart types in both two- and three-dimensional designs. You can use a 3-D design to give your chart a more sophisticated look.

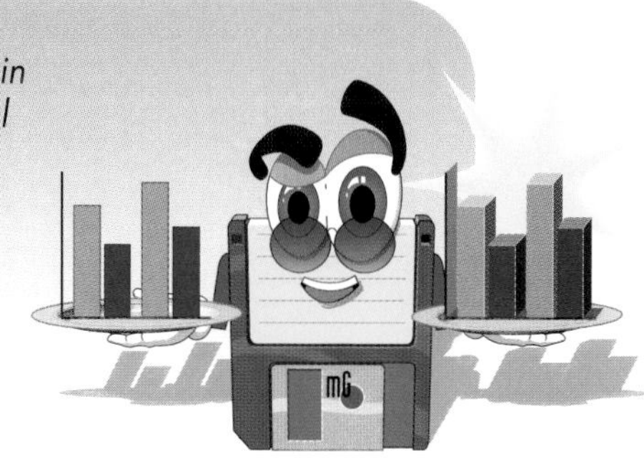

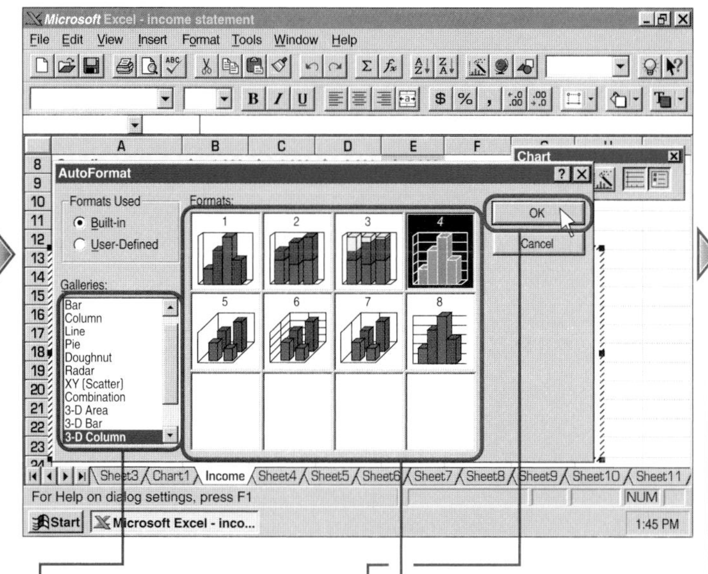

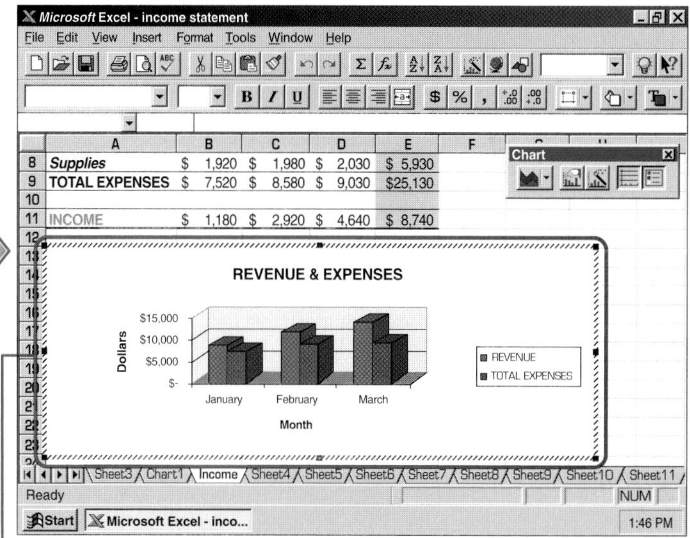

4 Move the mouse over the chart type you want to use and then press the left button.

Note: To view all the available chart types, use the scroll bar. For more information, refer to page 14.

5 Move the mouse over the design you want to use and then press the left button.

6 To apply the design to your worksheet, move the mouse over **OK** and then press the left button.

■ The chart displays the design you selected.

ADD A TEXT BOX

ADD A TEXT BOX

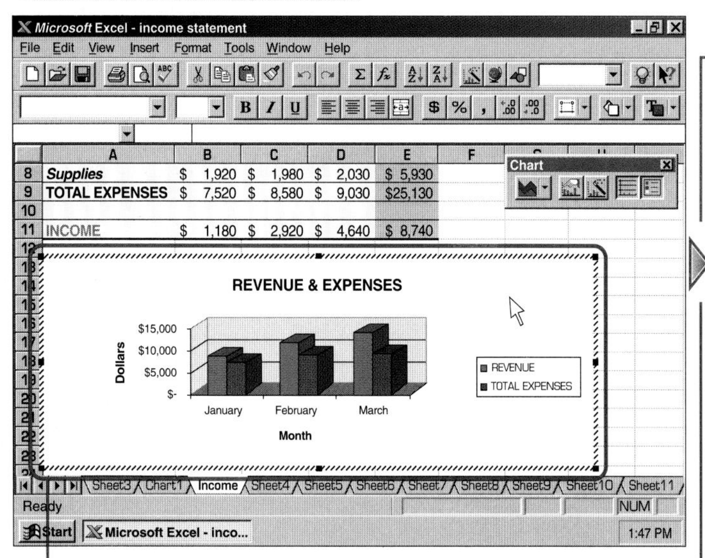

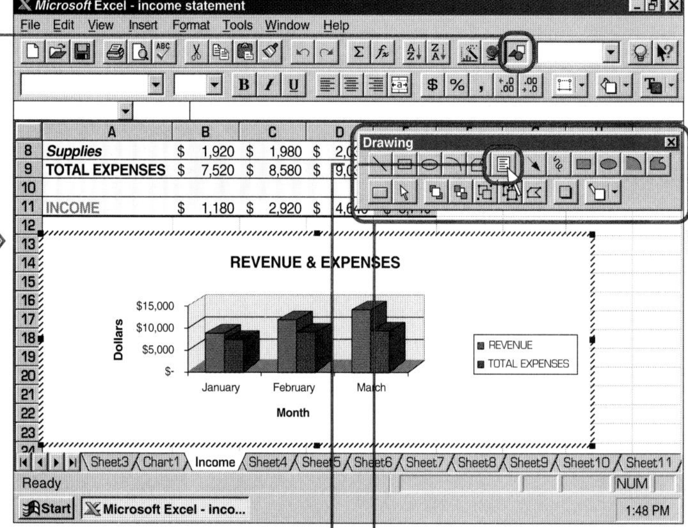

1 To add a text box to a chart, move the mouse over the chart and then quickly press the left button twice. This activates the chart.

■ To add a text box to the worksheet, move the mouse over any cell and then press the left button.

2 To display the **Drawing** toolbar, move the mouse over and then press the left button.

■ The **Drawing** toolbar appears.

3 Move the mouse over and then press the left button (changes to +).

You can move, size or delete a text box as you would a chart in your worksheet.

■ *To change a text box in a chart, you must first activate the chart. To do so, move the mouse ↖ over the chart and then quickly press the left button twice.*

■ *To move or size a chart, refer to page 170. To delete a chart, refer to page 178.*

Note: You cannot move a text box outside the chart area.

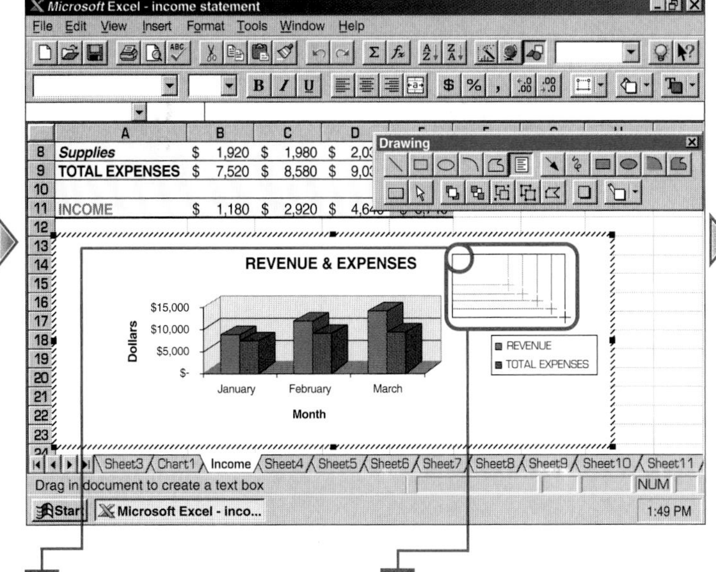

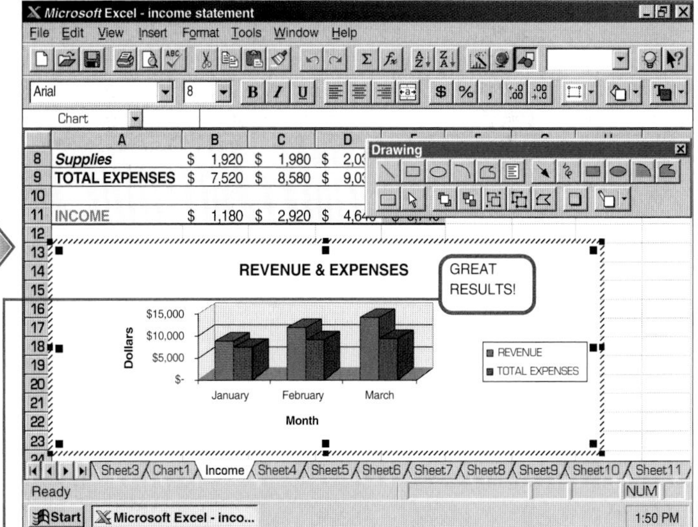

4 Move the mouse + to where you want the top left corner of the text box to appear.

5 Press and hold down the left button as you move the mouse + until the text box is the size you want. Then release the button.

6 Type the text you want to appear in the text box.

7 When you finish typing the text, move the mouse ↖ outside the text box area and then press the left button.

8 To hide the **Drawing** toolbar, repeat step **2**.

In this chapter you will learn how to manage large collections of information.
Last Name First Name Product Units Sold
Gresh Ric A 685
Smith Michael C 934
Hughes Susan A 812
Kilkenny Greg C 1625
Smith Linda B 598
Ratoff Ron A 632
Farance Kim C 795
Balin Sandy B 956
Smith Jill A 578
Farance Kim C 795
Kilkenny Greg C 1625
Smith Michael C 934
mG
Sales for Product C

CHAPTER 12

MANAGE DATA IN A LIST

Introduction

Create a List

Filter a List

Sort Data in a List

Add Subtotals to a List

Hide or Display Subtotaled Data

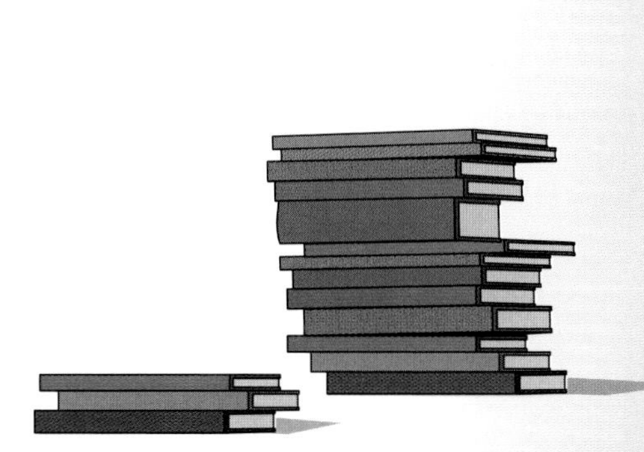

INTRODUCTION

Excel provides powerful tools for organizing, managing, sorting and retrieving data from a large collection of information.

Common lists include mailing lists, library book catalogs and product listings.

STORE DATA

You can keep your data in an organized and up-to-date list. For example, you can create a list to keep track of the names and addresses of all your employees.

SORT DATA

You can change the order of data in a list. Excel lets you sort data by letter, number or date. For example, you can alphabetically sort all employees by last name.

FIND DATA

You can quickly find specific data in a list. You can then compare and analyze the data. For example, you can display only the employees who sold more than 1000 units last month.

ADD SUBTOTALS TO DATA

You can subtotal the items in your list. For example, you can display the total number of units sold for each product in your list.

Last Name	First Name	Product	Units Sold
Gresh	Ric	A	685
Hughes	Susan	A	812
Ratoff	Ron	A	632
Smith	Jill	A	578
		A Total	2707
Balin	Sandy	B	956
Smith	Linda	B	598
		B Total	1554
Farance	Kim	C	795
Kilkenny	Greg	C	1625
nith	Michael	C	934
		C Total	3354
		Grand Total	7615

CREATE A LIST

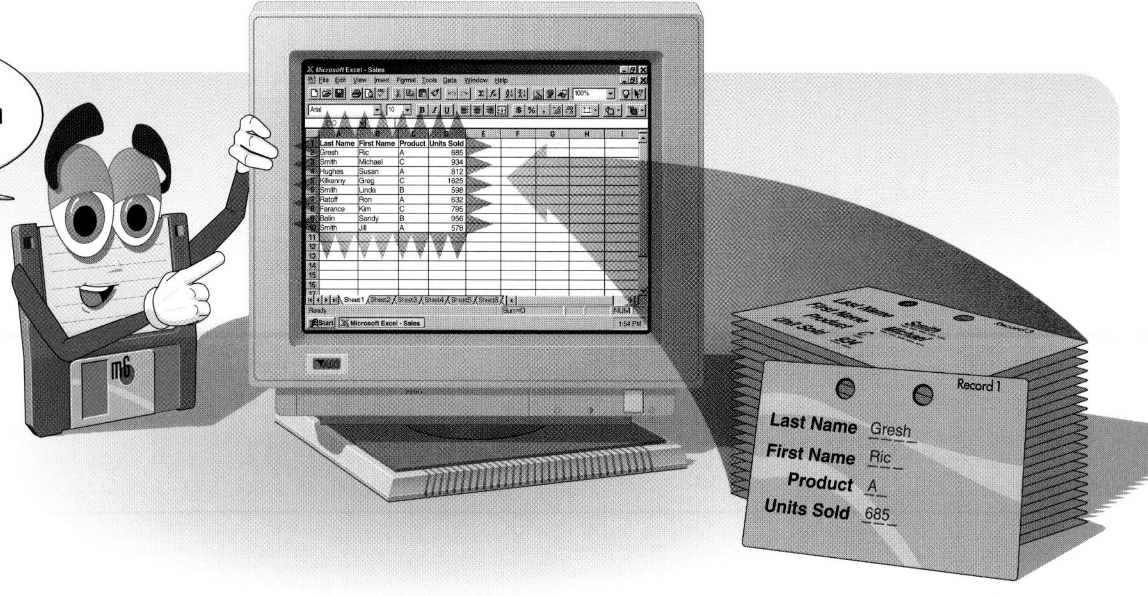

You can create and store a list in a workbook.
Record 1
Last Name Gresh
First Name Ric
Product A
Units Sold 685

CREATE A LIST

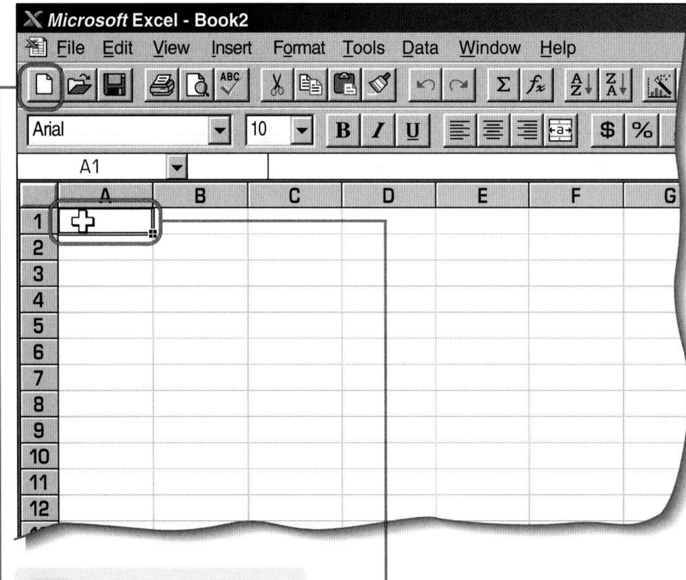

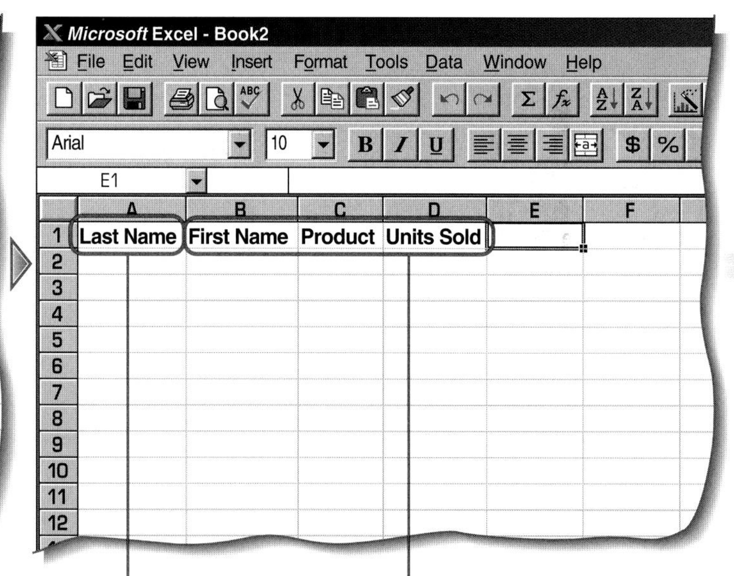

1 To create a new workbook for the list, move the mouse over and then press the left button.

2 Move the mouse over the cell where you want to begin the list and then press the left button.

3 Type a label to describe the data you will enter into the column.

4 Press → on your keyboard to enter the column label and move to the next cell.

5 Repeat steps **3** and **4** until you have entered labels for all the columns.

Note: To bold the column labels, refer to page 88. To change the column width, refer to page 80.

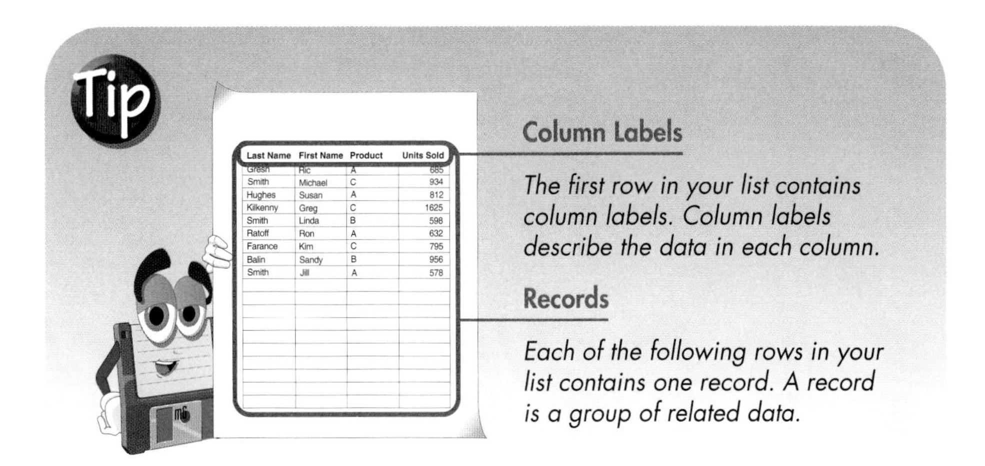

Column Labels

The first row in your list contains column labels. Column labels describe the data in each column.

Records

Each of the following rows in your list contains one record. A record is a group of related data.

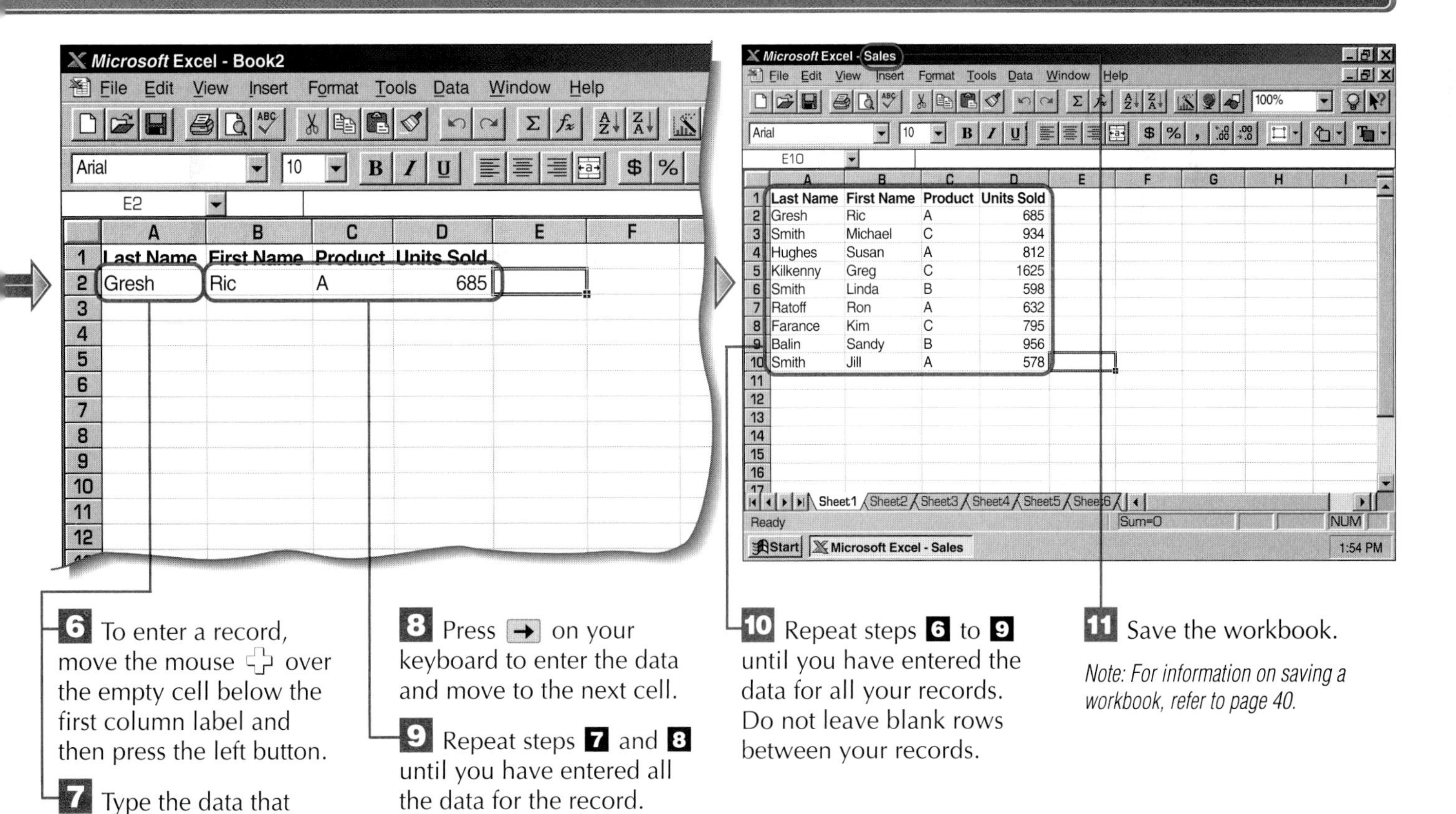

6 To enter a record, move the mouse over the empty cell below the first column label and then press the left button.

7 Type the data that corresponds to the column label.

8 Press → on your keyboard to enter the data and move to the next cell.

9 Repeat steps **7** and **8** until you have entered all the data for the record.

10 Repeat steps **6** to **9** until you have entered the data for all your records. Do not leave blank rows between your records.

11 Save the workbook.

Note: For information on saving a workbook, refer to page 40.

FILTER A LIST

You can filter your list to display only the records that contain the data you want to analyze.
Sales for Product C

FILTER A LIST

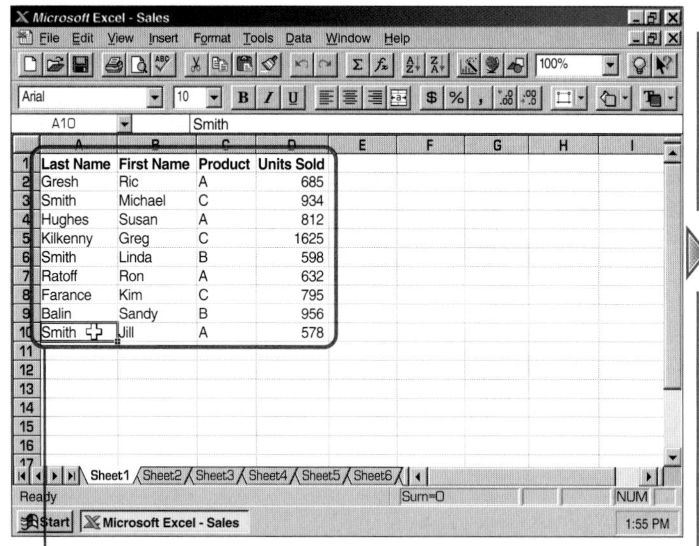

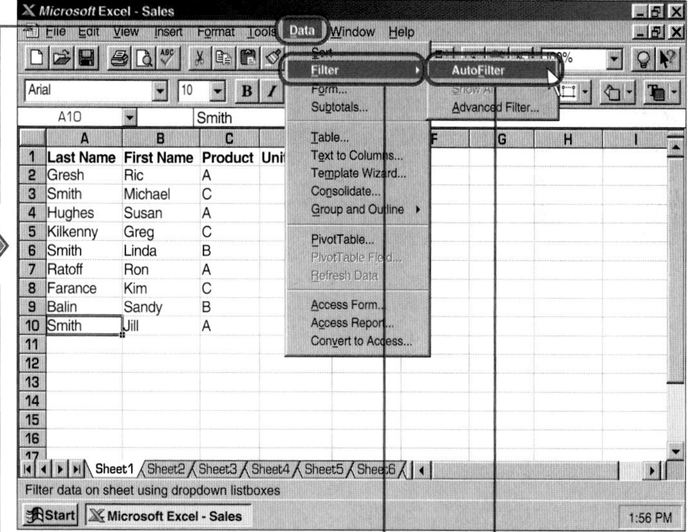

1 Move the mouse over any cell in the list and then press the left button.

2 Move the mouse over **Data** and then press the left button.

3 Move the mouse over **Filter**.

4 Move the mouse over **AutoFilter** and then press the left button.

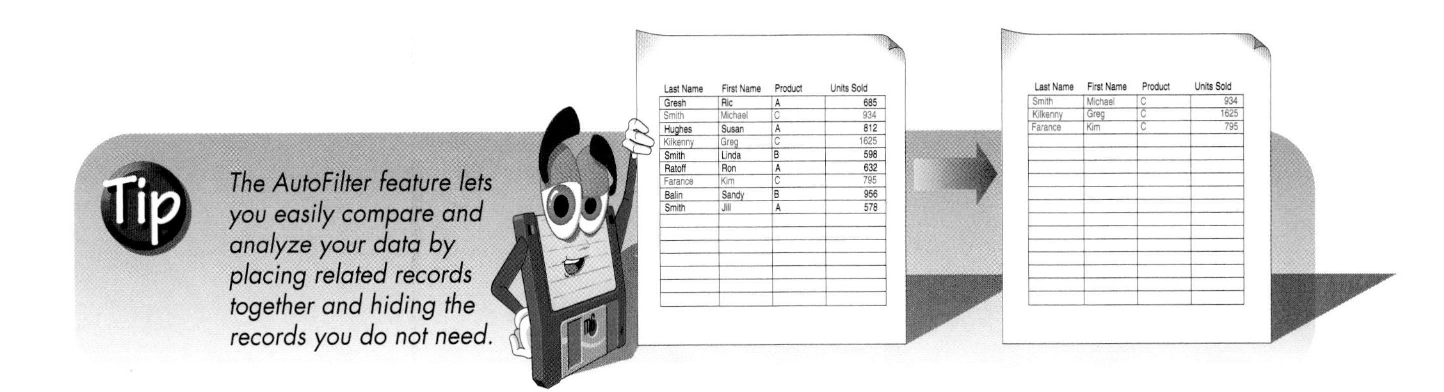

Tip
The AutoFilter feature lets you easily compare and analyze your data by placing related records together and hiding the records you do not need.

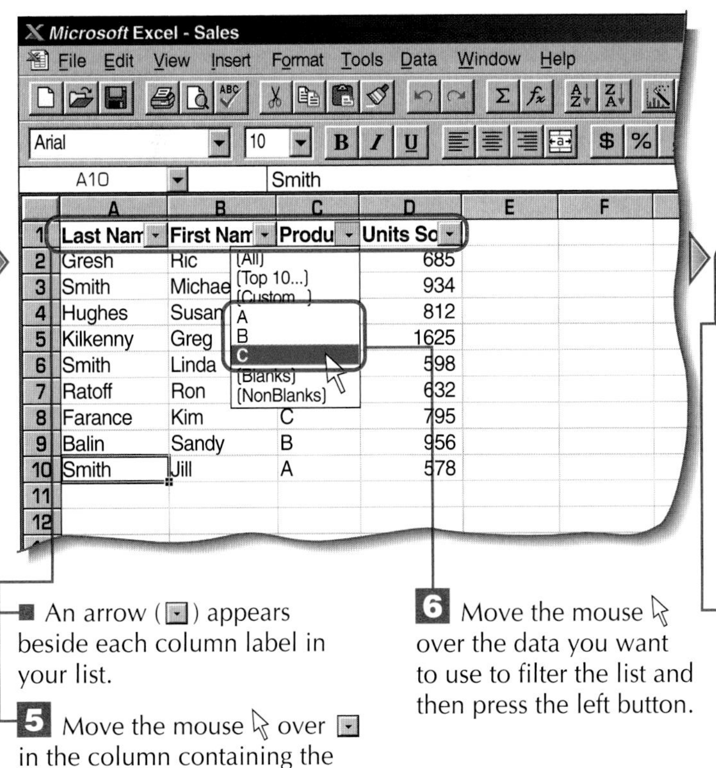

■ An arrow (▼) appears beside each column label in your list.

5 Move the mouse over ▼ in the column containing the data you want to use to filter the list and then press the left button.

6 Move the mouse over the data you want to use to filter the list and then press the left button.

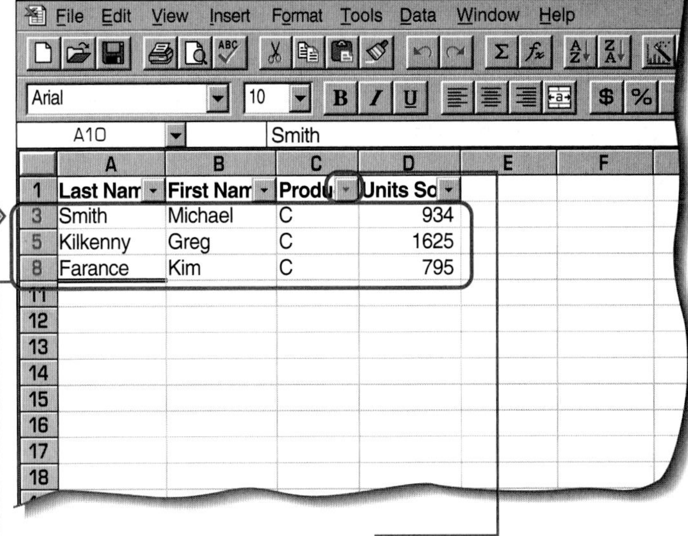

■ The list displays only the records containing the data you specified. The other records are temporarily hidden.

Note: In this example, the list displays only the records containing product C.

■ The arrow (▼) in the column you used to filter the list changes color.

■ To turn off the AutoFilter feature and redisplay the entire list, repeat steps **2** to **4**.

FILTER A LIST

> You can filter your list to display only records containing data within a specific range.

FILTER A LIST (USING COMPARISON OPERATORS)

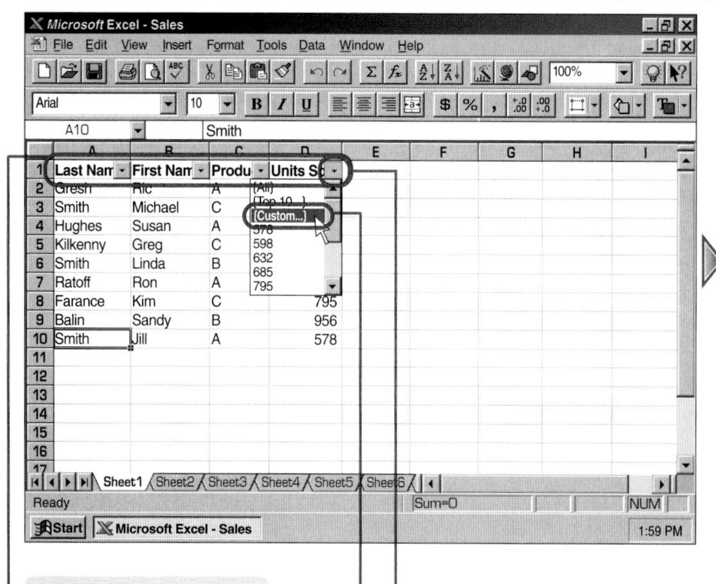

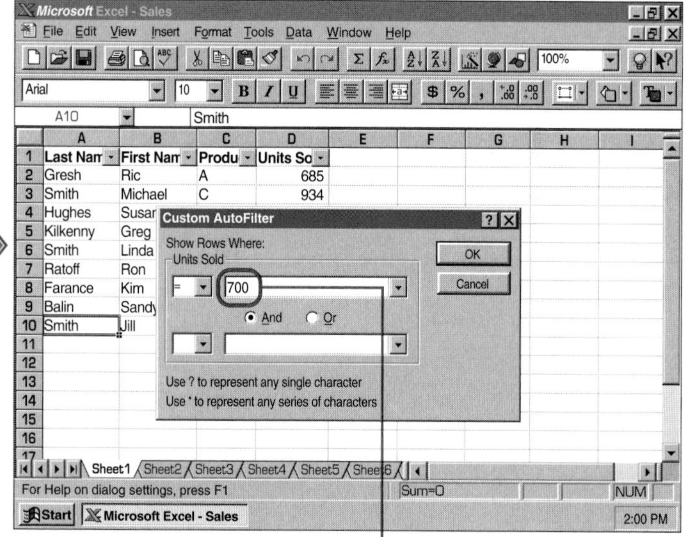

1 To turn on the AutoFilter feature, perform steps **1** to **4** on page 192.

■ An arrow (▾) appears beside each column label in your list.

2 Move the mouse over ▾ in the column containing the data you want to use to filter the list and then press the left button.

3 Move the mouse over **(Custom...)** and then press the left button.

■ The **Custom AutoFilter** dialog box appears.

4 Type the data you want to base the range on.

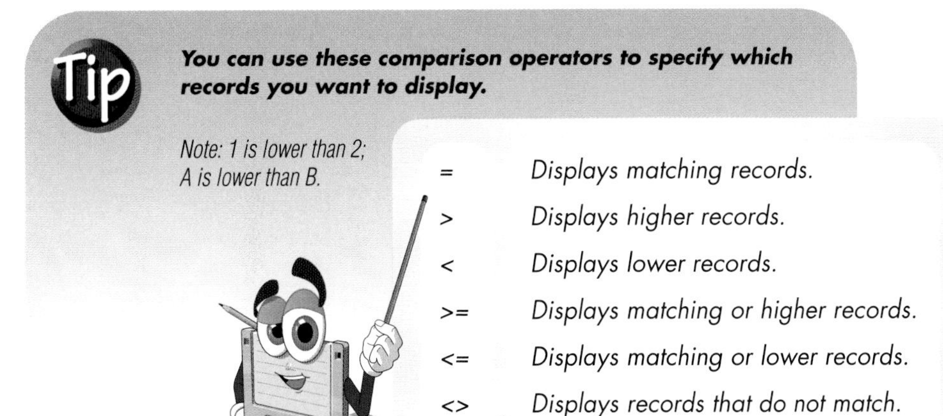

Tip

You can use these comparison operators to specify which records you want to display.

Note: 1 is lower than 2; A is lower than B.

Operator	Result
=	*Displays matching records.*
>	*Displays higher records.*
<	*Displays lower records.*
>=	*Displays matching or higher records.*
<=	*Displays matching or lower records.*
<>	*Displays records that do not match.*

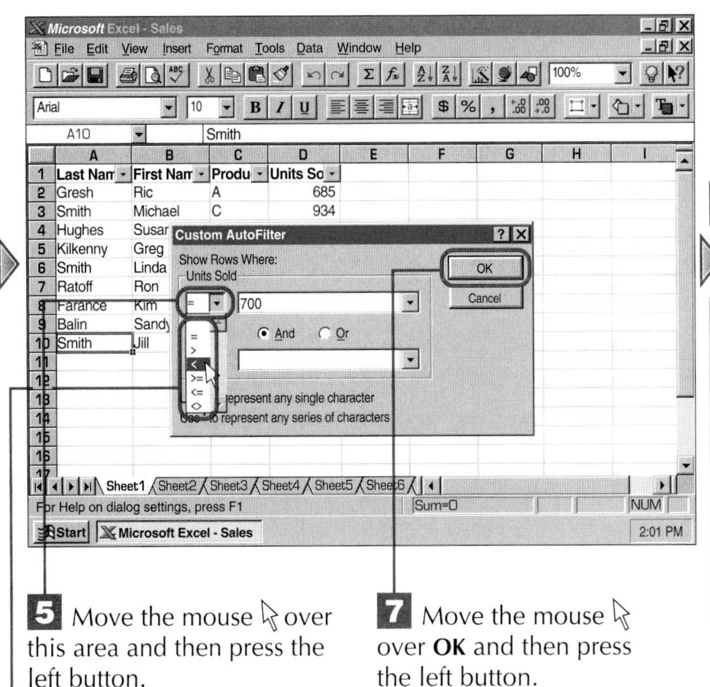

5 Move the mouse over this area and then press the left button.

6 Move the mouse over the comparison operator you want to use and then press the left button.

7 Move the mouse over **OK** and then press the left button.

■ The list displays only the records containing the data in the range you specified. The other records are temporarily hidden.

Note: In this example, the list displays only the records showing less than 700 units sold.

■ The arrow (▾) in the column you used to filter the list changes color.

■ To turn off the AutoFilter feature and redisplay the entire list, perform steps **2** to **4** on page 192.

SORT DATA IN A LIST

You should save your workbook before sorting, in case you do not like the results of the sort.

Note: To save a workbook, refer to page 40.

SORT BY ONE COLUMN

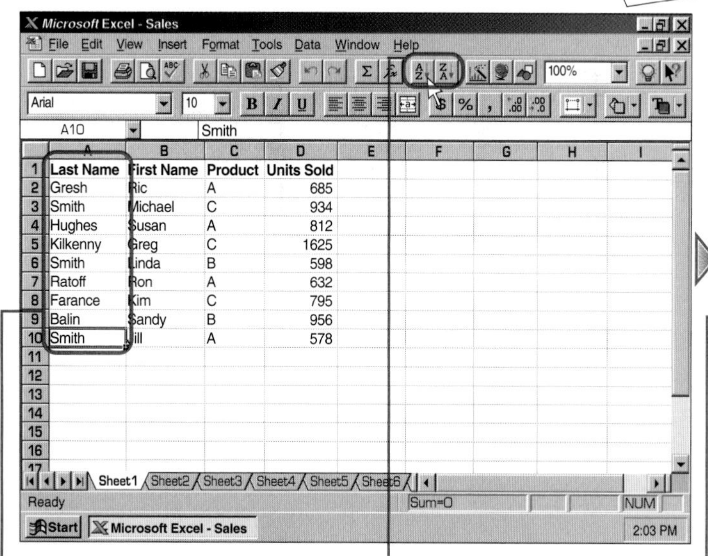

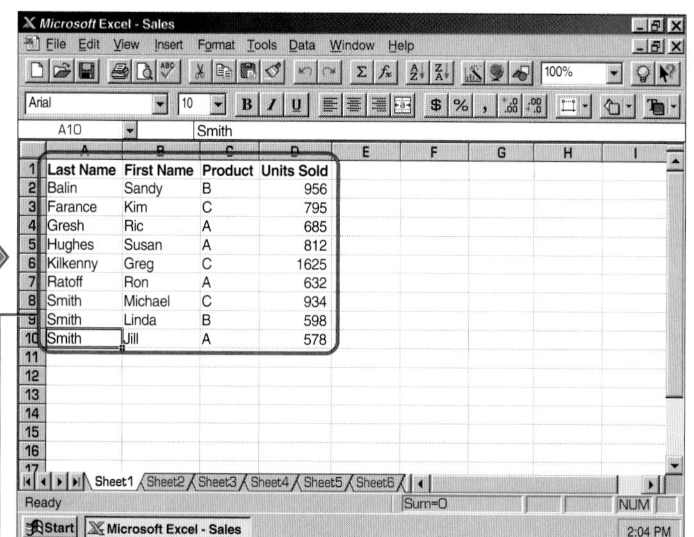

1 Move the mouse over any cell in the column you want to base the sort on and then press the left button.

2 Move the mouse over the way you want to sort the data and then press the left button.

- Sorts A to Z, 0 to 9.
- Sorts Z to A, 9 to 0.

■ The list appears in the new order.

Note: In this example, the records are sorted alphabetically by last name.

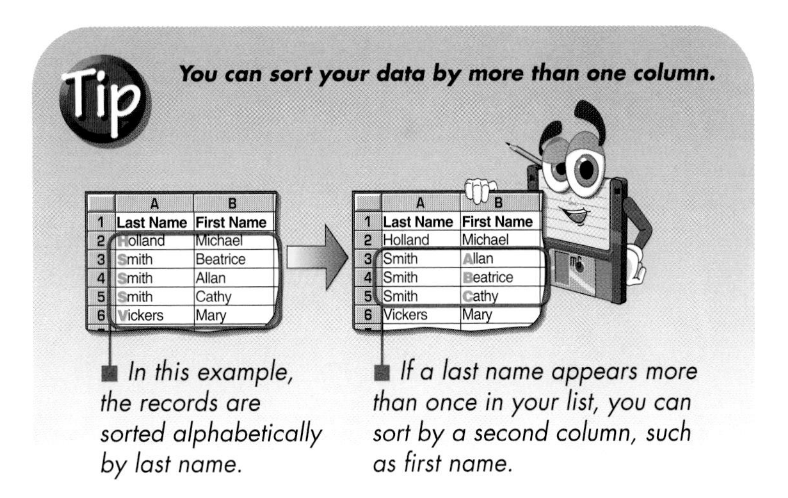

	A	B
1	Last Name	First Name
2	Holland	Michael
3	Smith	Beatrice
4	Smith	Allan
5	Smith	Cathy
6	Vickers	Mary

	A	B
1	Last Name	First Name
2	Holland	Michael
3	Smith	Allan
4	Smith	Beatrice
5	Smith	Cathy
6	Vickers	Mary

In this example, the records are sorted alphabetically by last name.

If a last name appears more than once in your list, you can sort by a second column, such as first name.

SORT BY TWO COLUMNS

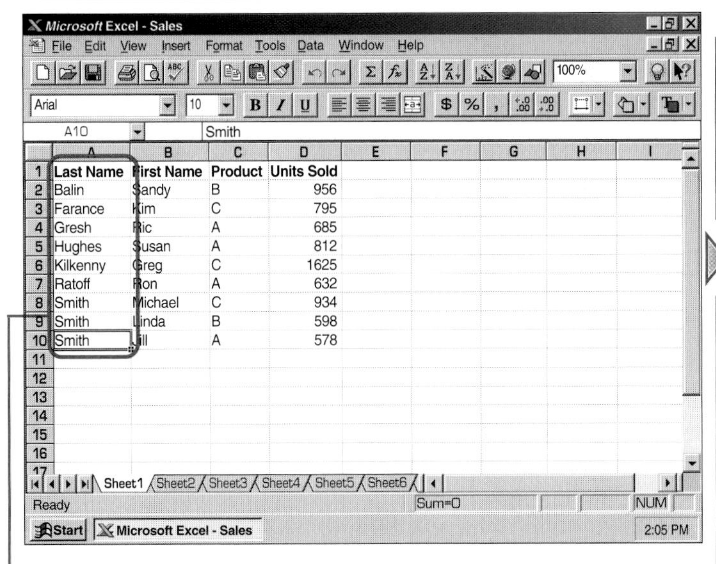

	A	B	C	D
1	Last Name	First Name	Product	Units Sold
2	Balin	Sandy	B	956
3	Farance	Kim	C	795
4	Gresh	Ric	A	685
5	Hughes	Susan	A	812
6	Kilkenny	Greg	C	1625
7	Ratoff	Ron	A	632
8	Smith	Michael	C	934
9	Smith	Linda	B	598
10	Smith	Jill	A	578

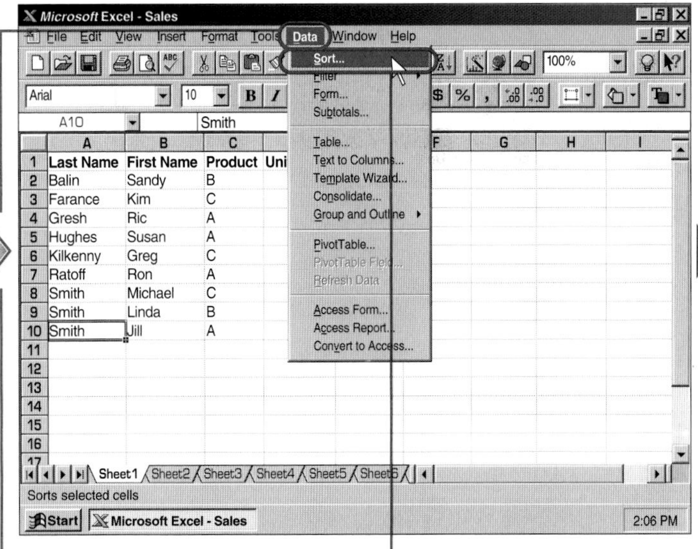

1 To identify the first column you want to base the sort on, move the mouse over any cell in the column and then press the left button.

2 Move the mouse over **Data** and then press the left button.

3 Move the mouse over **Sort** and then press the left button.

SORT DATA IN A LIST

You can sort the data in your list by letter, number or date.
NAME
Allan
Beatrice
Cathy
Derek
Evelyn
Frank
Gretchen
Harry
NUMBER
100
200
300
400
500
600
700
800
DATE
Jan-95
Feb-95
Mar-95
Apr-95
May-95
Jun-95
Jul-95
Aug-95

SORT BY TWO COLUMNS (CONTINUED)

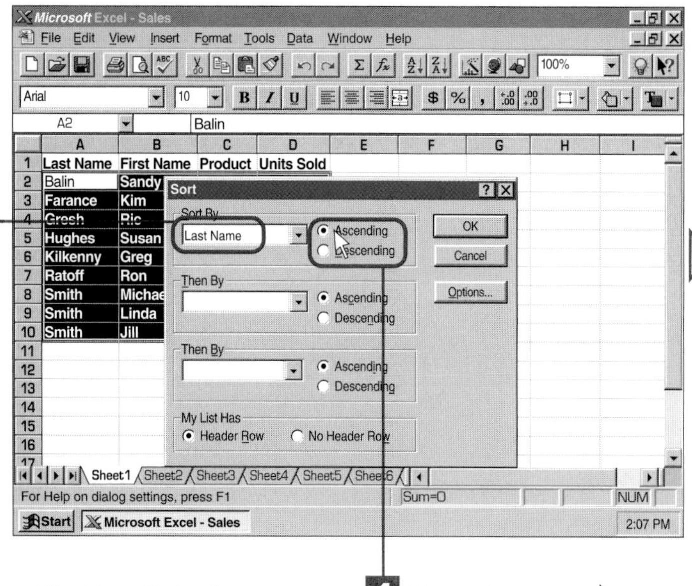

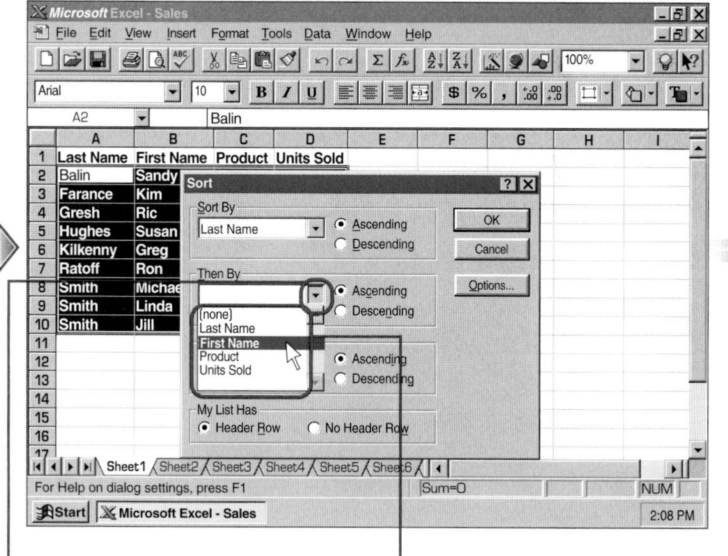

■ The **Sort** dialog box appears.

■ This area displays the label for the column you identified in step **1**.

4 Move the mouse over the way you want to sort the first column and then press the left button (○ changes to ◉).

Ascending
Sorts A to Z, 0 to 9.

Descending
Sorts Z to A, 9 to 0.

5 To identify the second column you want to base the sort on, move the mouse over ▾ in this area and then press the left button.

6 Move the mouse over the label of the second column you want to base the sort on and then press the left button.

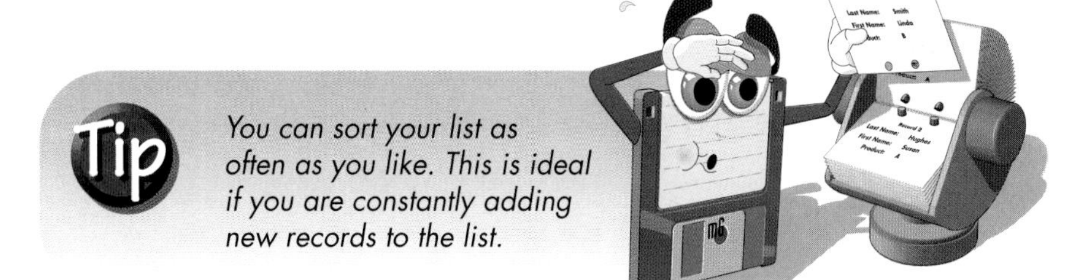

Tip You can sort your list as often as you like. This is ideal if you are constantly adding new records to the list.

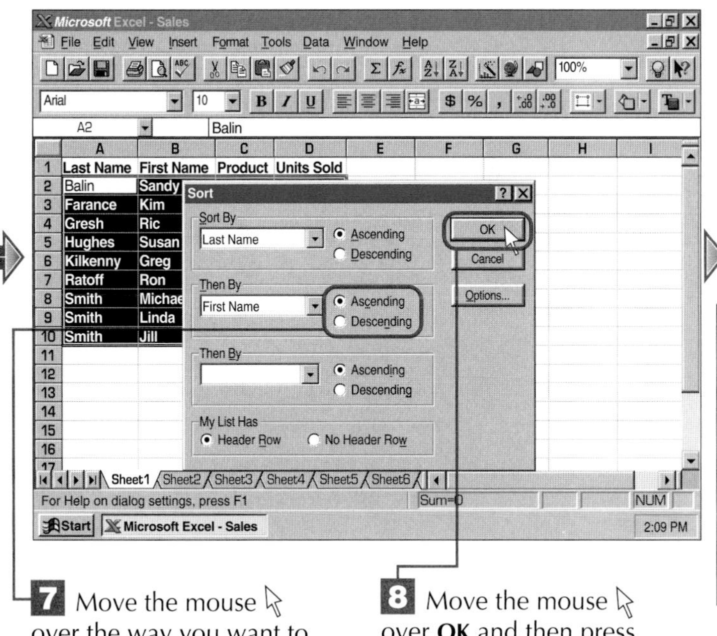

7 Move the mouse over the way you want to sort the second column and then press the left button (○ changes to ◉).

8 Move the mouse over **OK** and then press the left button.

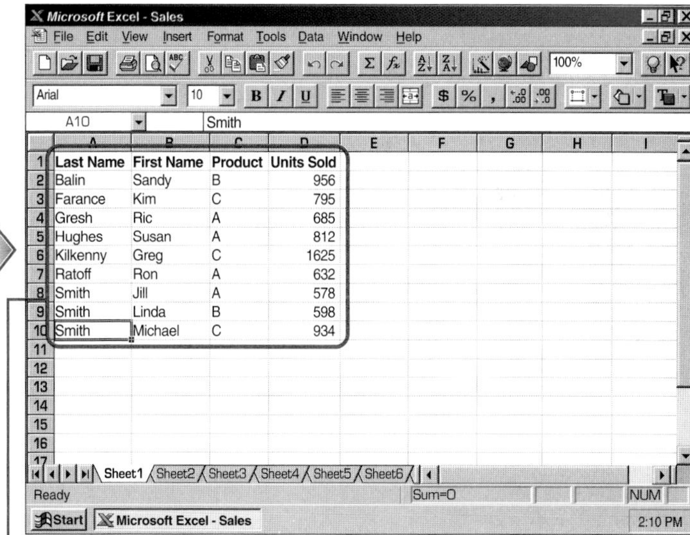

■ The list appears in the new order.

Note: In this example, the data is sorted by last name. All records with the same last name are then sorted by first name.

ADD SUBTOTALS TO A LIST

You can quickly summarize data by adding subtotals to your list.
Last Name
Gresh Ric
Hughes Susan
Ratoff Ron
Smith Jill 578
2707
Balin Sandy B 956
Smith Linda B 598
B Total 1554
Farance Kim C 795
Kilkenny Greg C 1625
Smith Michael C 934
C Total 3354
Grand Total 7615

ADD SUBTOTALS TO A LIST

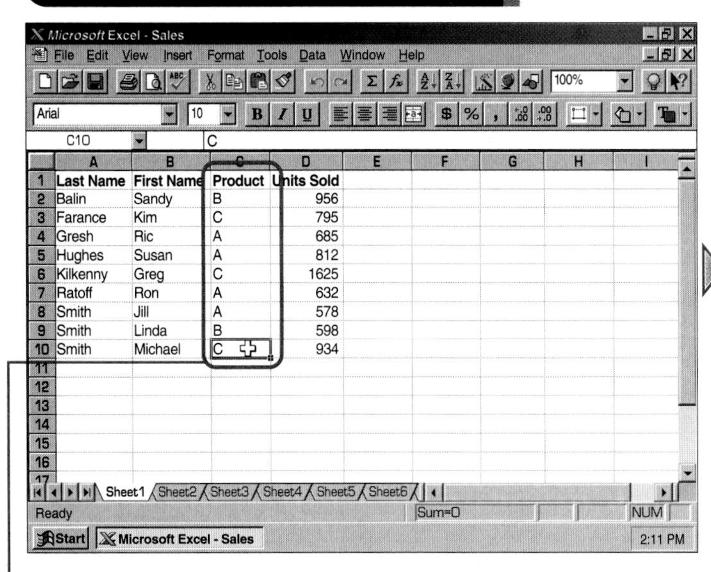

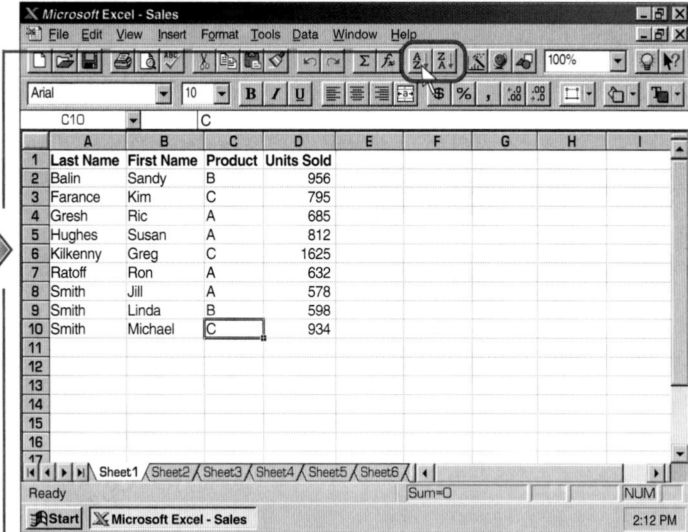

1 To sort the column you want to display subtotals for, move the mouse over any cell in the column and then press the left button.

2 Move the mouse over the way you want to sort the data and then press the left button.

- Sorts A to Z, 0 to 9.
- Sorts Z to A, 9 to 0.

Tip
After adding subtotals to your list, you can use the subtotals to quickly create reports and charts.
SALES
Total A
Total B
Total C

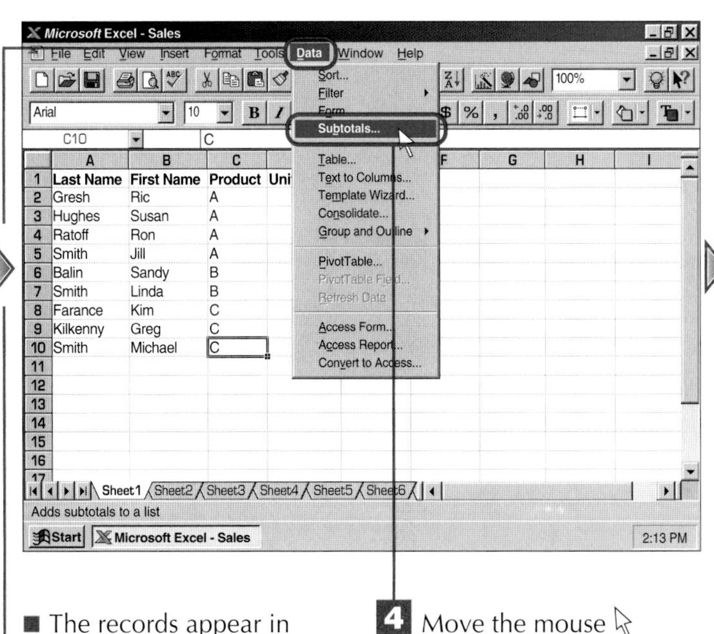

■ The records appear in the new order.

3 Move the mouse over **Data** and then press the left button.

4 Move the mouse over **Subtotals** and then press the left button.

■ The **Subtotal** dialog box appears.

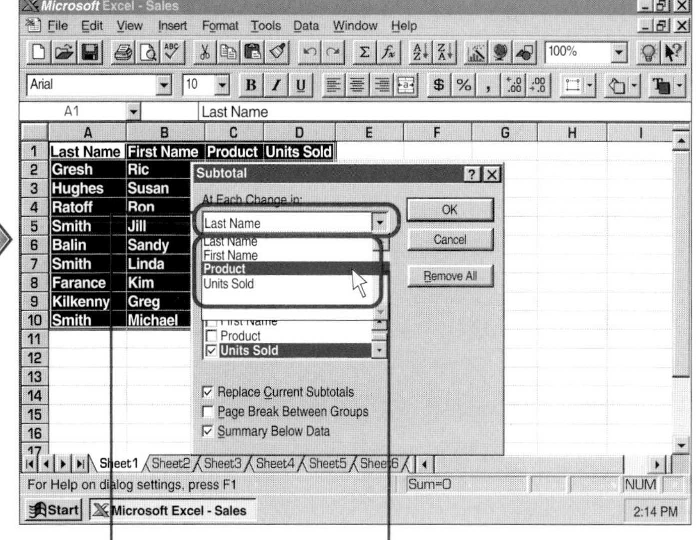

5 To display the column labels from your list, move the mouse over this area and then press the left button.

6 Move the mouse over the label of the column you want to display subtotals for and then press the left button.

ADD SUBTOTALS TO A LIST

You can choose from several types of calculations when you use the Subtotal feature.
MAX
AVERAGE
MIN

ADD SUBTOTALS TO A LIST (CONTINUED)

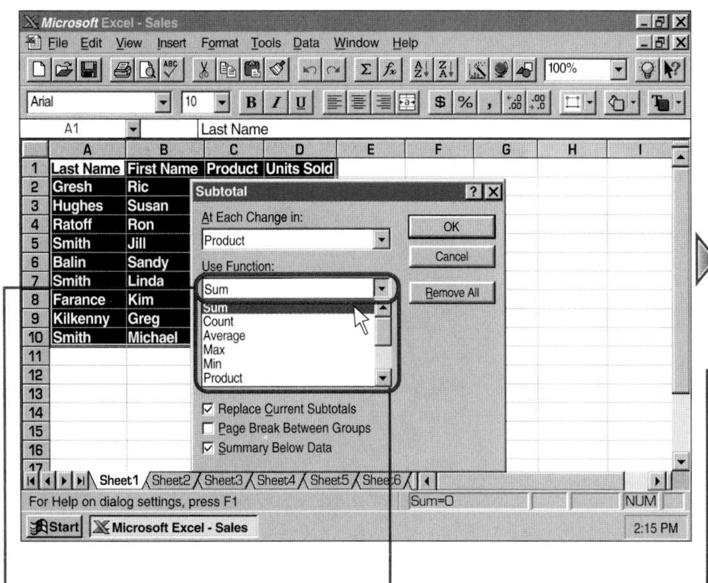

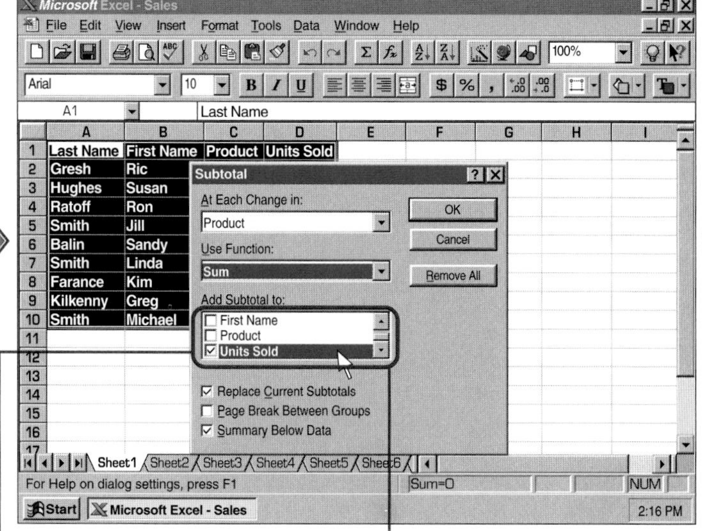

7 To display a list of the calculations Excel can perform, move the mouse over this area and then press the left button.

8 Move the mouse over the calculation you want to perform and then press the left button.

■ This area displays the column labels from your list. A check mark (✓) appears beside the label of the column Excel will subtotal.

9 To add or remove a check mark, move the mouse over the label of the column and then press the left button.

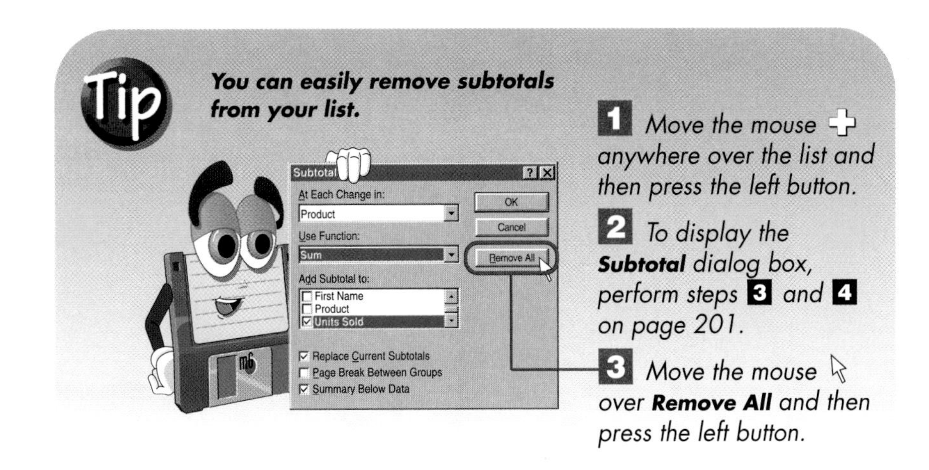

You can easily remove subtotals from your list.

1 *Move the mouse anywhere over the list and then press the left button.*

2 *To display the* ***Subtotal*** *dialog box, perform steps* **3** *and* **4** *on page 201.*

3 *Move the mouse over* ***Remove All*** *and then press the left button.*

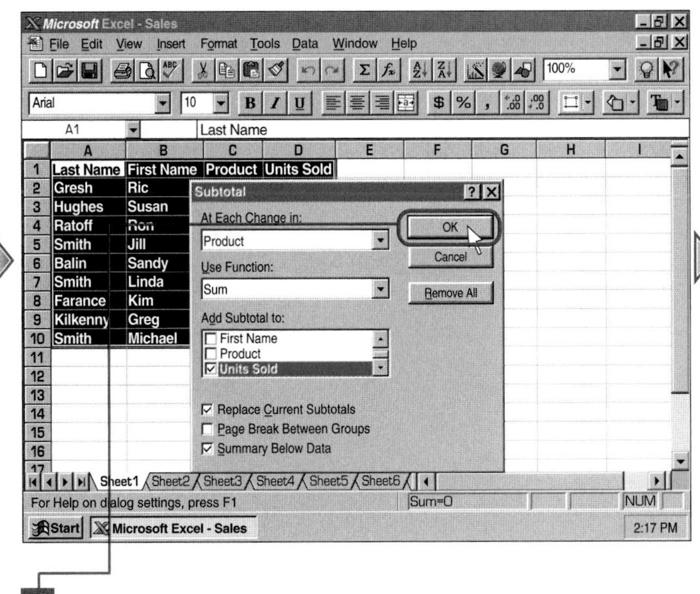

10 To add the subtotals to your list, move the mouse over **OK** and then press the left button.

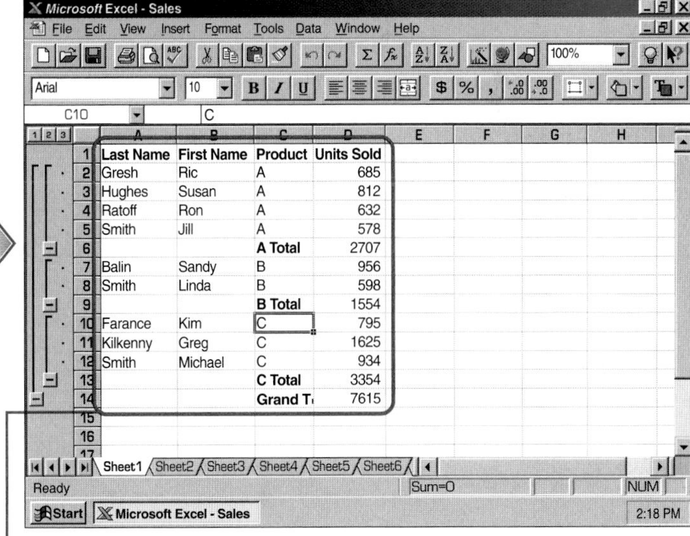

■ The list displays subtotals and a grand total.

HIDE OR DISPLAY SUBTOTALED DATA

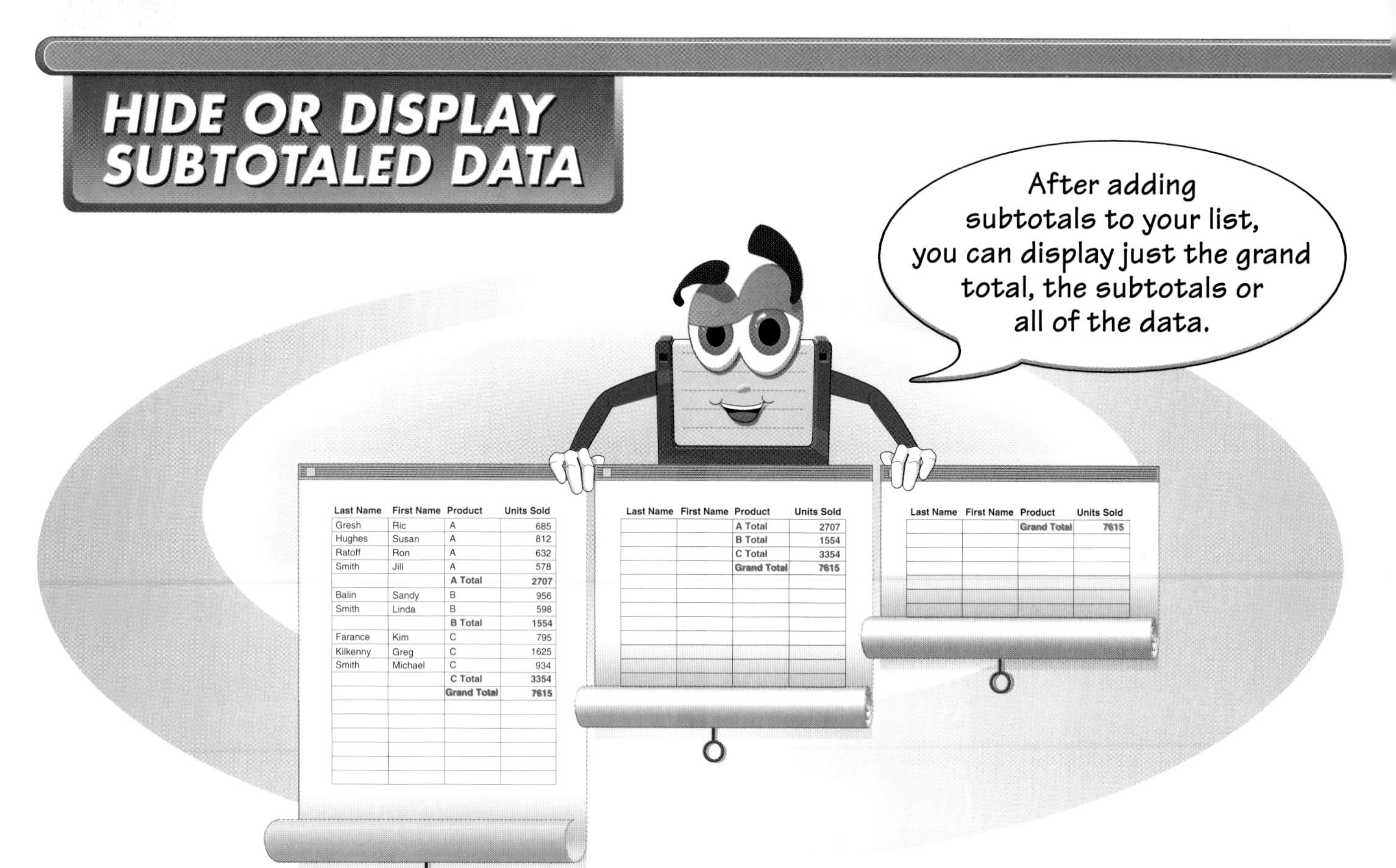

After adding subtotals to your list, you can display just the grand total, the subtotals or all of the data.

HIDE OR DISPLAY SUBTOTALED DATA

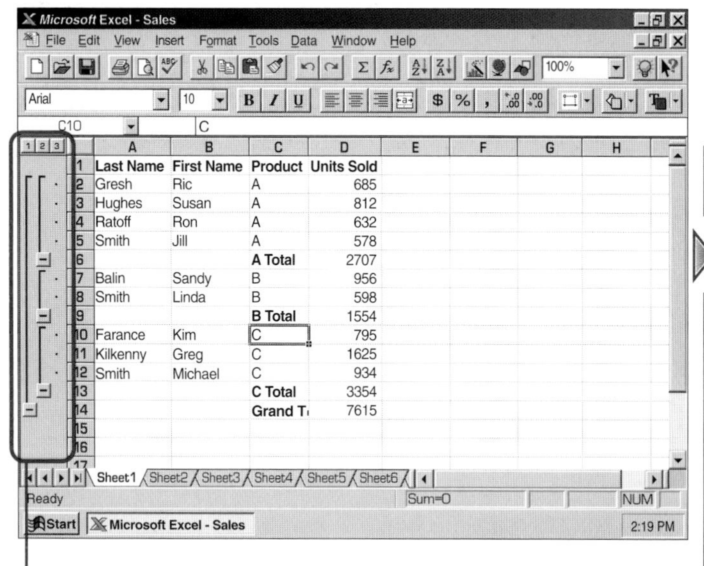

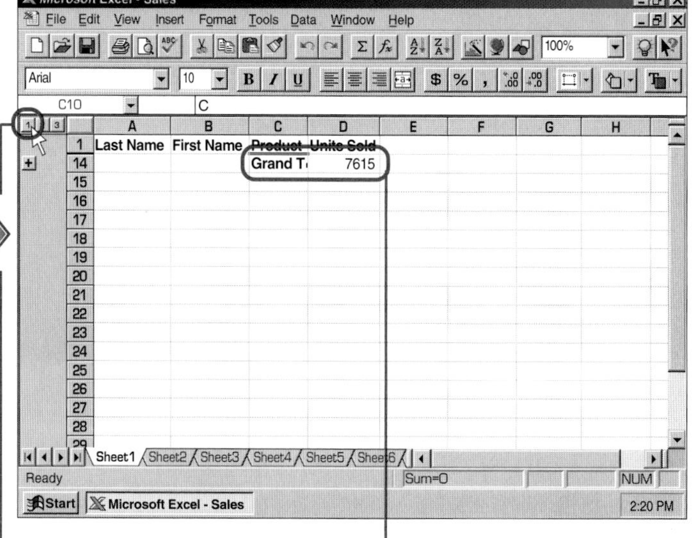

■ After you add subtotals to a list, these symbols appear to help you work with the data.

Note: To add subtotals to a list, refer to page 200.

1 To hide all data except the grand total, move the mouse over 1 and then press the left button.

■ The list displays only the grand total.

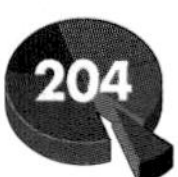

Hiding all the data in a list except the subtotals and the grand total lets you instantly view a summary of your data.

A Total 2707
B Total 1554
C Total 3354
Grand Total 7615

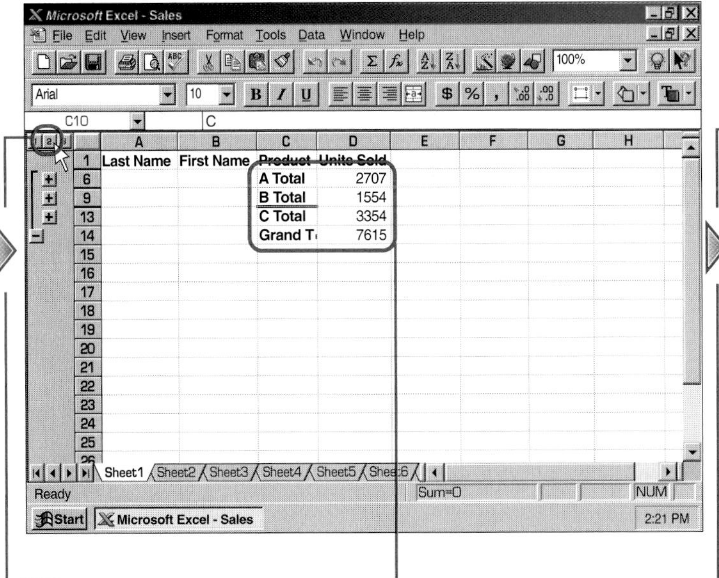

2 To hide all data except the subtotals and the grand total, move the mouse over **2** and then press the left button.

■ The list displays only the subtotals and the grand total.

3 To display all the data in the list, including subtotals and the grand total, move the mouse over **3** and then press the left button.

■ The list displays all the data.

*Note: To remove subtotals from your list, refer to the **Tip** on page 203.*

INDEX

A

B

C

D

E

INDEX

M

N

O

P

INDEX

INCOME STATEMENT
January
February
March
REVENUE
11500
13670
Payroll
3850
4850
5250
1750
1750
1750
1920
1980
2030
TOTAL EXPENSES
INCOME